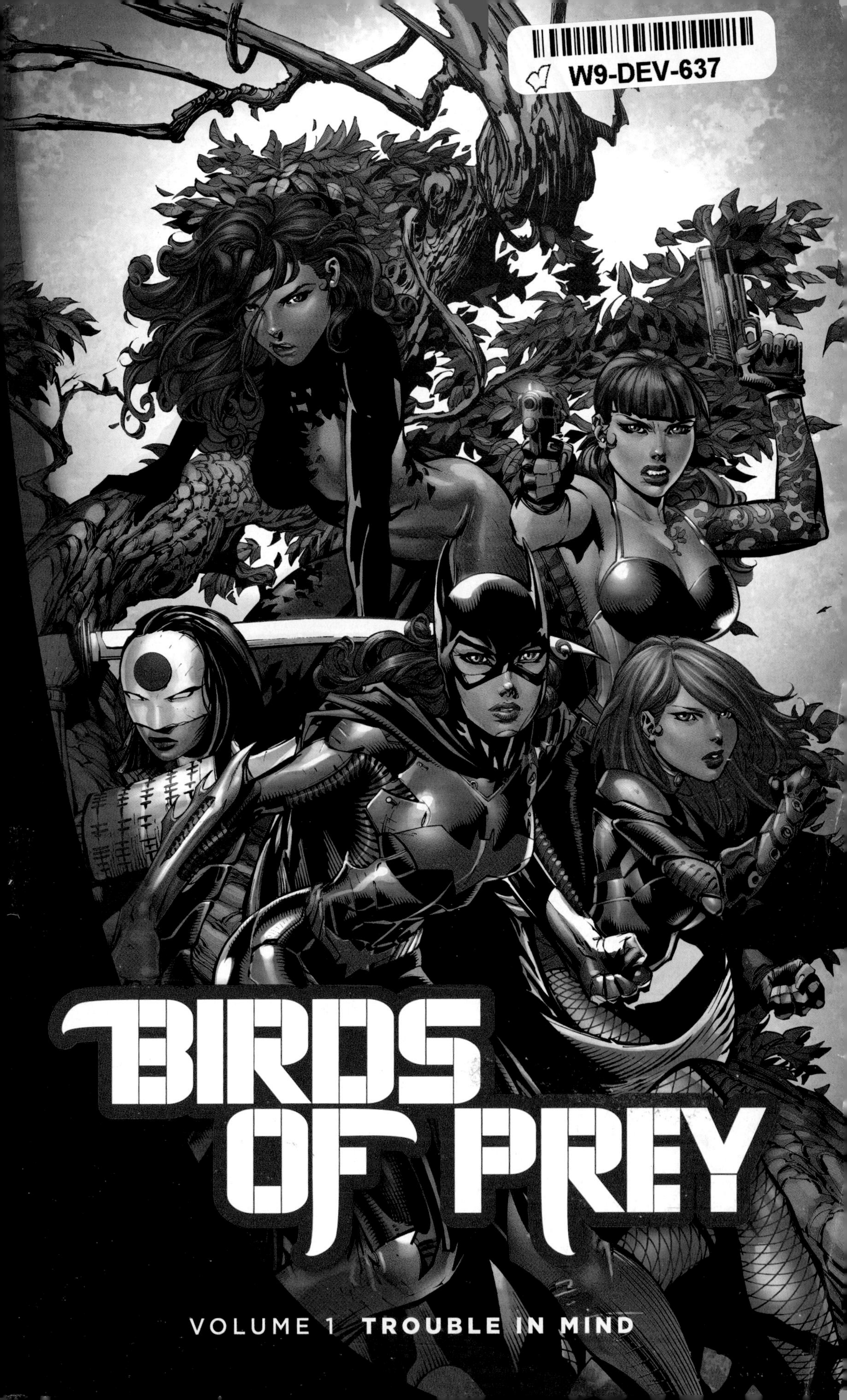

BIRDS OF PREY

VOLUME 1 TROUBLE IN MIND

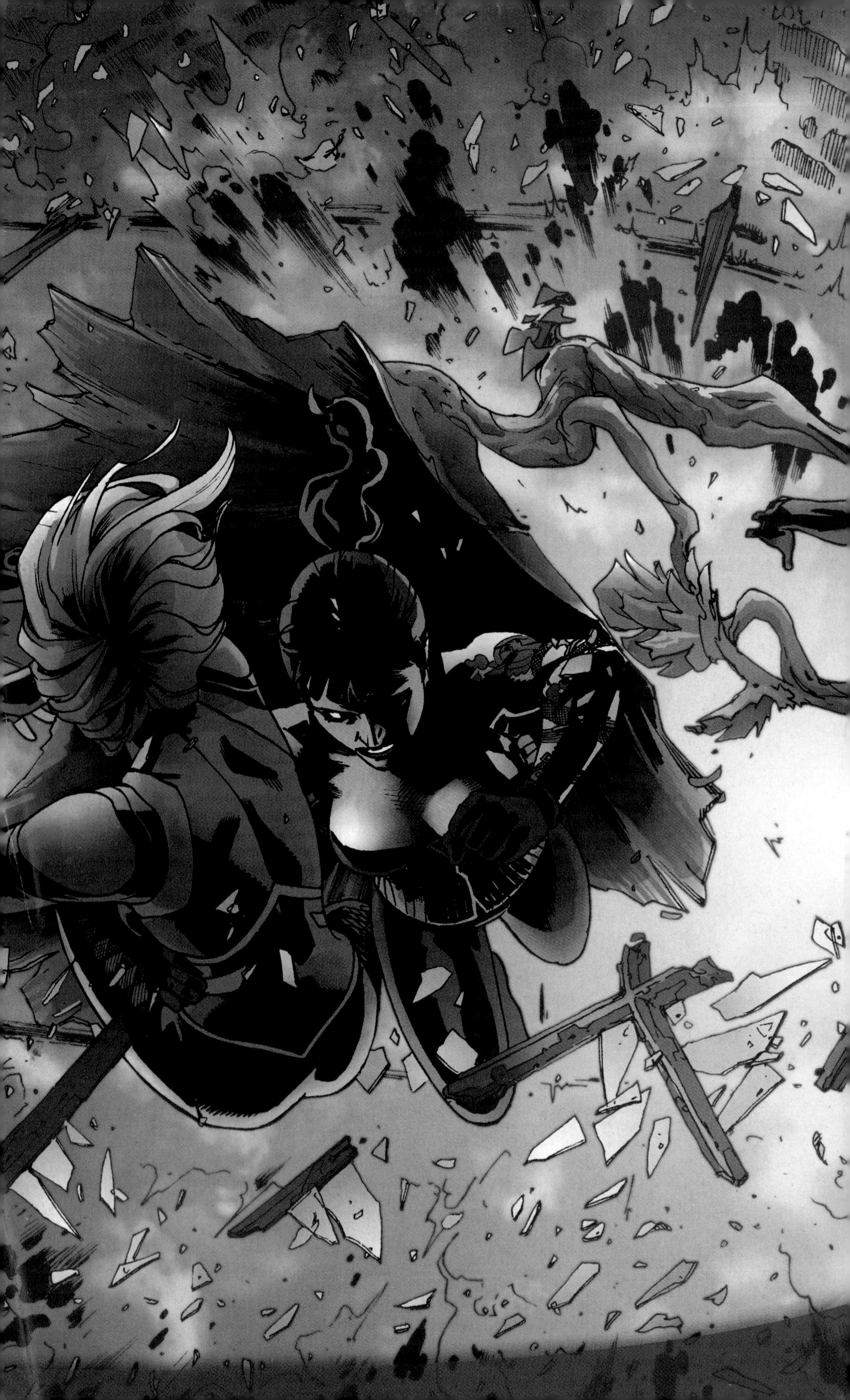

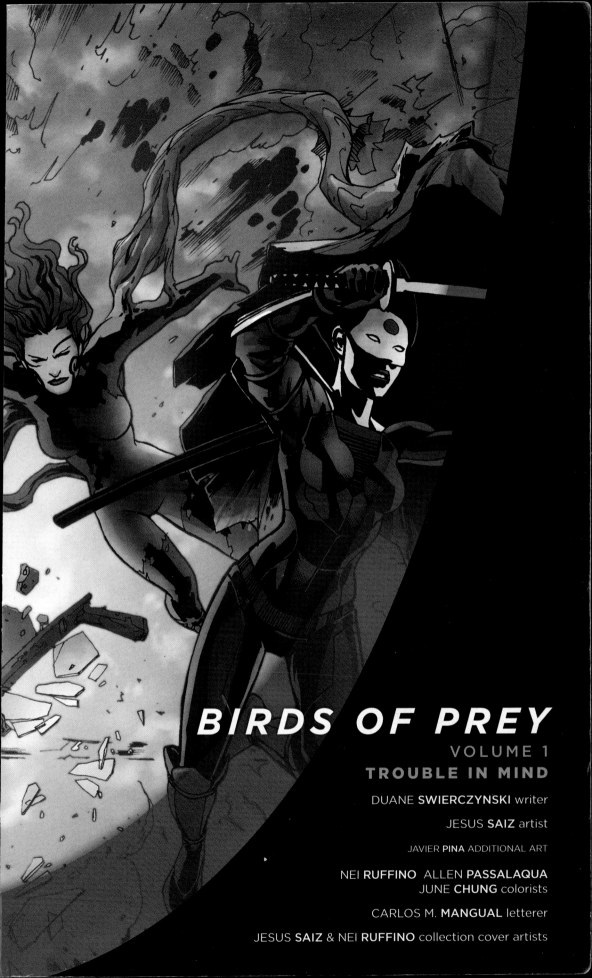

BIRDS OF PREY

VOLUME 1
TROUBLE IN MIND

DUANE **SWIERCZYNSKI** writer

JESUS **SAIZ** artist

JAVIER **PINA** ADDITIONAL ART

NEI **RUFFINO** ALLEN **PASSALAQUA**
JUNE **CHUNG** colorists

CARLOS M. **MANGUAL** letterer

JESUS **SAIZ** & NEI **RUFFINO** collection cover artists

JANELLE ASSELIN BOBBIE CHASE Editors – Original Series KATIE KUBERT Assistant Editor – Original Series
ROWENA YOW Editor ROBBIN BROSTERMAN Design Director – Books
ROBBIE BIEDERMAN Publication Design

BOB HARRAS VP – Editor-in-Chief

DIANE NELSON President DAN DIDIO and JIM LEE Co-Publishers
GEOFF JOHNS Chief Creative Officer
JOHN ROOD Executive VP – Sales, Marketing and Business Development
AMY GENKINS Senior VP – Business and Legal Affairs NAIRI GARDINER Senior VP – Finance
JEFF BOISON VP – Publishing Operations MARK CHIARELLO VP – Art Direction and Design
JOHN CUNNINGHAM VP – Marketing TERRI CUNNINGHAM VP – Talent Relations and Services
ALISON GILL Senior VP – Manufacturing and Operations HANK KANALZ Senior VP – Digital
JAY KOGAN VP – Business and Legal Affairs, Publishing JACK MAHAN VP – Business Affairs, Talent
NICK NAPOLITANO VP – Manufacturing Administration SUE POHJA VP – Book Sales
COURTNEY SIMMONS Senior VP – Publicity BOB WAYNE Senior VP – Sales

BIRDS OF PREY VOLUME 1: TROUBLE IN MIND

DC Comics, 1700 Broadway, New York, NY 10019
A Warner Bros. Entertainment Company.
Printed by RR Donnelley, Salem, VA, USA. 8/10/12. First Printing.

ISBN: 978-1-4012-3699-1

Library of Congress Cataloging-in-Publication Data

Swierczynski, Duane.
Birds of prey. Volume 1, Trouble in mind / Duane Swierczynski, Jesus Saiz.
p. cm.
"Originally published in single magazine form in BIRDS OF PREY 1-7."
ISBN 978-1-4012-3699-1
1. Graphic novels. I. Saiz, Jesus. II. Title. III. Title: Trouble in mind.
PN6728.B497S93 2012
741.5'973—dc23
2012018772

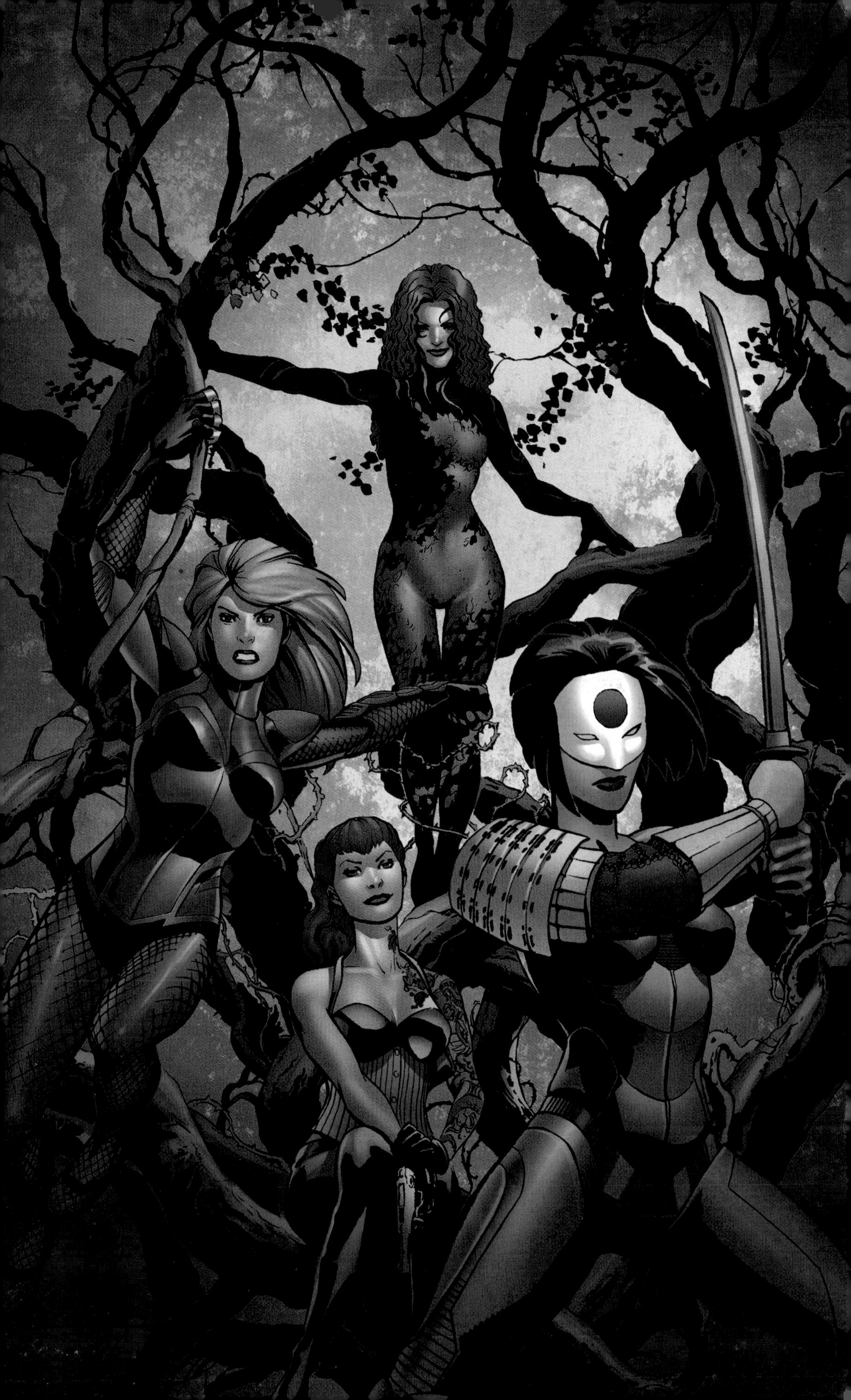

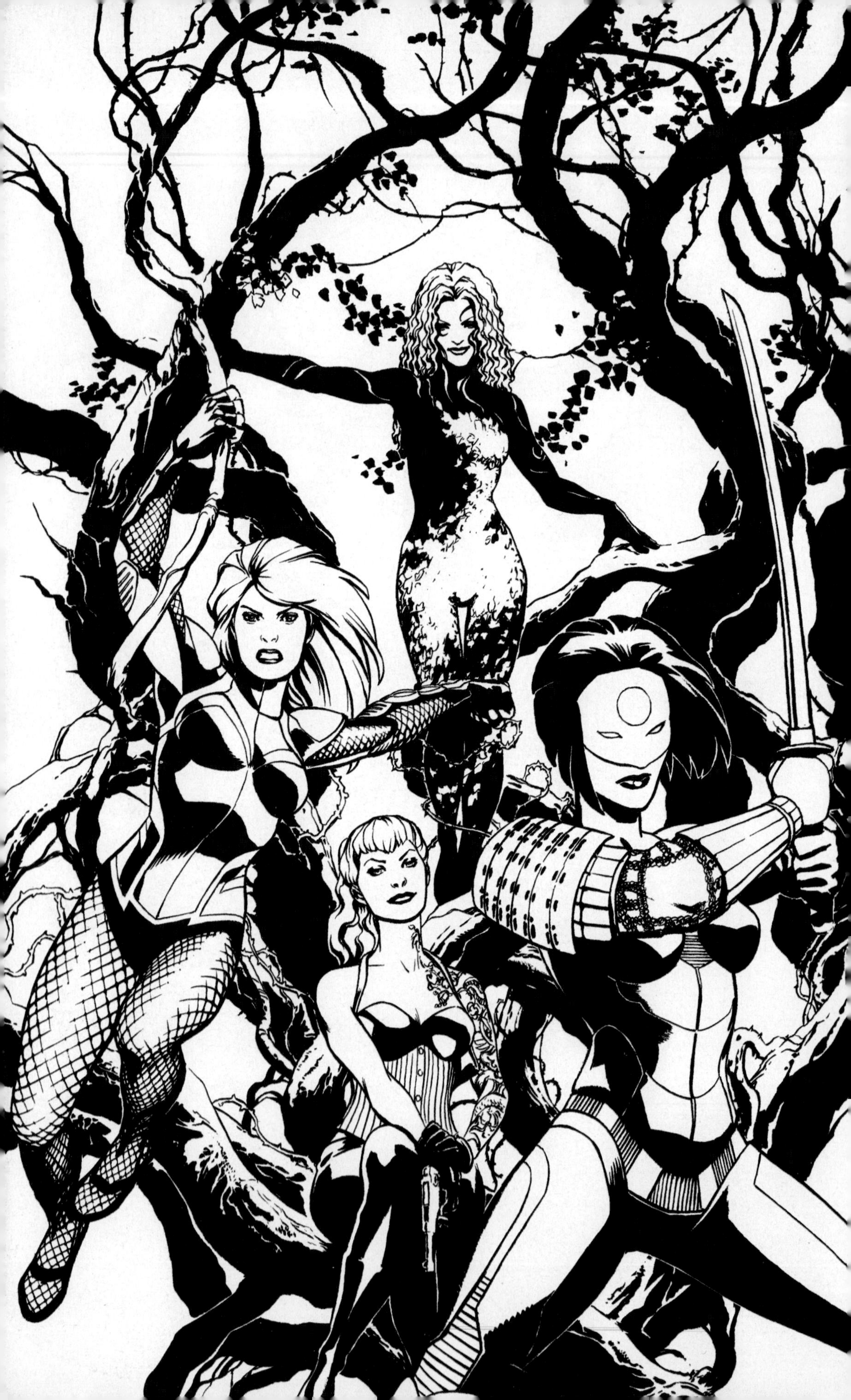

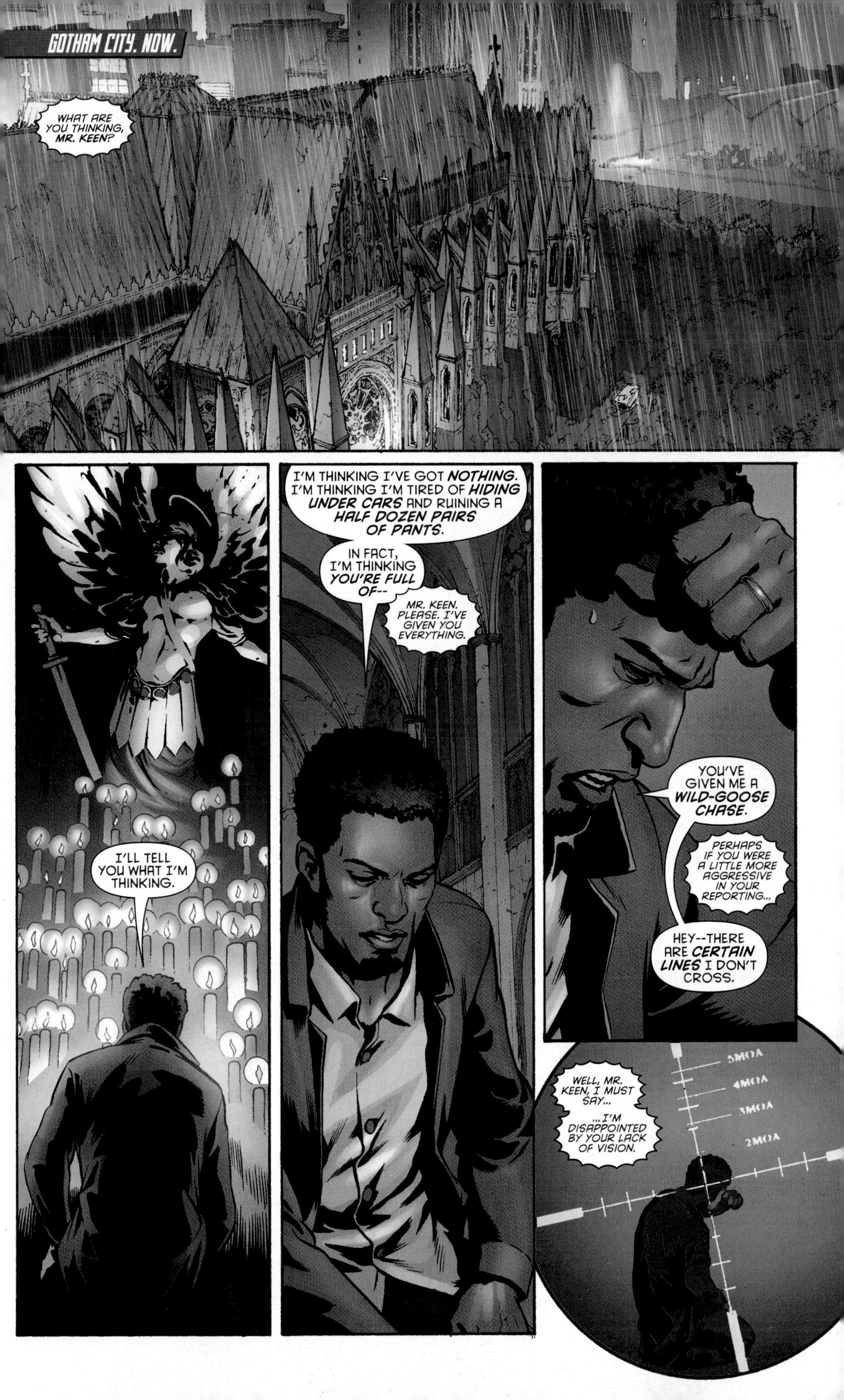
GOTHAM CITY. NOW.
WHAT ARE YOU THINKING, MR. KEEN?
I'LL TELL YOU WHAT I'M THINKING.
I'M THINKING I'VE GOT NOTHING. I'M THINKING I'M TIRED OF HIDING UNDER CARS AND RUINING A HALF DOZEN PAIRS OF PANTS.
IN FACT, I'M THINKING YOU'RE FULL OF--
MR. KEEN. PLEASE. I'VE GIVEN YOU EVERYTHING.
YOU'VE GIVEN ME A WILD-GOOSE CHASE.
PERHAPS IF YOU WERE A LITTLE MORE AGGRESSIVE IN YOUR REPORTING...
HEY--THERE ARE CERTAIN LINES I DON'T CROSS.
WELL, MR. KEEN, I MUST SAY...
...I'M DISAPPOINTED BY YOUR LACK OF VISION.
5MOA
4MOA
3MOA
2MOA

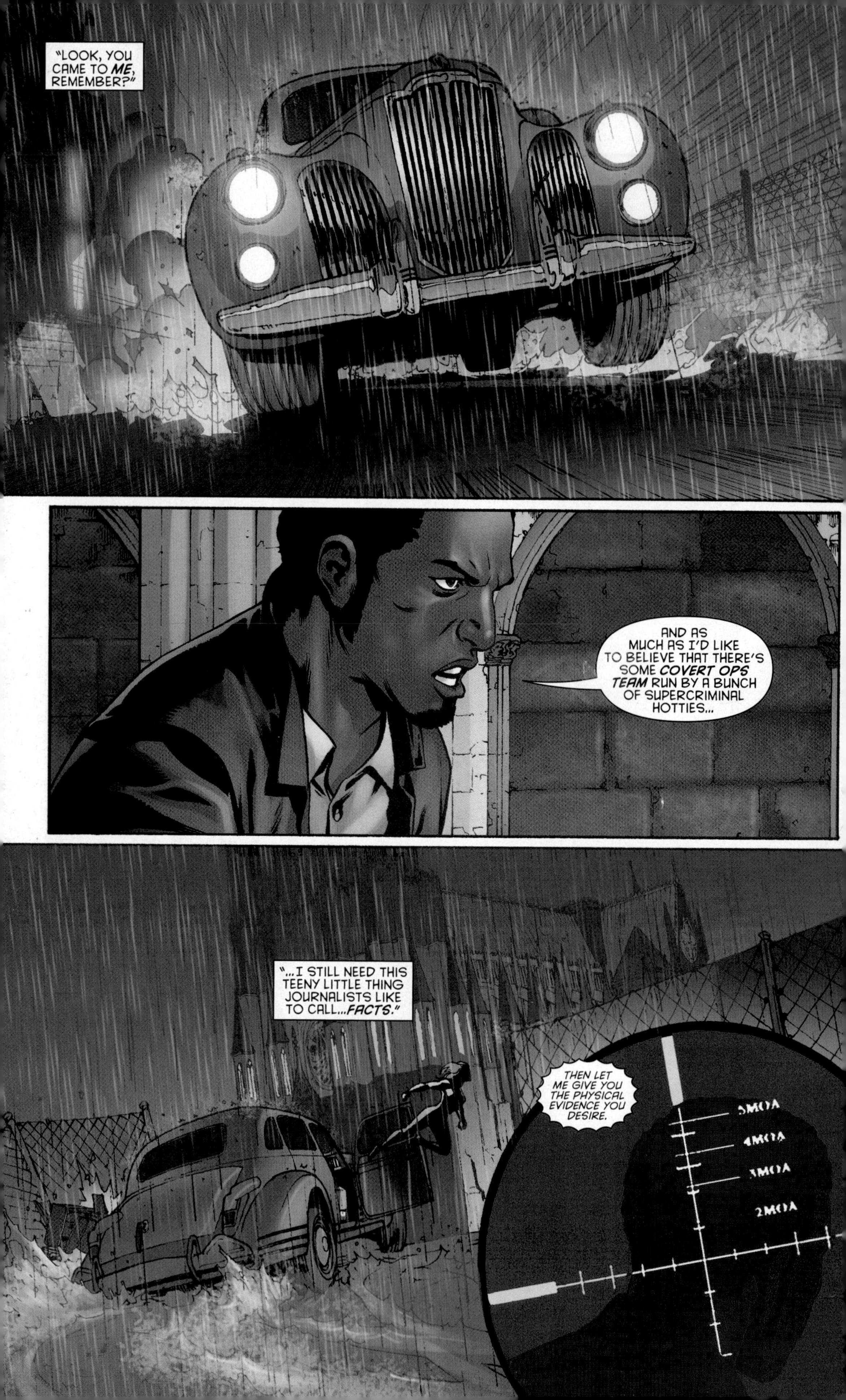
"LOOK, YOU CAME TO *ME*, REMEMBER?"
AND AS MUCH AS I'D LIKE TO BELIEVE THAT THERE'S SOME *COVERT OPS TEAM* RUN BY A BUNCH OF SUPERCRIMINAL HOTTIES...
"...I STILL NEED THIS TEENY LITTLE THING JOURNALISTS LIKE TO CALL...*FACTS*."
THEN LET ME GIVE YOU THE PHYSICAL EVIDENCE YOU DESIRE.
5MOA
4MOA
3MOA
2MOA

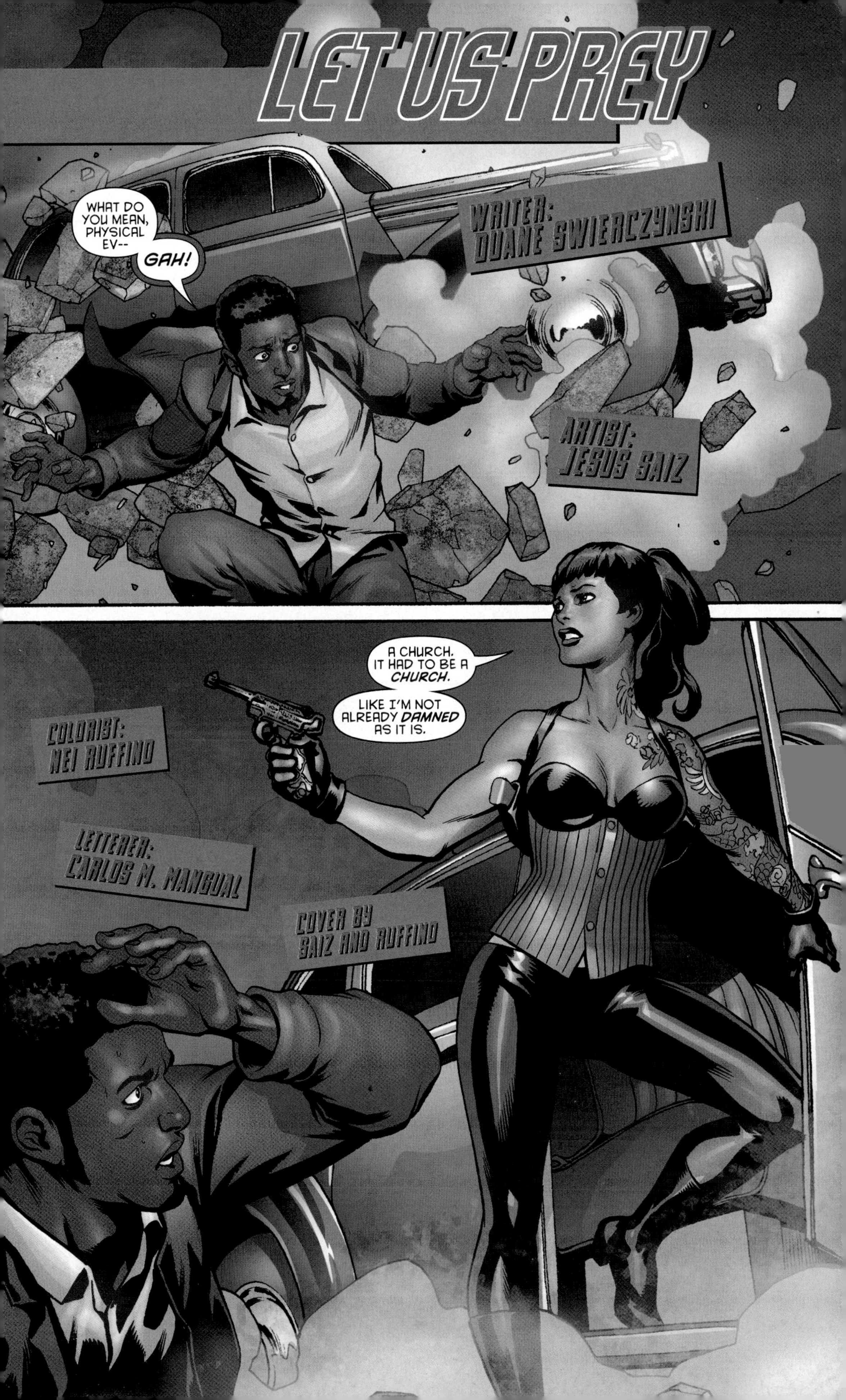
LET US PREY
WHAT DO YOU MEAN, PHYSICAL EV--
GAH!
WRITER: DUANE SWIERCZYNSKI
ARTIST: JESUS SAIZ
A CHURCH. IT HAD TO BE A CHURCH.
LIKE I'M NOT ALREADY DAMNED AS IT IS.
COLORIST: NEI RUFFINO
LETTERER: CARLOS M. MANGUAL
COVER BY SAIZ AND RUFFINO

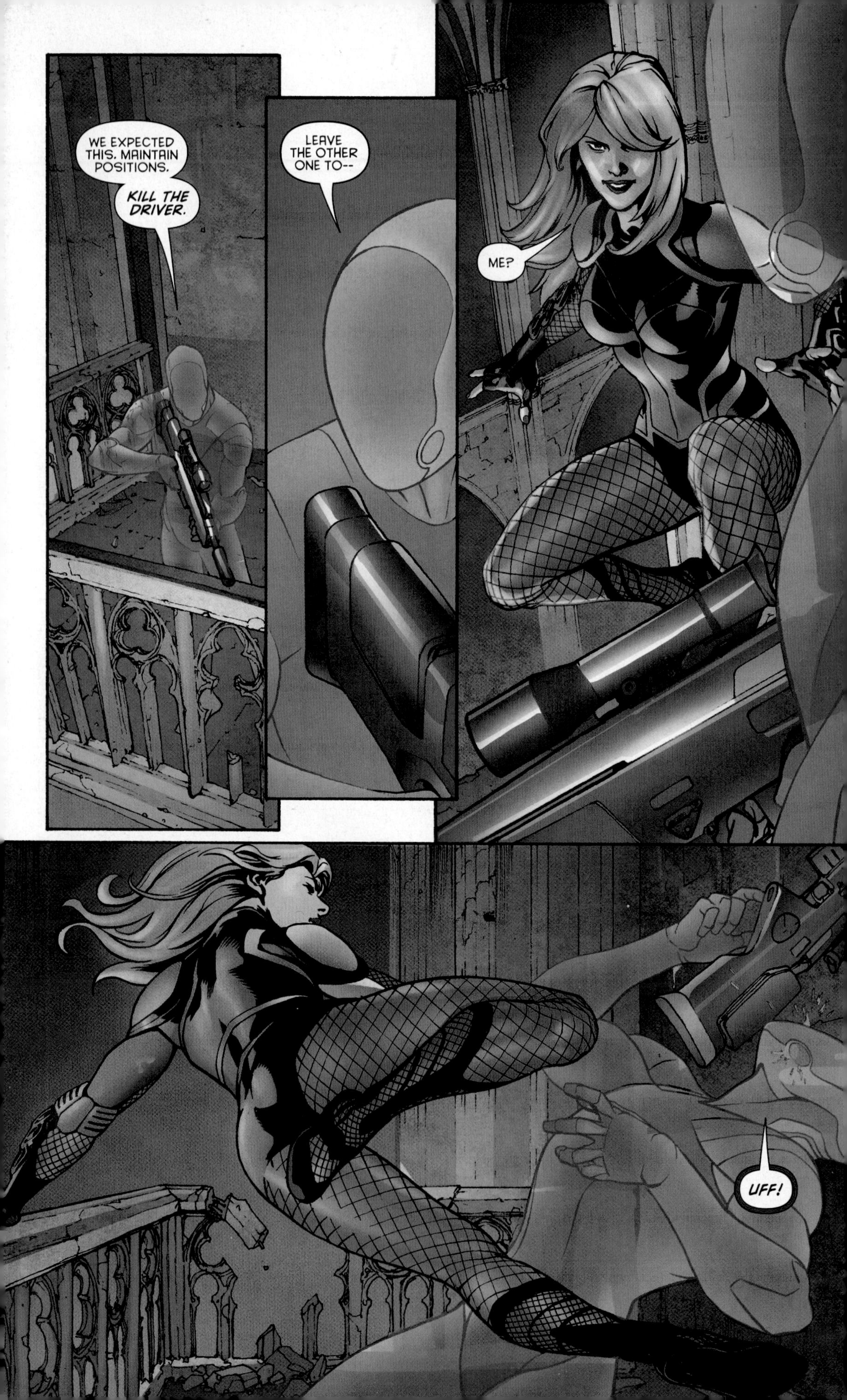
WE EXPECTED THIS. MAINTAIN POSITIONS.
KILL THE DRIVER.
LEAVE THE OTHER ONE TO--
ME?
UFF!

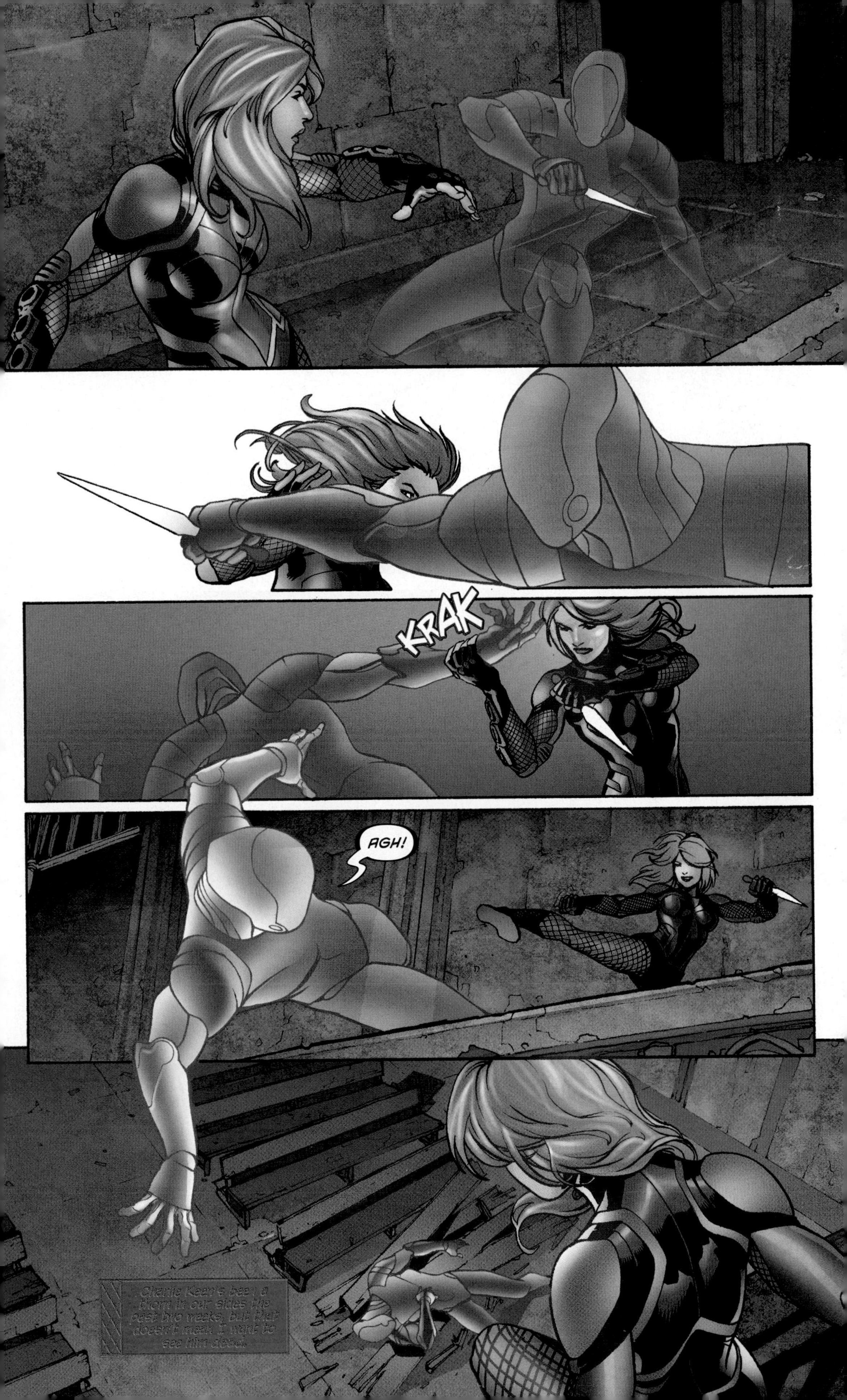
KRAK
AGH!
Charlie Keen's been a thorn in our sides the past two weeks, but that doesn't mean I want to see him dead.

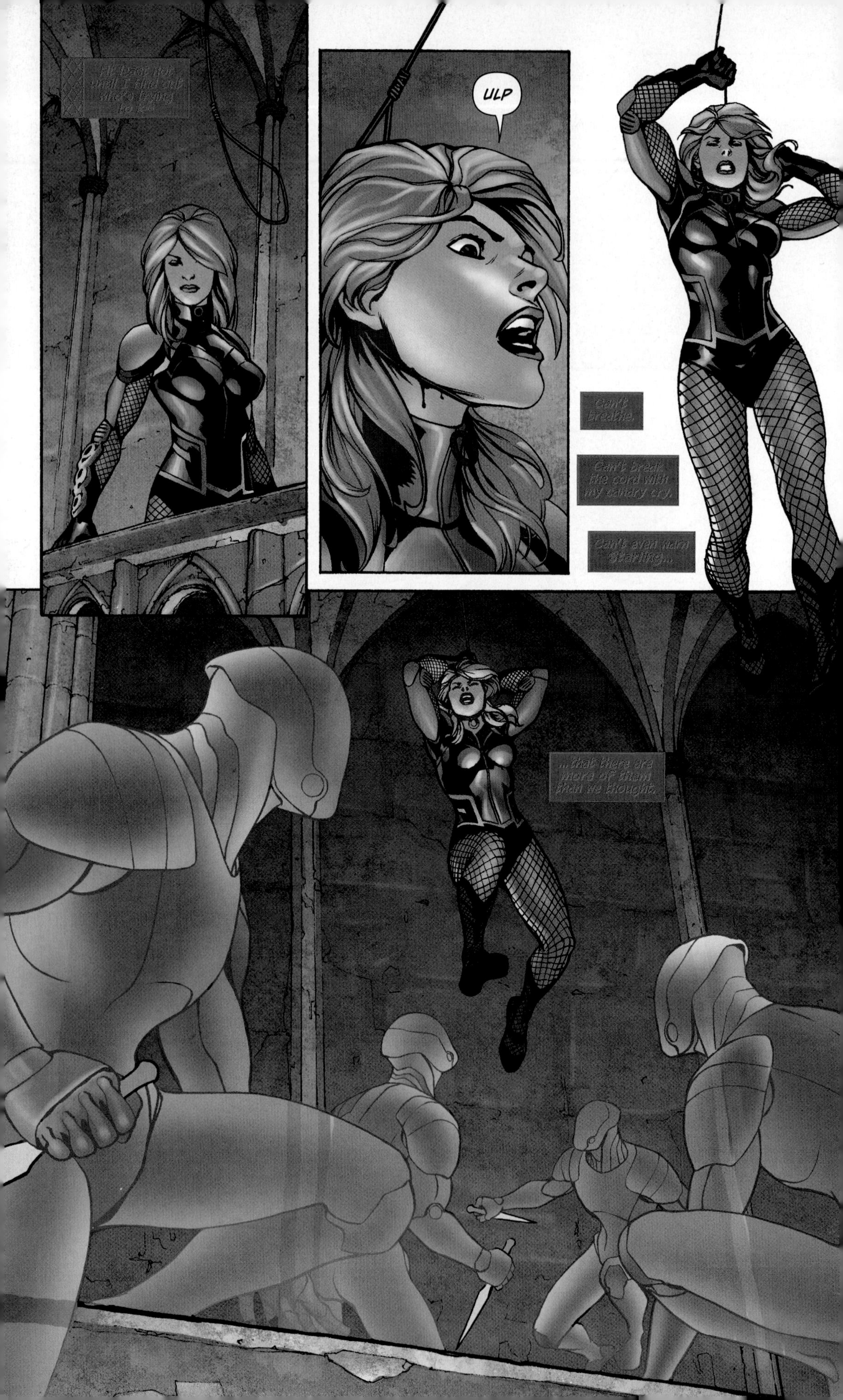
ULP
Can't breathe.
Can't break the cord with my canary cry.
Can't even warn Starling...
...that there are more of them than we thought.

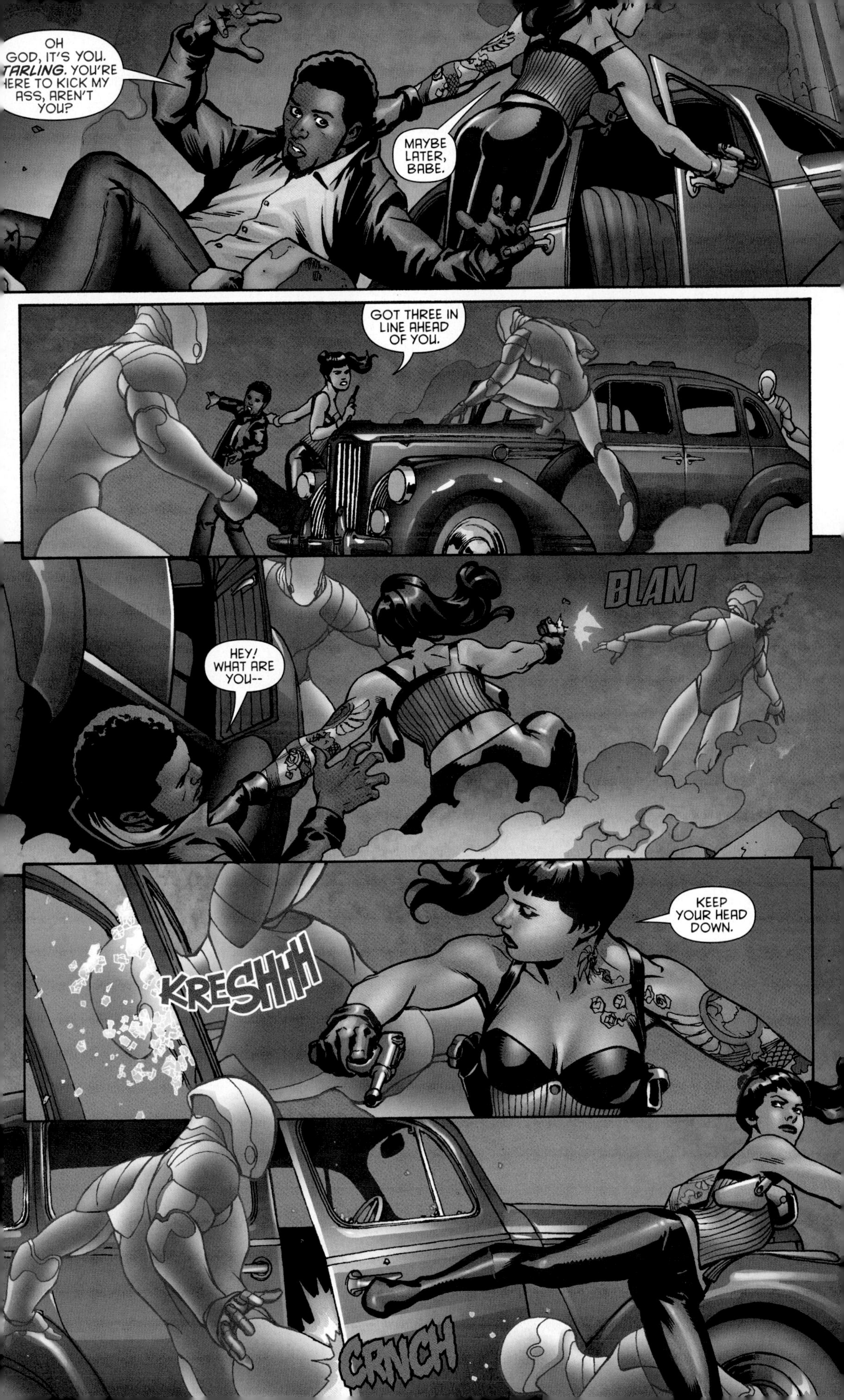

OH GOD, IT'S YOU. STARLING. YOU'RE HERE TO KICK MY ASS, AREN'T YOU?
MAYBE LATER, BABE.
GOT THREE IN LINE AHEAD OF YOU.
BLAM
HEY! WHAT ARE YOU--
KEEP YOUR HEAD DOWN.
KRESHHH
CRNCH

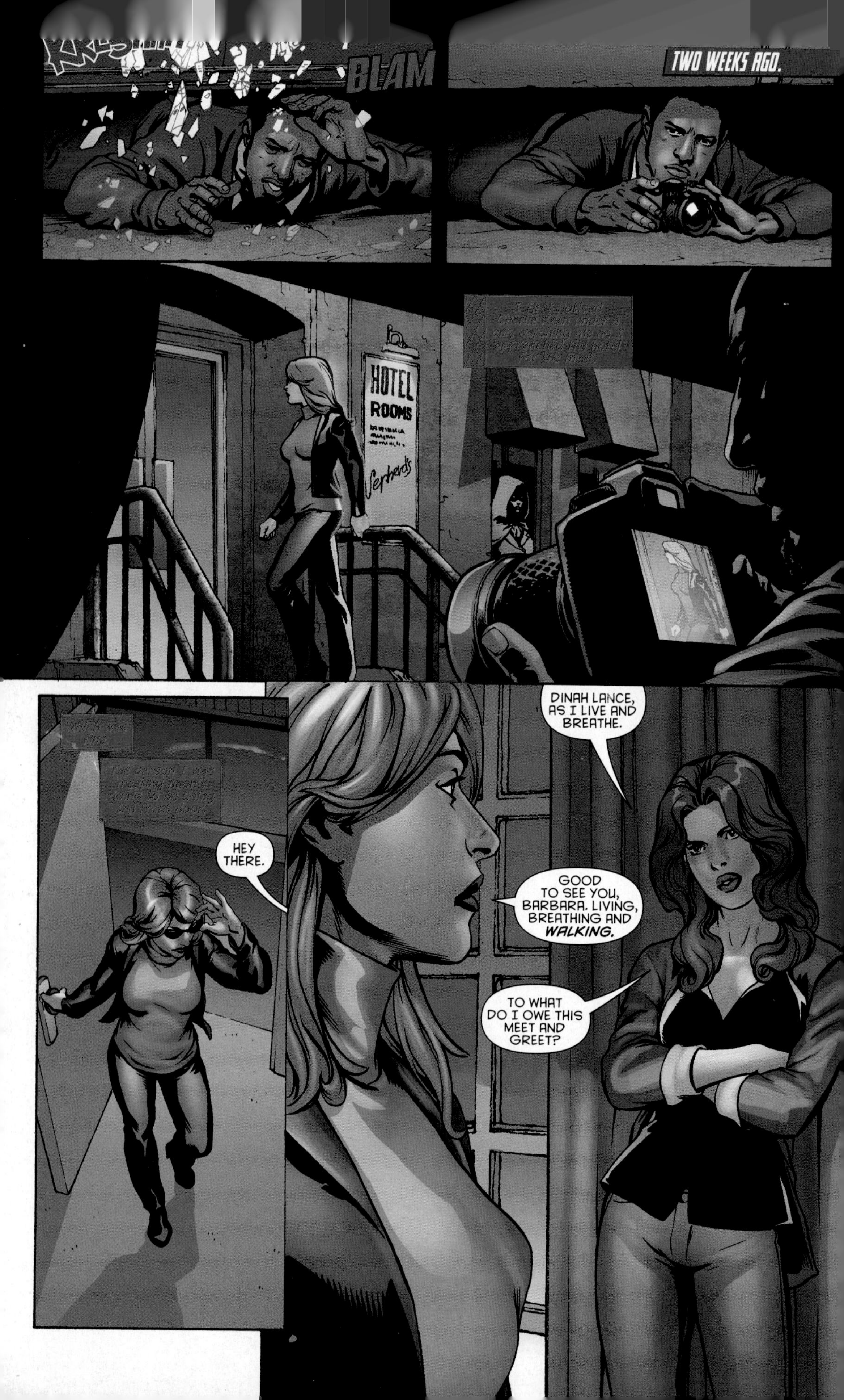

BLAM
TWO WEEKS AGO.
HOTEL
ROOMS
HEY THERE.
DINAH LANCE, AS I LIVE AND BREATHE.
GOOD TO SEE YOU, BARBARA. LIVING, BREATHING AND *WALKING.*
TO WHAT DO I OWE THIS MEET AND GREET?

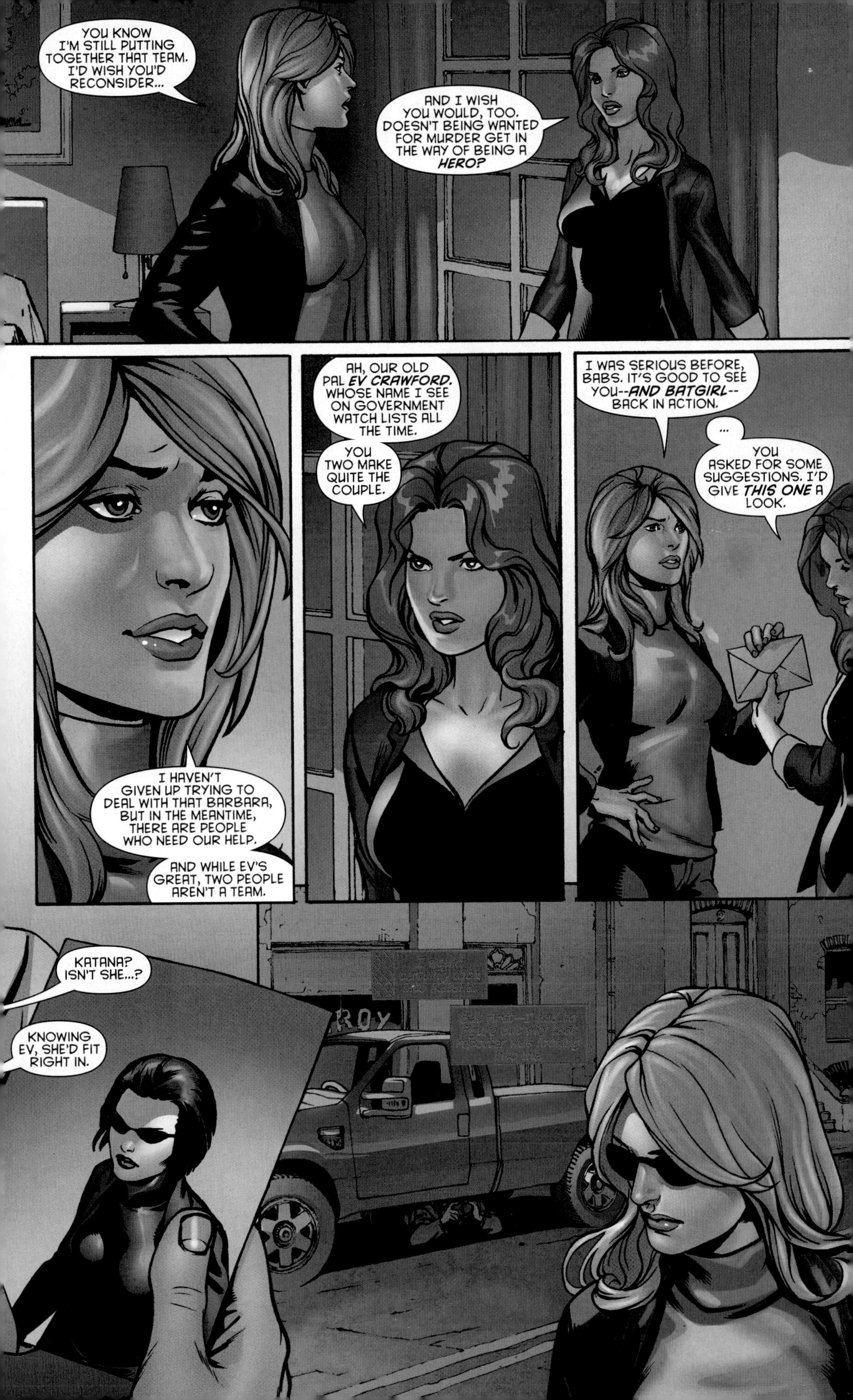
YOU KNOW I'M STILL PUTTING TOGETHER THAT TEAM. I'D WISH YOU'D RECONSIDER...
AND I WISH YOU WOULD, TOO. DOESN'T BEING WANTED FOR MURDER GET IN THE WAY OF BEING A HERO?
I HAVEN'T GIVEN UP TRYING TO DEAL WITH THAT BARBARA, BUT IN THE MEANTIME, THERE ARE PEOPLE WHO NEED OUR HELP.
AND WHILE EV'S GREAT, TWO PEOPLE AREN'T A TEAM.
AH, OUR OLD PAL EV CRAWFORD. WHOSE NAME I SEE ON GOVERNMENT WATCH LISTS ALL THE TIME.
YOU TWO MAKE QUITE THE COUPLE.
I WAS SERIOUS BEFORE, BABS. IT'S GOOD TO SEE YOU--AND BATGIRL--BACK IN ACTION.
...
YOU ASKED FOR SOME SUGGESTIONS. I'D GIVE THIS ONE A LOOK.
KATANA? ISN'T SHE...?
KNOWING EV, SHE'D FIT RIGHT IN.

SCRRRRRREEEEEEEEZEE

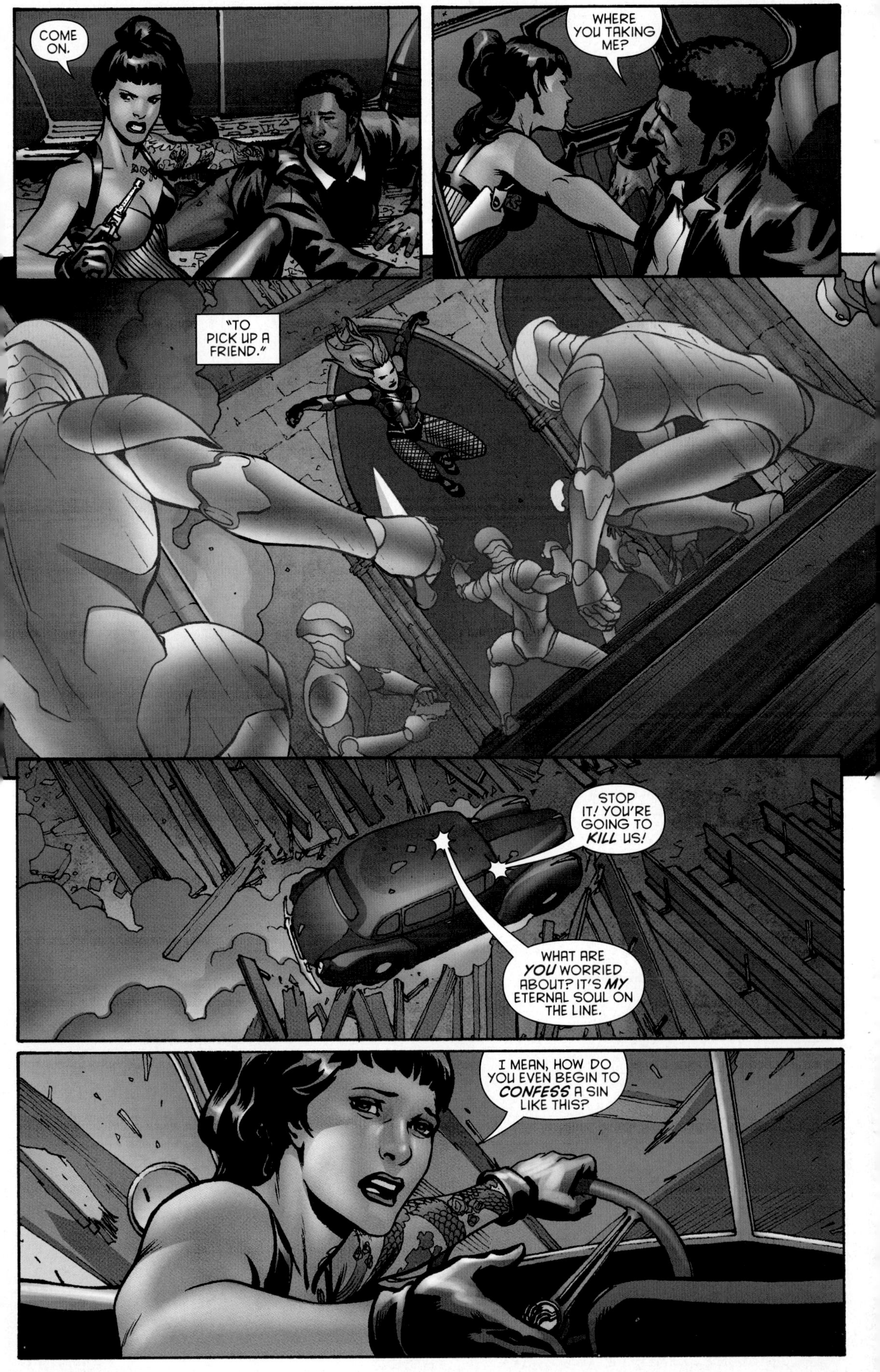
COME ON.
WHERE YOU TAKING ME?
"TO PICK UP A FRIEND."
STOP IT! YOU'RE GOING TO KILL US!
WHAT ARE YOU WORRIED ABOUT? IT'S MY ETERNAL SOUL ON THE LINE.
I MEAN, HOW DO YOU EVEN BEGIN TO CONFESS A SIN LIKE THIS?

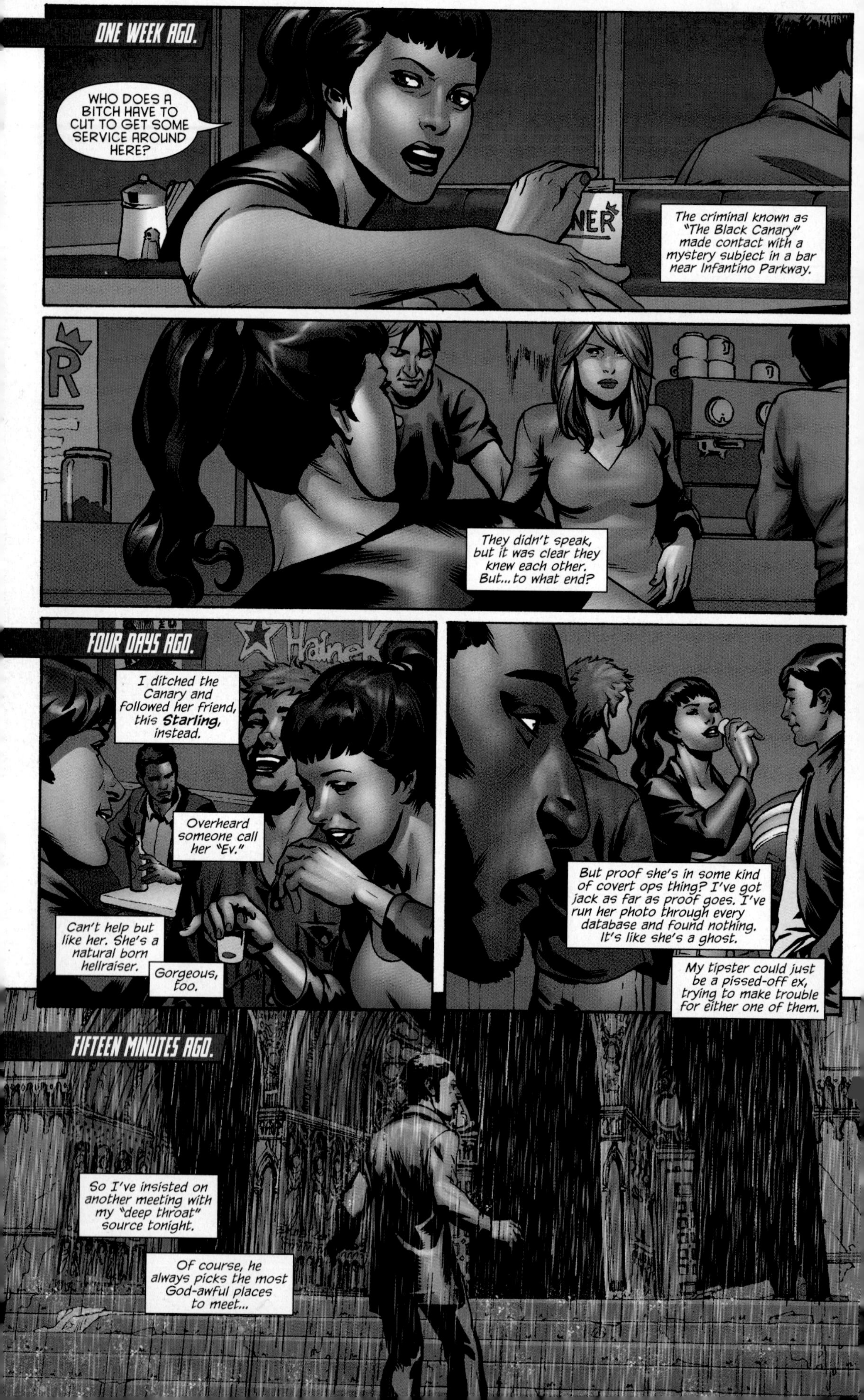
ONE WEEK AGO.
WHO DOES A BITCH HAVE TO CUT TO GET SOME SERVICE AROUND HERE?
The criminal known as "The Black Canary" made contact with a mystery subject in a bar near Infantino Parkway.
They didn't speak, but it was clear they knew each other. But...to what end?
FOUR DAYS AGO.
I ditched the Canary and followed her friend, this Starling, instead.
Overheard someone call her "Ev."
Can't help but like her. She's a natural born hellraiser.
Gorgeous, too.
But proof she's in some kind of covert ops thing? I've got jack as far as proof goes. I've run her photo through every database and found nothing. It's like she's a ghost.
My tipster could just be a pissed-off ex, trying to make trouble for either one of them.
FIFTEEN MINUTES AGO.
So I've insisted on another meeting with my "deep throat" source tonight.
Of course, he always picks the most God-awful places to meet...

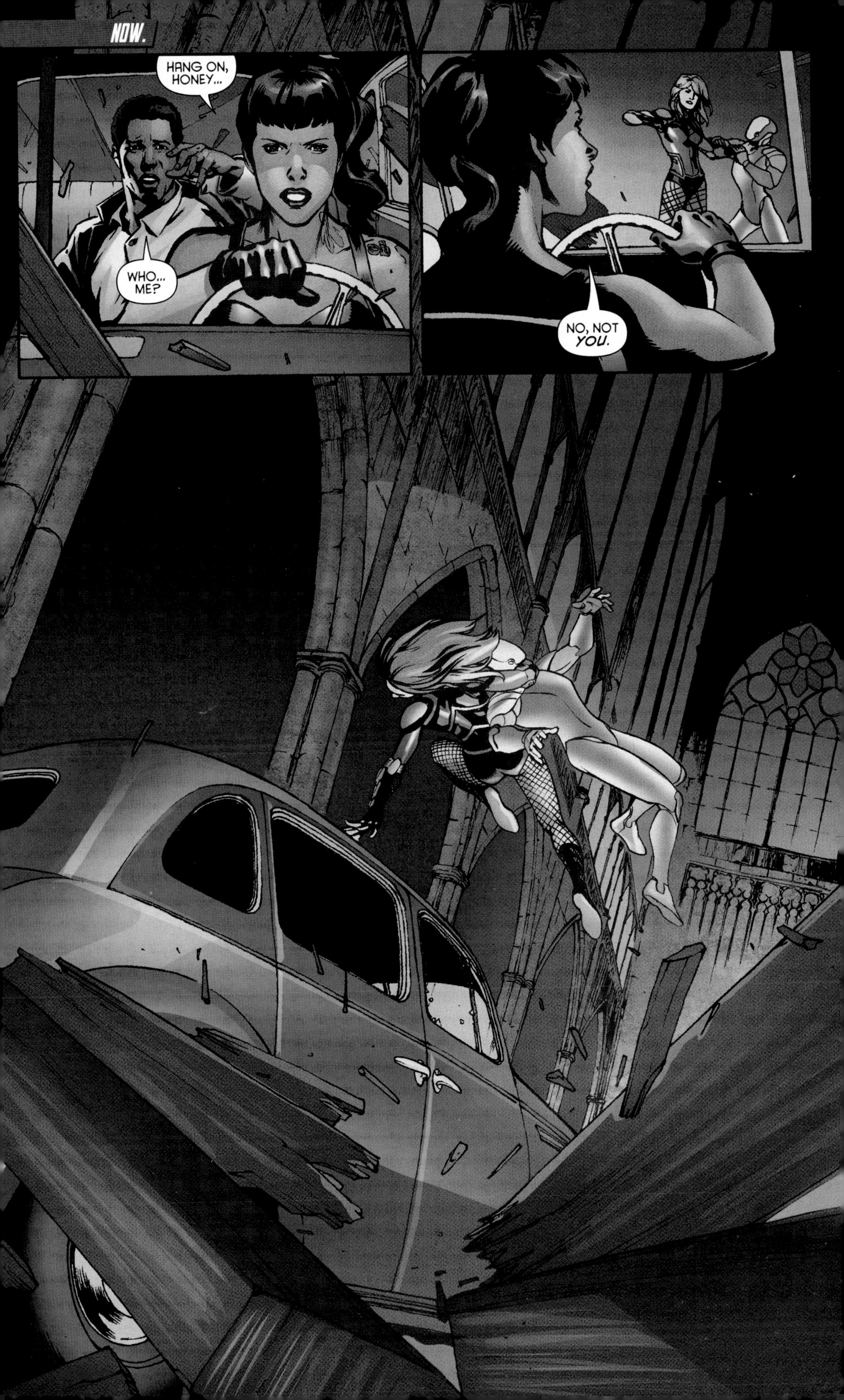
NOW.
HANG ON, HONEY...
WHO... ME?
NO, NOT YOU.

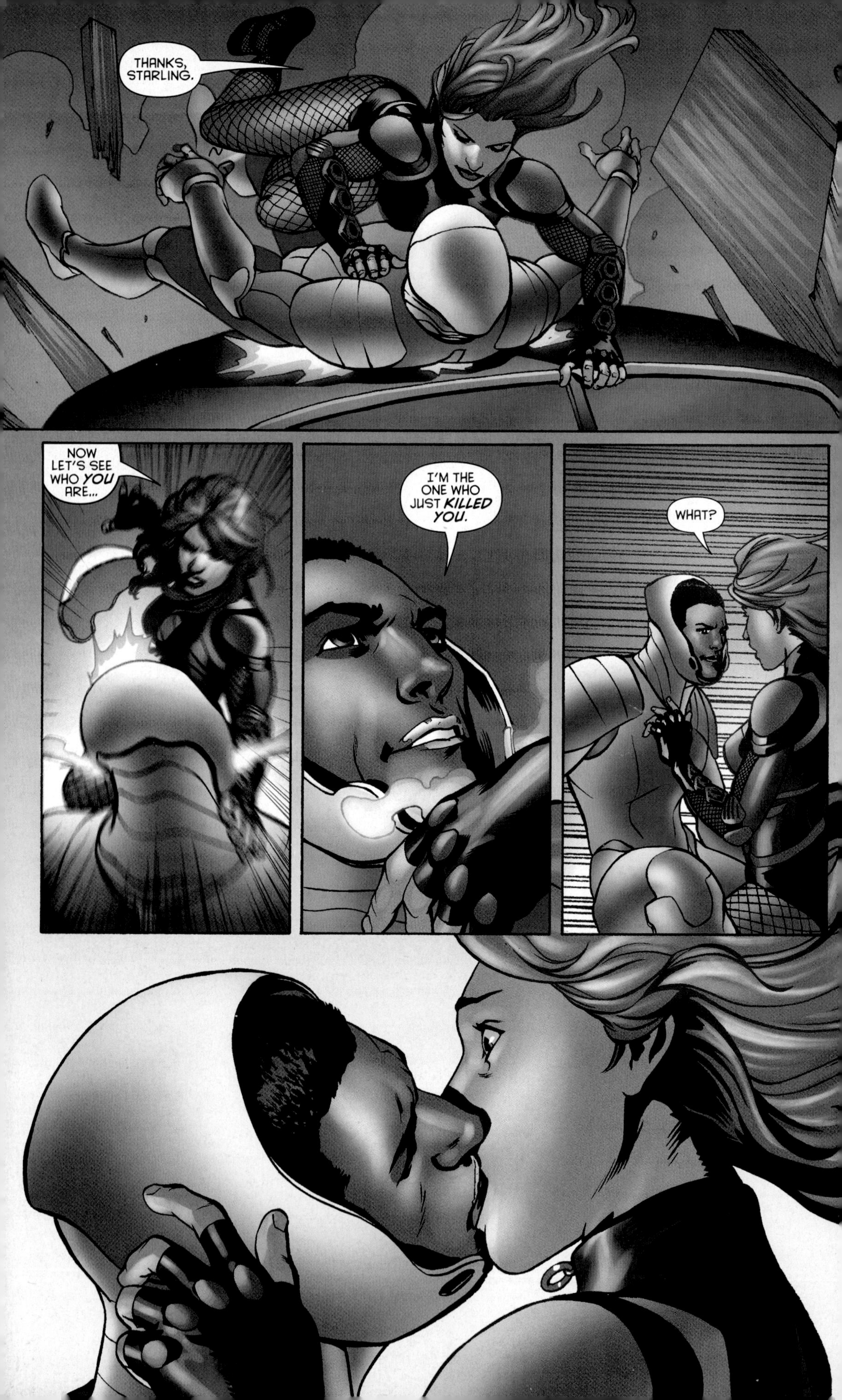
THANKS, STARLING.
NOW LET'S SEE WHO *YOU* ARE...
I'M THE ONE WHO JUST *KILLED YOU*.
WHAT?

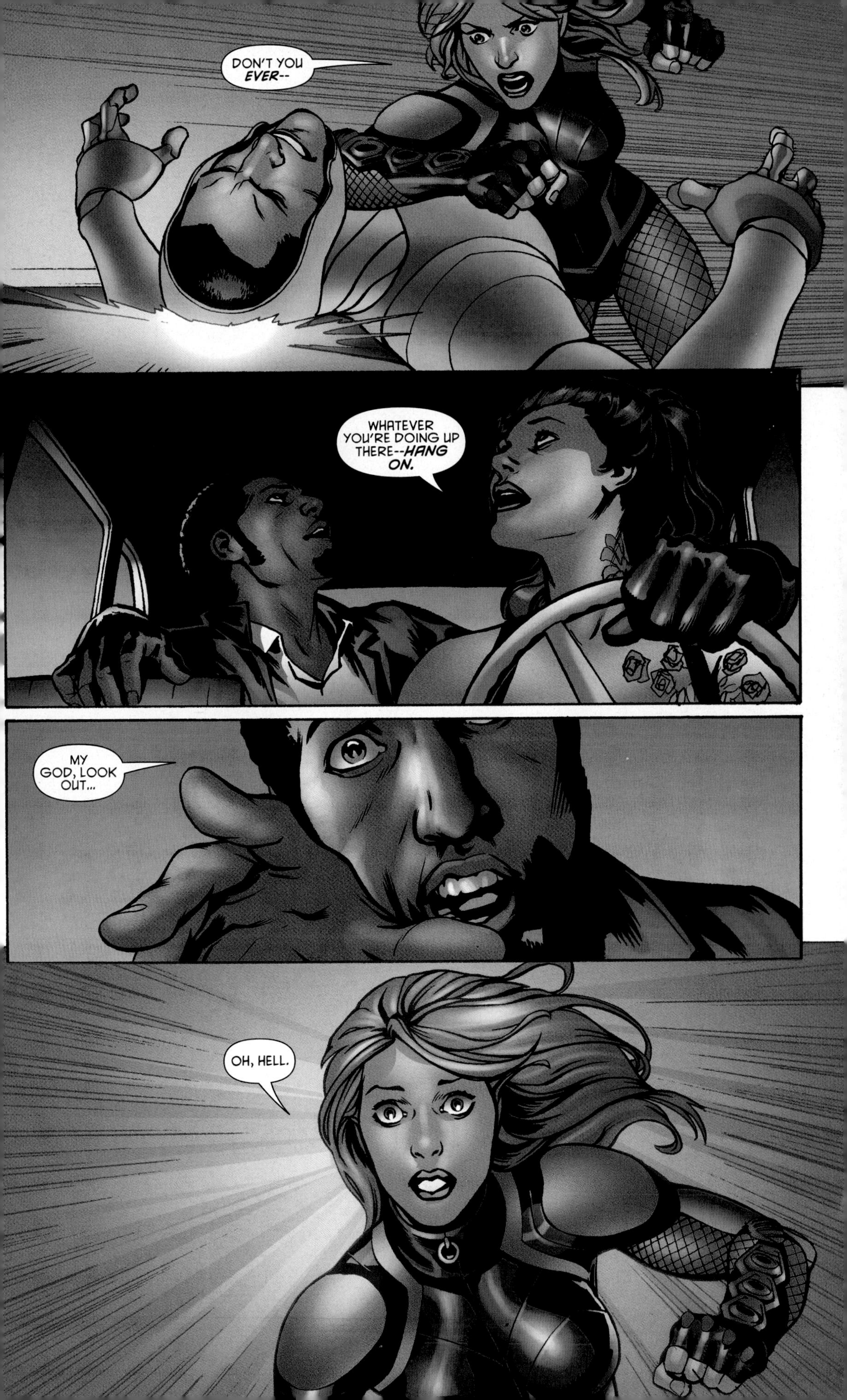
DON'T YOU *EVER*--
WHATEVER YOU'RE DOING UP THERE--*HANG ON.*
MY GOD, LOOK OUT...
OH, HELL.

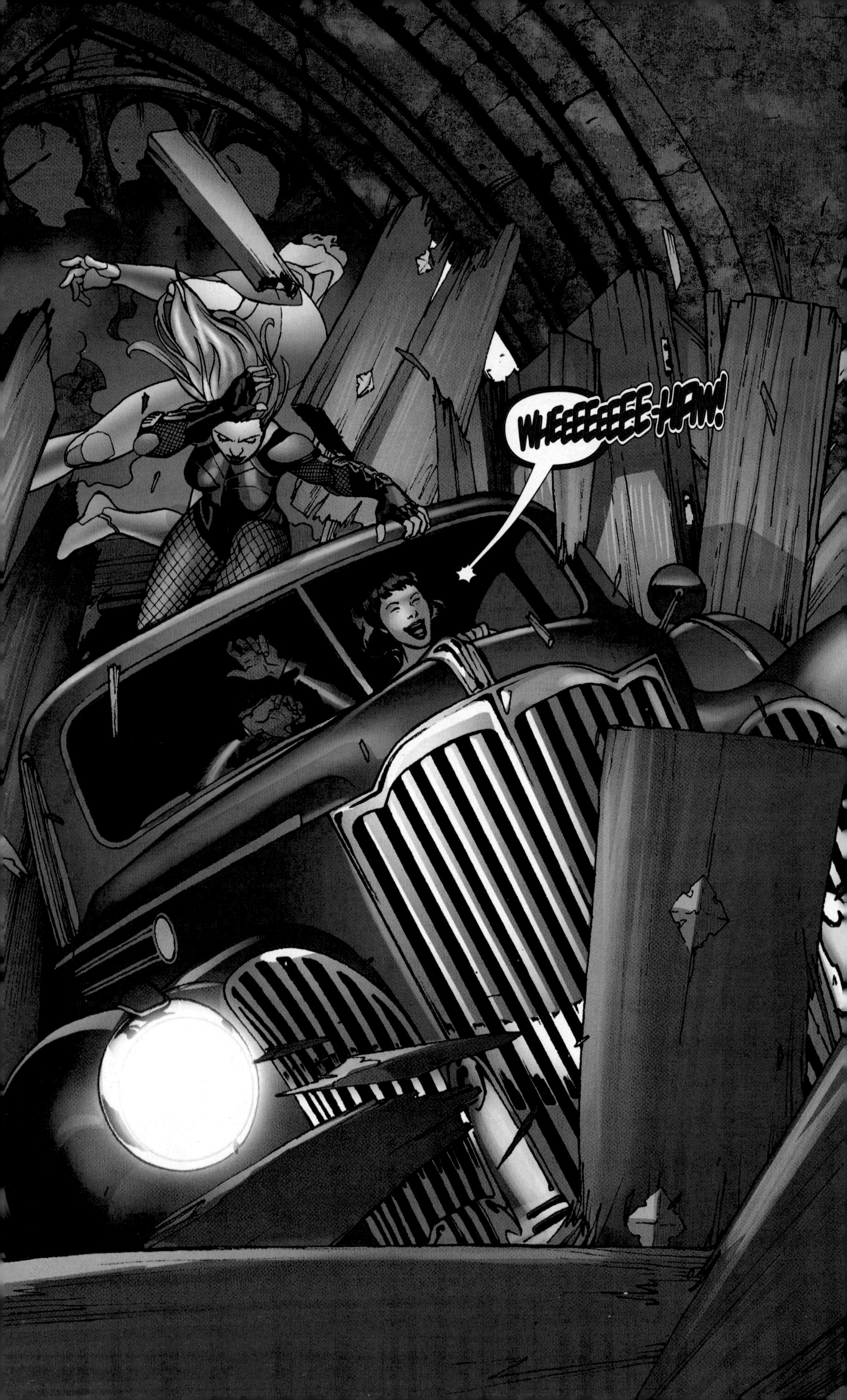
WHEEEEEEEE-HAW!

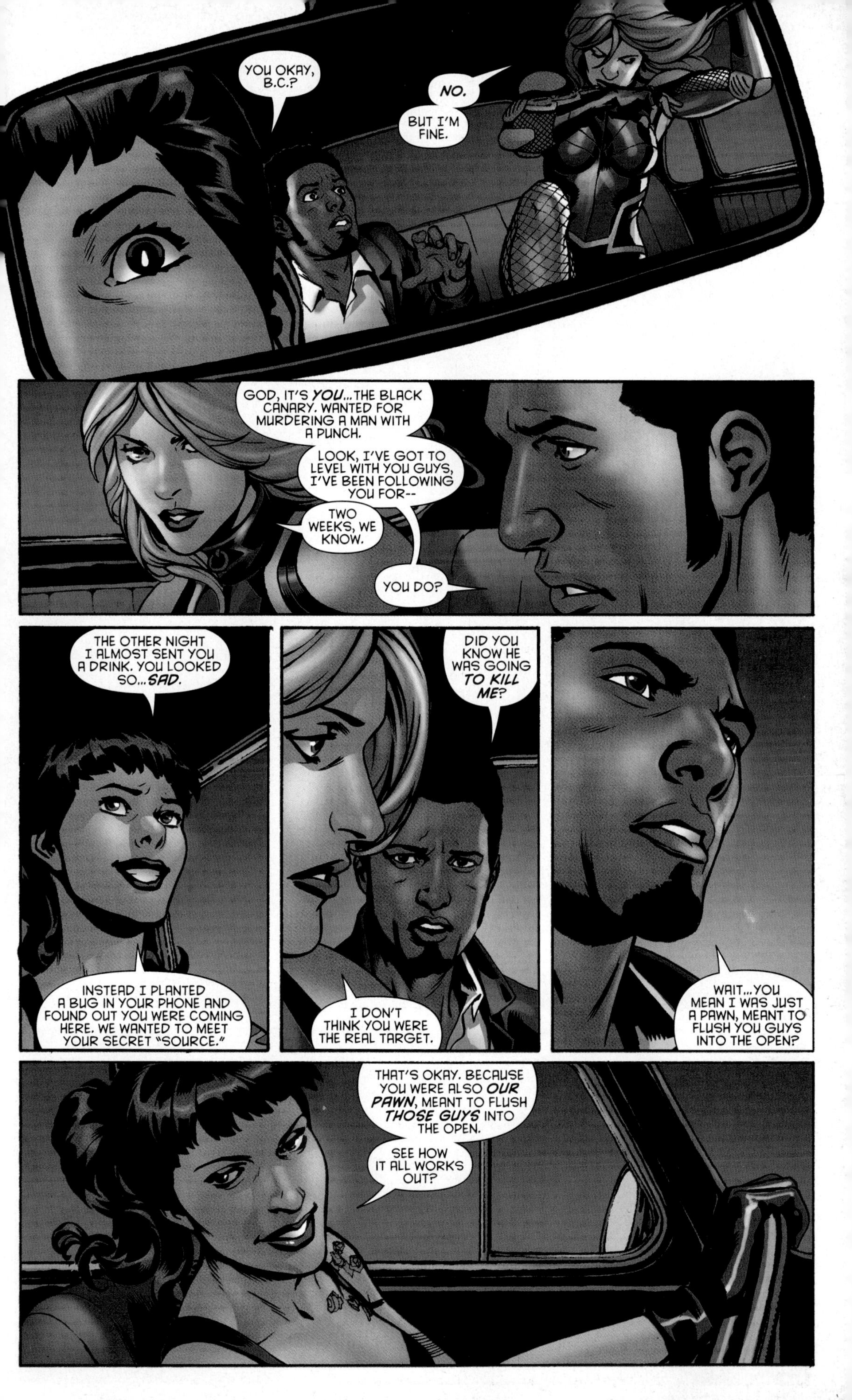

YOU OKAY, B.C.?
NO.
BUT I'M FINE.
GOD, IT'S YOU... THE BLACK CANARY. WANTED FOR MURDERING A MAN WITH A PUNCH.
LOOK, I'VE GOT TO LEVEL WITH YOU GUYS, I'VE BEEN FOLLOWING YOU FOR--
TWO WEEKS, WE KNOW.
YOU DO?
THE OTHER NIGHT I ALMOST SENT YOU A DRINK. YOU LOOKED SO...SAD.
INSTEAD I PLANTED A BUG IN YOUR PHONE AND FOUND OUT YOU WERE COMING HERE. WE WANTED TO MEET YOUR SECRET "SOURCE."
DID YOU KNOW HE WAS GOING TO KILL ME?
I DON'T THINK YOU WERE THE REAL TARGET.
WAIT...YOU MEAN I WAS JUST A PAWN, MEANT TO FLUSH YOU GUYS INTO THE OPEN?
THAT'S OKAY. BECAUSE YOU WERE ALSO OUR PAWN, MEANT TO FLUSH THOSE GUYS INTO THE OPEN.
SEE HOW IT ALL WORKS OUT?

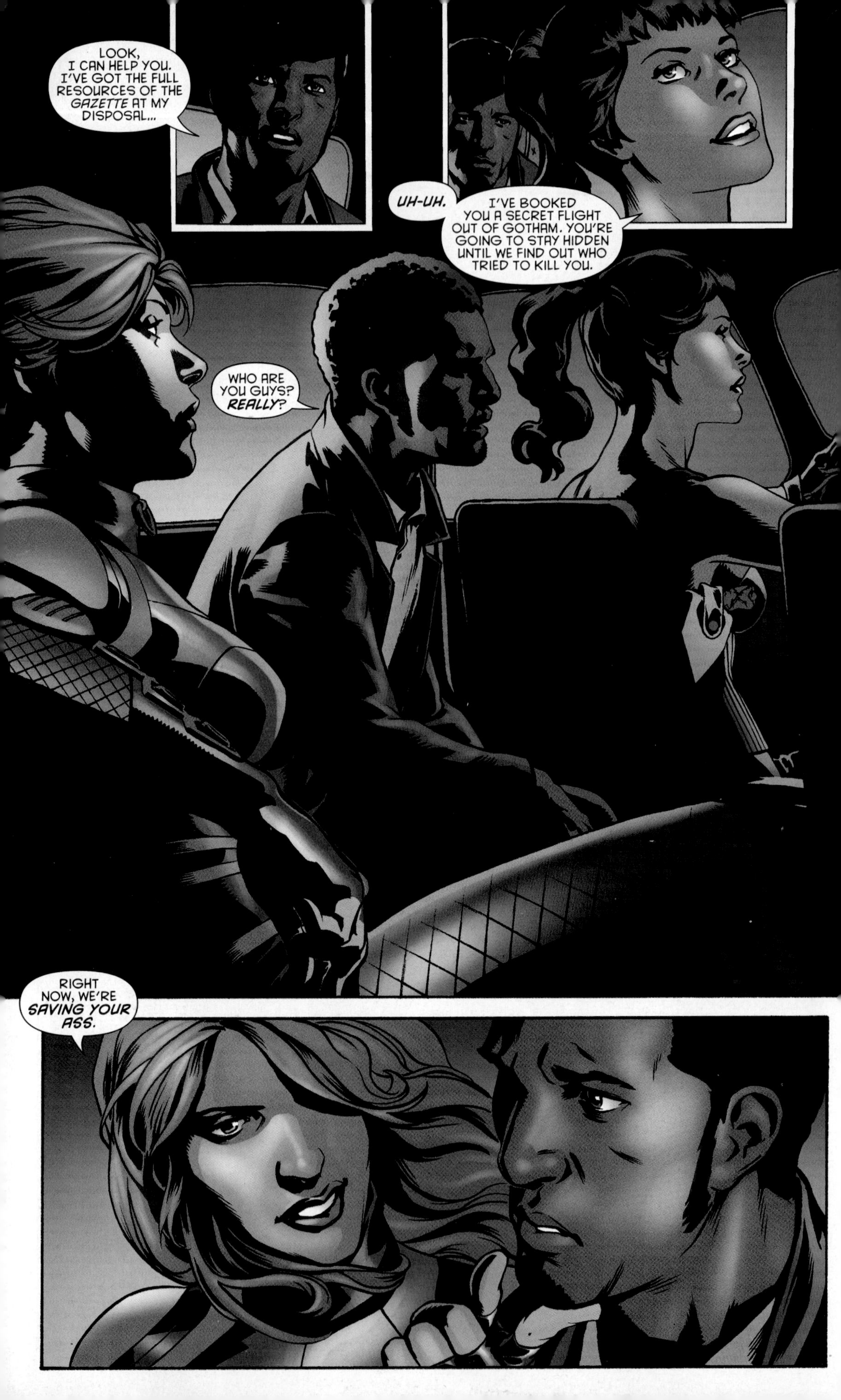
LOOK, I CAN HELP YOU. I'VE GOT THE FULL RESOURCES OF THE *GAZETTE* AT MY DISPOSAL...
UH-UH.
I'VE BOOKED YOU A SECRET FLIGHT OUT OF GOTHAM. YOU'RE GOING TO STAY HIDDEN UNTIL WE FIND OUT WHO TRIED TO KILL YOU.
WHO ARE YOU GUYS? *REALLY*?
RIGHT NOW, WE'RE *SAVING YOUR ASS*.

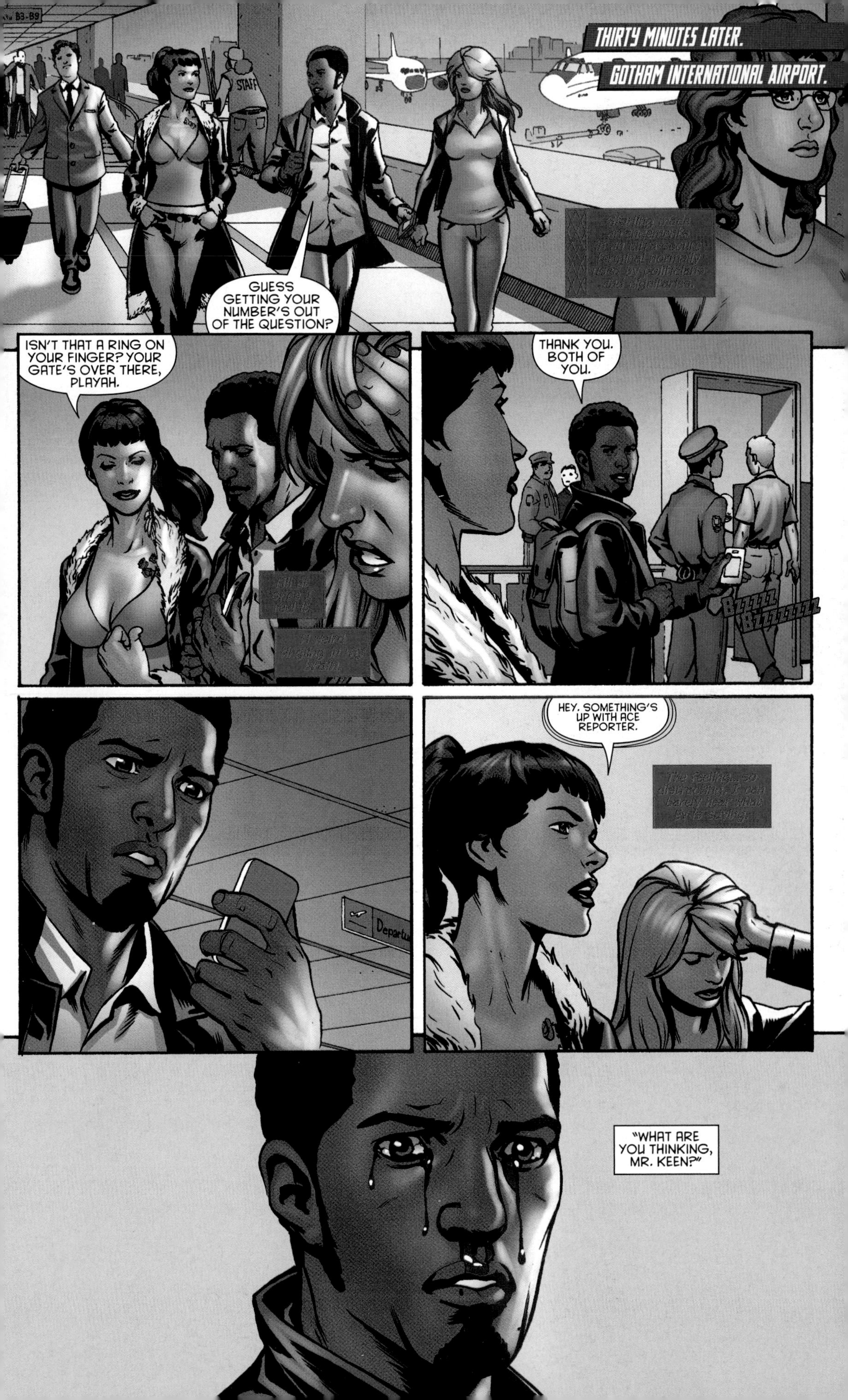
THIRTY MINUTES LATER.
GOTHAM INTERNATIONAL AIRPORT.
GUESS GETTING YOUR NUMBER'S OUT OF THE QUESTION?
ISN'T THAT A RING ON YOUR FINGER? YOUR GATE'S OVER THERE, PLAYAH.
THANK YOU. BOTH OF YOU.
HEY. SOMETHING'S UP WITH ACE REPORTER.
"WHAT ARE YOU THINKING, MR. KEEN?"

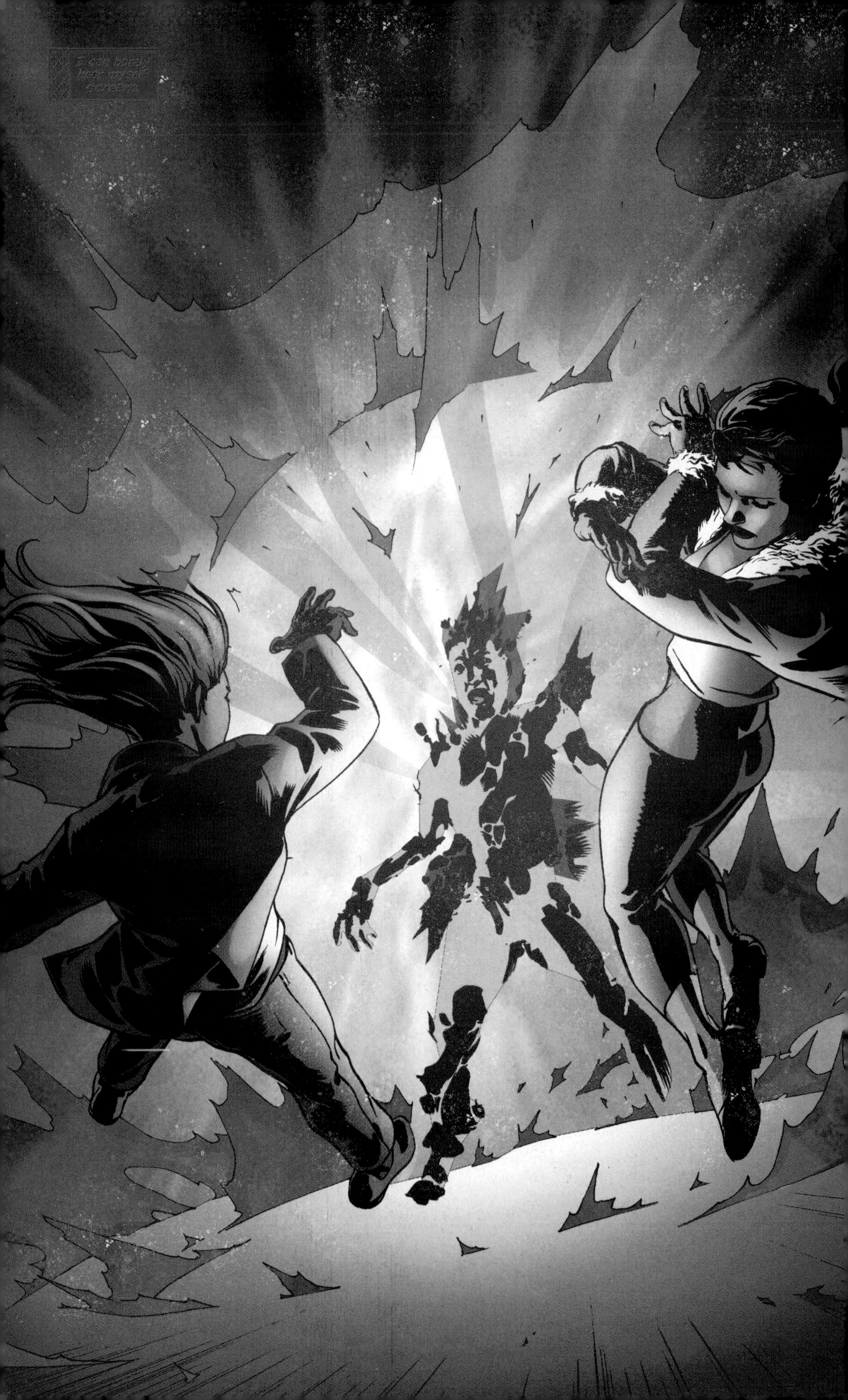
I can barely hear myself scream.

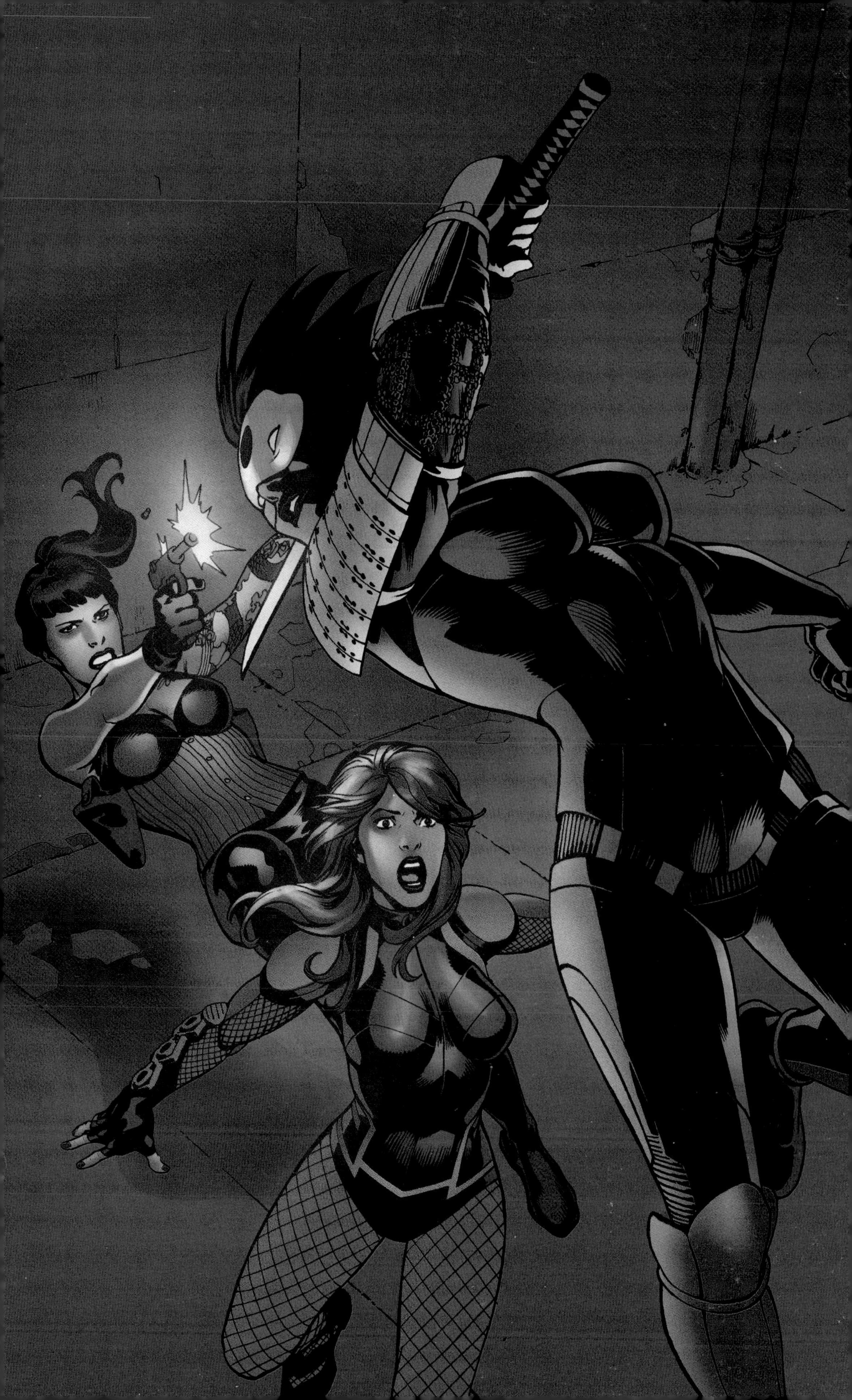

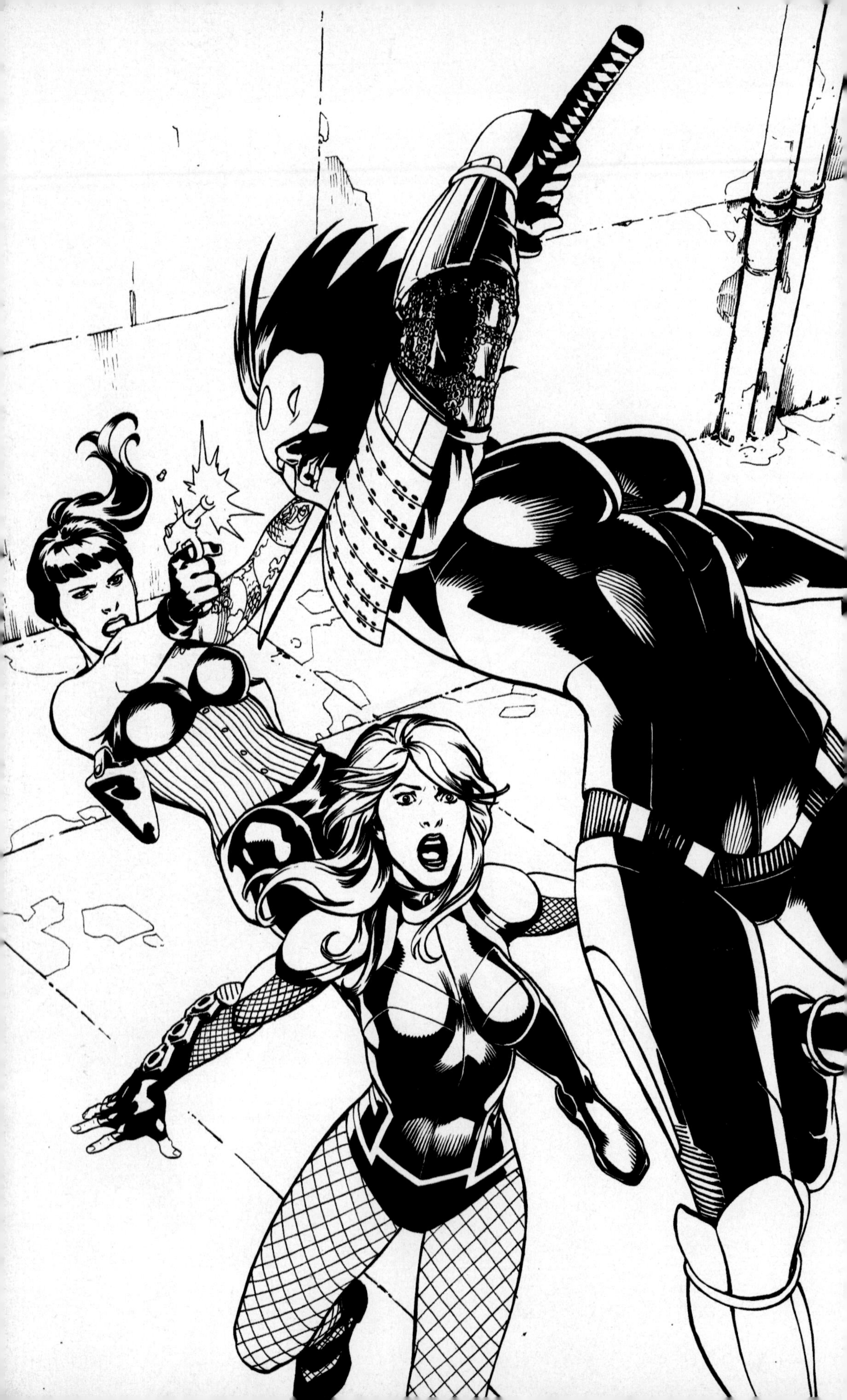

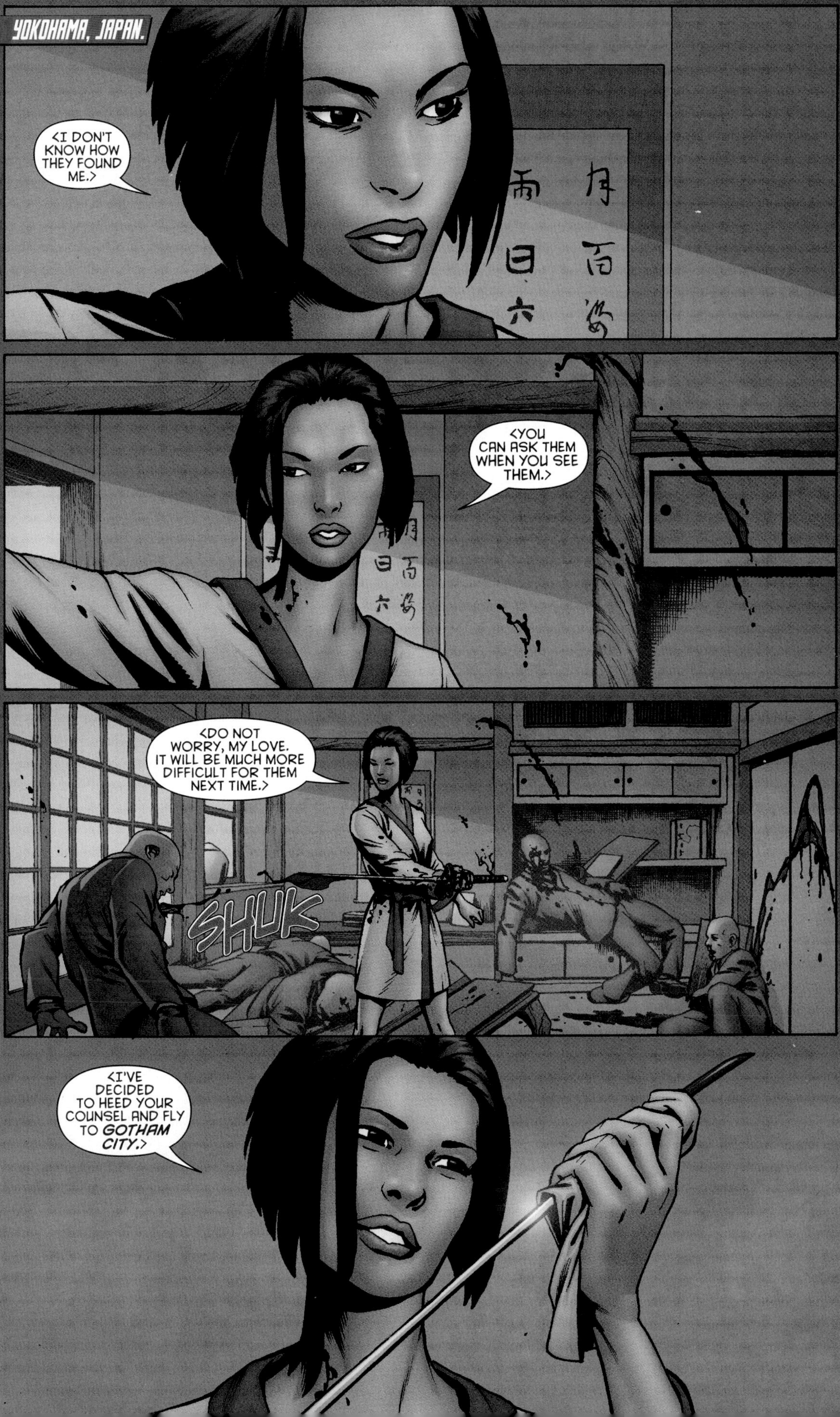
YOKOHAMA, JAPAN.
<I DON'T KNOW HOW THEY FOUND ME.>
<YOU CAN ASK THEM WHEN YOU SEE THEM.>
<DO NOT WORRY, MY LOVE. IT WILL BE MUCH MORE DIFFICULT FOR THEM NEXT TIME.>
SHUK
<I'VE DECIDED TO HEED YOUR COUNSEL AND FLY TO *GOTHAM CITY.*>

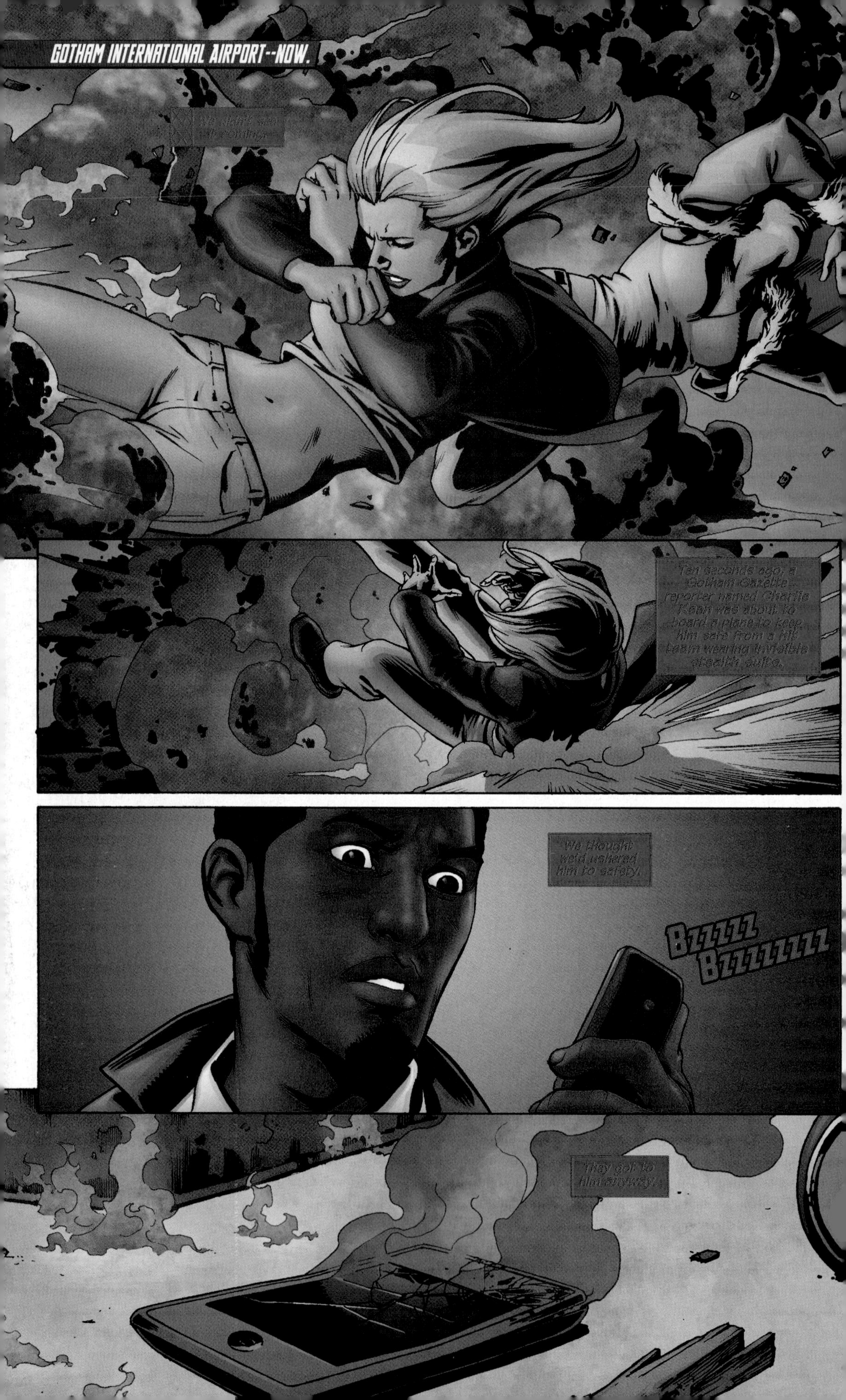
GOTHAM INTERNATIONAL AIRPORT--NOW.
We didn't see it coming.
Ten seconds ago, a Gotham Gazette reporter named Charlie Kean was about to board a plane to keep him safe from a hit team wearing invisible stealth suits.
We thought we'd ushered him to safety.
Bzzzzz Bzzzzzzzz
They got to him anyway.

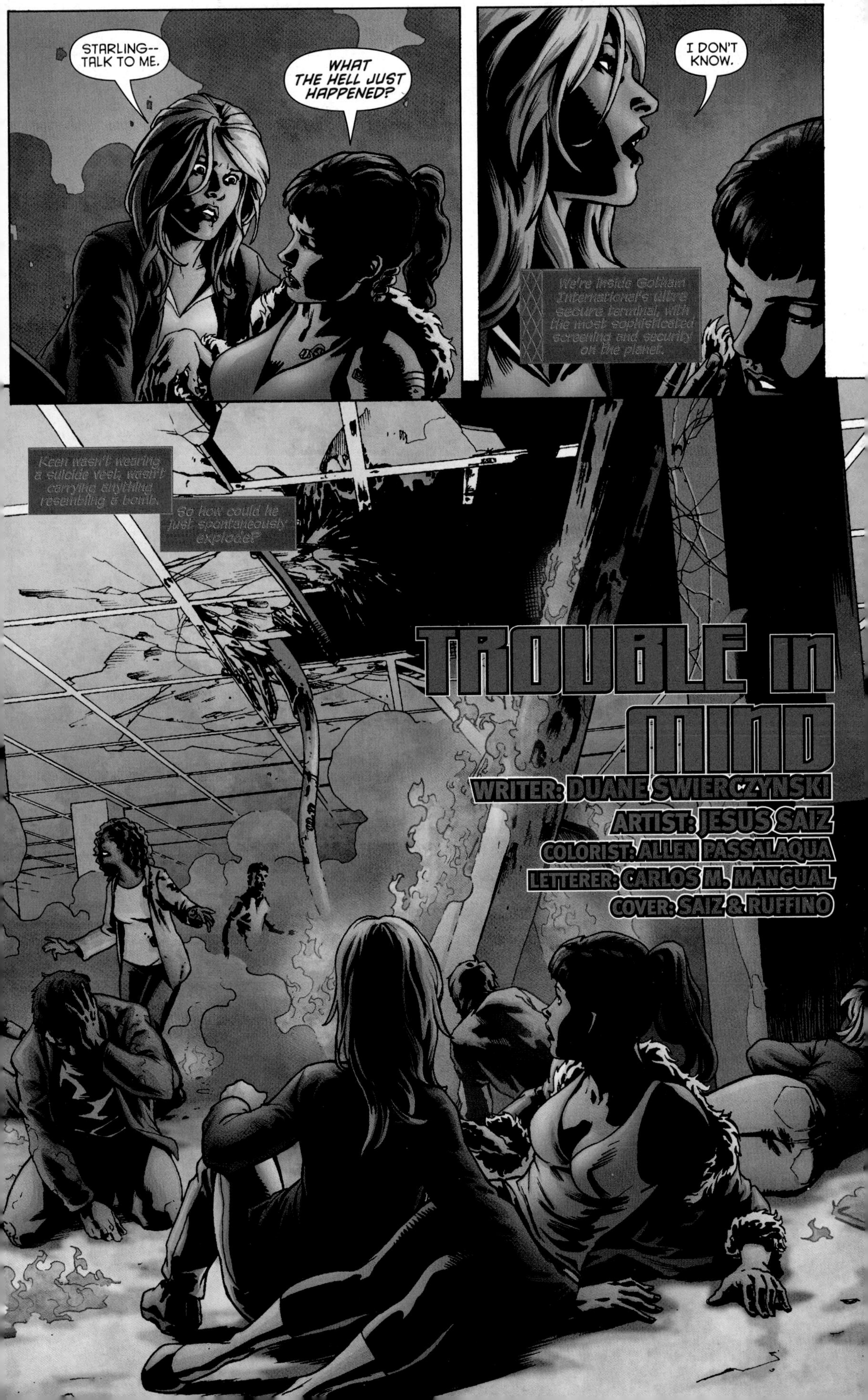
STARLING-- TALK TO ME.
WHAT THE HELL JUST HAPPENED?
I DON'T KNOW.
We're inside Gotham International's ultra secure terminal, with the most sophisticated screening and security on the planet.
Keen wasn't wearing a suicide vest, wasn't carrying anything resembling a bomb.
So how could he just spontaneously explode?
TROUBLE in MIND
WRITER: DUANE SWIERCZYNSKI
ARTIST: JESUS SAIZ
COLORIST: ALLEN PASSALAQUA
LETTERER: CARLOS M. MANGUAL
COVER: SAIZ & RUFFINO

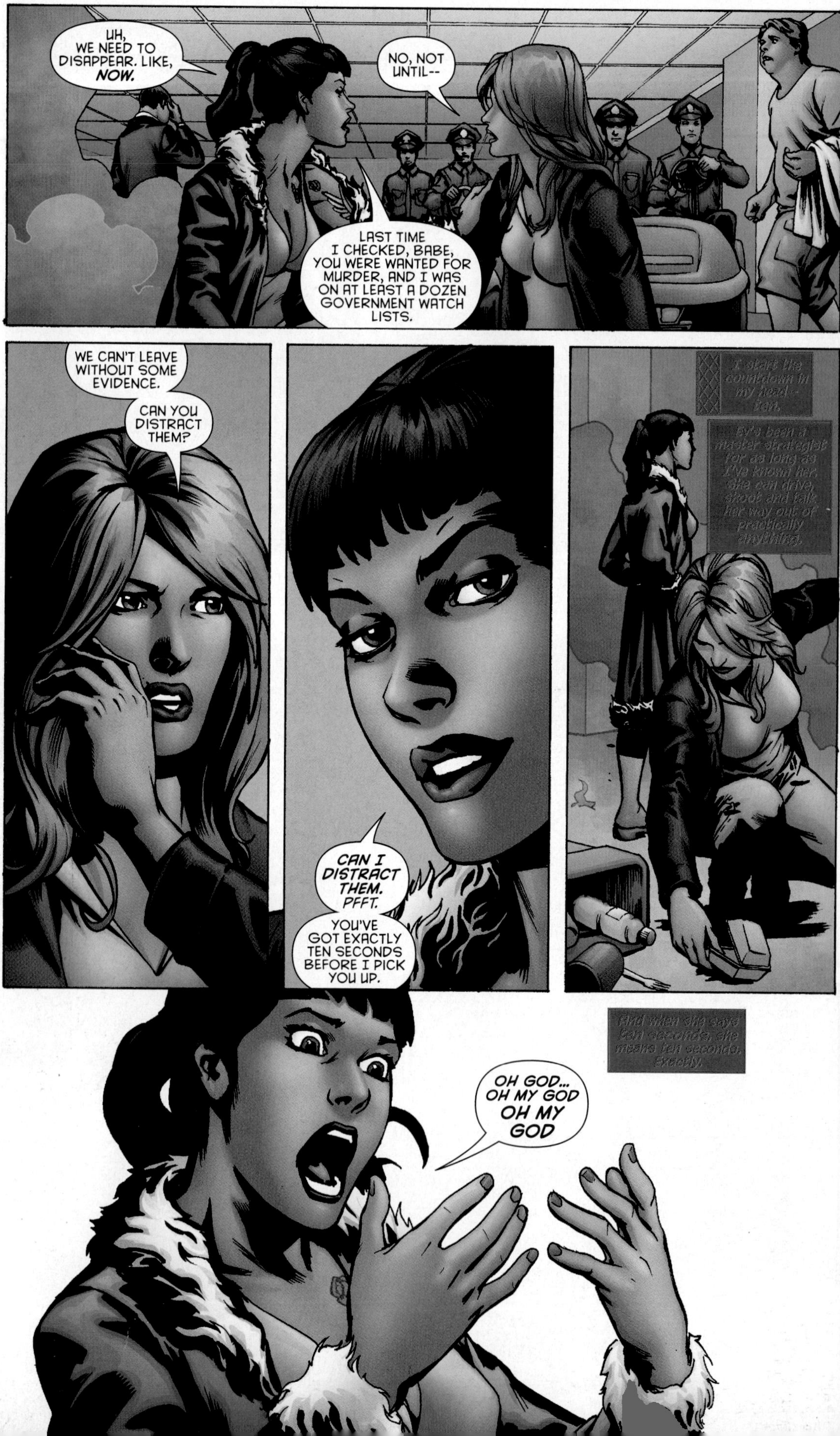

UH, WE NEED TO DISAPPEAR. LIKE, NOW.
NO, NOT UNTIL--
LAST TIME I CHECKED, BABE, YOU WERE WANTED FOR MURDER, AND I WAS ON AT LEAST A DOZEN GOVERNMENT WATCH LISTS.
WE CAN'T LEAVE WITHOUT SOME EVIDENCE.
CAN YOU DISTRACT THEM?
CAN I DISTRACT THEM. PFFT.
YOU'VE GOT EXACTLY TEN SECONDS BEFORE I PICK YOU UP.
I start the countdown in my head-- ten.
Ev's been a master strategist for as long as I've known her. She can drive, shoot and talk her way out of practically anything.
And when she says ten seconds, she means ten seconds. Exactly.
OH GOD... OH MY GOD OH MY GOD

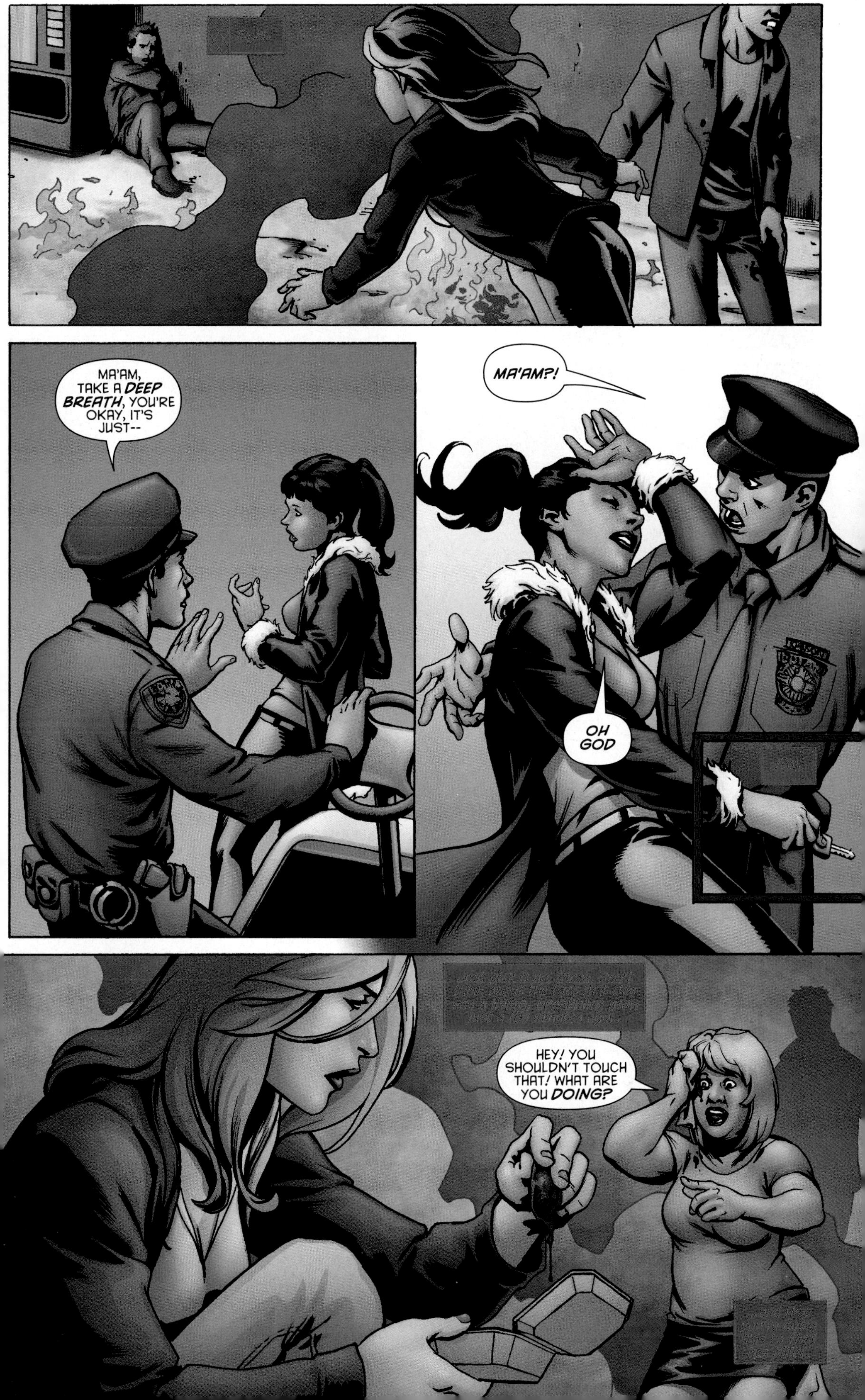

MA'AM, TAKE A DEEP BREATH, YOU'RE OKAY, IT'S JUST--
MA'AM?!
OH GOD
HEY! YOU SHOULDN'T TOUCH THAT! WHAT ARE YOU DOING?

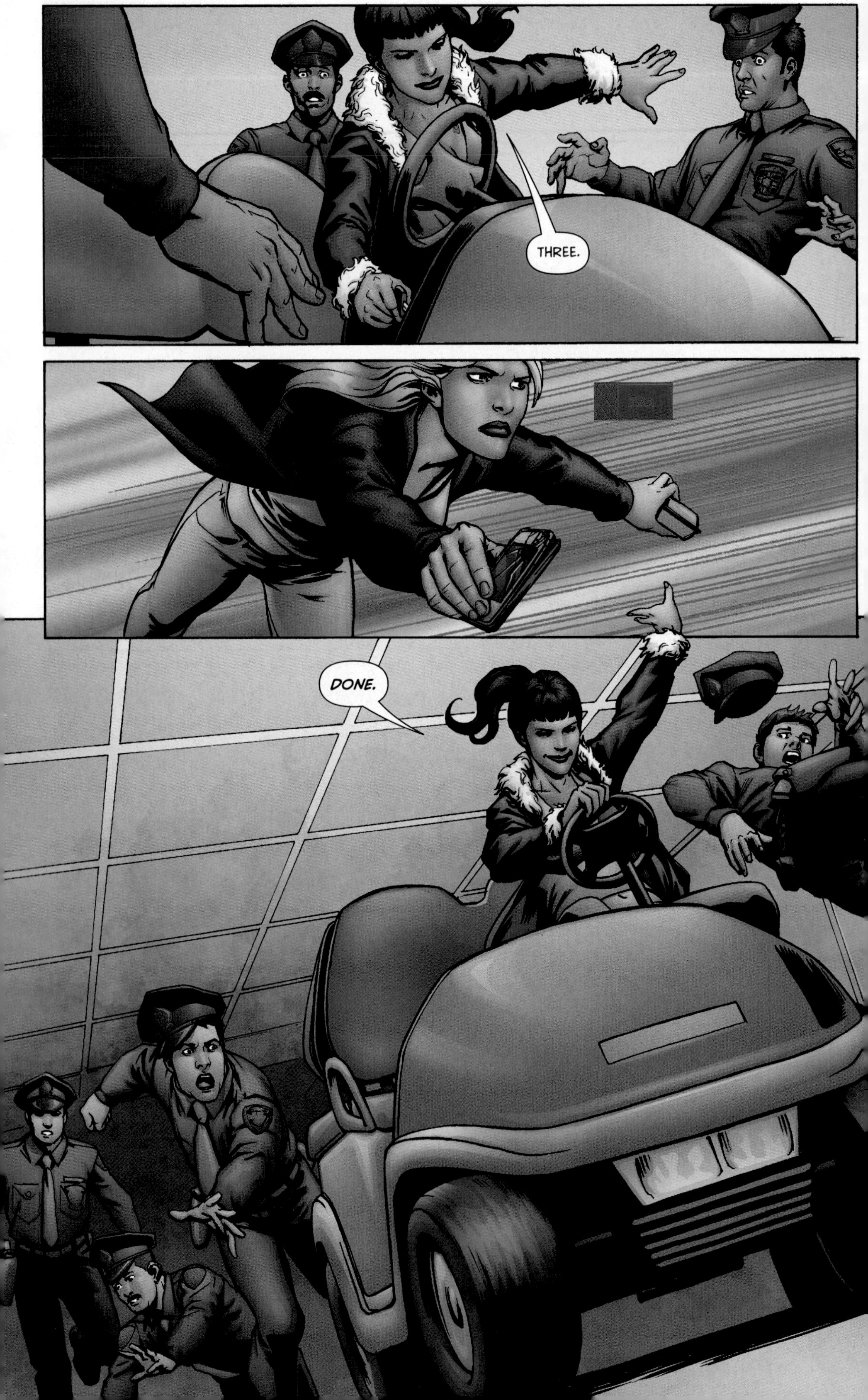
THREE.
DONE.

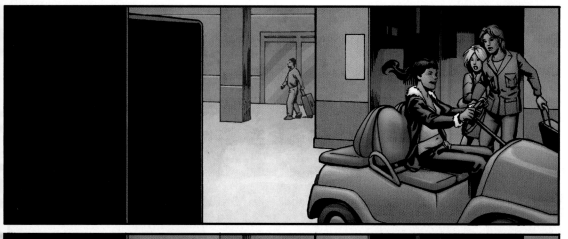

TEST COMPLETE, CARRIER ELIMINATED.

LANCE AND CRAWFORD ARE LEAVING THE SCENE.

KRESSSSHHH

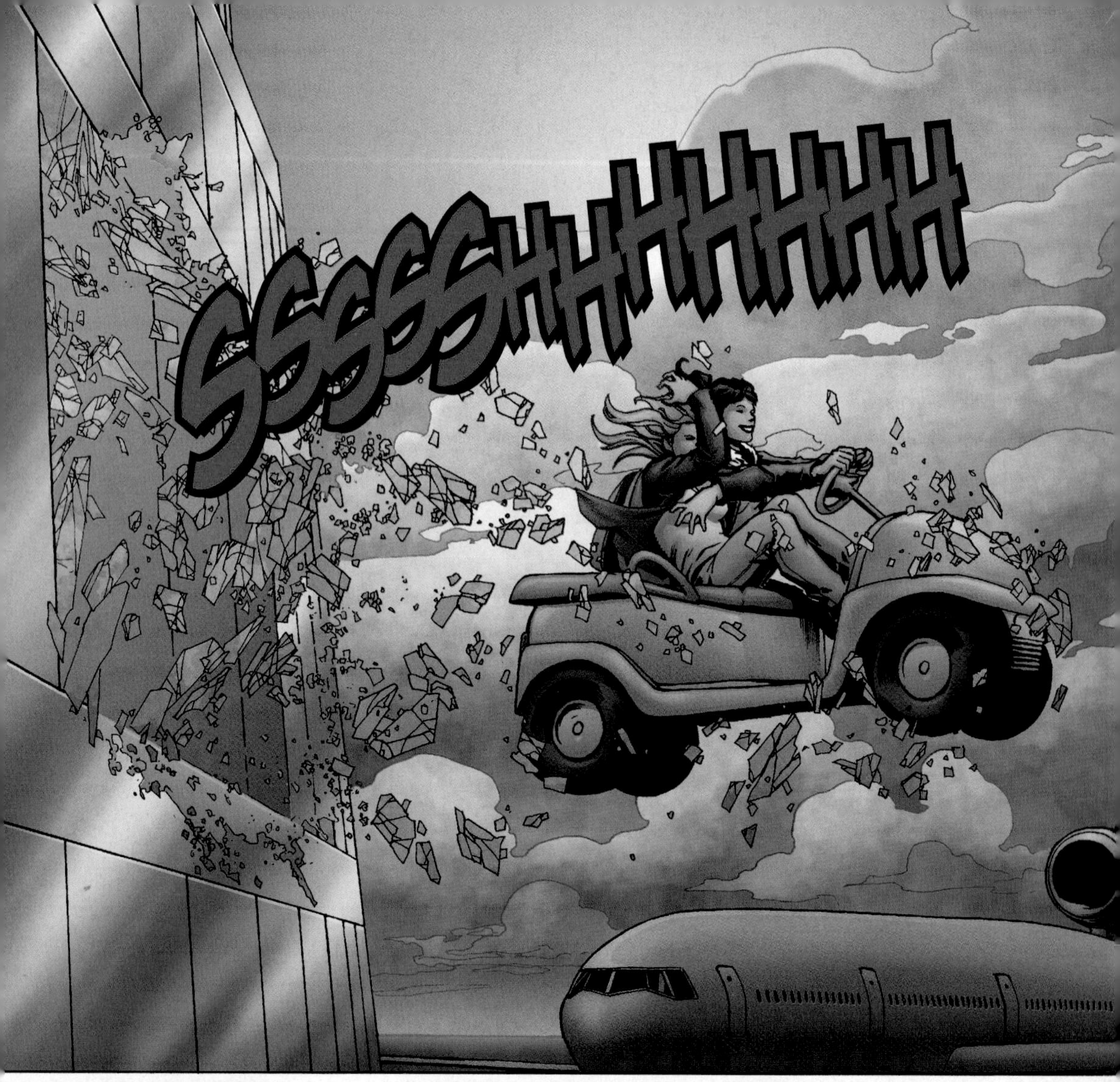
SSSSSHHHHHHHH

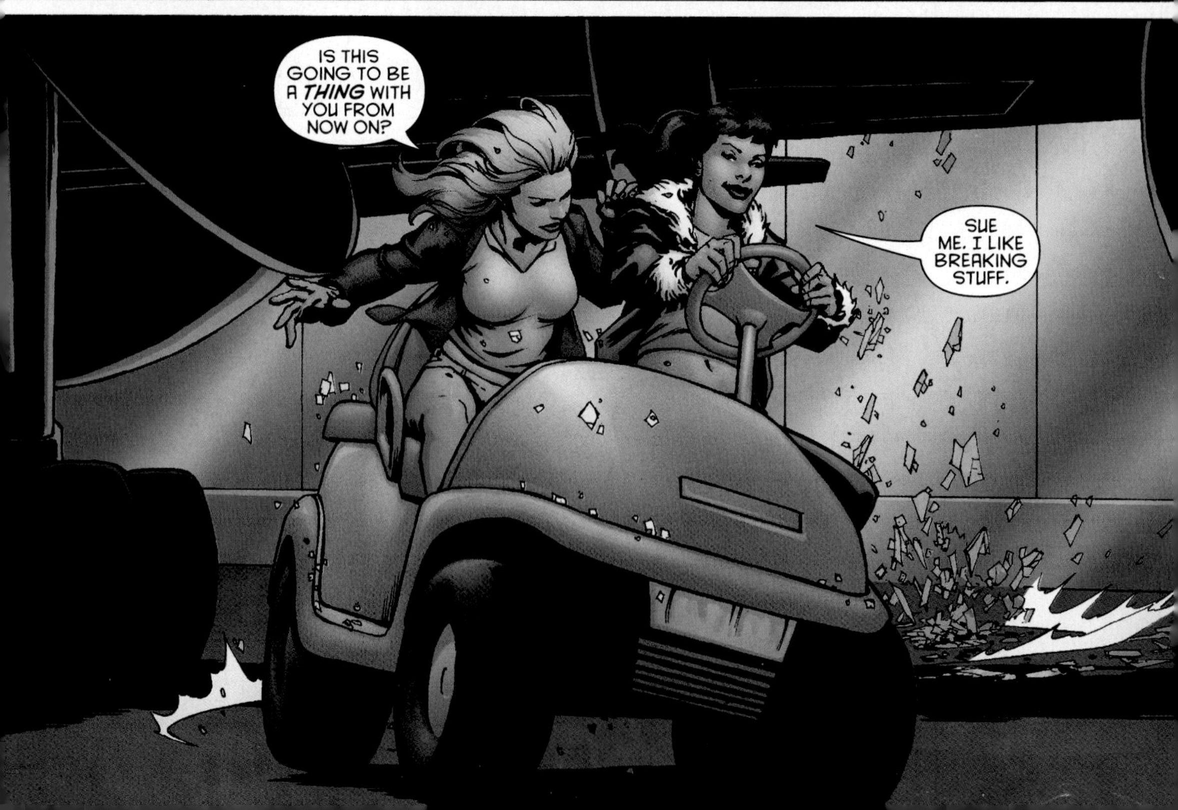
IS THIS GOING TO BE A *THING* WITH YOU FROM NOW ON?
SUE ME. I LIKE BREAKING STUFF.

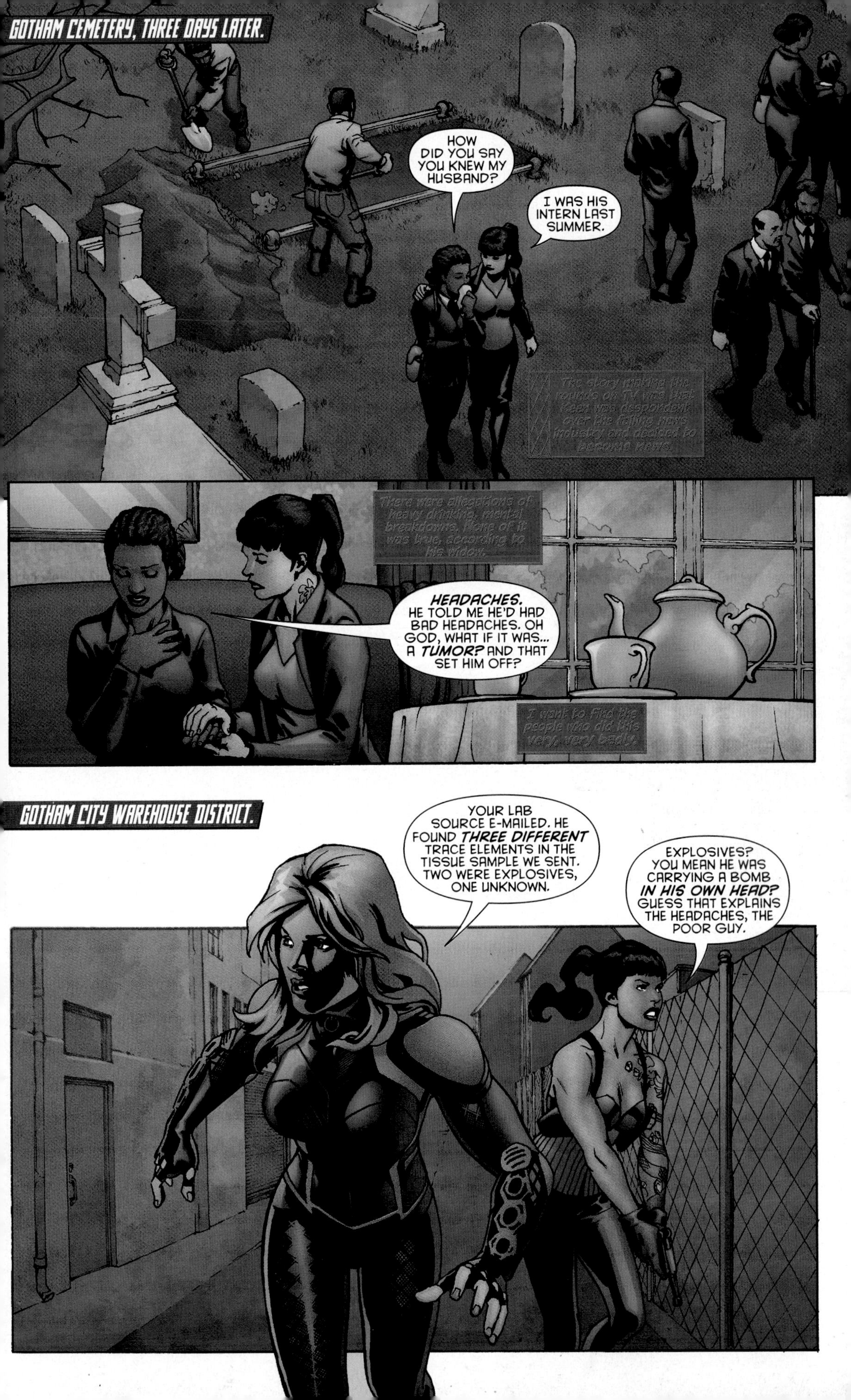
GOTHAM CEMETERY, THREE DAYS LATER.
HOW DID YOU SAY YOU KNEW MY HUSBAND?
I WAS HIS INTERN LAST SUMMER.
The story making the rounds on TV was that Keen was despondent over the failing news industry and decided to become news.
There were allegations of heavy drinking, mental breakdowns. None of it was true, according to his widow.
HEADACHES. HE TOLD ME HE'D HAD BAD HEADACHES. OH GOD, WHAT IF IT WAS... A TUMOR? AND THAT SET HIM OFF?
I want to find the people who did this very, very badly.
GOTHAM CITY WAREHOUSE DISTRICT.
YOUR LAB SOURCE E-MAILED. HE FOUND THREE DIFFERENT TRACE ELEMENTS IN THE TISSUE SAMPLE WE SENT. TWO WERE EXPLOSIVES, ONE UNKNOWN.
EXPLOSIVES? YOU MEAN HE WAS CARRYING A BOMB IN HIS OWN HEAD? GUESS THAT EXPLAINS THE HEADACHES, THE POOR GUY.

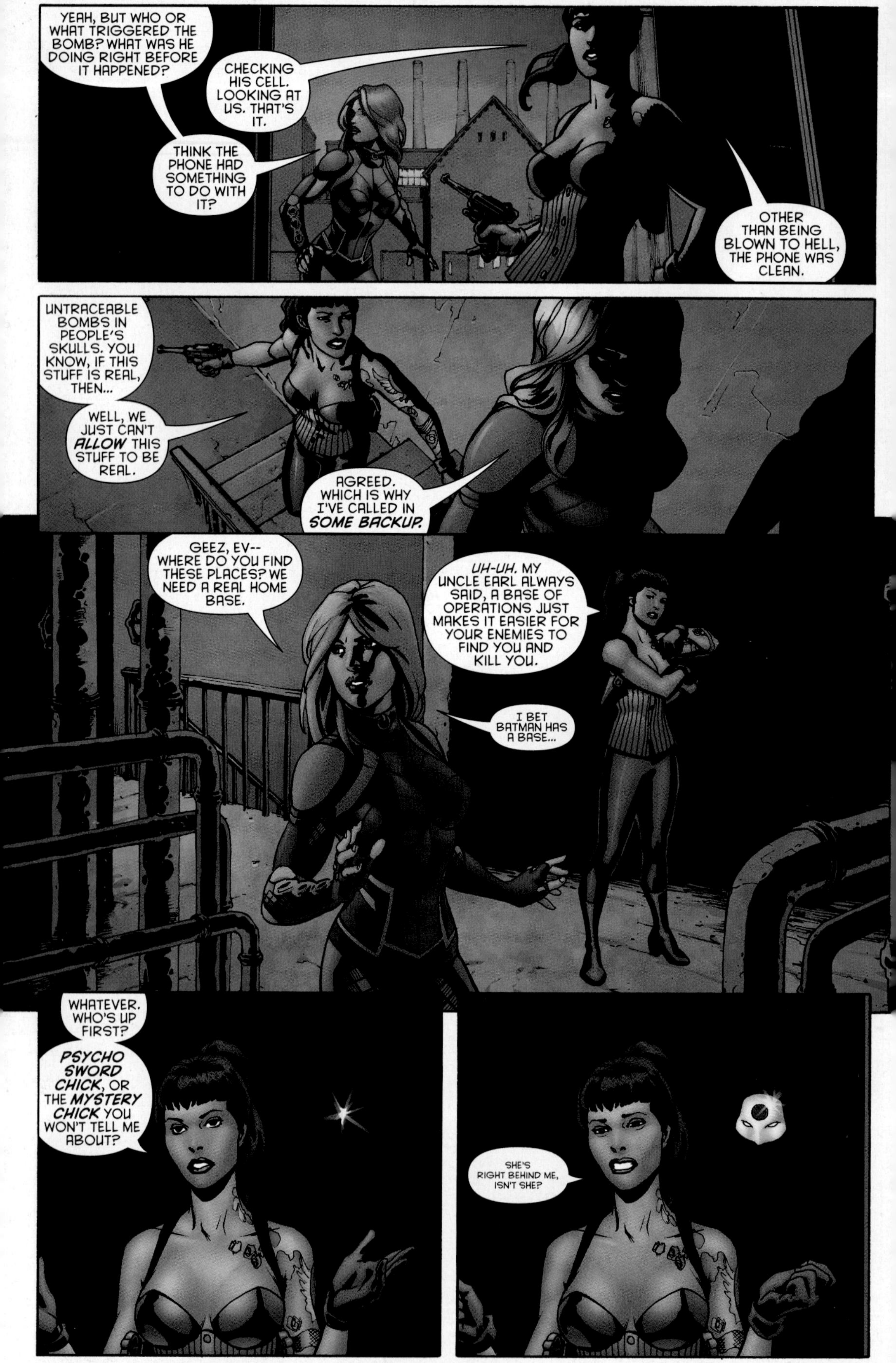
YEAH, BUT WHO OR WHAT TRIGGERED THE BOMB? WHAT WAS HE DOING RIGHT BEFORE IT HAPPENED?
CHECKING HIS CELL. LOOKING AT US. THAT'S IT.
THINK THE PHONE HAD SOMETHING TO DO WITH IT?
OTHER THAN BEING BLOWN TO HELL, THE PHONE WAS CLEAN.
UNTRACEABLE BOMBS IN PEOPLE'S SKULLS. YOU KNOW, IF THIS STUFF IS REAL, THEN...
WELL, WE JUST CAN'T *ALLOW* THIS STUFF TO BE REAL.
AGREED. WHICH IS WHY I'VE CALLED IN ***SOME BACKUP.***
GEEZ, EV-- WHERE DO YOU FIND THESE PLACES? WE NEED A REAL HOME BASE.
UH-UH. MY UNCLE EARL ALWAYS SAID, A BASE OF OPERATIONS JUST MAKES IT EASIER FOR YOUR ENEMIES TO FIND YOU AND KILL YOU.
I BET BATMAN HAS A BASE...
WHATEVER. WHO'S UP FIRST?
PSYCHO SWORD CHICK, OR THE ***MYSTERY CHICK*** YOU WON'T TELL ME ABOUT?
SHE'S RIGHT BEHIND ME, ISN'T SHE?

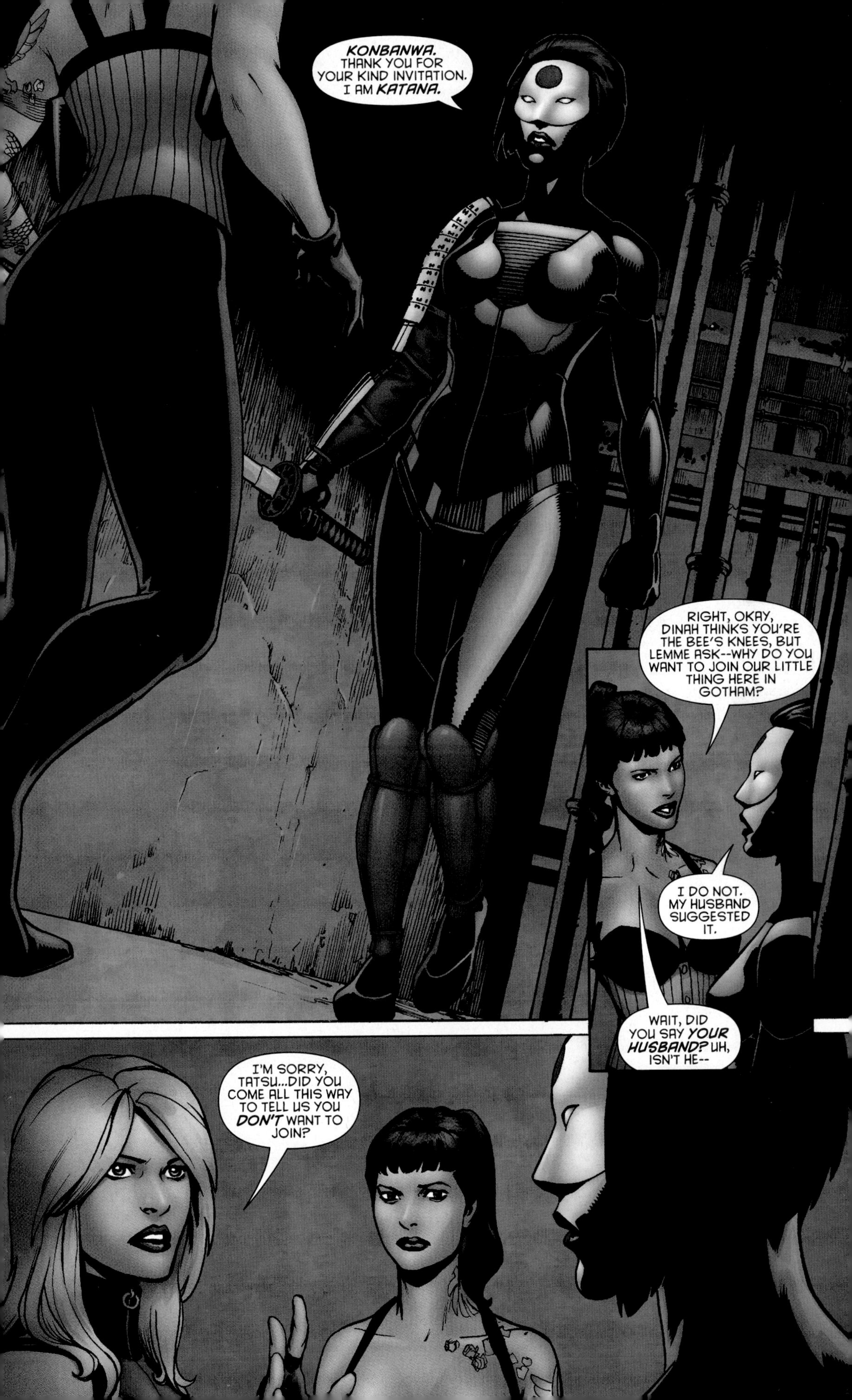

KONBANWA. THANK YOU FOR YOUR KIND INVITATION. I AM *KATANA.*
RIGHT, OKAY, DINAH THINKS YOU'RE THE BEE'S KNEES, BUT LEMME ASK--WHY DO YOU WANT TO JOIN OUR LITTLE THING HERE IN GOTHAM?
I DO NOT. MY HUSBAND SUGGESTED IT.
WAIT, DID YOU SAY *YOUR HUSBAND?* UH, ISN'T HE--
I'M SORRY, TATSU...DID YOU COME ALL THIS WAY TO TELL US YOU *DON'T* WANT TO JOIN?

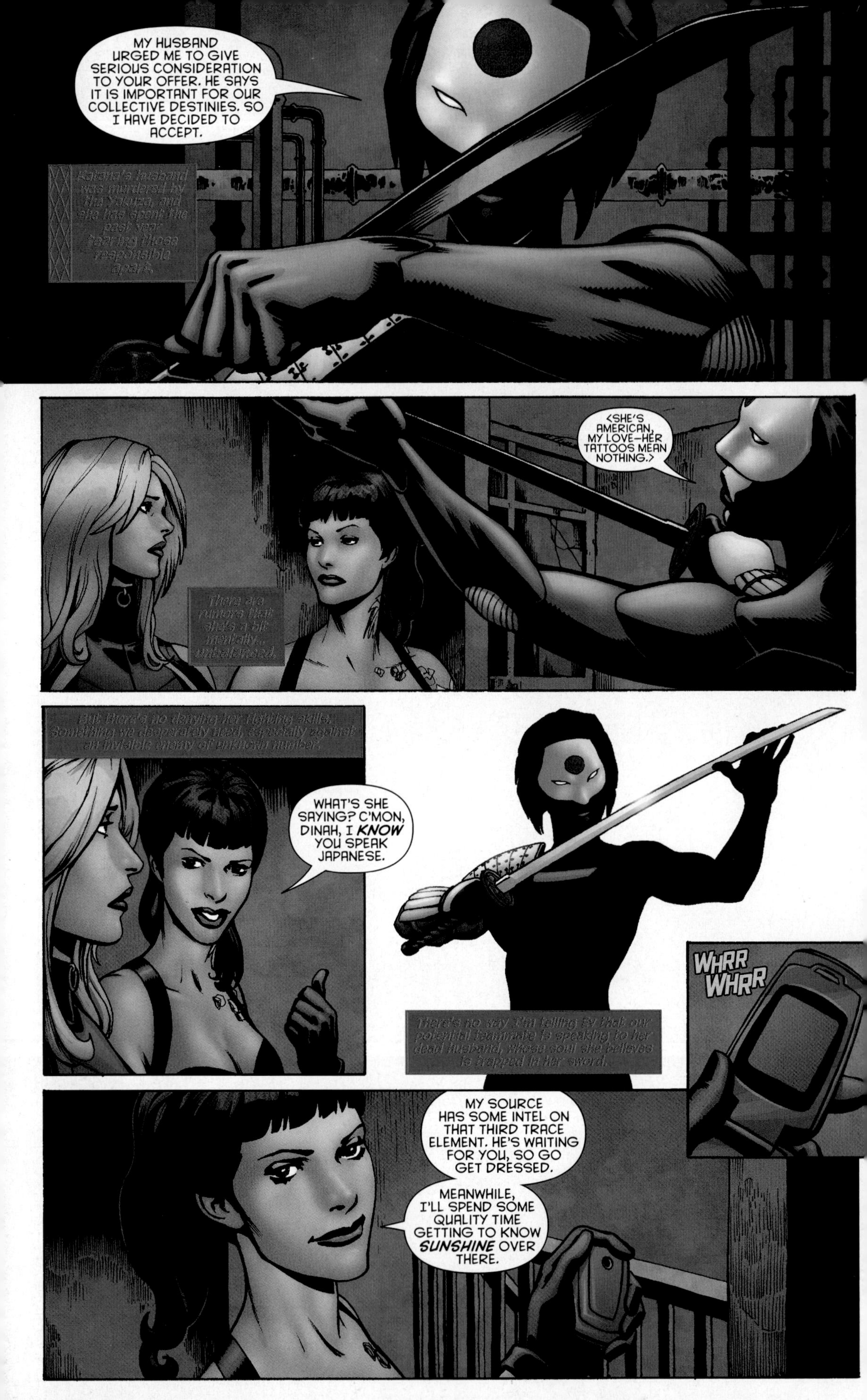

MY HUSBAND URGED ME TO GIVE SERIOUS CONSIDERATION TO YOUR OFFER. HE SAYS IT IS IMPORTANT FOR OUR COLLECTIVE DESTINIES. SO I HAVE DECIDED TO ACCEPT.
Katana's husband was murdered by the Yakuza, and she has spent the past year tearing those responsible apart.
<SHE'S AMERICAN, MY LOVE—HER TATTOOS MEAN NOTHING.>
There are rumors that she's a bit mentally... unbalanced.
But there's no denying her fighting skills. Something we desperately need, especially against an invisible enemy of unknown number.
WHAT'S SHE SAYING? C'MON, DINAH, I KNOW YOU SPEAK JAPANESE.
There's no way I'm telling Ev that our potential teammate is speaking to her dead husband, whose soul she believes is trapped in her sword.
WHRR WHRR
MY SOURCE HAS SOME INTEL ON THAT THIRD TRACE ELEMENT. HE'S WAITING FOR YOU, SO GO GET DRESSED.
MEANWHILE, I'LL SPEND SOME QUALITY TIME GETTING TO KNOW SUNSHINE OVER THERE.

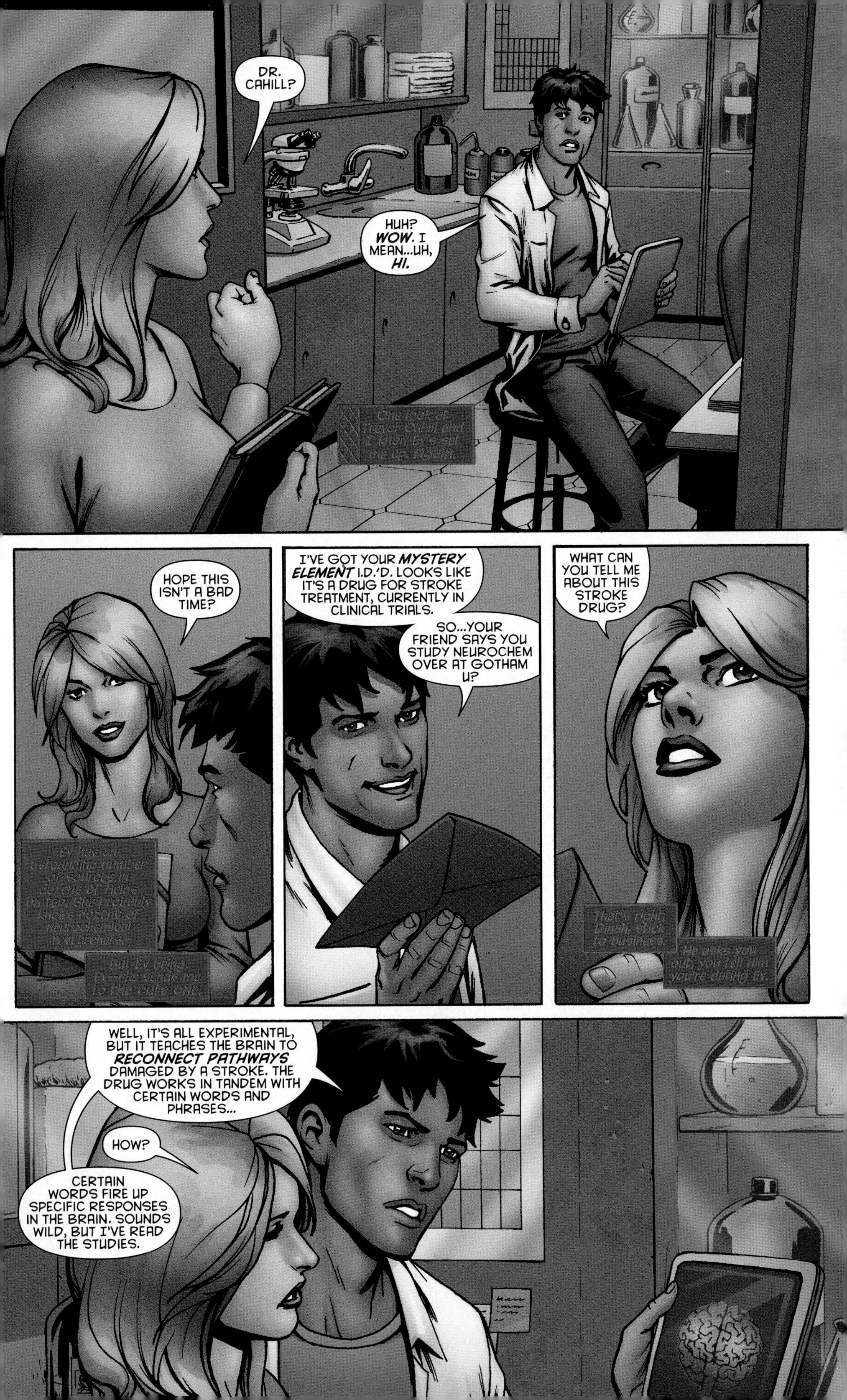
DR. CAHILL?
HUH? WOW. I MEAN...UH, HI.
One look at Trevor Cahill and I know Ev's set me up. Again.
HOPE THIS ISN'T A BAD TIME?
Ev has an astounding number of sources in dozens of fields on tap. She probably knows dozens of neurochemical researchers.
But Ev being Ev--she sends me to the cute one.
I'VE GOT YOUR MYSTERY ELEMENT I.D.'D. LOOKS LIKE IT'S A DRUG FOR STROKE TREATMENT, CURRENTLY IN CLINICAL TRIALS.
SO...YOUR FRIEND SAYS YOU STUDY NEUROCHEM OVER AT GOTHAM U?
WHAT CAN YOU TELL ME ABOUT THIS STROKE DRUG?
That's right, Dinah, stick to business.
He asks you out, you tell him you're dating Ev.
WELL, IT'S ALL EXPERIMENTAL, BUT IT TEACHES THE BRAIN TO RECONNECT PATHWAYS DAMAGED BY A STROKE. THE DRUG WORKS IN TANDEM WITH CERTAIN WORDS AND PHRASES...
HOW?
CERTAIN WORDS FIRE UP SPECIFIC RESPONSES IN THE BRAIN. SOUNDS WILD, BUT I'VE READ THE STUDIES.

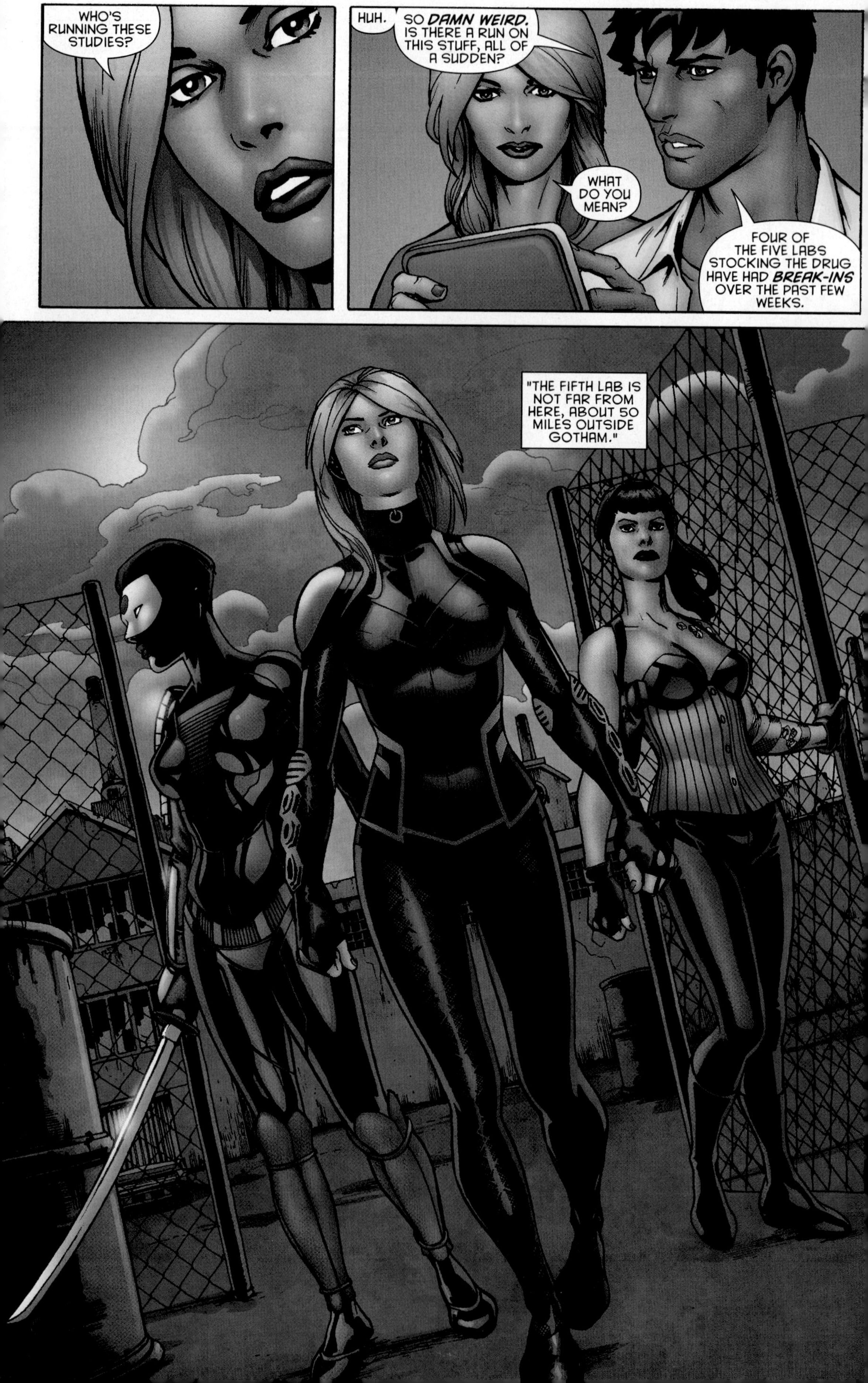
WHO'S RUNNING THESE STUDIES?
HUH.
SO DAMN WEIRD. IS THERE A RUN ON THIS STUFF, ALL OF A SUDDEN?
WHAT DO YOU MEAN?
FOUR OF THE FIVE LABS STOCKING THE DRUG HAVE HAD BREAK-INS OVER THE PAST FEW WEEKS.
"THE FIFTH LAB IS NOT FAR FROM HERE, ABOUT 50 MILES OUTSIDE GOTHAM."

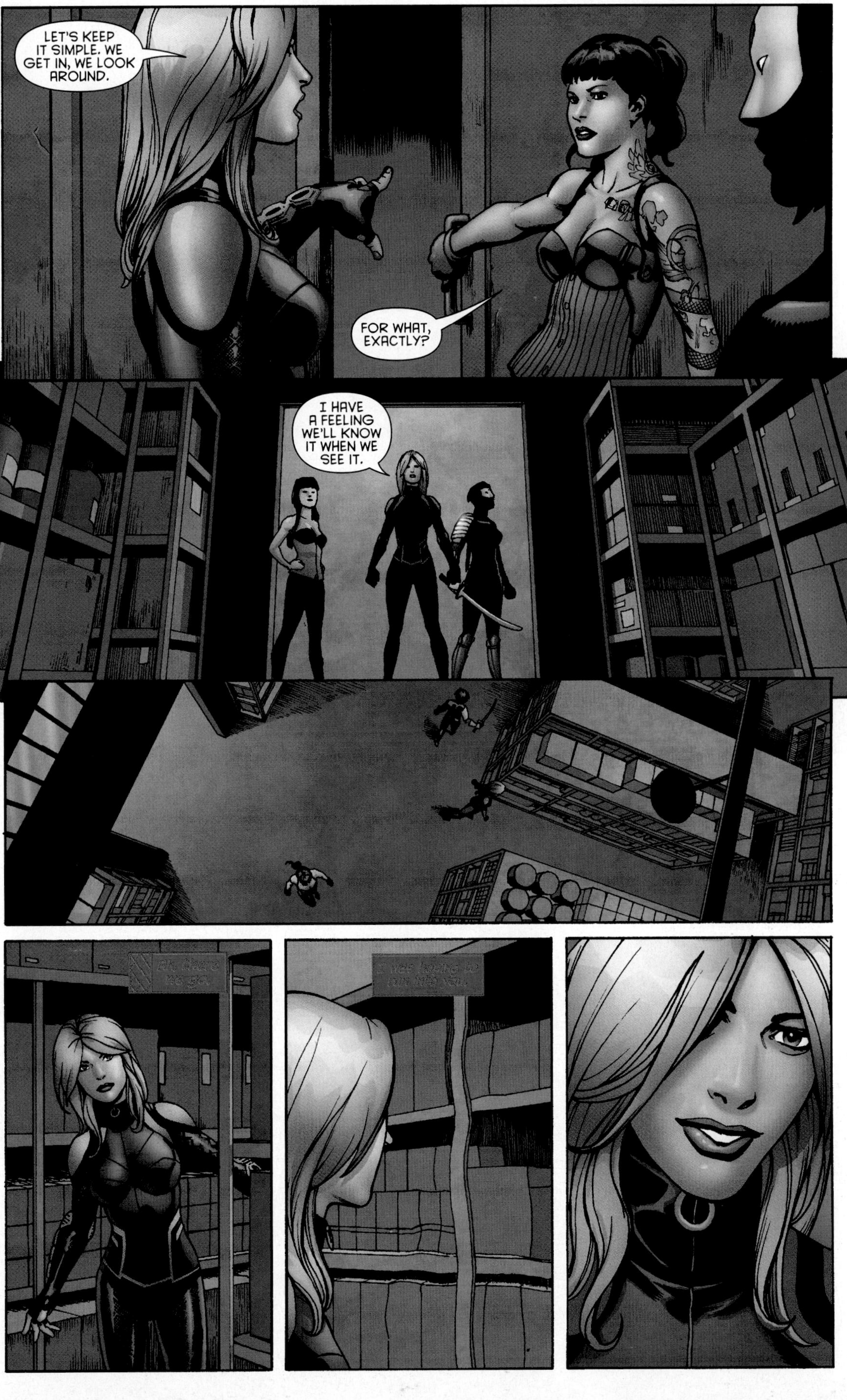
LET'S KEEP IT SIMPLE. WE GET IN, WE LOOK AROUND.
FOR WHAT, EXACTLY?
I HAVE A FEELING WE'LL KNOW IT WHEN WE SEE IT.

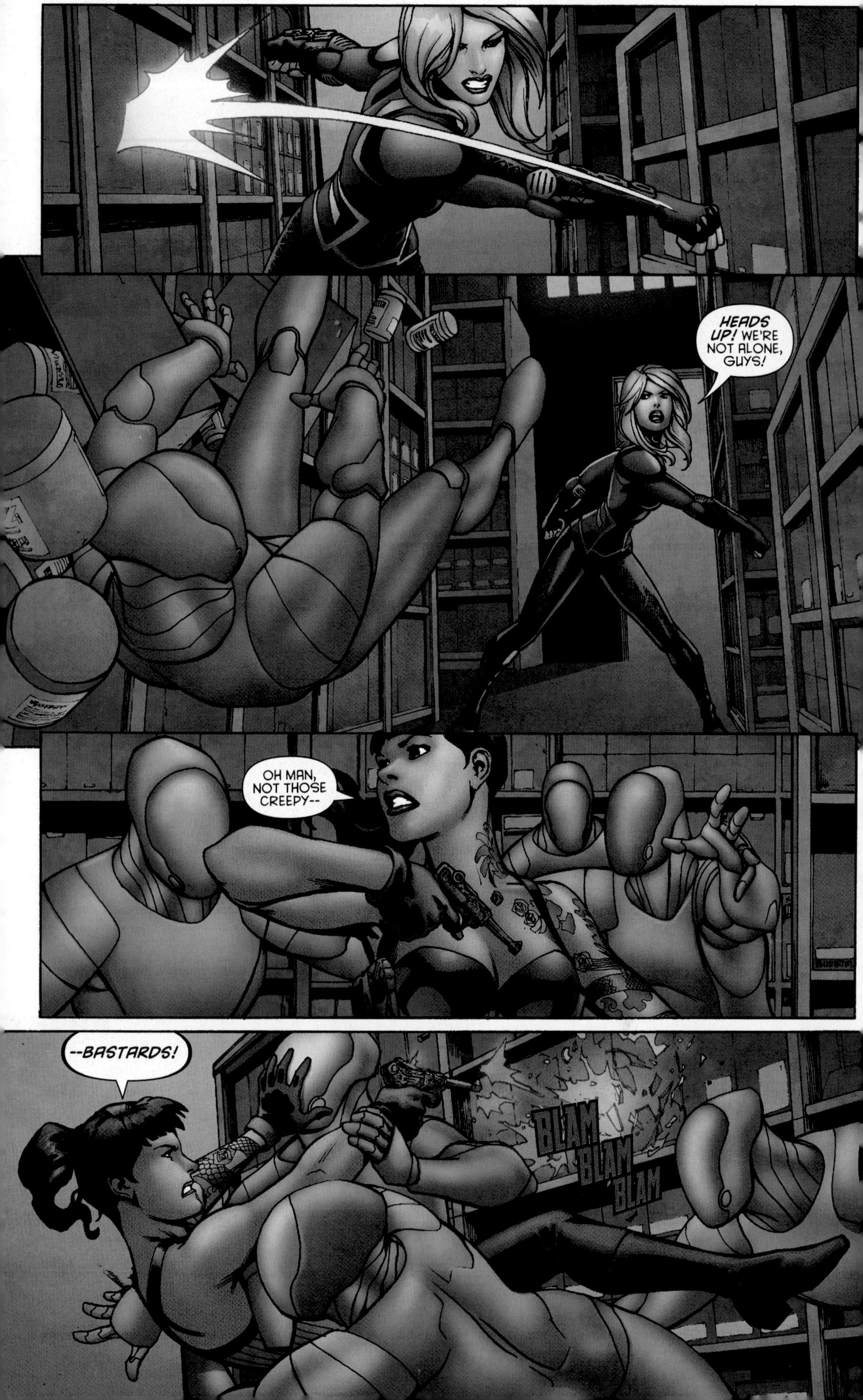
HEADS UP! WE'RE NOT ALONE, GUYS!
OH MAN, NOT THOSE CREEPY--
--BASTARDS!
BLAM
BLAM
BLAM

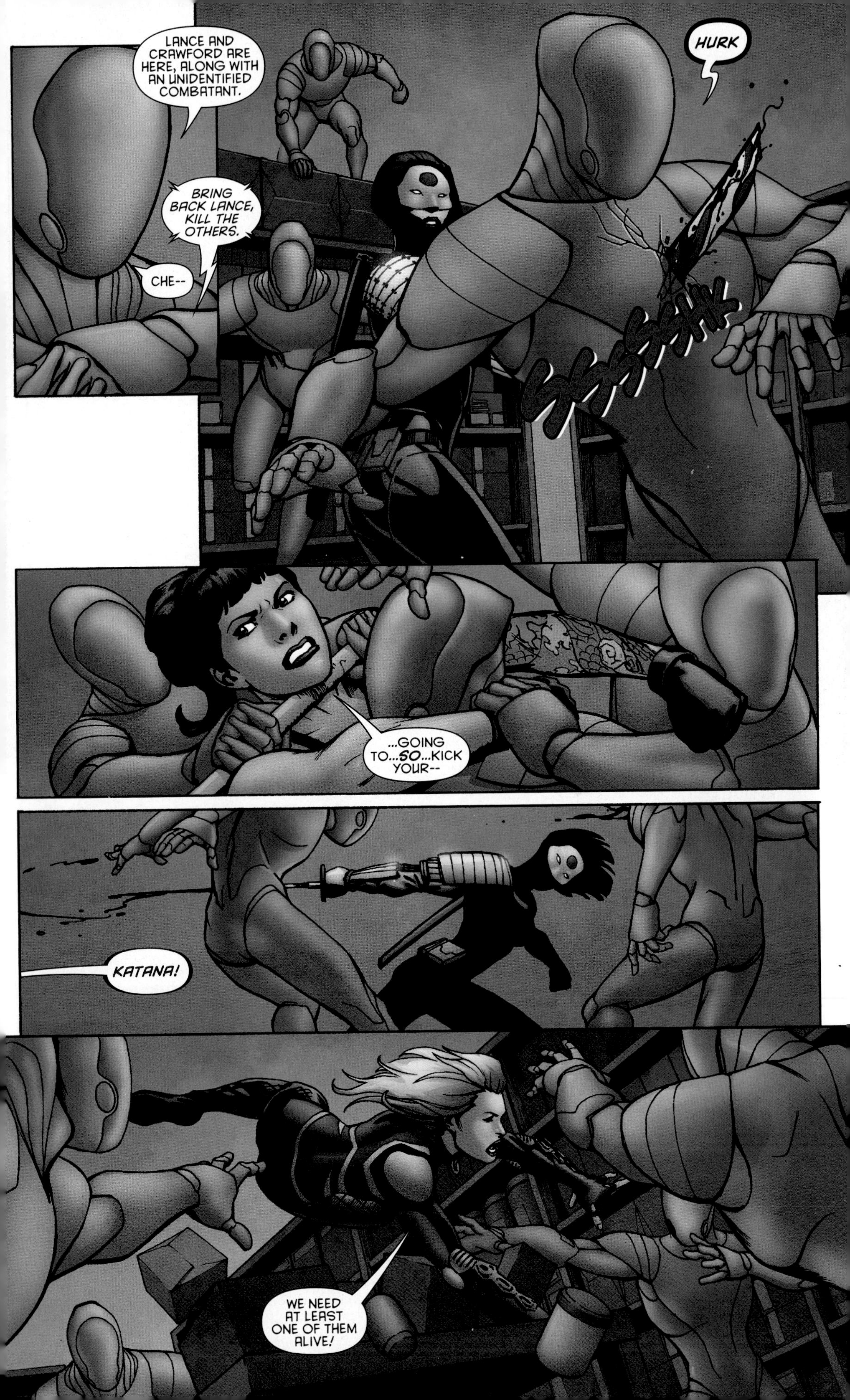
LANCE AND CRAWFORD ARE HERE, ALONG WITH AN UNIDENTIFIED COMBATANT.
BRING BACK LANCE, KILL THE OTHERS.
CHE--
HURK
SHHHSHHHK
...GOING TO...SO...KICK YOUR--
KATANA!
WE NEED AT LEAST ONE OF THEM ALIVE!

SCREEEEEEEEEE

OH HELL-- EV?

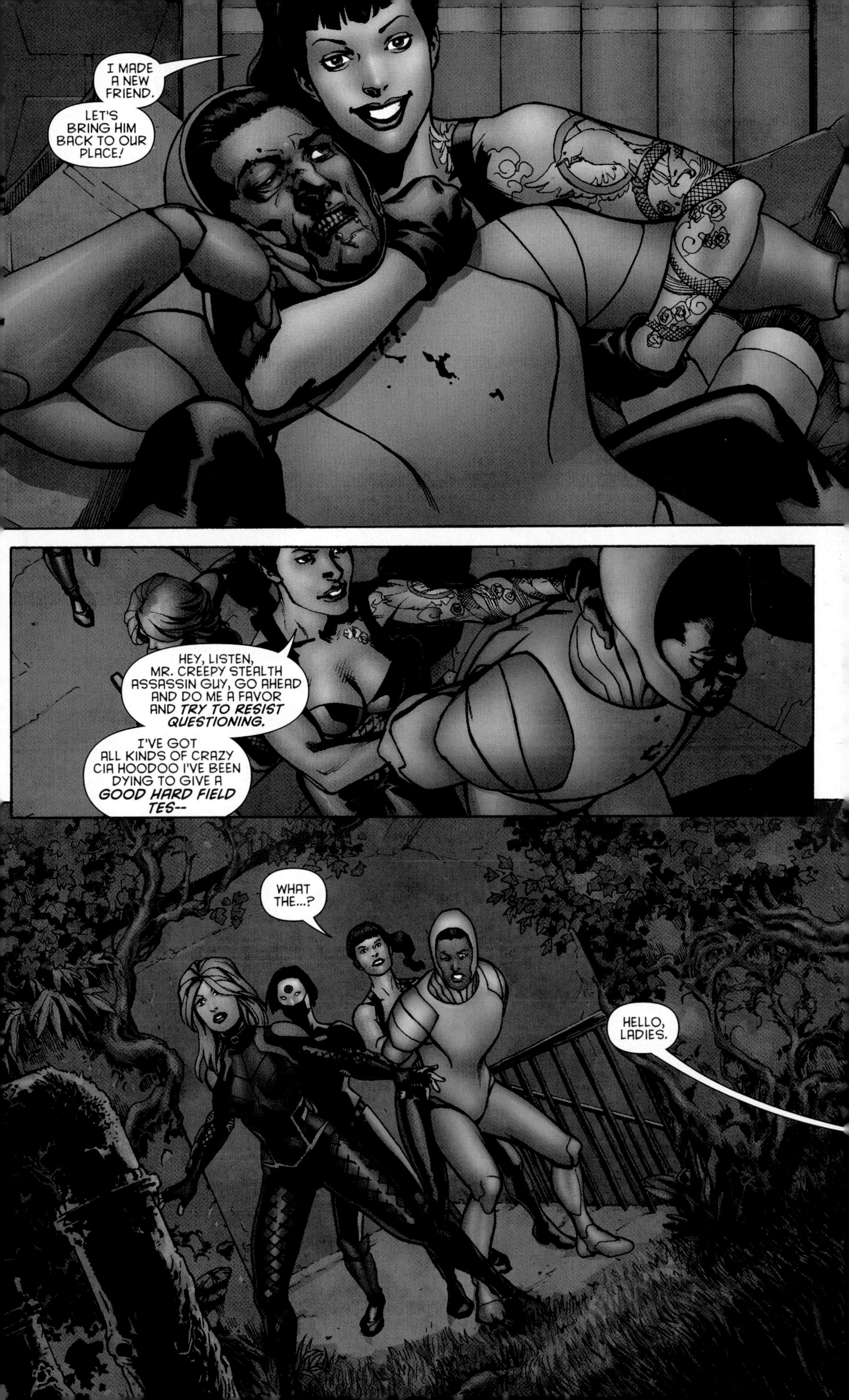
I MADE A NEW FRIEND.
LET'S BRING HIM BACK TO OUR PLACE!
HEY, LISTEN, MR. CREEPY STEALTH ASSASSIN GUY, GO AHEAD AND DO ME A FAVOR AND *TRY TO RESIST QUESTIONING.*
I'VE GOT ALL KINDS OF CRAZY CIA HOODOO I'VE BEEN DYING TO GIVE A *GOOD HARD FIELD TES--*
WHAT THE...?
HELLO, LADIES.

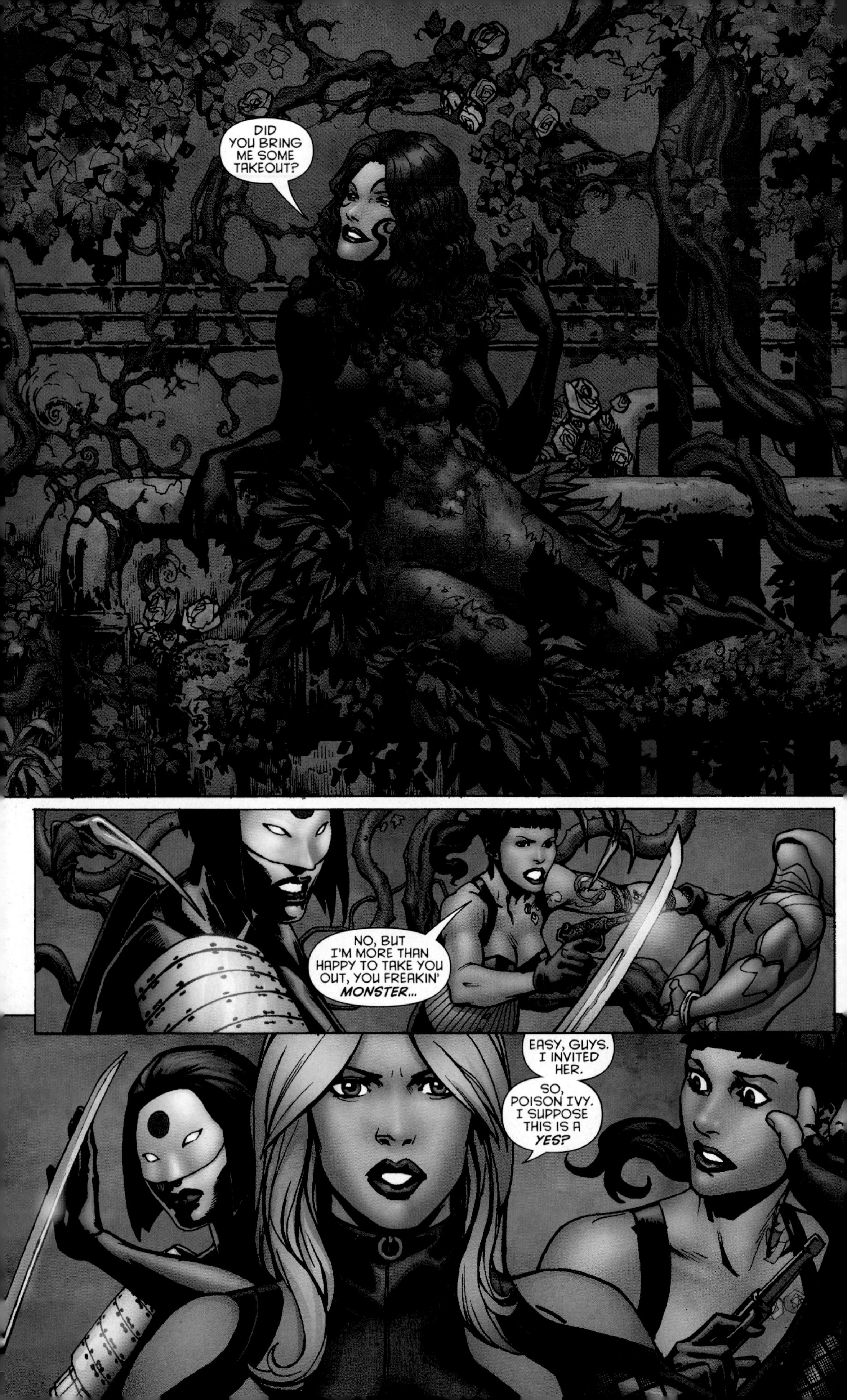
DID YOU BRING ME SOME TAKEOUT?
NO, BUT I'M MORE THAN HAPPY TO TAKE YOU OUT, YOU FREAKIN' *MONSTER*...
EASY, GUYS. I INVITED HER.
SO, POISON IVY. I SUPPOSE THIS IS A *YES?*

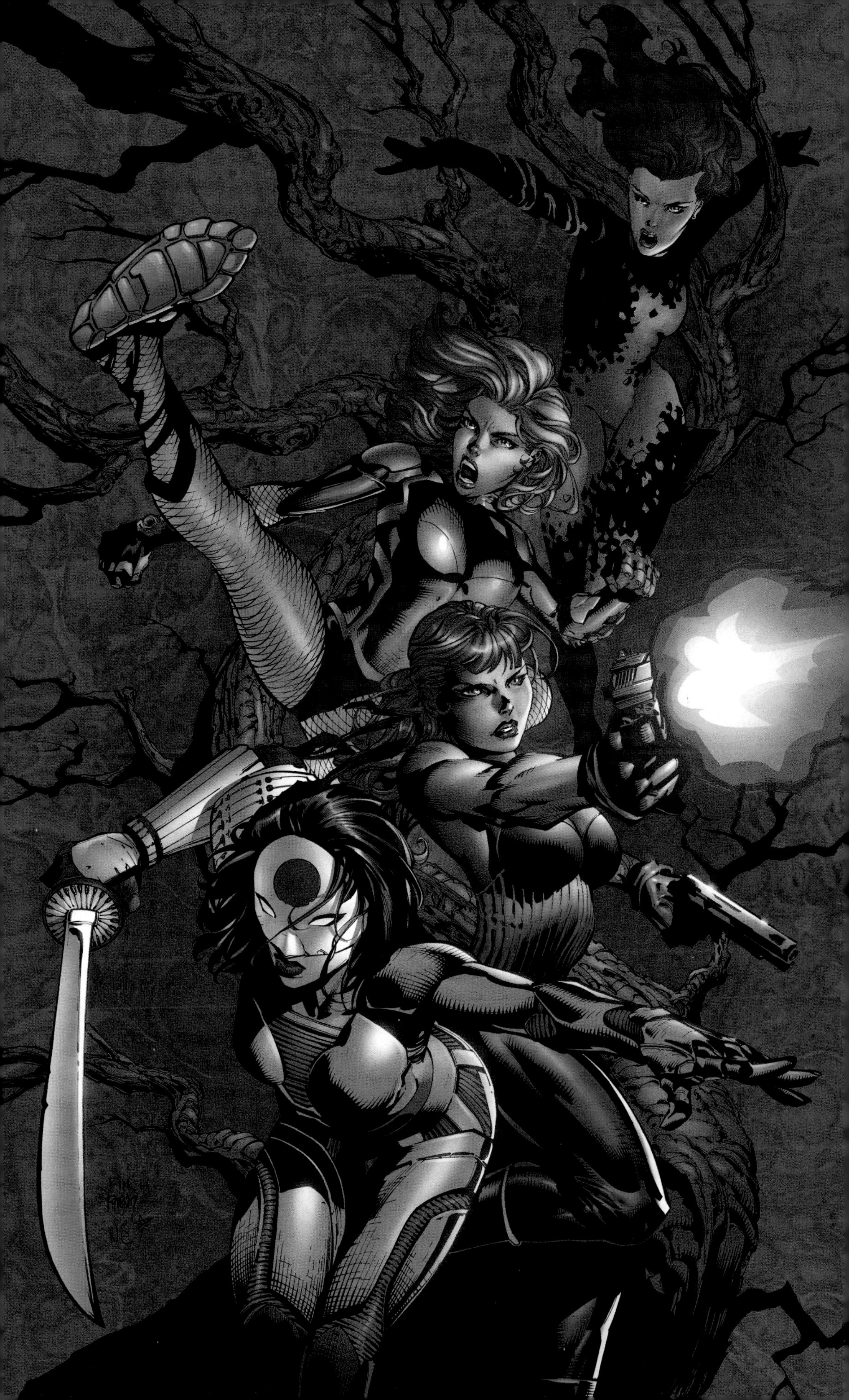

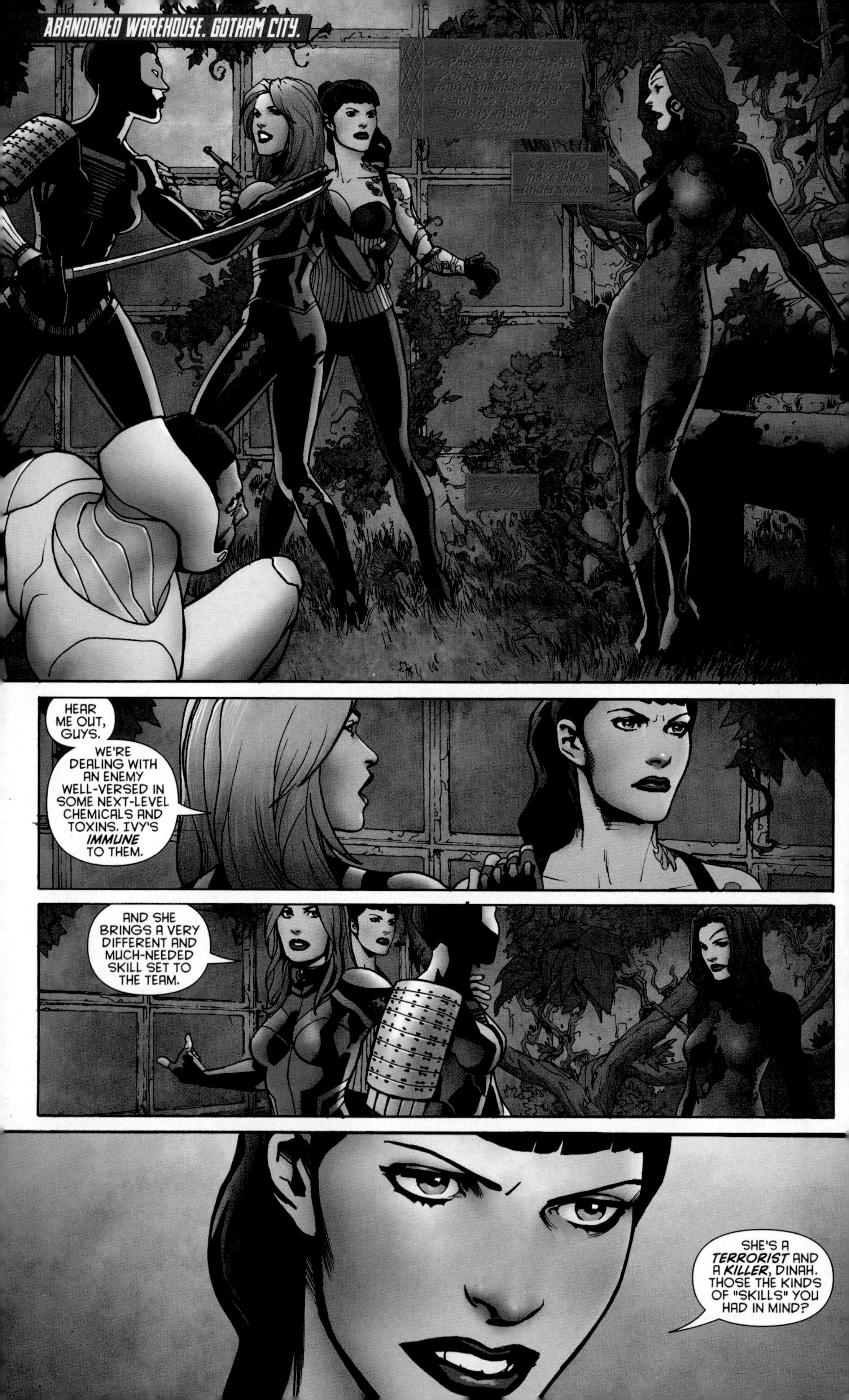
ABANDONED WAREHOUSE. GOTHAM CITY.
My choice of Dr. Pamela Isley—A.K.A. Poison Ivy—as the fourth member of our team has gone over pretty much as expected.
I need to make them understand.
Badly.
HEAR ME OUT, GUYS.
WE'RE DEALING WITH AN ENEMY WELL-VERSED IN SOME NEXT-LEVEL CHEMICALS AND TOXINS. IVY'S IMMUNE TO THEM.
AND SHE BRINGS A VERY DIFFERENT AND MUCH-NEEDED SKILL SET TO THE TEAM.
SHE'S A TERRORIST AND A KILLER, DINAH. THOSE THE KINDS OF "SKILLS" YOU HAD IN MIND?

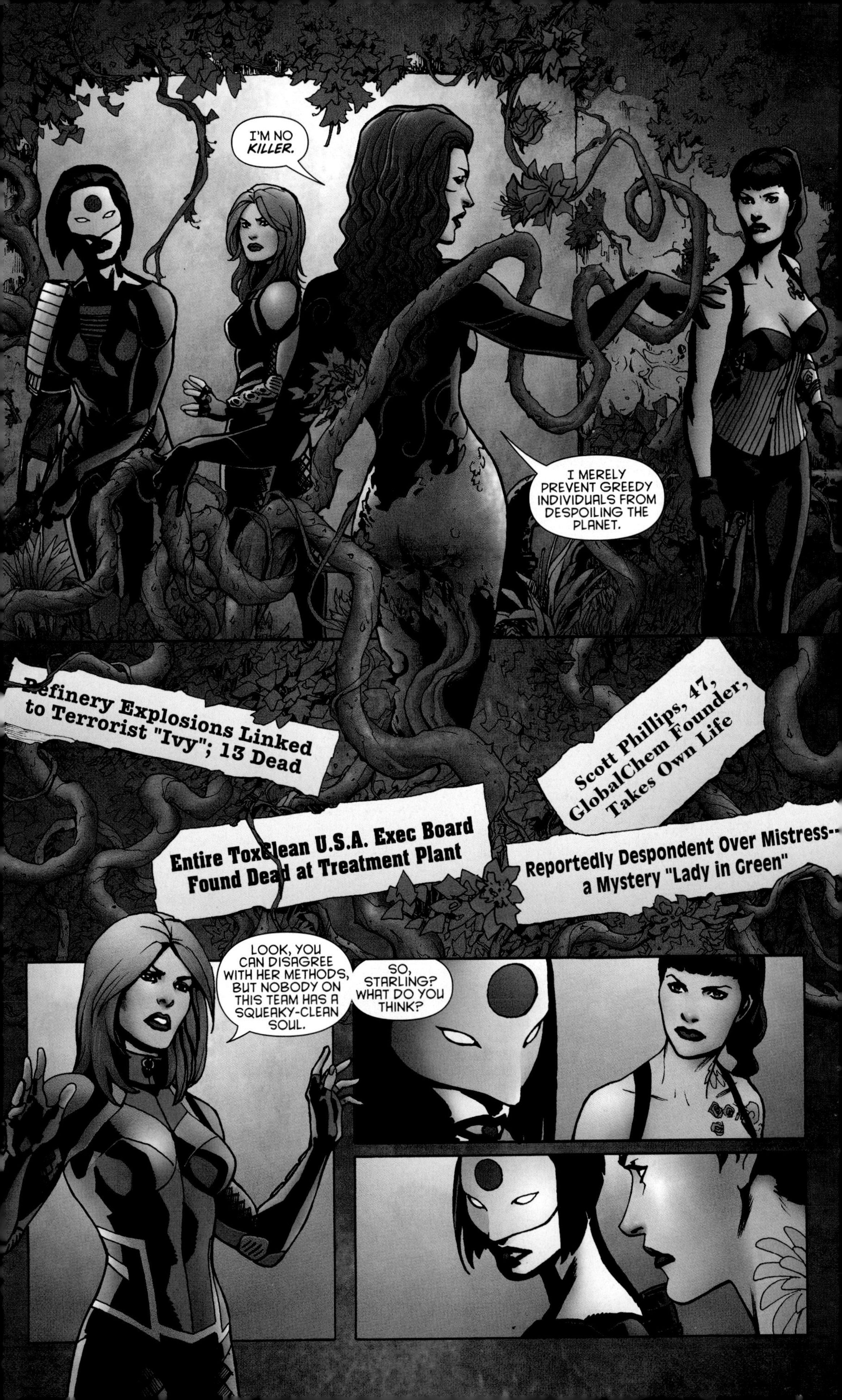

I'M NO KILLER.
I MERELY PREVENT GREEDY INDIVIDUALS FROM DESPOILING THE PLANET.
Refinery Explosions Linked to Terrorist "Ivy"; 13 Dead
Scott Phillips, 47, GlobalChem Founder, Takes Own Life
Entire ToxClean U.S.A. Exec Board Found Dead at Treatment Plant
Reportedly Despondent Over Mistress-- a Mystery "Lady in Green"
LOOK, YOU CAN DISAGREE WITH HER METHODS, BUT NOBODY ON THIS TEAM HAS A SQUEAKY-CLEAN SOUL.
SO, STARLING? WHAT DO YOU THINK?

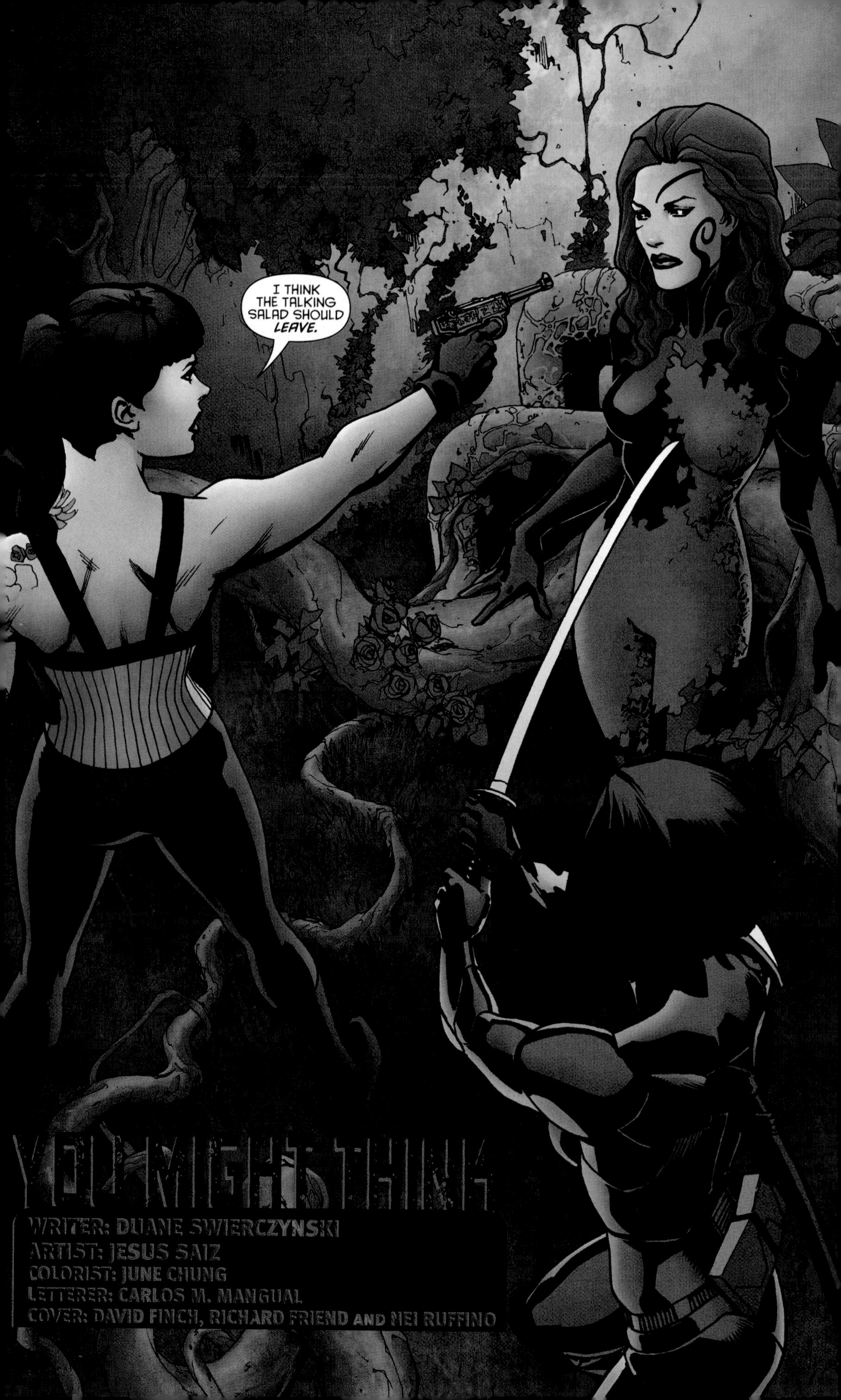
I THINK THE TALKING SALAD SHOULD *LEAVE.*
YOU MIGHT THINK
WRITER: DUANE SWIERCZYNSKI
ARTIST: JESUS SAIZ
COLORIST: JUNE CHUNG
LETTERER: CARLOS M. MANGUAL
COVER: DAVID FINCH, RICHARD FRIEND AND NEI RUFFINO

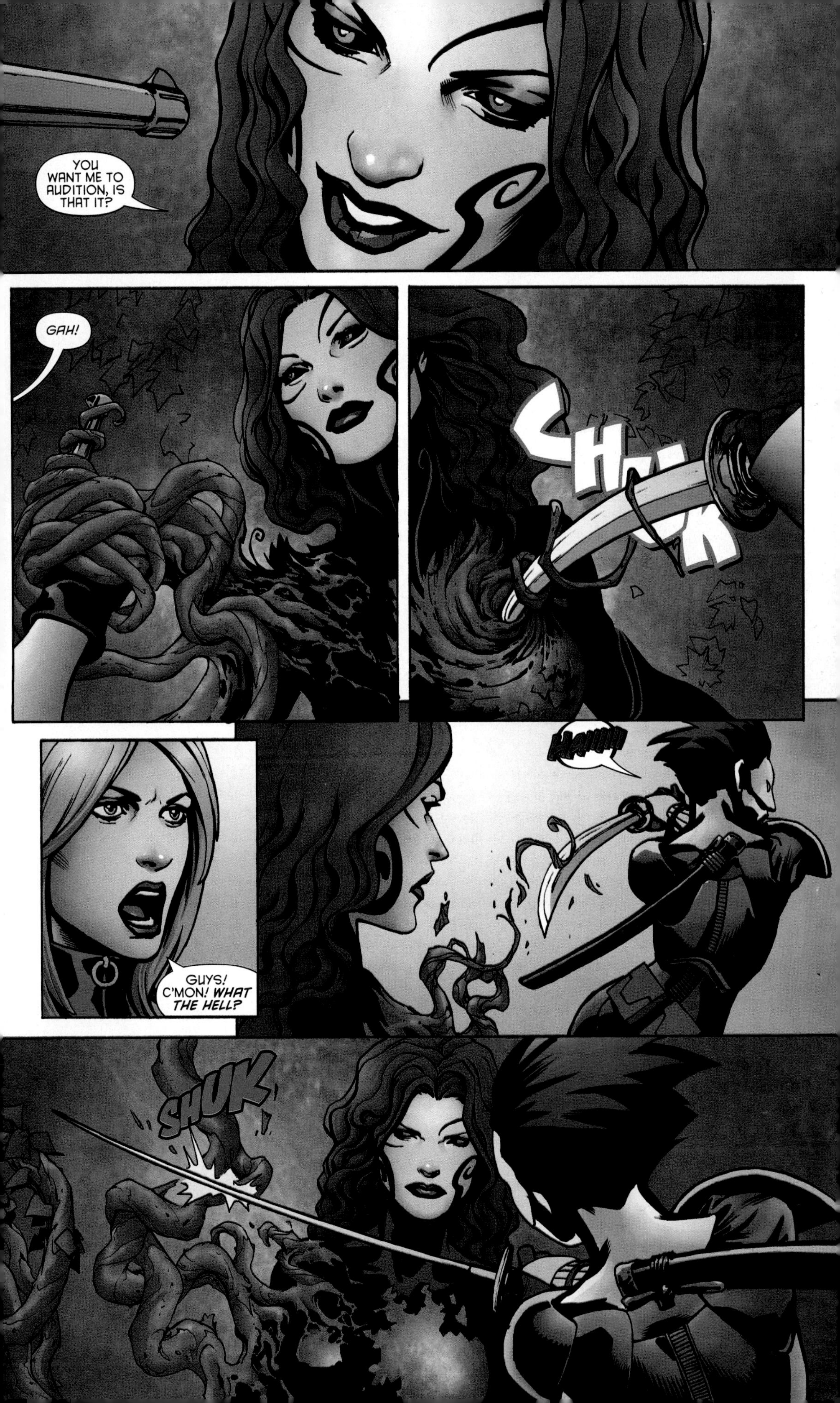

YOU WANT ME TO AUDITION, IS THAT IT?
GAH!
CHUNK
GUYS! C'MON! WHAT THE HELL?
SHUK

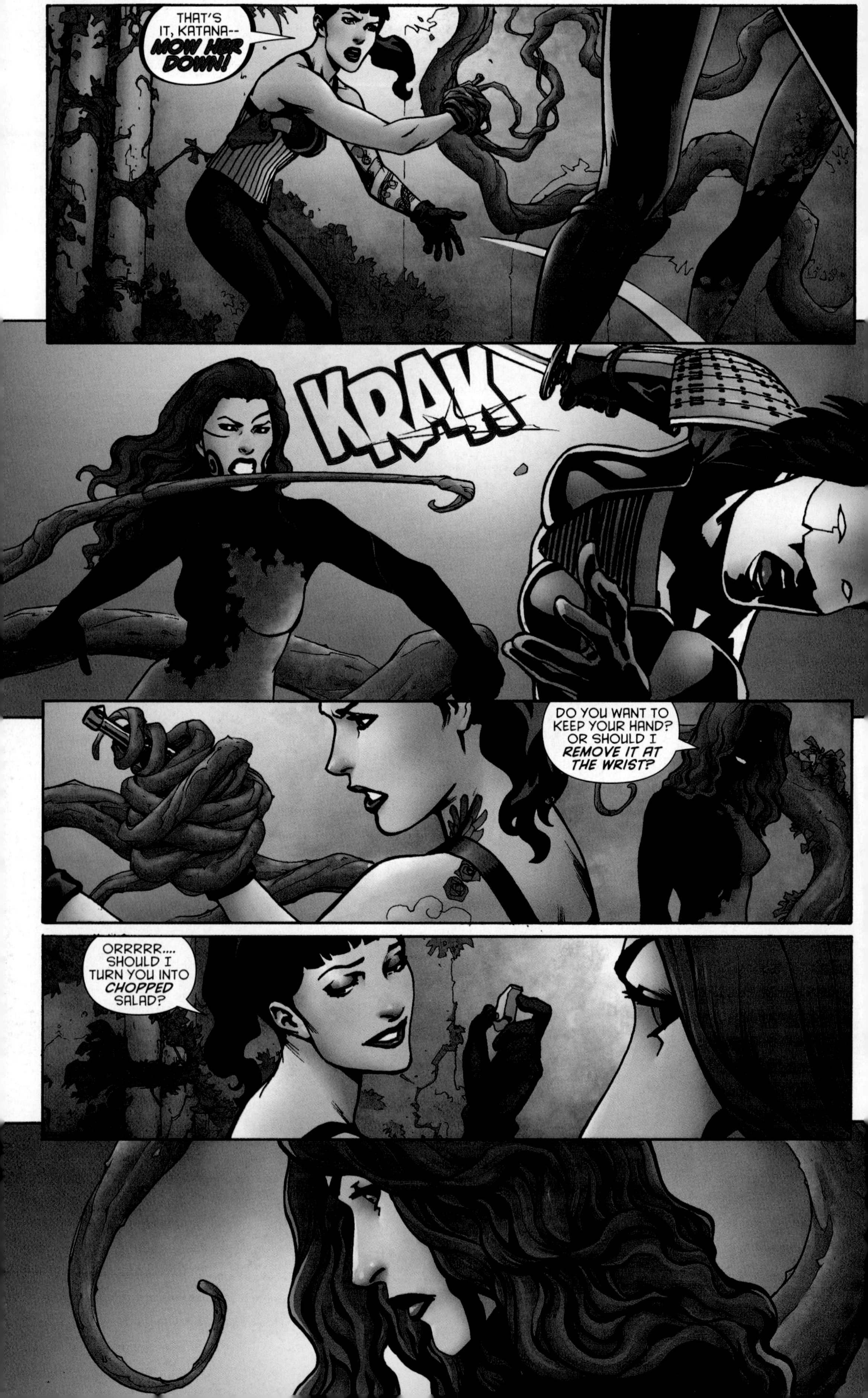
THAT'S IT, KATANA-- MOW HER DOWN!
KRAK
DO YOU WANT TO KEEP YOUR HAND? OR SHOULD I REMOVE IT AT THE WRIST?
ORRRRR.... SHOULD I TURN YOU INTO CHOPPED SALAD?

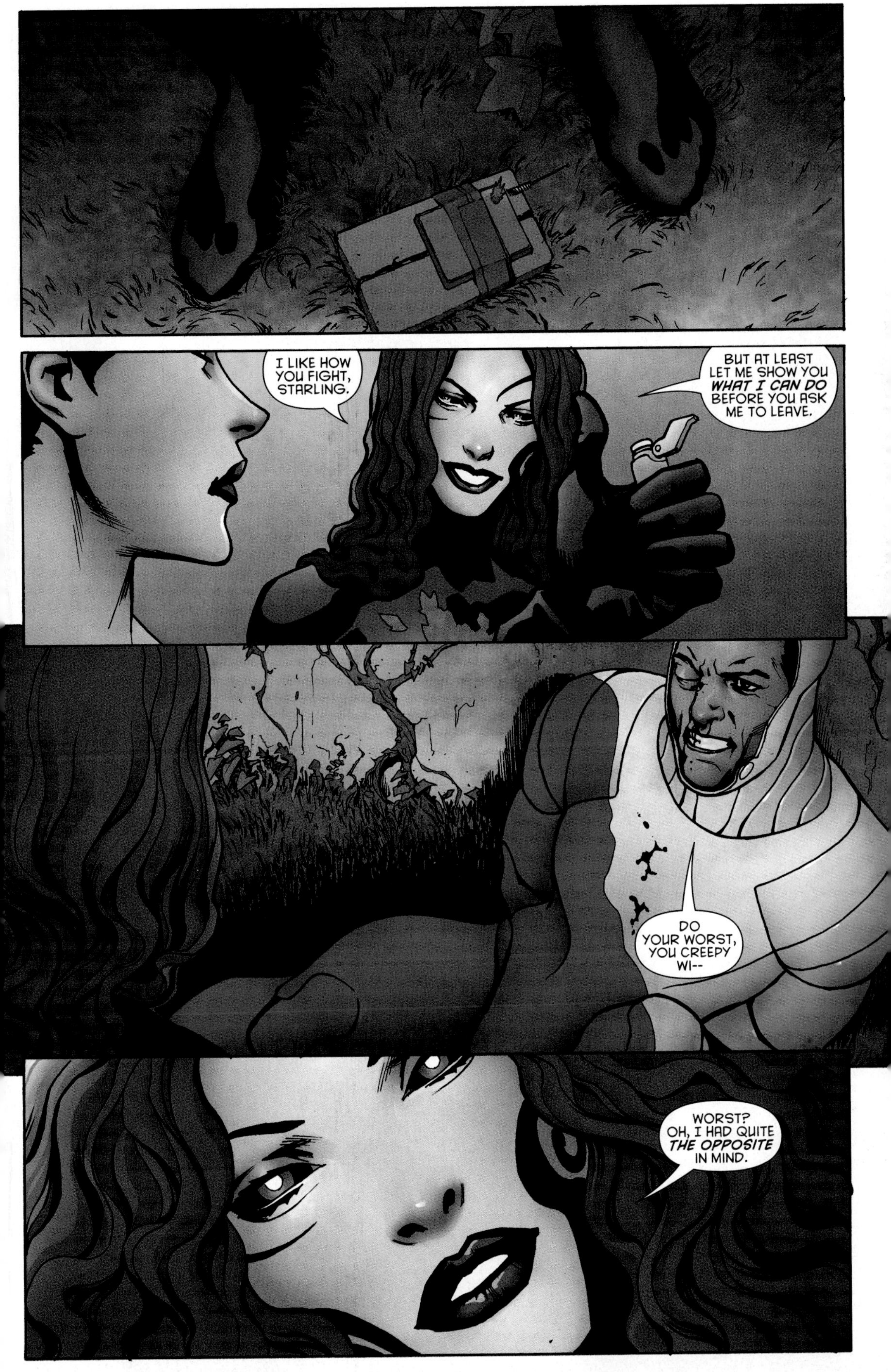
I LIKE HOW YOU FIGHT, STARLING.
BUT AT LEAST LET ME SHOW YOU *WHAT I CAN DO* BEFORE YOU ASK ME TO LEAVE.
DO YOUR WORST, YOU CREEPY WI--
WORST? OH, I HAD QUITE *THE OPPOSITE* IN MIND.

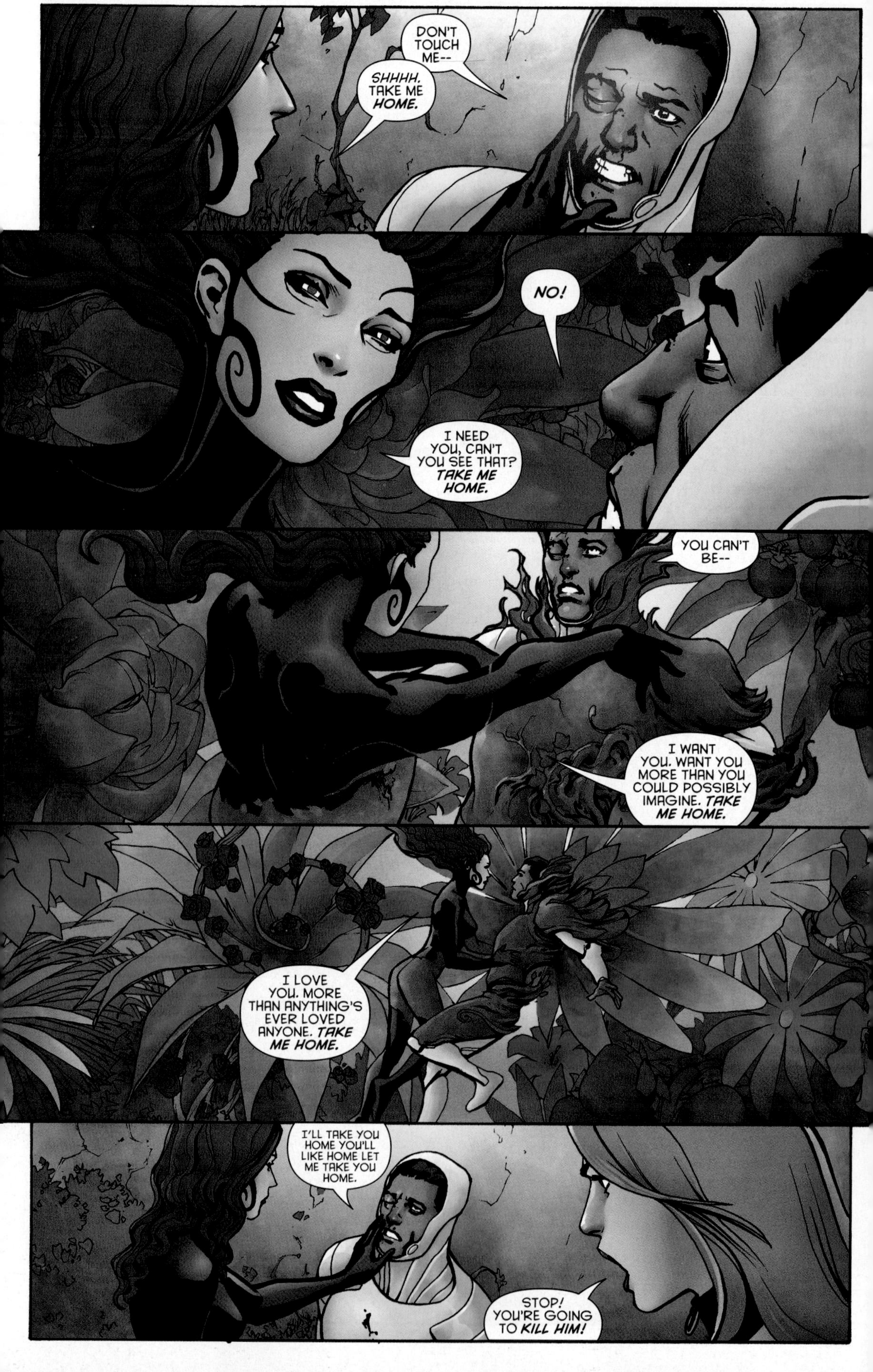
DON'T TOUCH ME--
SHHHH. TAKE ME HOME.
NO!
I NEED YOU, CAN'T YOU SEE THAT? TAKE ME HOME.
YOU CAN'T BE--
I WANT YOU. WANT YOU MORE THAN YOU COULD POSSIBLY IMAGINE. TAKE ME HOME.
I LOVE YOU. MORE THAN ANYTHING'S EVER LOVED ANYONE. TAKE ME HOME.
I'LL TAKE YOU HOME YOU'LL LIKE HOME LET ME TAKE YOU HOME.
STOP! YOU'RE GOING TO KILL HIM!

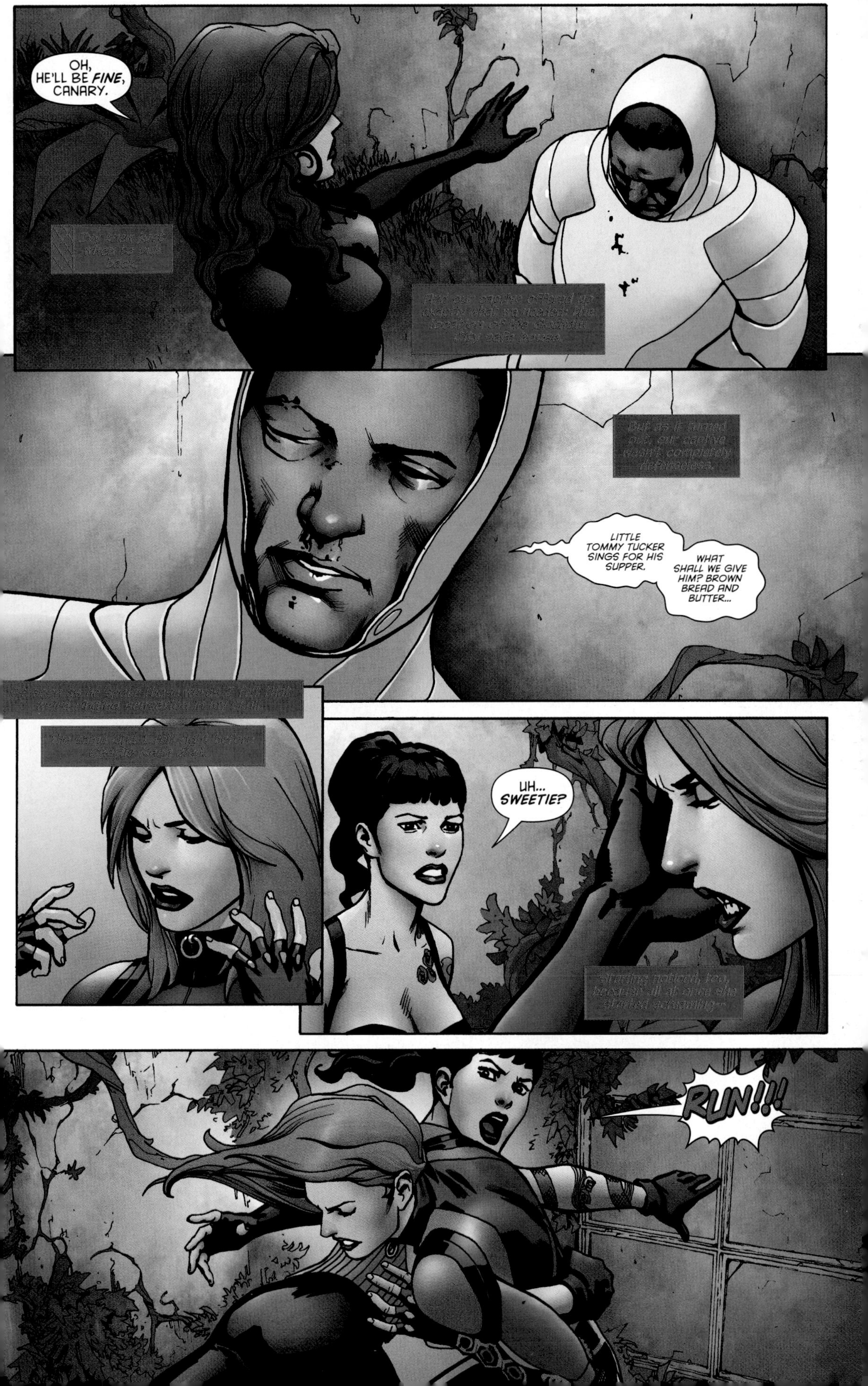
OH, HE'LL BE FINE, CANARY.
And our captive offered up exactly what we needed: the location of the Gotham City safe house.
But as it turned out, our captive wasn't completely defenseless.
LITTLE TOMMY TUCKER SINGS FOR HIS SUPPER.
WHAT SHALL WE GIVE HIM? BROWN BREAD AND BUTTER...
UH... SWEETIE?
RUN!!!

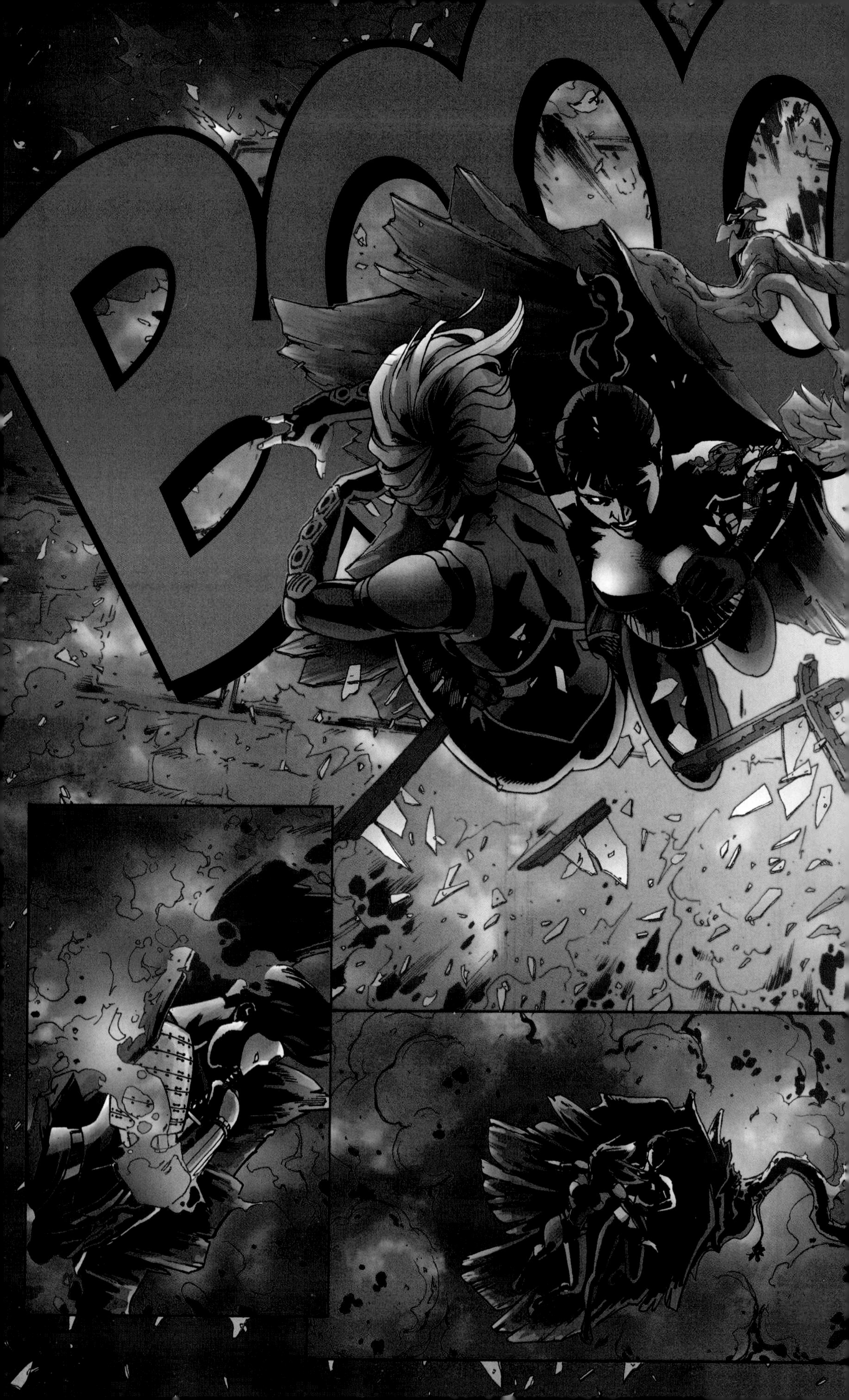
BOOO

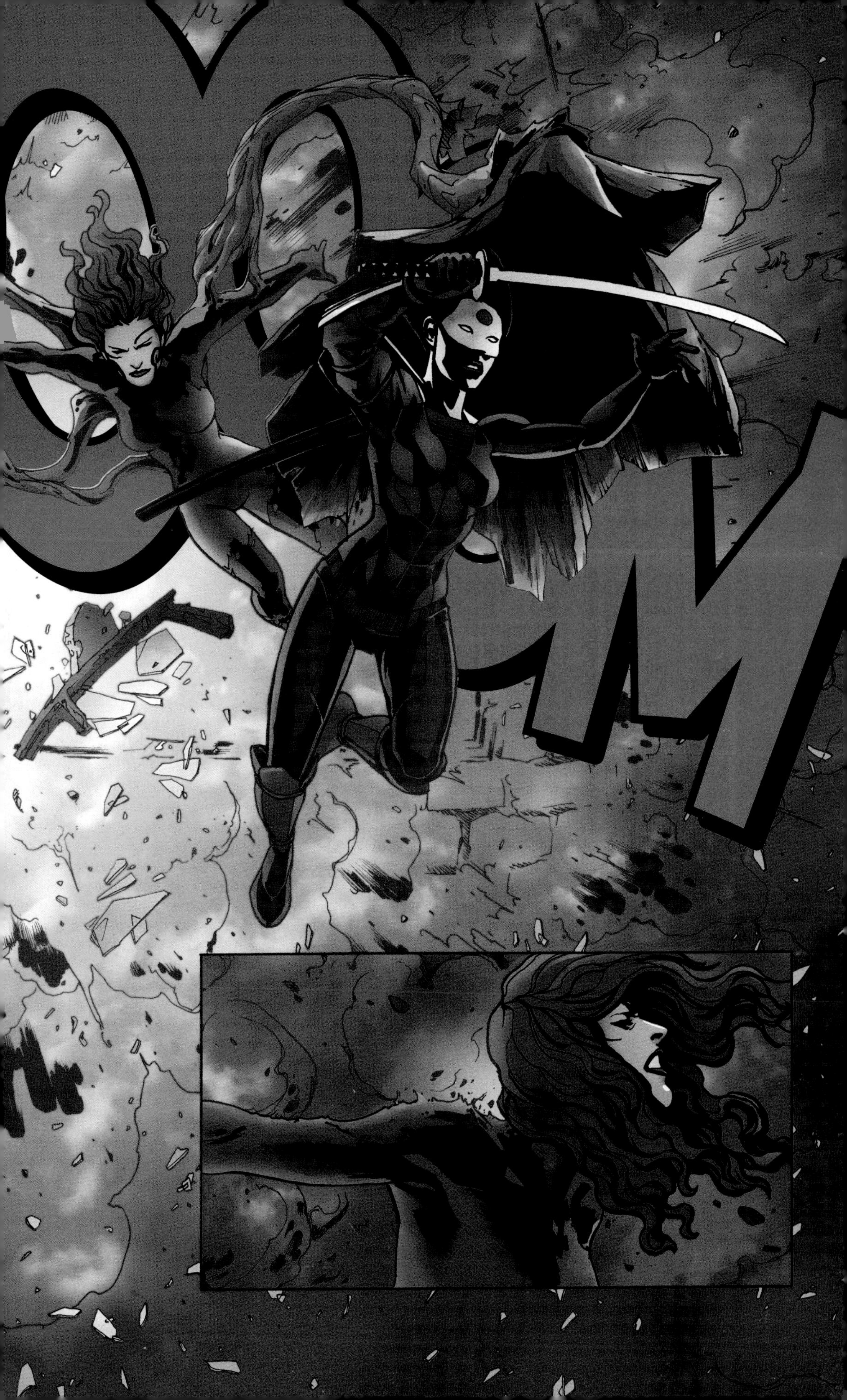
OOM

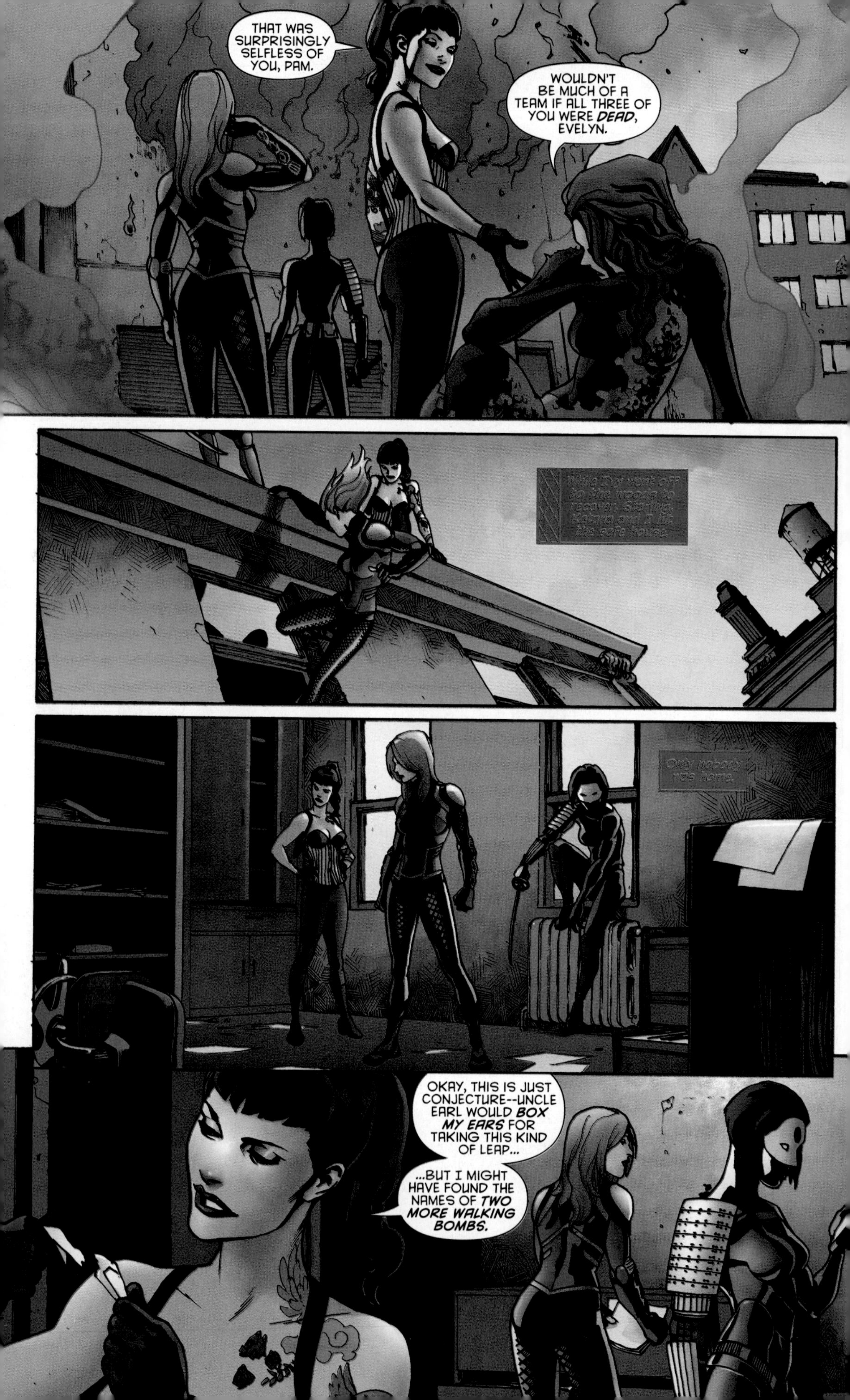

THAT WAS SURPRISINGLY SELFLESS OF YOU, PAM.
WOULDN'T BE MUCH OF A TEAM IF ALL THREE OF YOU WERE *DEAD*, EVELYN.
While Ivy went off to the woods to recover, Starling, Katana and I hit the safe house.
Only nobody was home.
OKAY, THIS IS JUST CONJECTURE--UNCLE EARL WOULD *BOX MY EARS* FOR TAKING THIS KIND OF LEAP...
...BUT I MIGHT HAVE FOUND THE NAMES OF *TWO MORE WALKING BOMBS*.

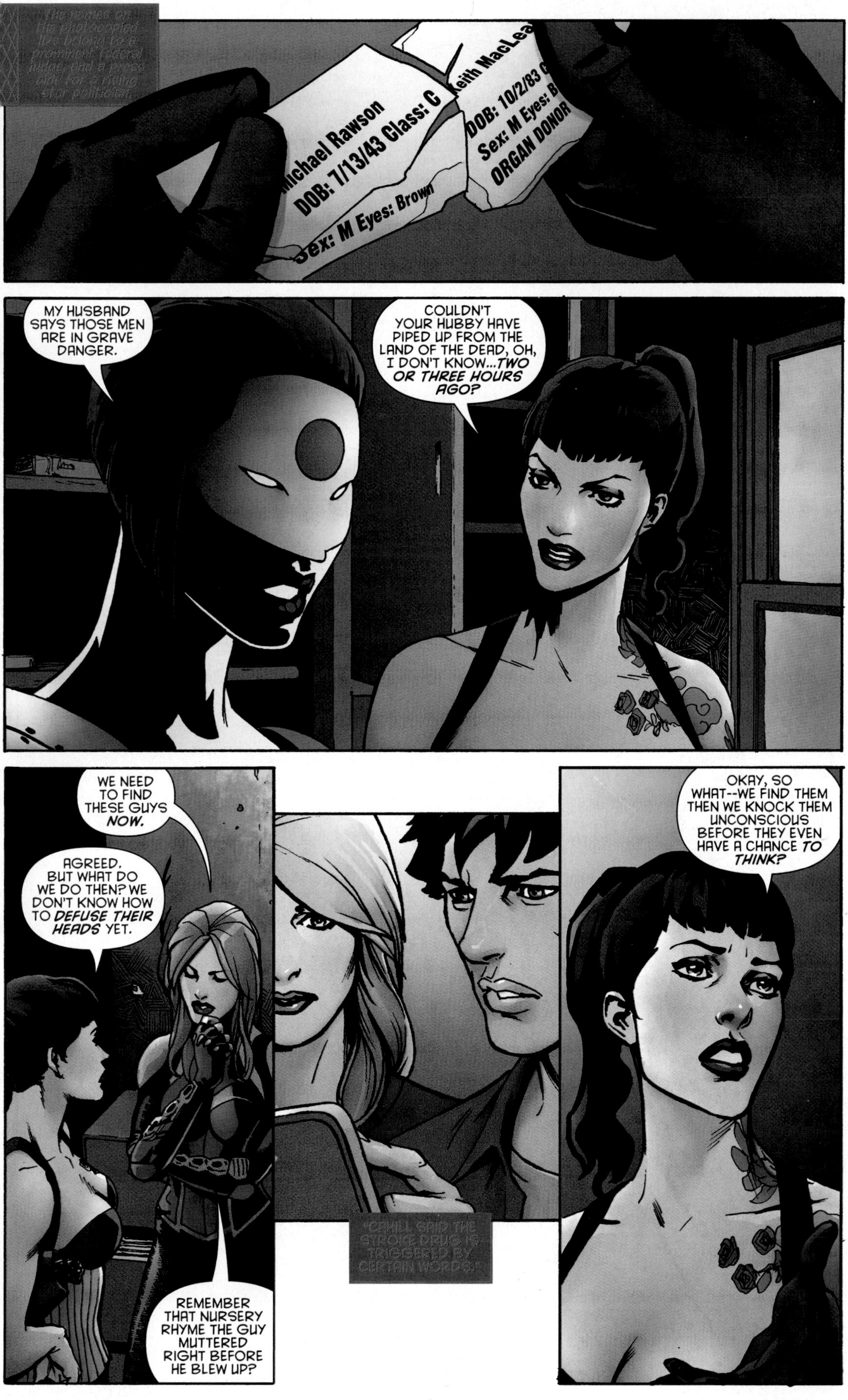
The names on the photocopied ID's belong to a prominent federal judge and a press aide for a rising star politician.
Michael Rawson
DOB: 7/13/43 Class: C
Sex: M Eyes: Brown
Keith MacLea
DOB: 10/2/83
Sex: M Eyes: B
ORGAN DONOR
MY HUSBAND SAYS THOSE MEN ARE IN GRAVE DANGER.
COULDN'T YOUR HUBBY HAVE PIPED UP FROM THE LAND OF THE DEAD, OH, I DON'T KNOW...TWO OR THREE HOURS AGO?
WE NEED TO FIND THESE GUYS NOW.
AGREED. BUT WHAT DO WE DO THEN? WE DON'T KNOW HOW TO DEFUSE THEIR HEADS YET.
REMEMBER THAT NURSERY RHYME THE GUY MUTTERED RIGHT BEFORE HE BLEW UP?
"CAHILL SAID THE STROKE DRUG IS TRIGGERED BY CERTAIN WORDS."
OKAY, SO WHAT--WE FIND THEM THEN WE KNOCK THEM UNCONSCIOUS BEFORE THEY EVEN HAVE A CHANCE TO THINK?

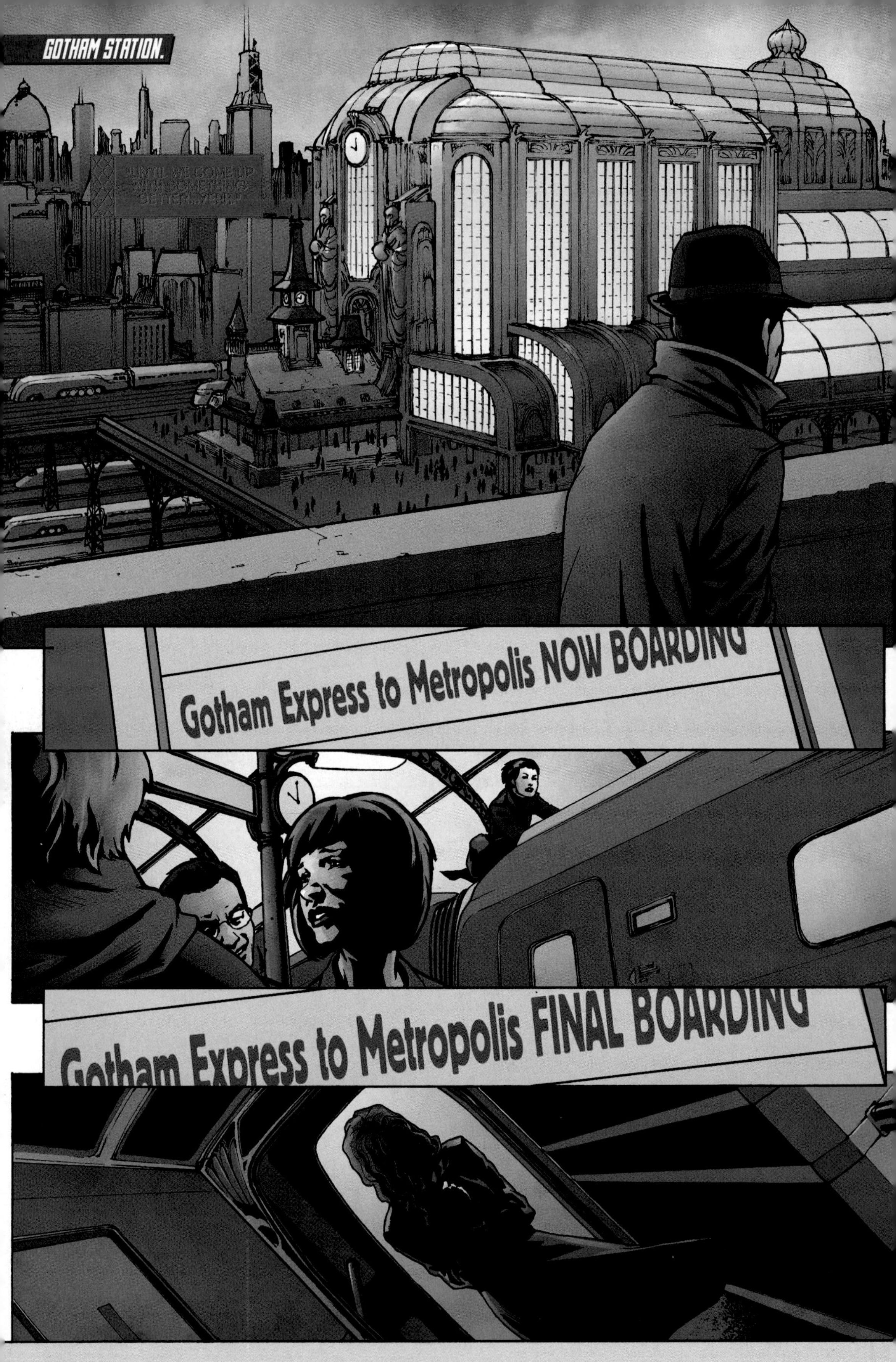
GOTHAM STATION.
Gotham Express to Metropolis NOW BOARDING
Gotham Express to Metropolis FINAL BOARDING

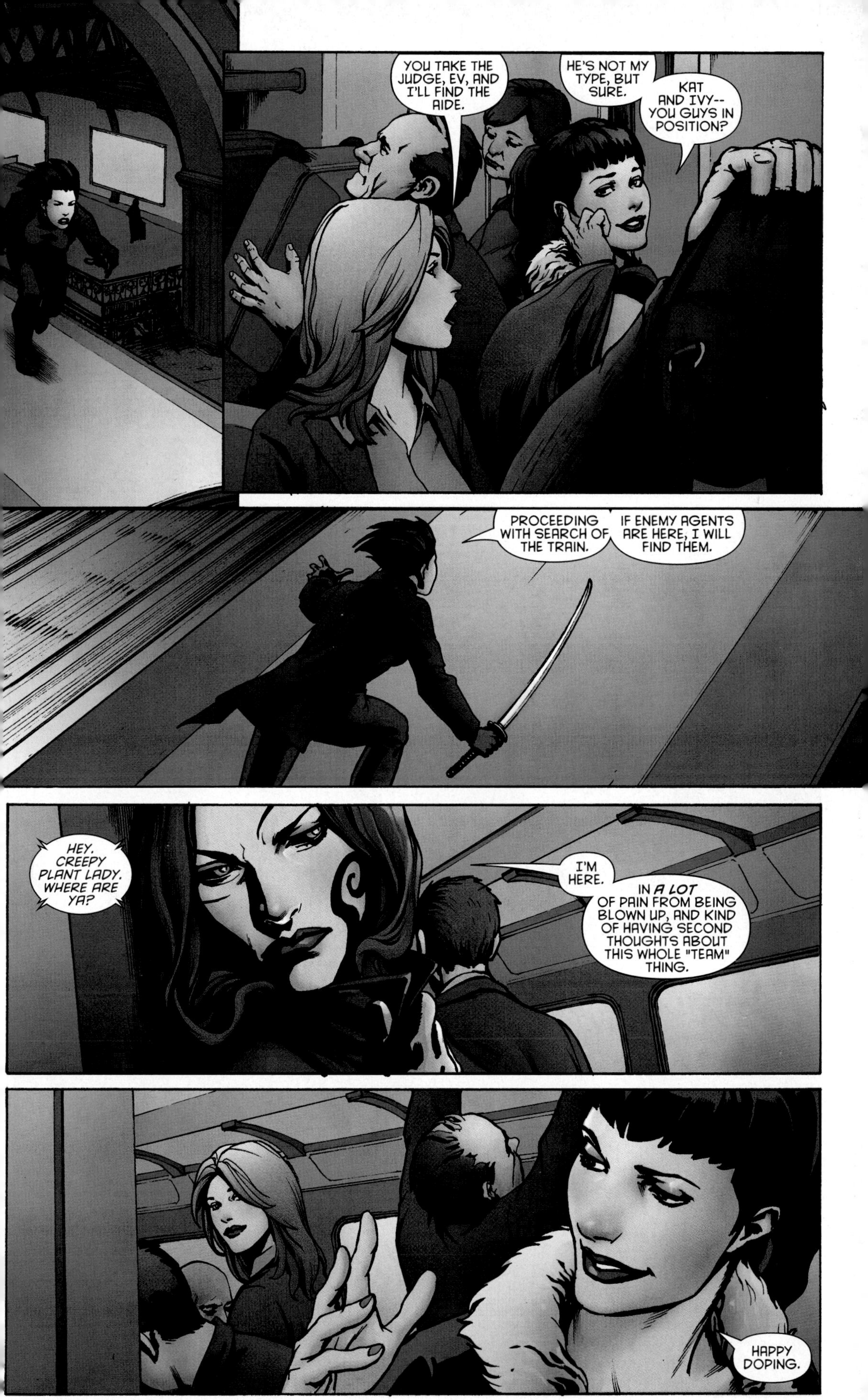
YOU TAKE THE JUDGE, EV, AND I'LL FIND THE AIDE.
HE'S NOT MY TYPE, BUT SURE.
KAT AND IVY-- YOU GUYS IN POSITION?
PROCEEDING WITH SEARCH OF THE TRAIN.
IF ENEMY AGENTS ARE HERE, I WILL FIND THEM.
HEY. CREEPY PLANT LADY. WHERE ARE YA?
I'M HERE.
IN A LOT OF PAIN FROM BEING BLOWN UP, AND KIND OF HAVING SECOND THOUGHTS ABOUT THIS WHOLE "TEAM" THING.
HAPPY DOPING.

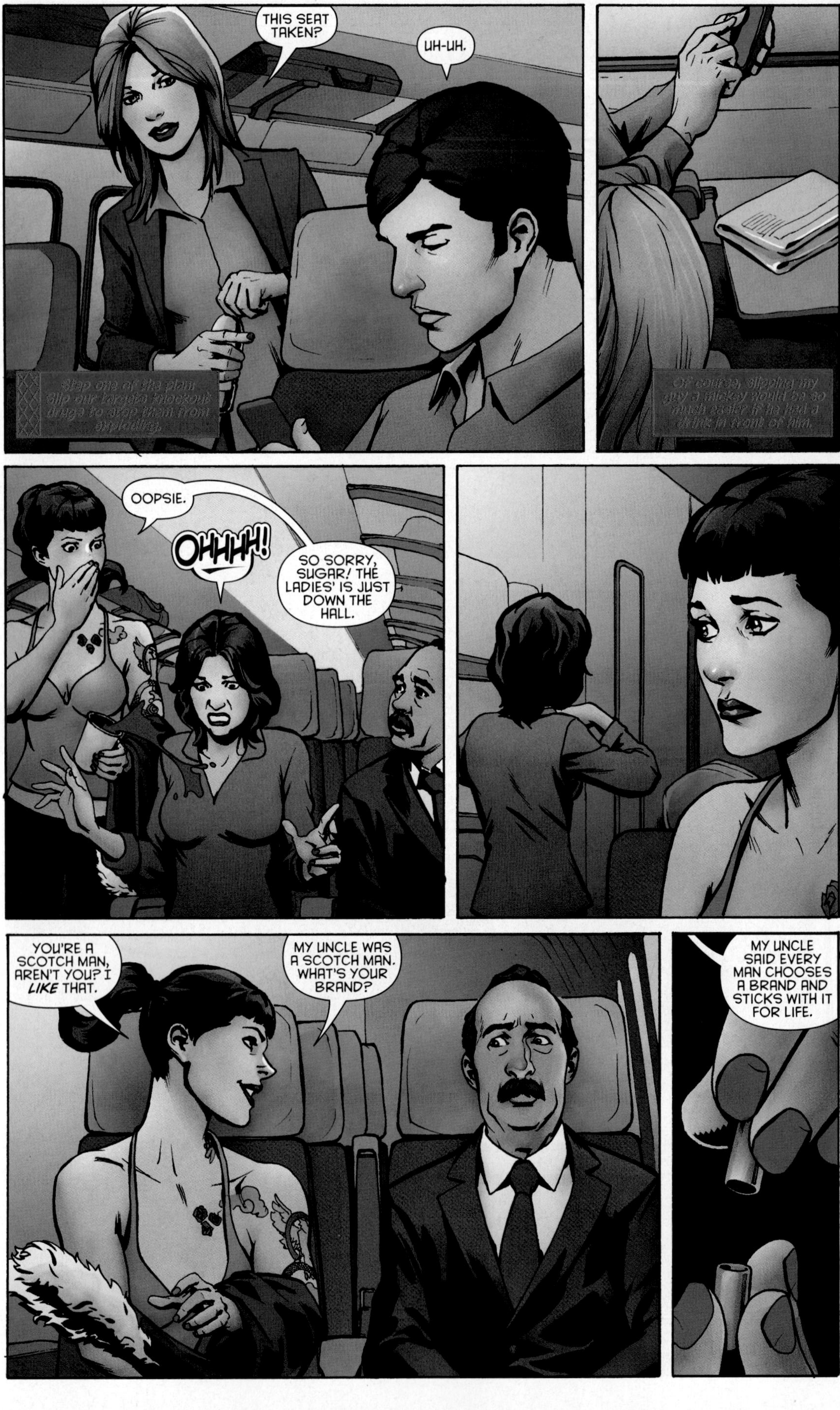
THIS SEAT TAKEN?
UH-UH.
Step one of the plan: Slip our targets knockout drugs to stop them from exploding.
Of course, slipping my guy a mickey would be so much easier if he had a drink in front of him.
OOPSIE.
OHHHH!
SO SORRY, SUGAR! THE LADIES' IS JUST DOWN THE HALL.
YOU'RE A SCOTCH MAN, AREN'T YOU? I *LIKE* THAT.
MY UNCLE WAS A SCOTCH MAN. WHAT'S YOUR BRAND?
MY UNCLE SAID EVERY MAN CHOOSES A BRAND AND STICKS WITH IT FOR LIFE.

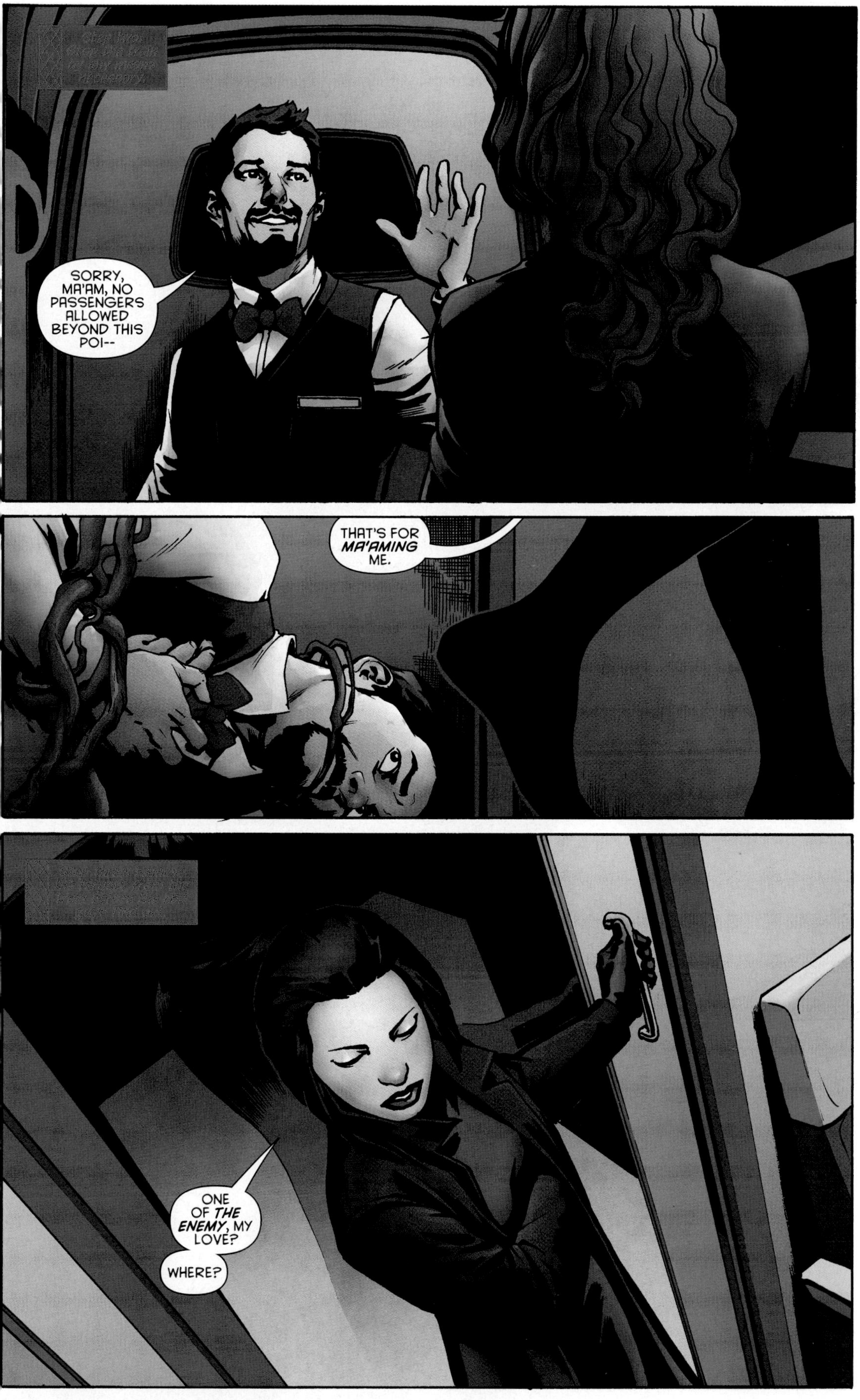
SORRY, MA'AM, NO PASSENGERS ALLOWED BEYOND THIS POI--
THAT'S FOR *MA'AMING* ME.
ONE OF *THE ENEMY*, MY LOVE?
WHERE?

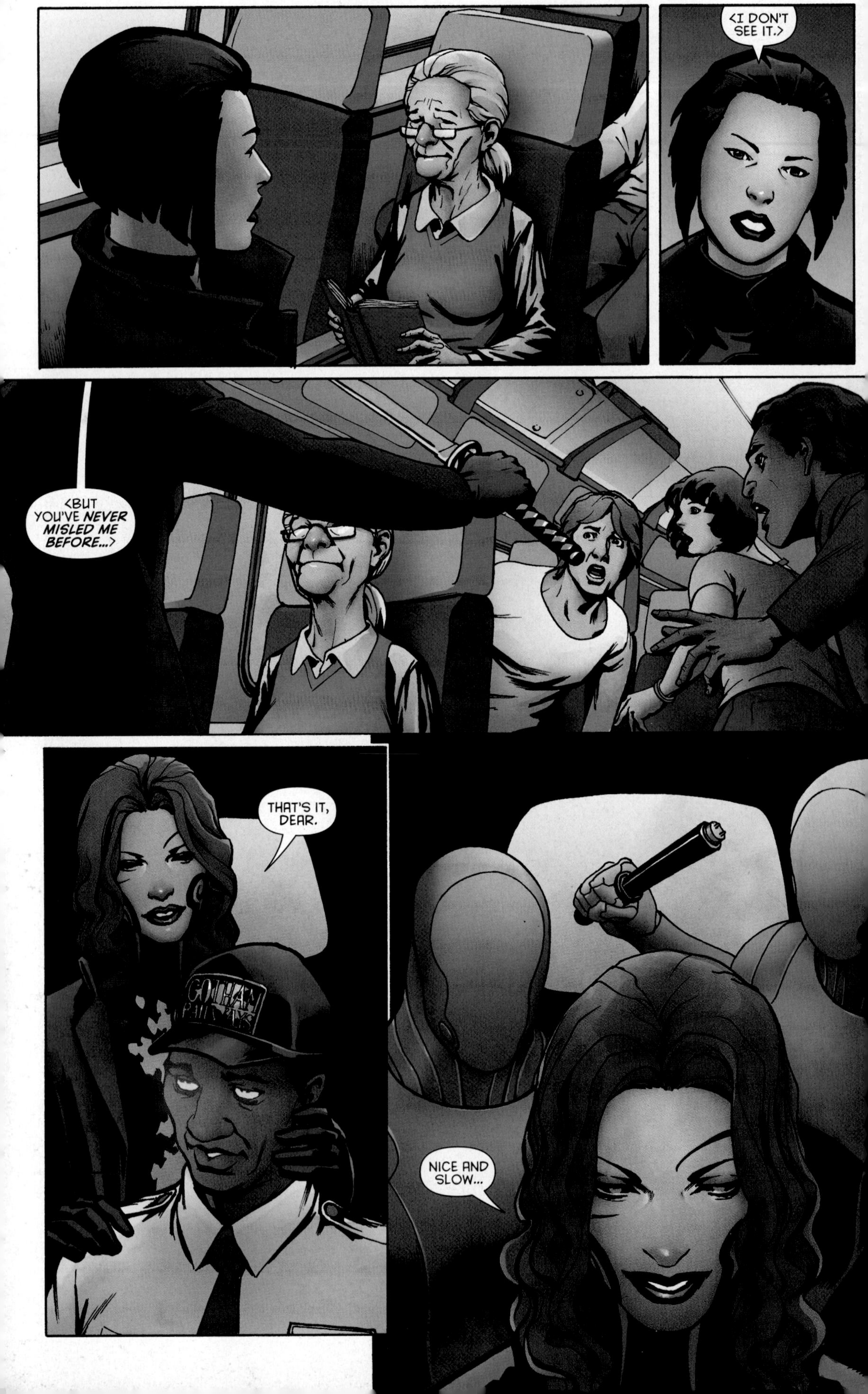
<I DON'T SEE IT.>
<BUT YOU'VE *NEVER MISLED* ME BEFORE...>
THAT'S IT, DEAR.
NICE AND SLOW...

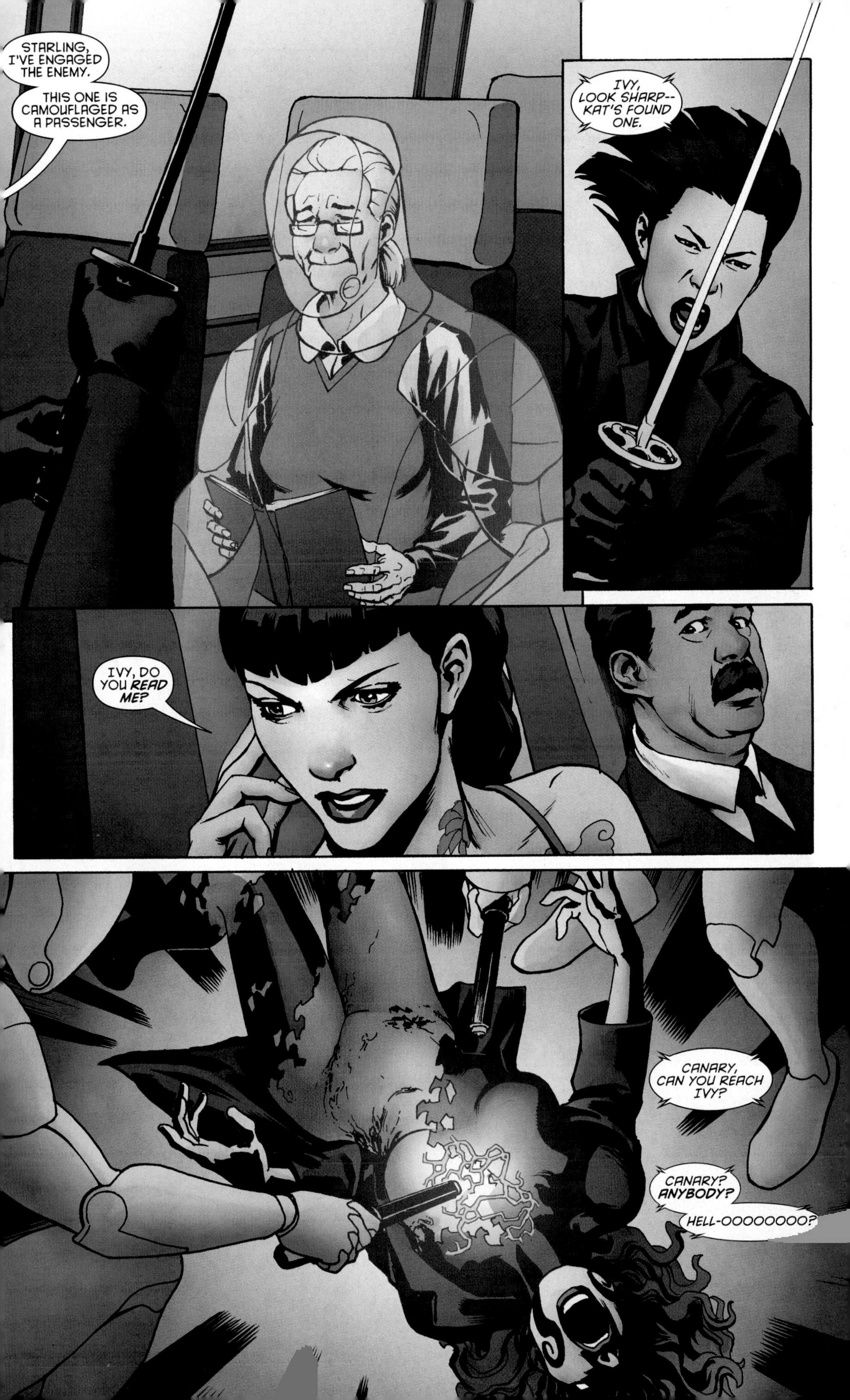
STARLING, I'VE ENGAGED THE ENEMY.
THIS ONE IS CAMOUFLAGED AS A PASSENGER.
IVY, LOOK SHARP-- KAT'S FOUND ONE.
IVY, DO YOU *READ ME?*
CANARY, CAN YOU REACH IVY?
CANARY? **ANYBODY?**
HELL-OOOOOOOO?

HELLO, DINAH.

WHAT--

SHHH NOW. THERE'S NO TIME. CALL OFF YOUR TEAM OR EVERYONE DIES.

WHERE ARE YOU?

DON'T YOU KNOW BY NOW THAT WE ARE EVERY-WHERE?

I'M NOT GOING TO LET YOU HURT THESE PEOPLE.

YES YOU ARE, DINAH. BECAUSE THERE'S ANOTHER BOMB. AND IT'S IN YOUR BRAIN.

WE PLANTED THE COMPONENTS DURING OUR FIRST ENCOUNTER.

DON'T YOU REMEMBER THE THREE TIMES WE TOUCHED YOU?

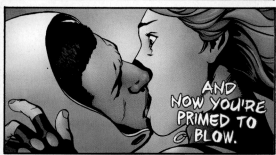

AND NOW YOU'RE PRIMED TO BLOW.

HEY, ARE YOU... ARE YOU OKAY?

UGH...

DO IT NOW. CALL THEM OFF. OR YOU AN EVERYONE ELS ON THIS TRAIN DIES.

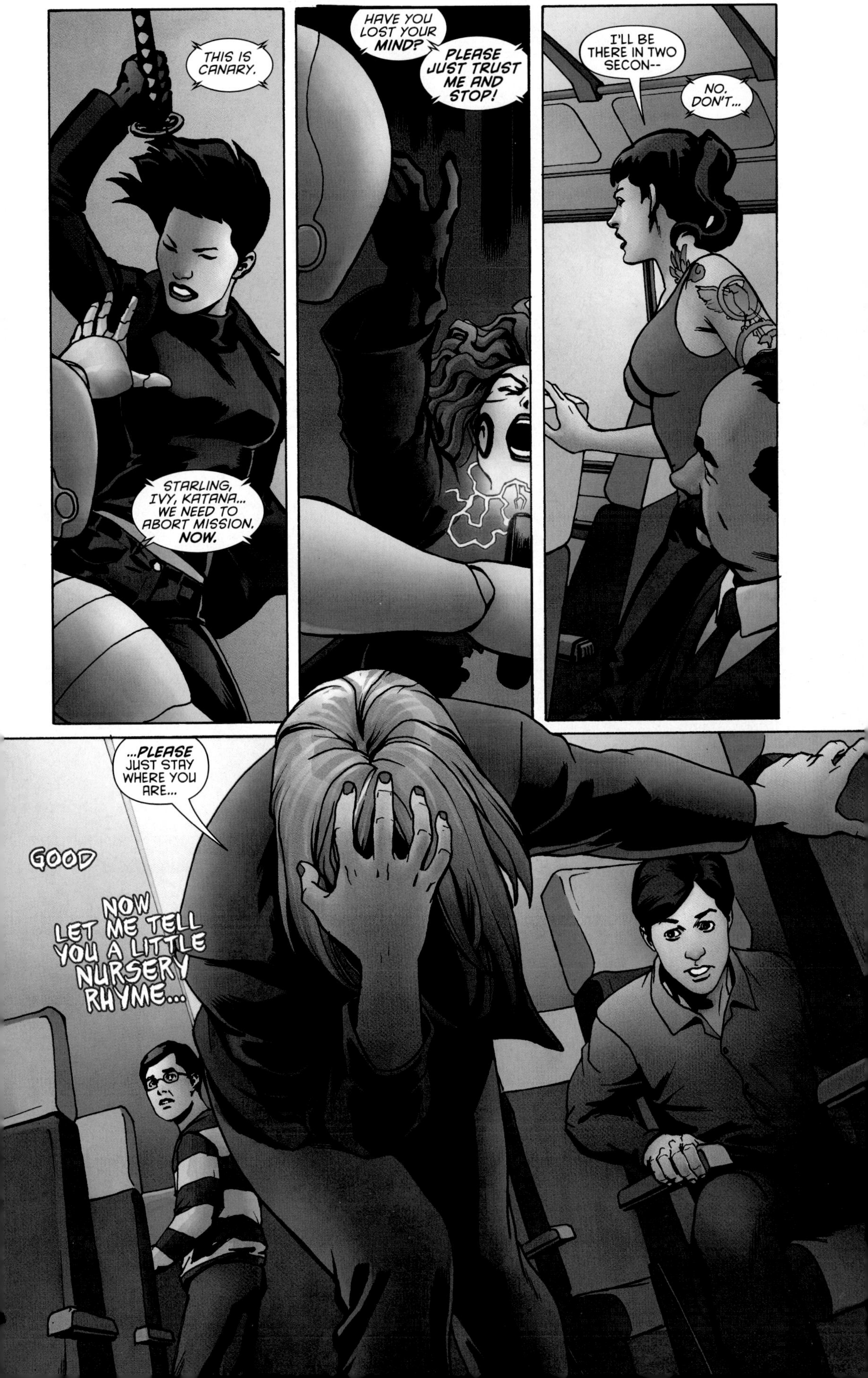
THIS IS CANARY.
STARLING, IVY, KATANA... WE NEED TO ABORT MISSION. NOW.
HAVE YOU LOST YOUR MIND?
PLEASE JUST TRUST ME AND STOP!
I'LL BE THERE IN TWO SECON--
NO. DON'T...
...PLEASE JUST STAY WHERE YOU ARE...
GOOD
NOW LET ME TELL YOU A LITTLE NURSERY RHYME...

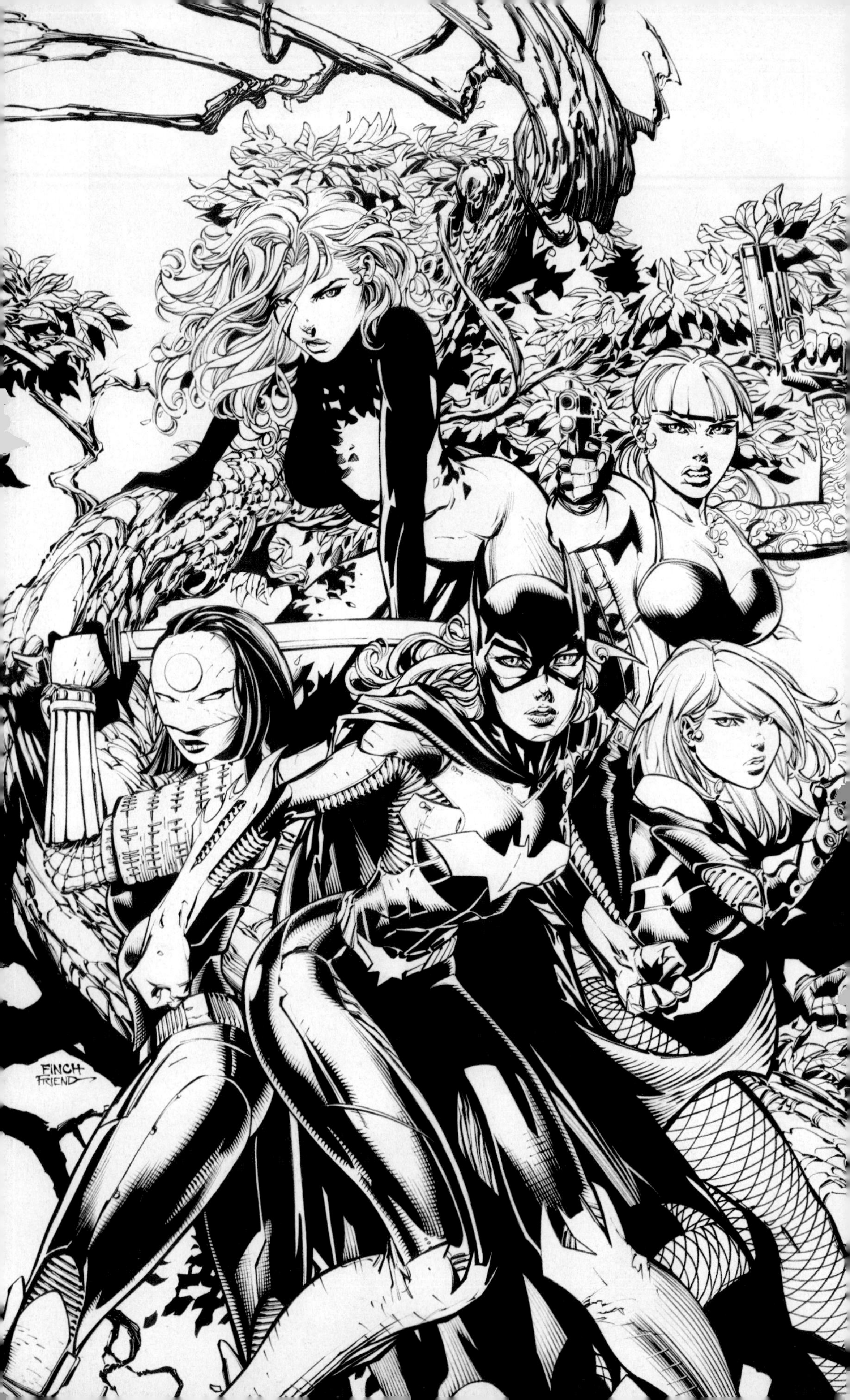
FINCH
FRIEND

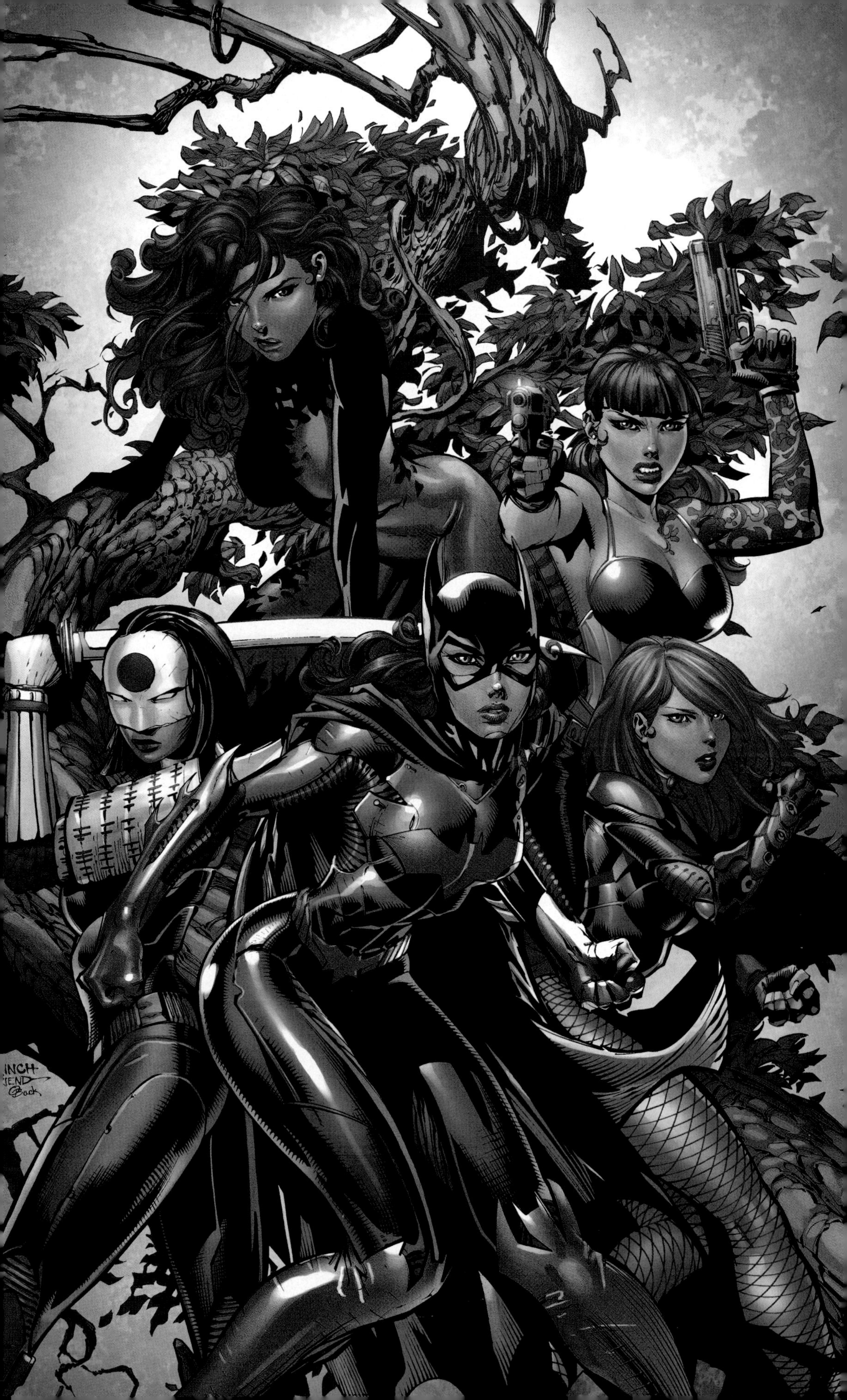

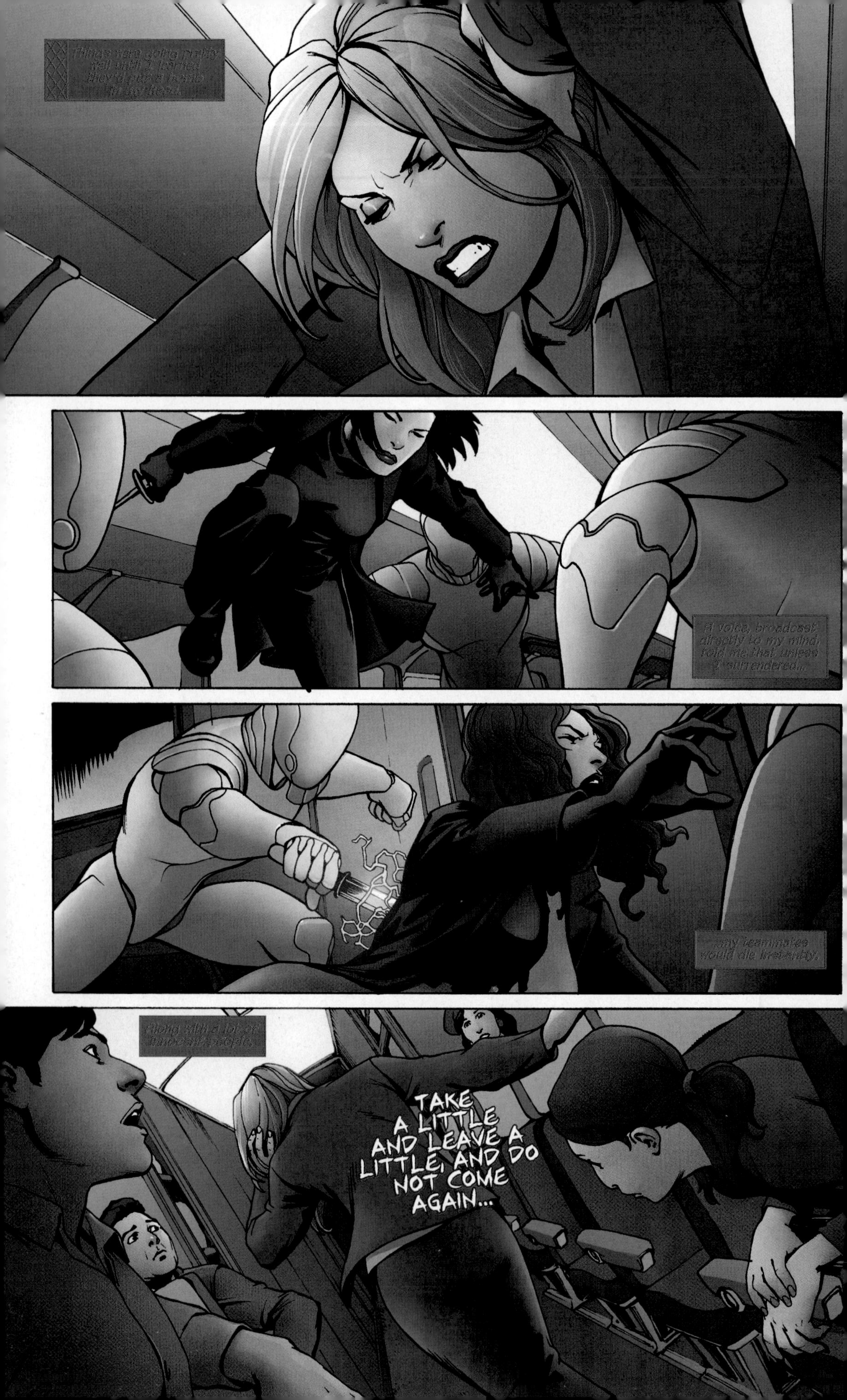
Things were going pretty well until I learned they'd put a bomb in my head.
A voice, broadcast directly to my mind, told me that unless I surrendered...
...my teammates would die instantly.
Along with a lot of innocent people.
TAKE A LITTLE AND LEAVE A LITTLE, AND DO NOT COME AGAIN...

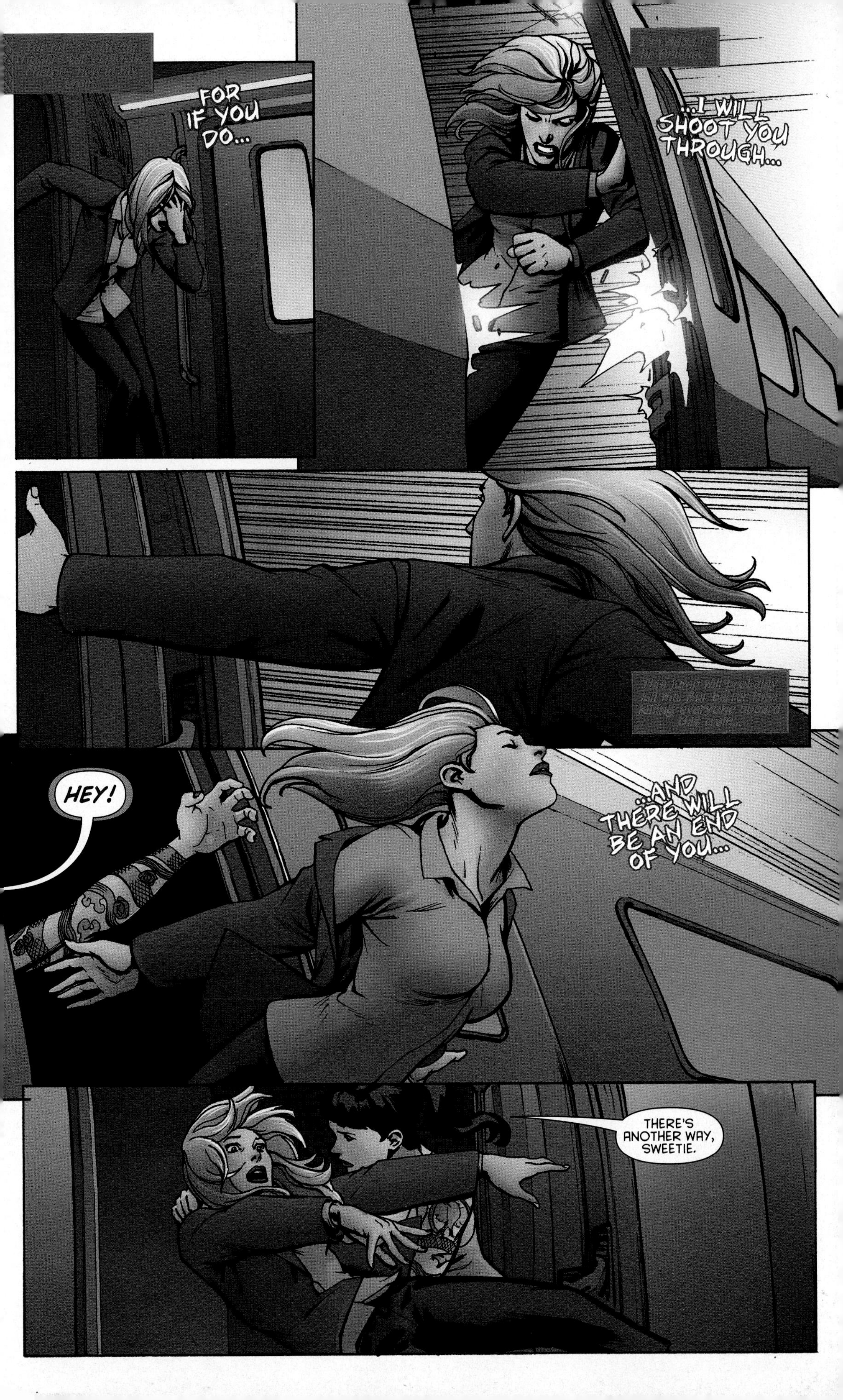
The nursery rhyme triggers the explosive charges now in my brain...
FOR IF YOU DO...
...I WILL SHOOT YOU THROUGH...
This jump will probably kill me. But better than killing everyone aboard this train...
HEY!
...AND THERE WILL BE AN END OF YOU...
THERE'S ANOTHER WAY, SWEETIE.

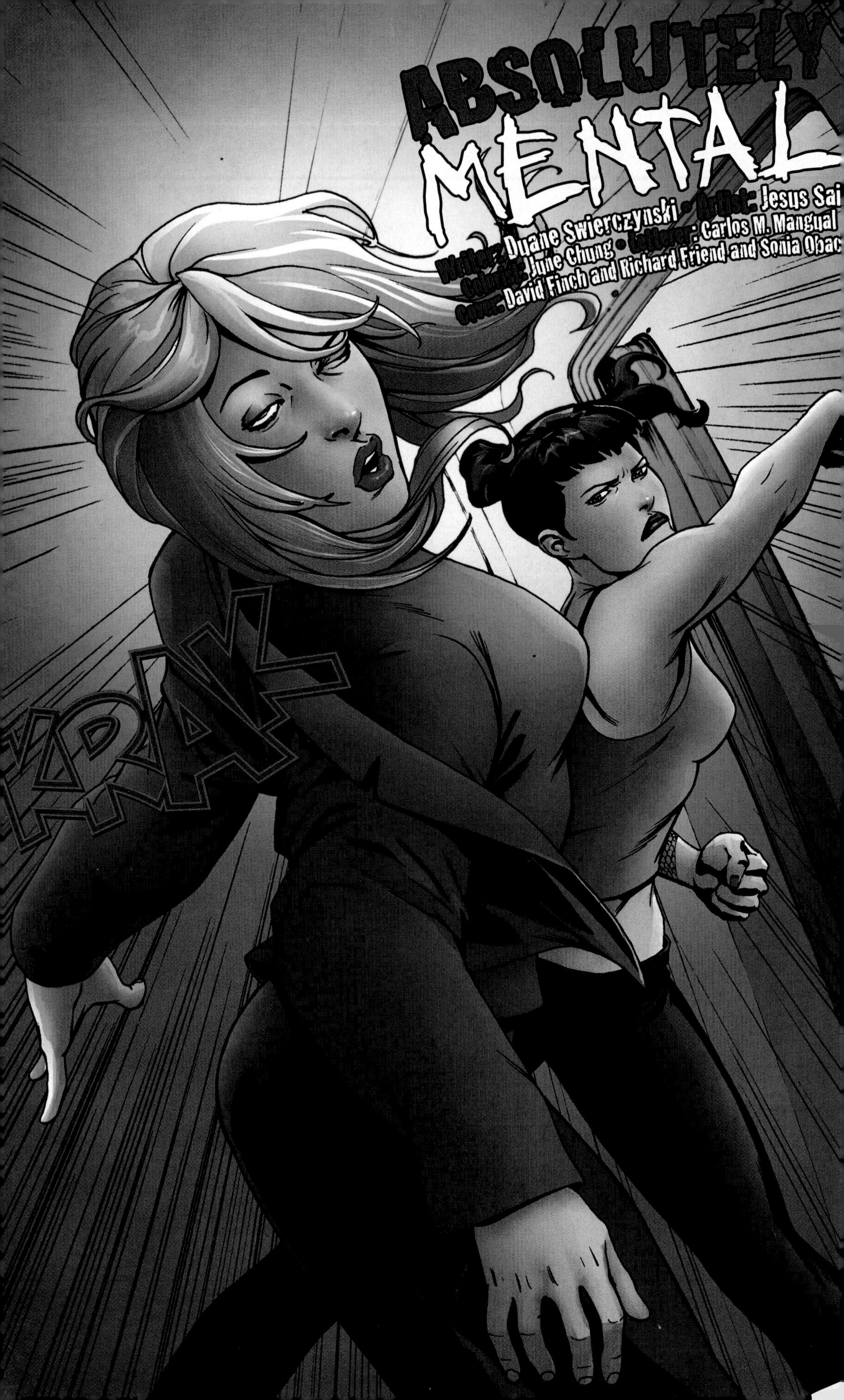
ABSOLUTELY MENTAL
Writer: Duane Swierczynski • Artist: Jesus Sai
Colorist: June Chung • Letterer: Carlos M. Mangual
Cover: David Finch and Richard Friend and Sonia Obac
KRAK

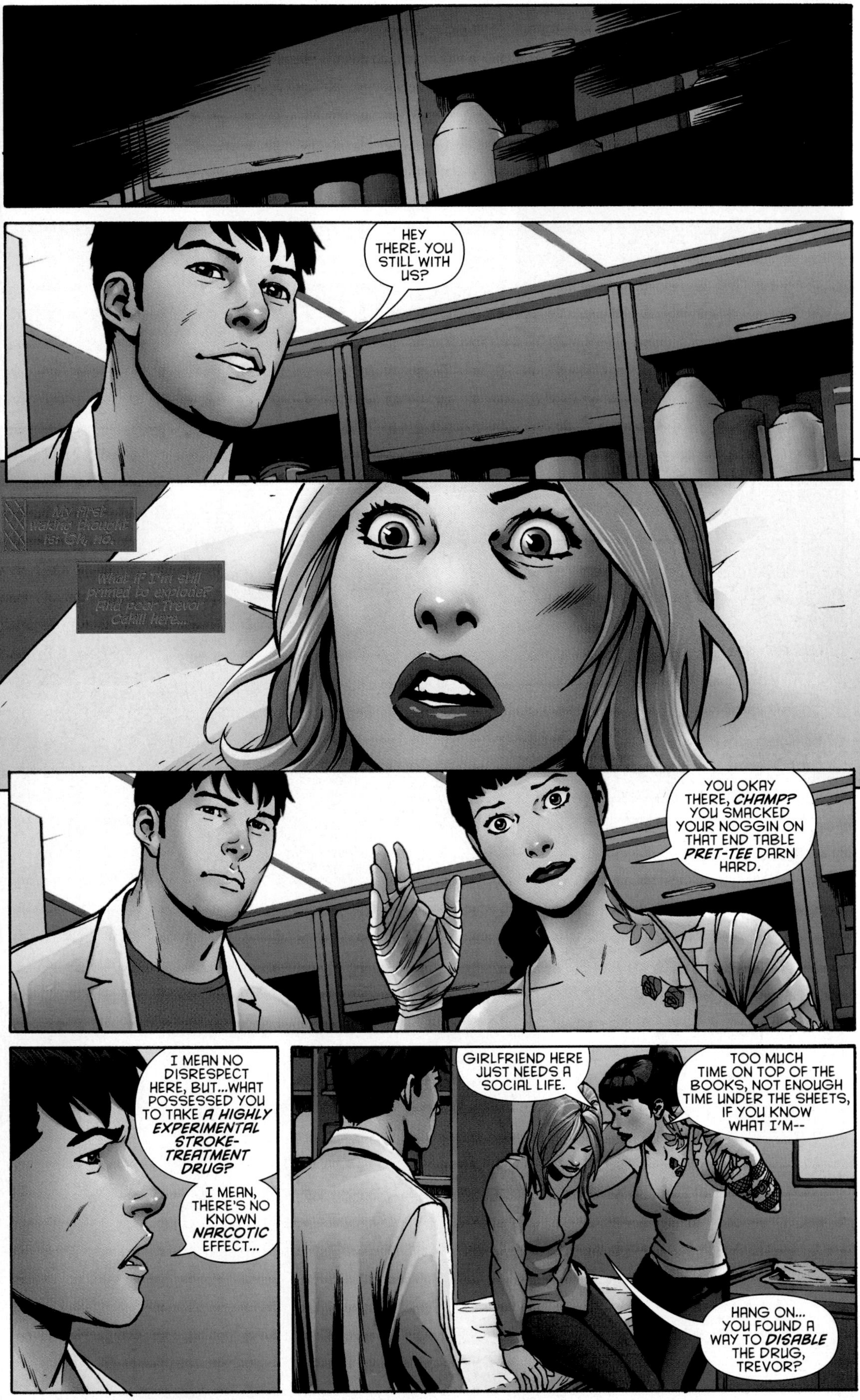
HEY THERE. YOU STILL WITH US?
My first waking thought is: Oh, no.
What if I'm still primed to explode? And poor Trevor Cahill here...
YOU OKAY THERE, CHAMP? YOU SMACKED YOUR NOGGIN ON THAT END TABLE PRET-TEE DARN HARD.
I MEAN NO DISRESPECT HERE, BUT...WHAT POSSESSED YOU TO TAKE A HIGHLY EXPERIMENTAL STROKE-TREATMENT DRUG?
I MEAN, THERE'S NO KNOWN NARCOTIC EFFECT...
GIRLFRIEND HERE JUST NEEDS A SOCIAL LIFE.
TOO MUCH TIME ON TOP OF THE BOOKS, NOT ENOUGH TIME UNDER THE SHEETS, IF YOU KNOW WHAT I'M--
HANG ON... YOU FOUND A WAY TO DISABLE THE DRUG, TREVOR?

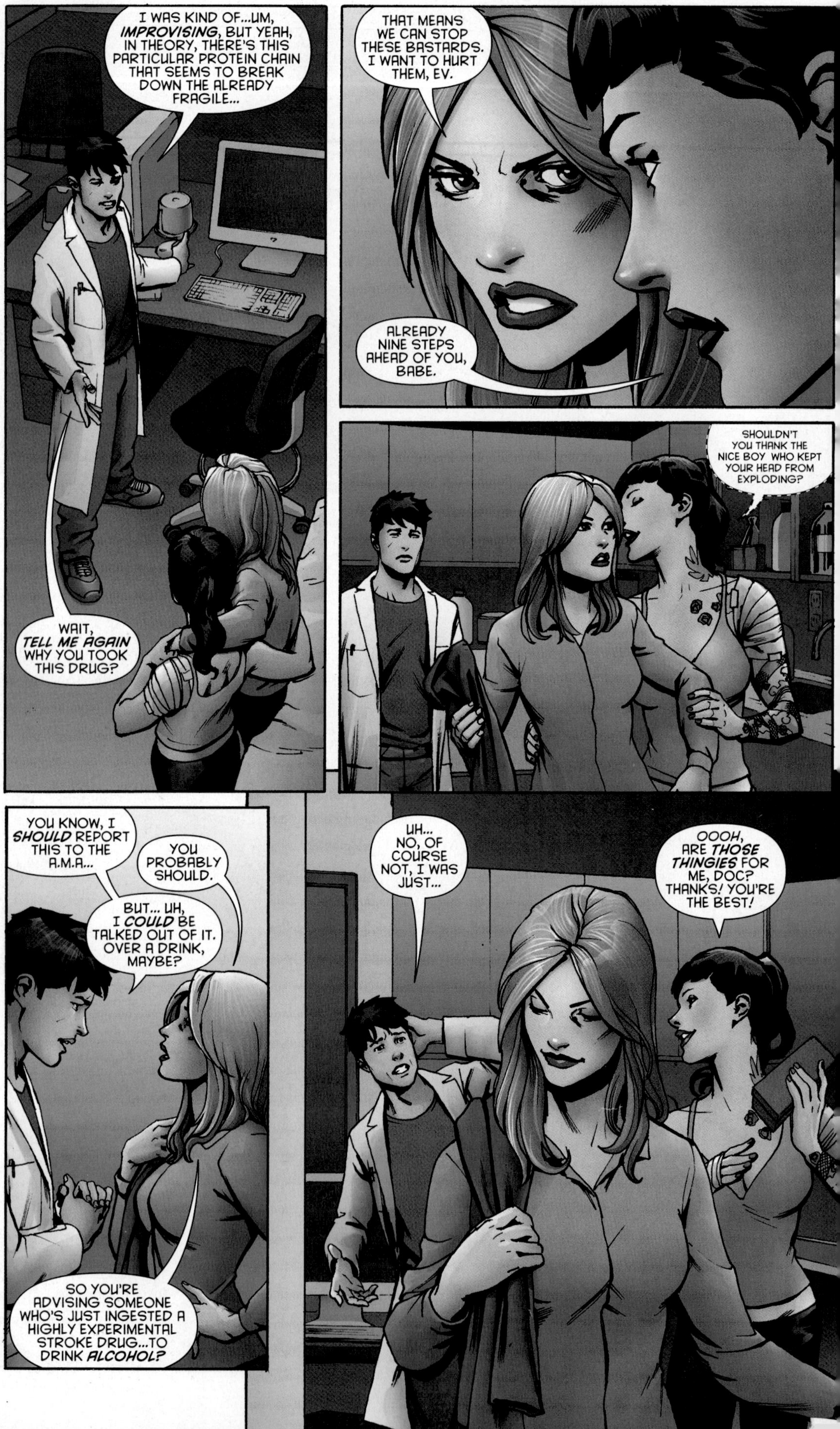
I WAS KIND OF...UM, IMPROVISING, BUT YEAH, IN THEORY, THERE'S THIS PARTICULAR PROTEIN CHAIN THAT SEEMS TO BREAK DOWN THE ALREADY FRAGILE...
WAIT, TELL ME AGAIN WHY YOU TOOK THIS DRUG?
THAT MEANS WE CAN STOP THESE BASTARDS. I WANT TO HURT THEM, EV.
ALREADY NINE STEPS AHEAD OF YOU, BABE.
SHOULDN'T YOU THANK THE NICE BOY WHO KEPT YOUR HEAD FROM EXPLODING?
YOU KNOW, I SHOULD REPORT THIS TO THE A.M.A...
YOU PROBABLY SHOULD.
BUT... UH, I COULD BE TALKED OUT OF IT. OVER A DRINK, MAYBE?
SO YOU'RE ADVISING SOMEONE WHO'S JUST INGESTED A HIGHLY EXPERIMENTAL STROKE DRUG...TO DRINK ALCOHOL?
UH... NO, OF COURSE NOT, I WAS JUST...
OOOH, ARE THOSE THINGIES FOR ME, DOC? THANKS! YOU'RE THE BEST!

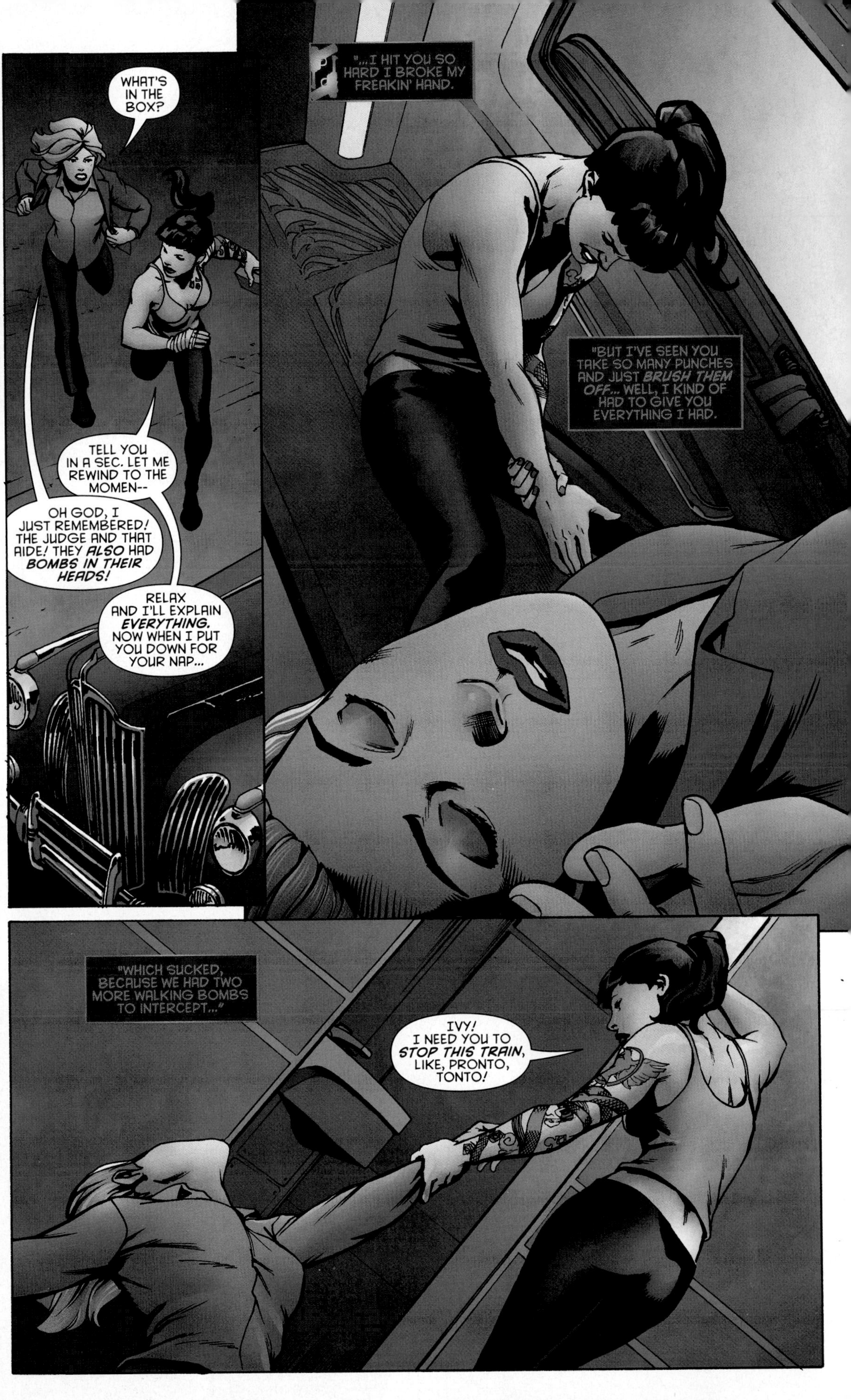
WHAT'S IN THE BOX?
TELL YOU IN A SEC. LET ME REWIND TO THE MOMEN--
OH GOD, I JUST REMEMBERED! THE JUDGE AND THAT AIDE! THEY ALSO HAD BOMBS IN THEIR HEADS!
RELAX AND I'LL EXPLAIN EVERYTHING. NOW WHEN I PUT YOU DOWN FOR YOUR NAP...
"...I HIT YOU SO HARD I BROKE MY FREAKIN' HAND.
"BUT I'VE SEEN YOU TAKE SO MANY PUNCHES AND JUST BRUSH THEM OFF... WELL, I KIND OF HAD TO GIVE YOU EVERYTHING I HAD.
"WHICH SUCKED, BECAUSE WE HAD TWO MORE WALKING BOMBS TO INTERCEPT..."
IVY! I NEED YOU TO STOP THIS TRAIN, LIKE, PRONTO, TONTO!

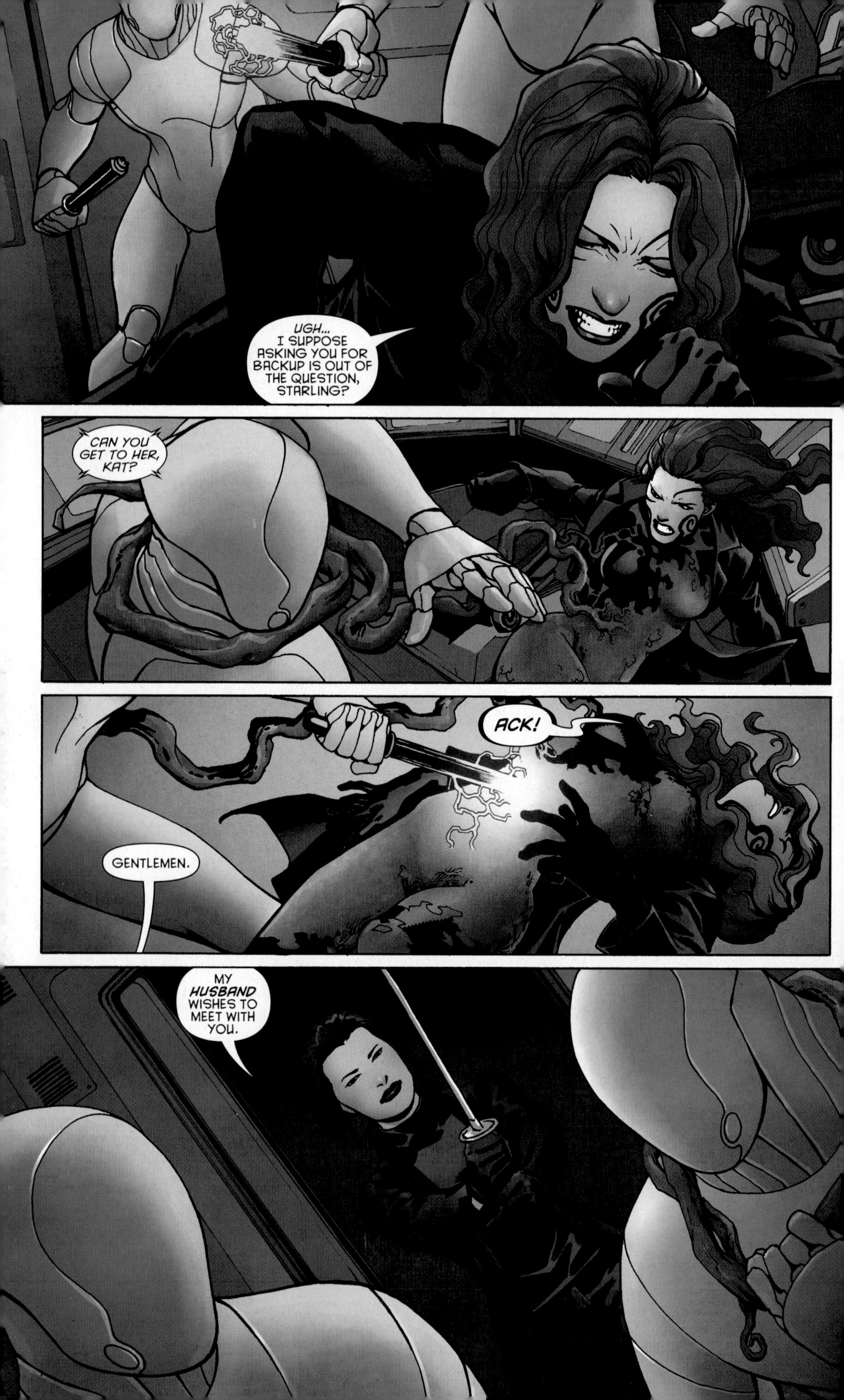
UGH... I SUPPOSE ASKING YOU FOR BACKUP IS OUT OF THE QUESTION, STARLING?
CAN YOU GET TO HER, KAT?
ACK!
GENTLEMEN.
MY HUSBAND WISHES TO MEET WITH YOU.

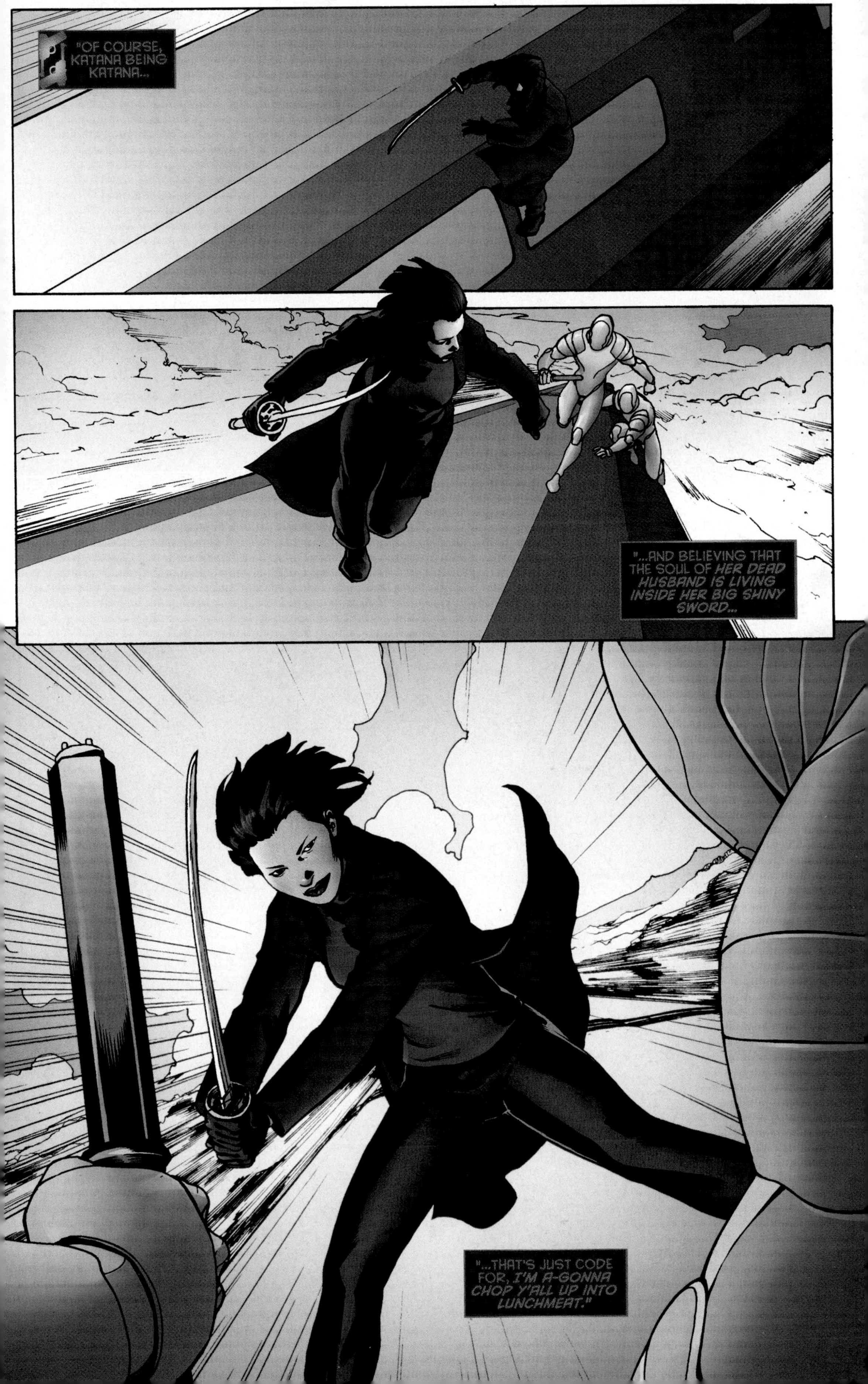
"OF COURSE, KATANA BEING KATANA...
"...AND BELIEVING THAT THE SOUL OF HER DEAD HUSBAND IS LIVING INSIDE HER BIG SHINY SWORD...
"...THAT'S JUST CODE FOR, I'M A-GONNA CHOP Y'ALL UP INTO LUNCHMEAT."

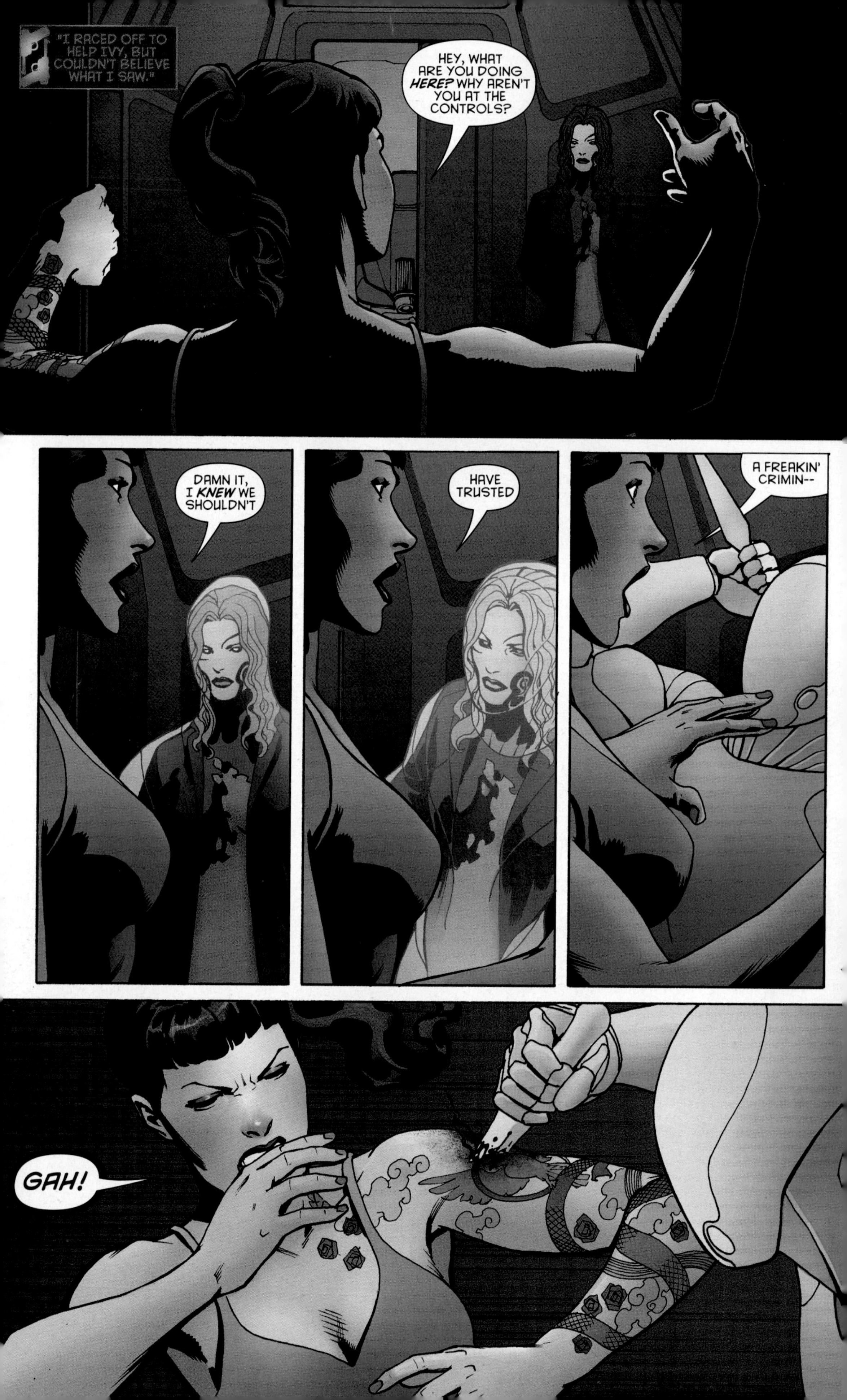
"I RACED OFF TO HELP IVY, BUT COULDN'T BELIEVE WHAT I SAW."
HEY, WHAT ARE YOU DOING *HERE?* WHY AREN'T YOU AT THE CONTROLS?
DAMN IT, I *KNEW* WE SHOULDN'T
HAVE TRUSTED
A FREAKIN' CRIMIN--
GAH!

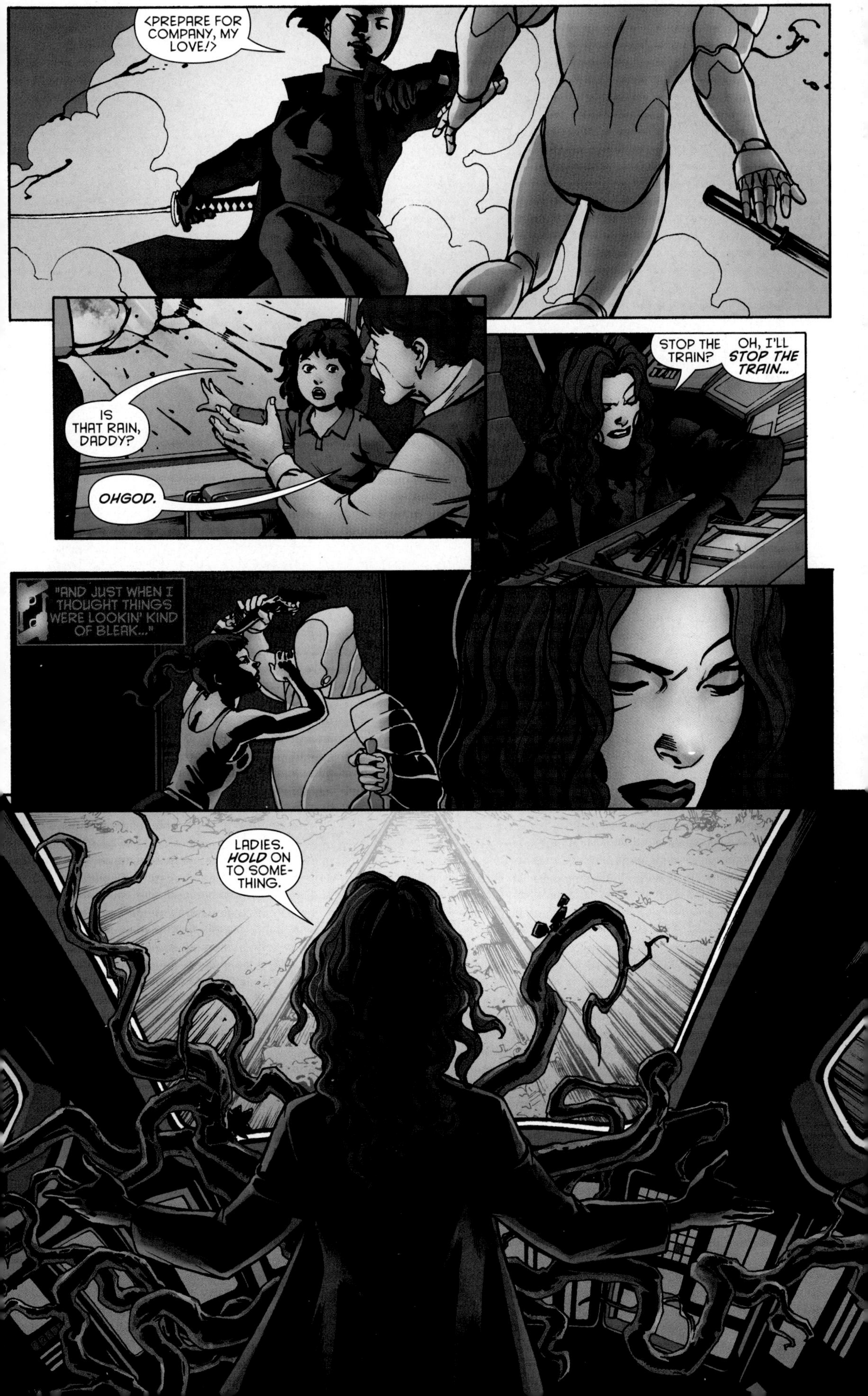
<PREPARE FOR COMPANY, MY LOVE!>
IS THAT RAIN, DADDY?
OHGOD.
STOP THE TRAIN?
OH, I'LL STOP THE TRAIN...
"AND JUST WHEN I THOUGHT THINGS WERE LOOKIN' KIND OF BLEAK..."
LADIES. HOLD ON TO SOME-THING.

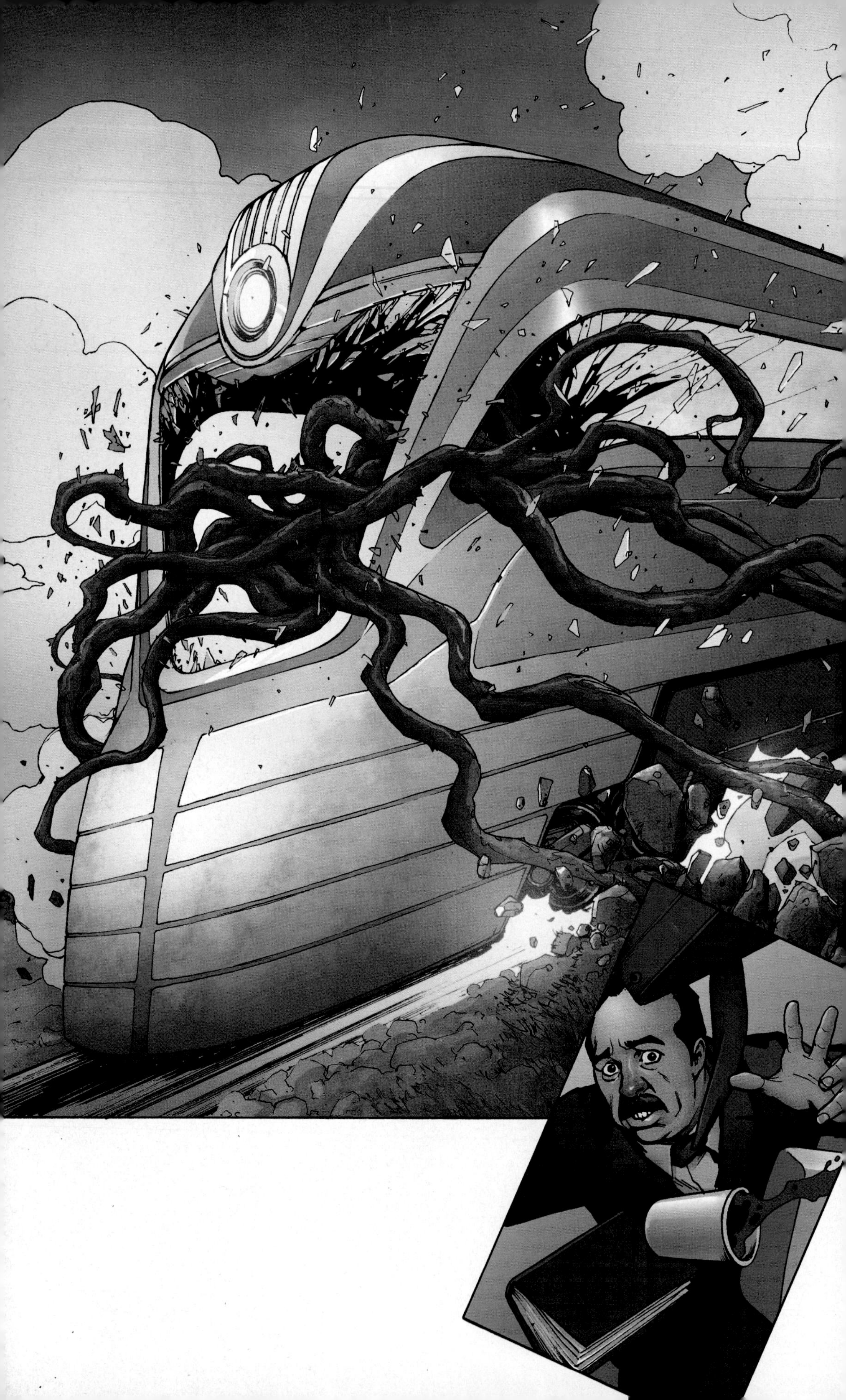

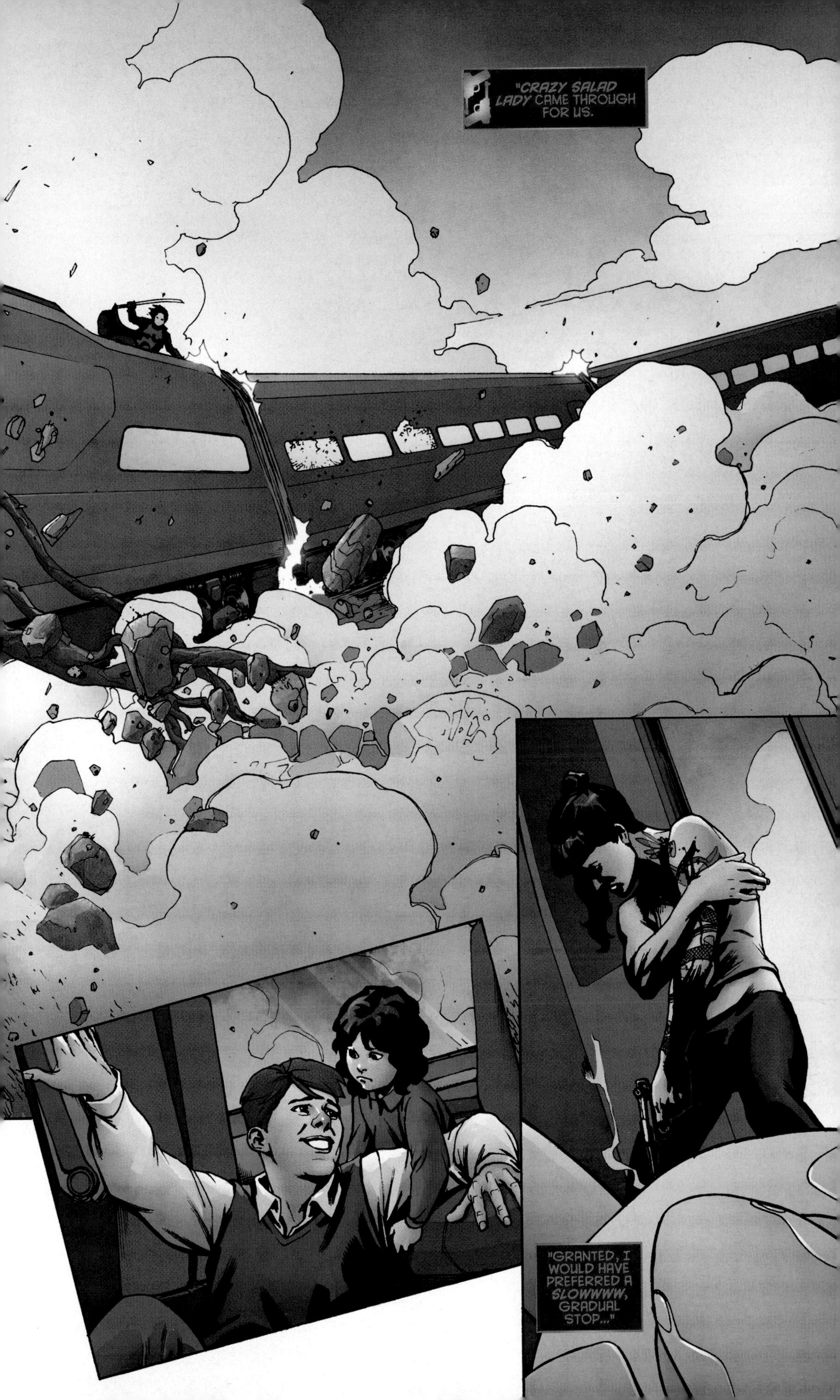
"CRAZY SALAD LADY CAME THROUGH FOR US.
"GRANTED, I WOULD HAVE PREFERRED A SLOWWWW, GRADUAL STOP..."

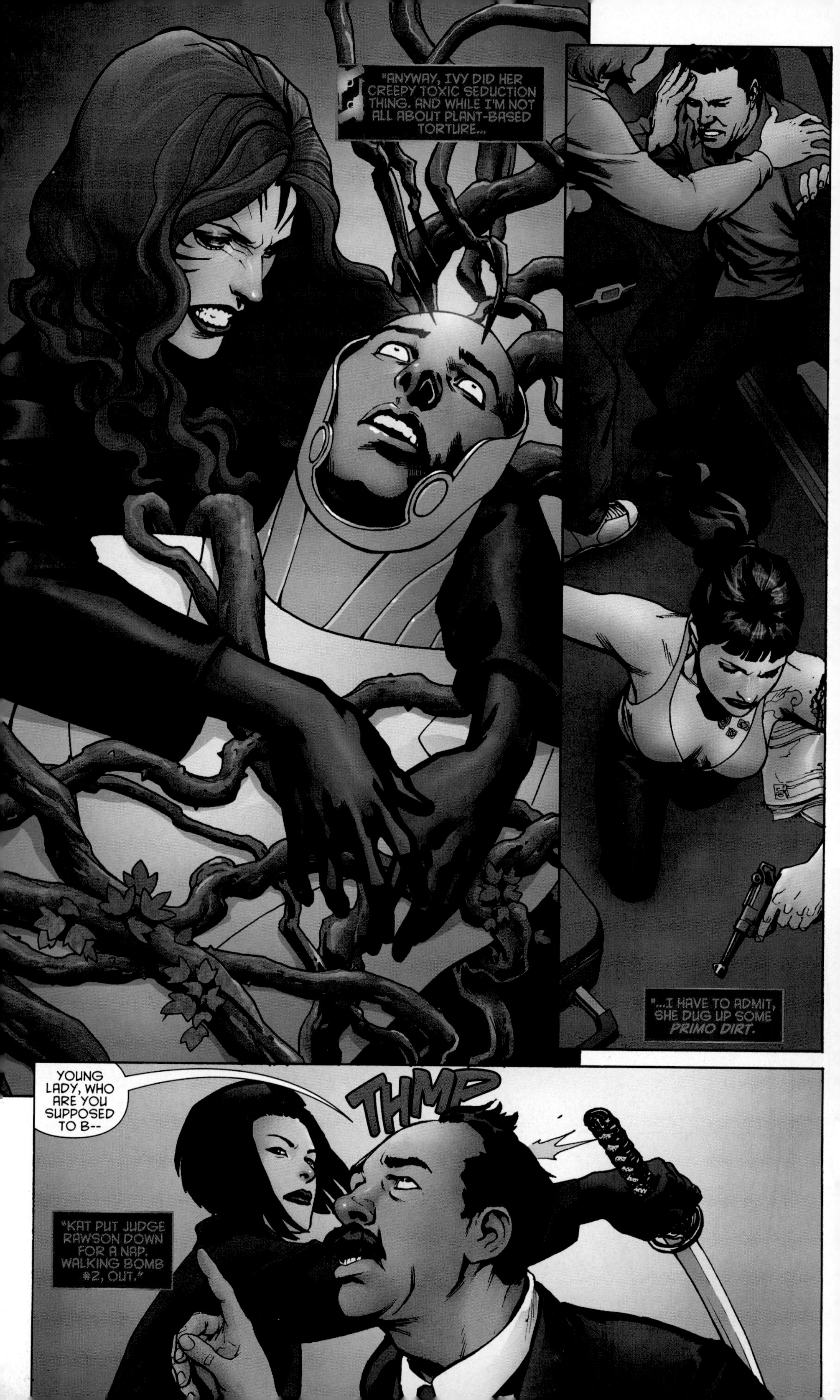
"ANYWAY, IVY DID HER CREEPY TOXIC SEDUCTION THING. AND WHILE I'M NOT ALL ABOUT PLANT-BASED TORTURE...
"...I HAVE TO ADMIT, SHE DUG UP SOME *PRIMO DIRT*.
YOUNG LADY, WHO ARE YOU SUPPOSED TO B--
THMP
"KAT PUT JUDGE RAWSON DOWN FOR A NAP. WALKING BOMB #2, OUT."

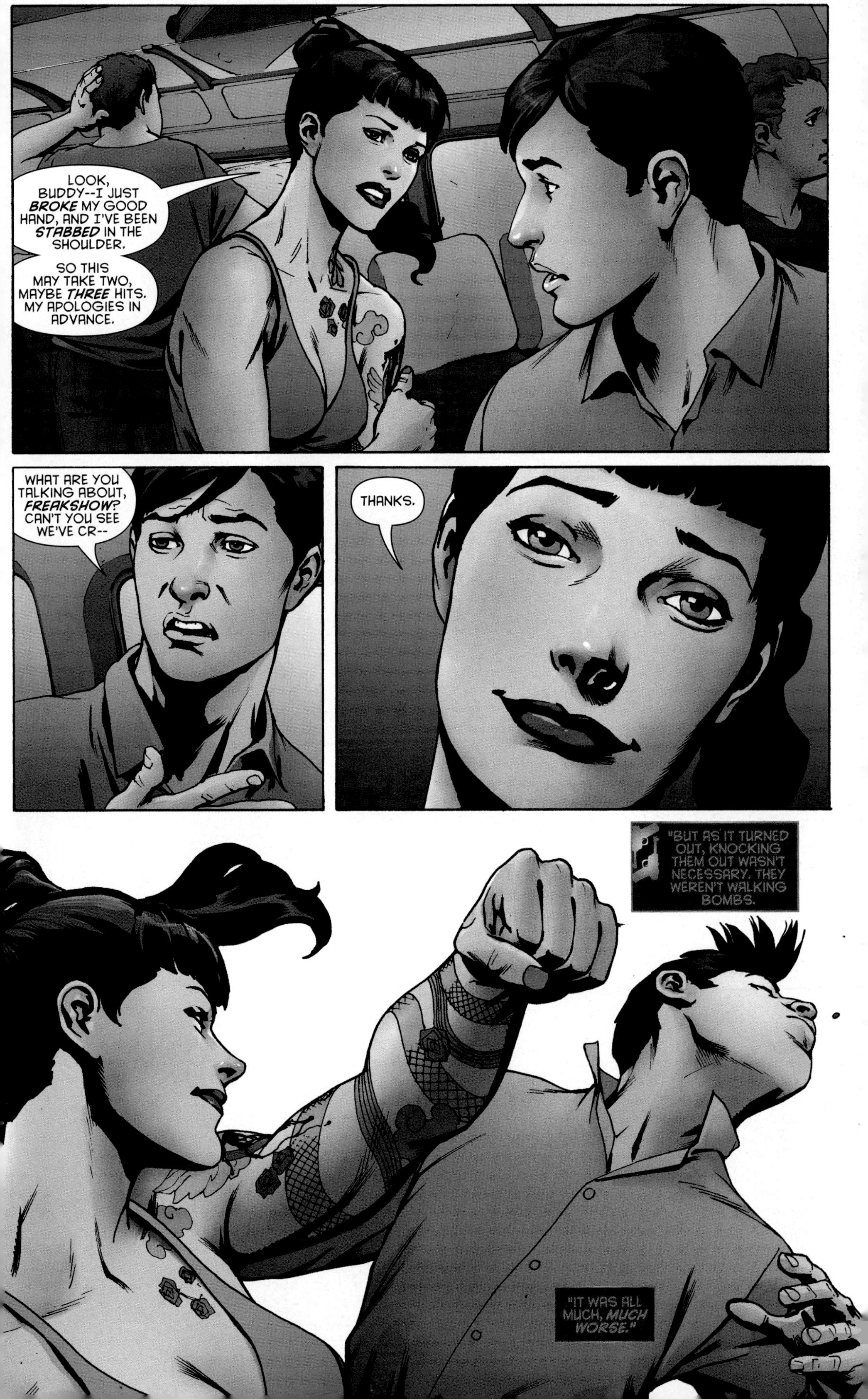

LOOK, BUDDY--I JUST BROKE MY GOOD HAND, AND I'VE BEEN STABBED IN THE SHOULDER.
SO THIS MAY TAKE TWO, MAYBE THREE HITS. MY APOLOGIES IN ADVANCE.
WHAT ARE YOU TALKING ABOUT, FREAKSHOW? CAN'T YOU SEE WE'VE CR--
THANKS.
"BUT AS IT TURNED OUT, KNOCKING THEM OUT WASN'T NECESSARY. THEY WEREN'T WALKING BOMBS.
"IT WAS ALL MUCH, MUCH WORSE."

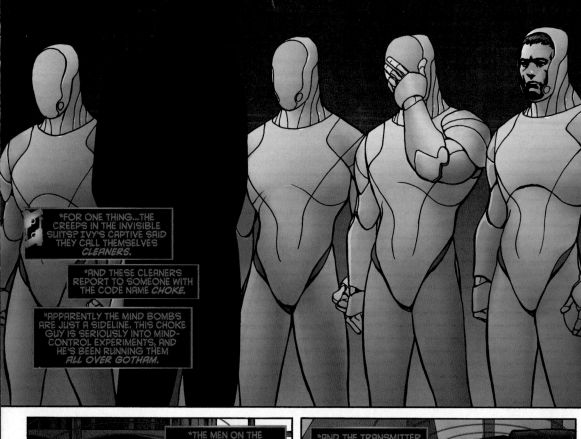

"FOR ONE THING...THE CREEPS IN THE INVISIBLE SUITS? IVY'S CAPTIVE SAID THEY CALL THEMSELVES *CLEANERS*.

"AND THESE CLEANERS REPORT TO SOMEONE WITH THE CODE NAME *CHOKE*.

"APPARENTLY THE MIND BOMBS ARE JUST A SIDELINE. THIS CHOKE GUY IS SERIOUSLY INTO MIND-CONTROL EXPERIMENTS, AND HE'S BEEN RUNNING THEM *ALL OVER GOTHAM*.

"THE MEN ON THE TRAIN WEREN'T WALKING BOMBS. THEY WERE LIVING MICROPHONES, BROADCASTING EVERYTHING THEY *SAW* AND *HEARD*.

"AND THE TRANSMITTER AND RECEIVERS ARE ESSENTIALLY *UNDETECTABLE* TO ALL BUG SWEEPERS AND ANTI-SPY GEAR."

I'VE GOT THE FEELING THIS IS ALL A WARM-UP FOR SOMETHING... BIG. LIKE, *SCARY BIG*.

PLEASE TELL ME IVY GOT AN ADDRESS OUT OF THE GUY.

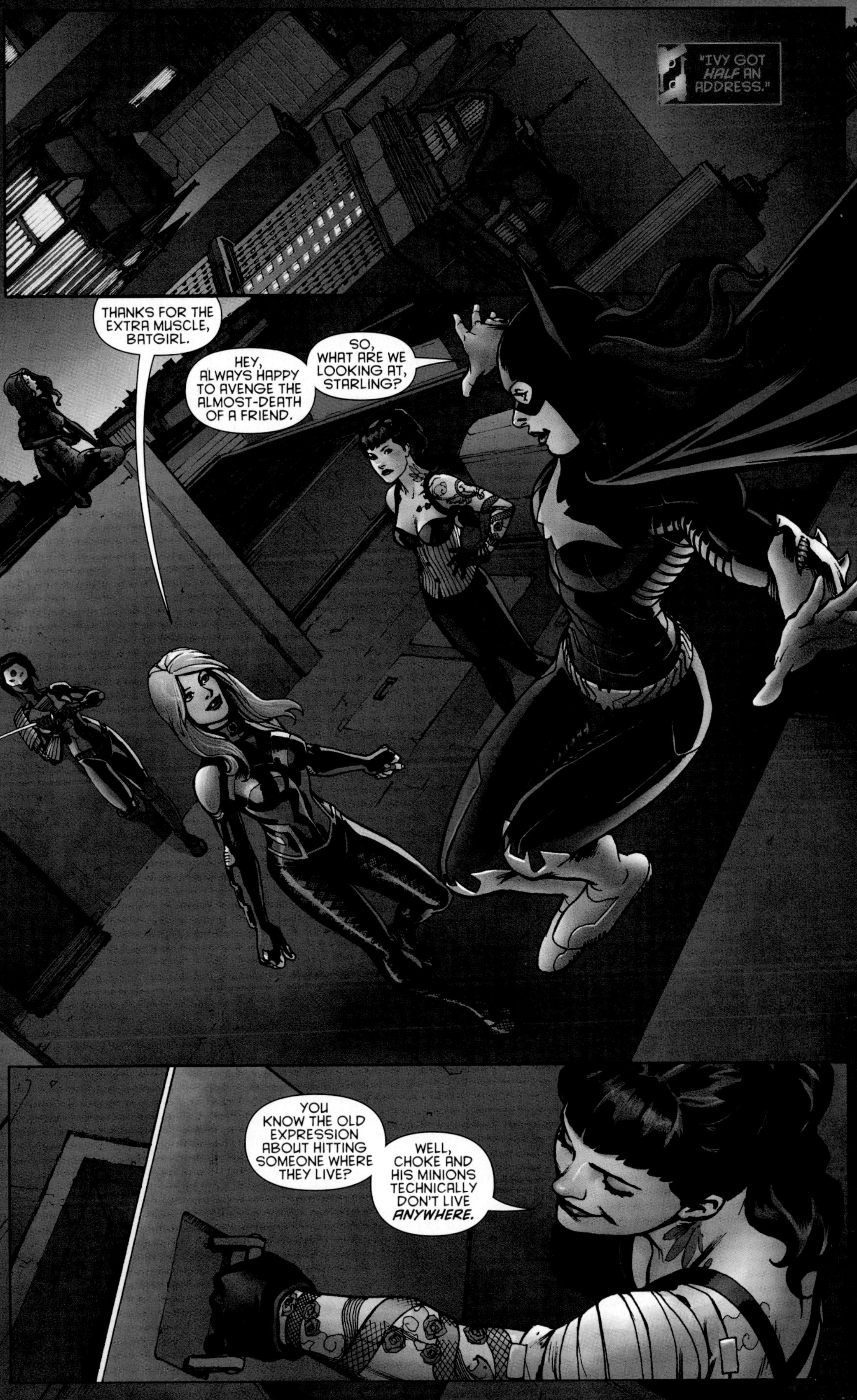
"IVY GOT HALF AN ADDRESS."
THANKS FOR THE EXTRA MUSCLE, BATGIRL.
HEY, ALWAYS HAPPY TO AVENGE THE ALMOST-DEATH OF A FRIEND.
SO, WHAT ARE WE LOOKING AT, STARLING?
YOU KNOW THE OLD EXPRESSION ABOUT HITTING SOMEONE WHERE THEY LIVE?
WELL, CHOKE AND HIS MINIONS TECHNICALLY DON'T LIVE ANYWHERE.

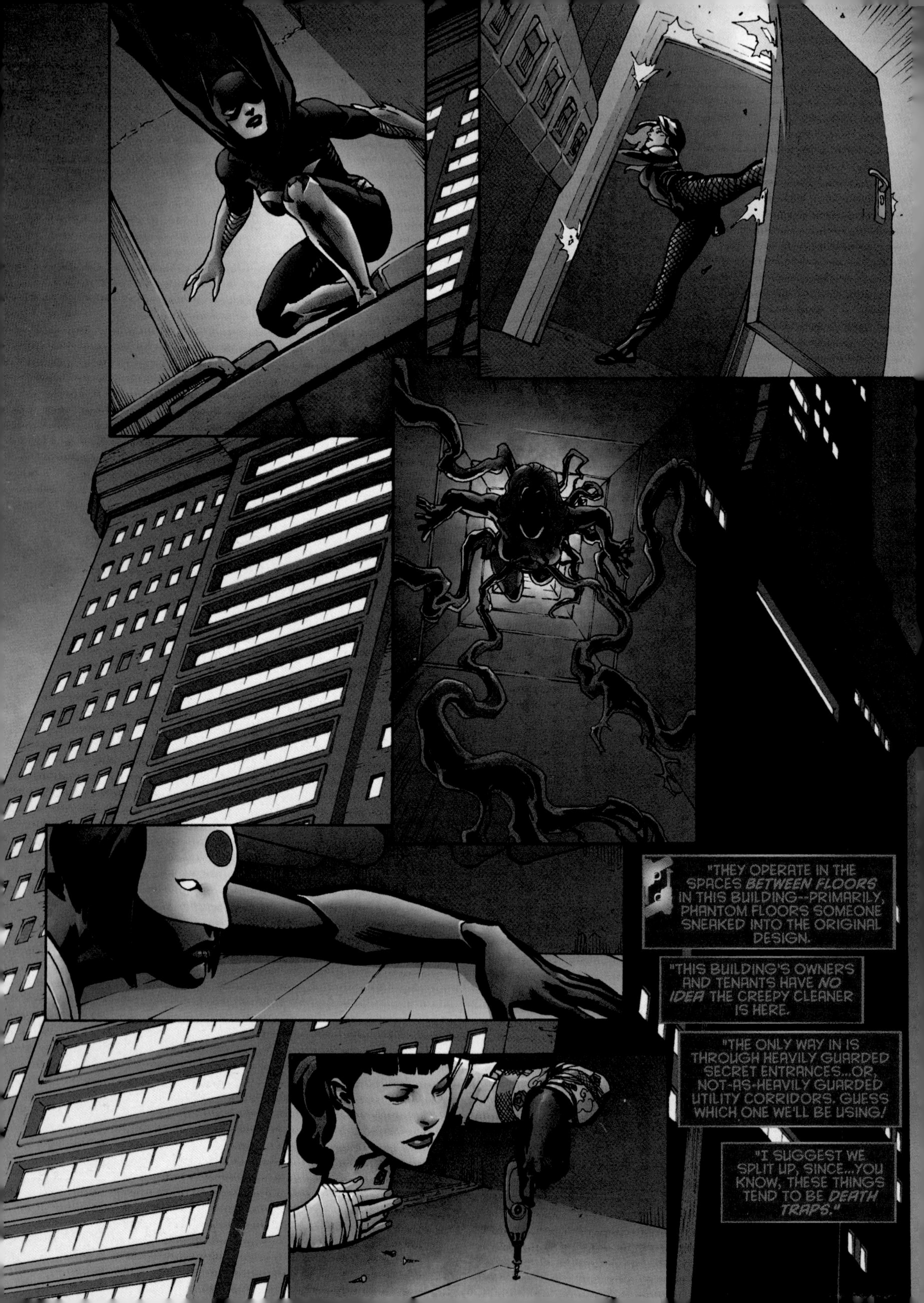
"THEY OPERATE IN THE SPACES *BETWEEN FLOORS* IN THIS BUILDING--PRIMARILY, PHANTOM FLOORS SOMEONE SNEAKED INTO THE ORIGINAL DESIGN.
"THIS BUILDING'S OWNERS AND TENANTS HAVE *NO IDEA* THE CREEPY CLEANER IS HERE.
"THE ONLY WAY IN IS THROUGH HEAVILY GUARDED SECRET ENTRANCES...OR, NOT-AS-HEAVILY GUARDED UTILITY CORRIDORS. GUESS WHICH ONE WE'LL BE USING!
"I SUGGEST WE SPLIT UP, SINCE...YOU KNOW, THESE THINGS TEND TO BE *DEATH TRAPS.*"

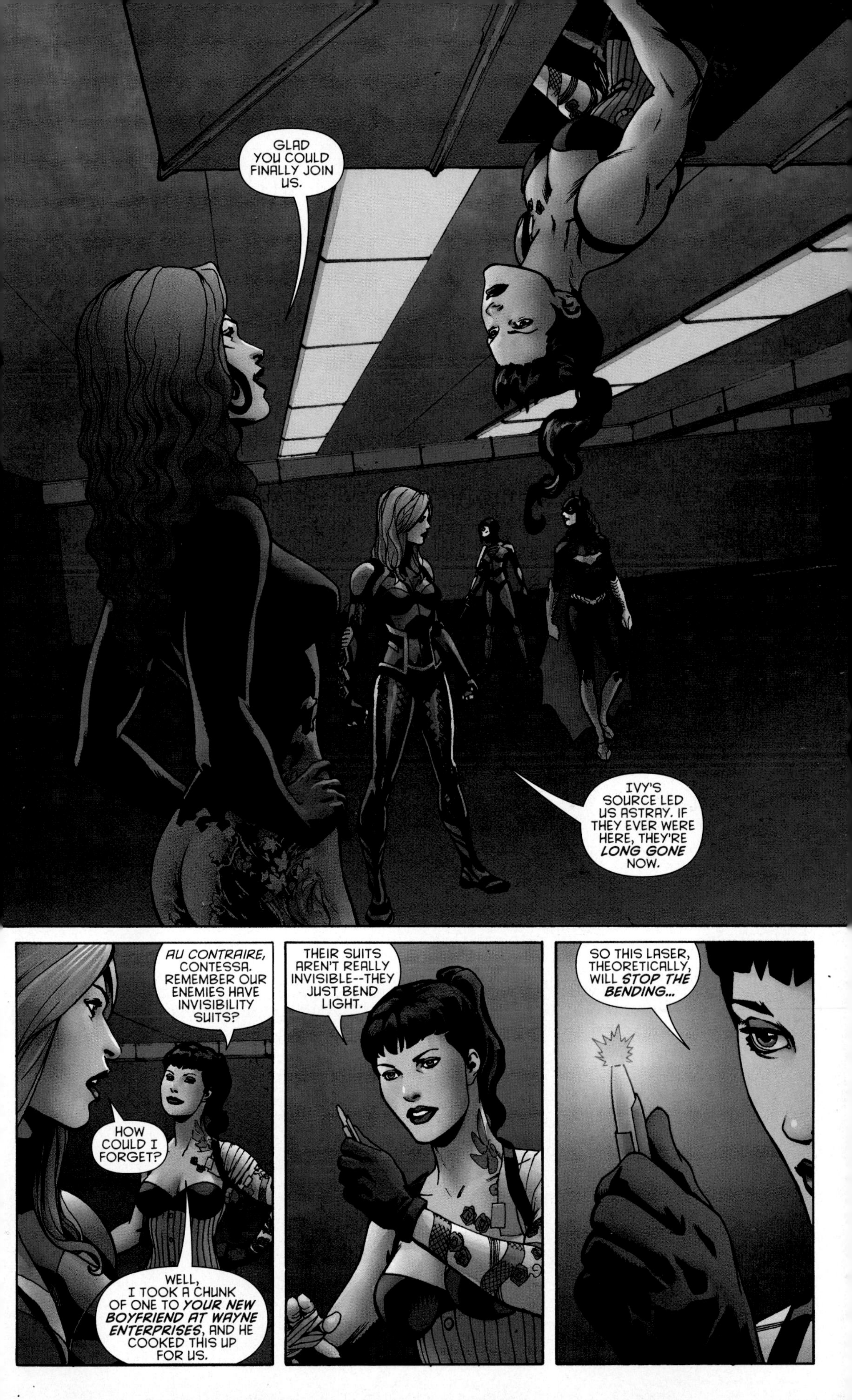
GLAD YOU COULD FINALLY JOIN US.
IVY'S SOURCE LED US ASTRAY. IF THEY EVER WERE HERE, THEY'RE *LONG GONE* NOW.
AU CONTRAIRE, CONTESSA. REMEMBER OUR ENEMIES HAVE INVISIBILITY SUITS?
HOW COULD I FORGET?
WELL, I TOOK A CHUNK OF ONE TO *YOUR NEW BOYFRIEND AT WAYNE ENTERPRISES,* AND HE COOKED THIS UP FOR US.
THEIR SUITS AREN'T REALLY INVISIBLE--THEY JUST BEND LIGHT.
SO THIS LASER, THEORETICALLY, WILL *STOP THE BENDING...*

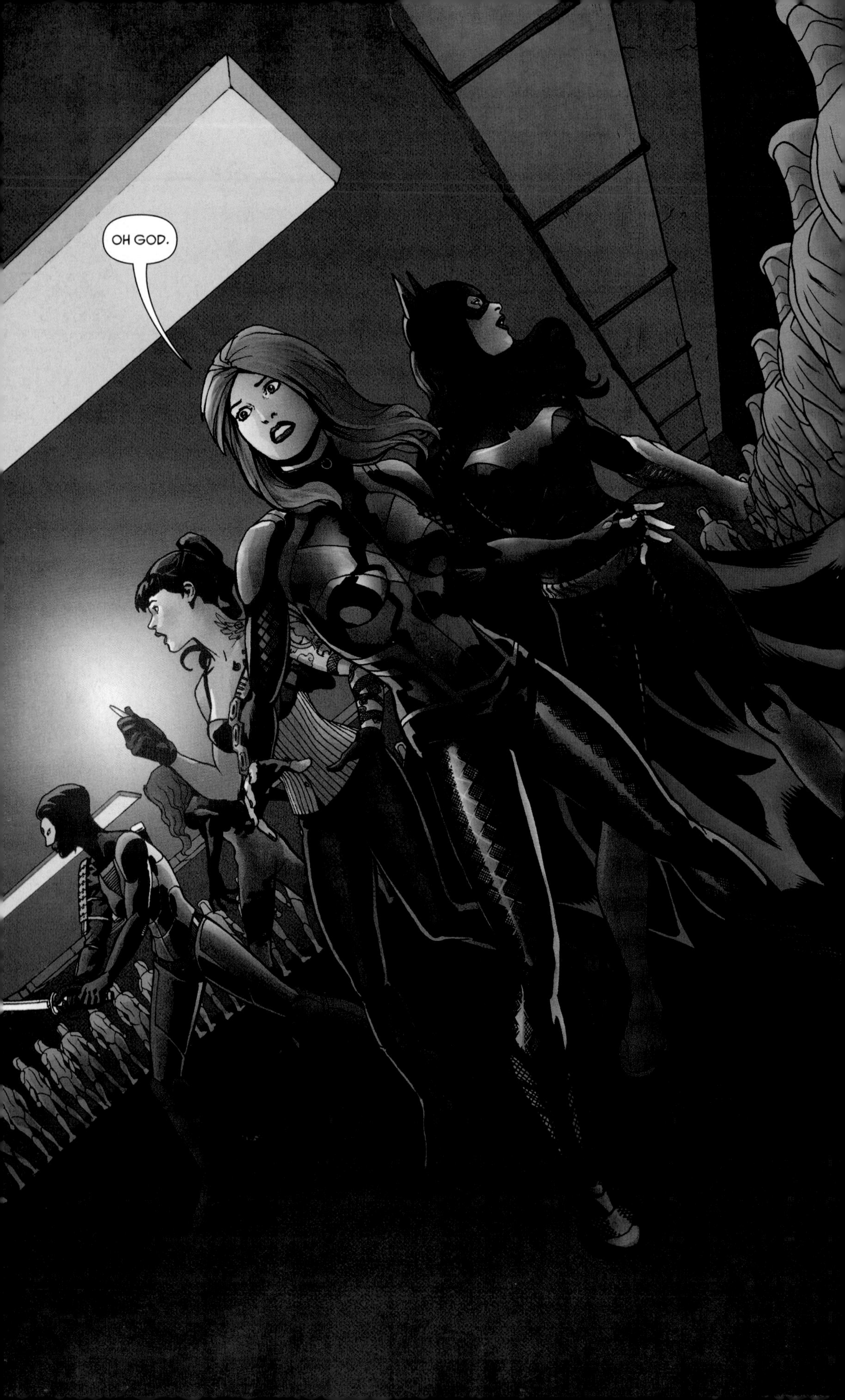
OH GOD.

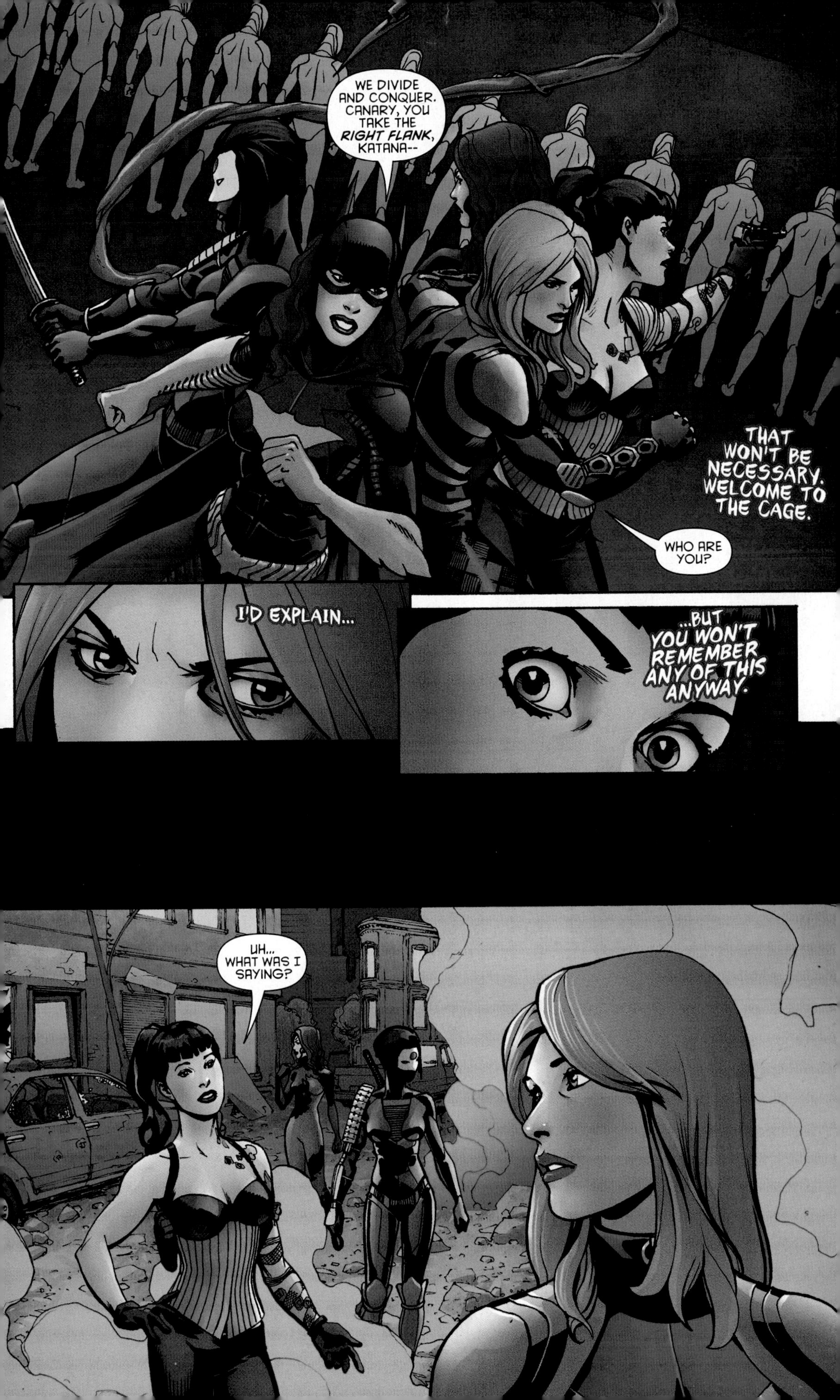
WE DIVIDE AND CONQUER. CANARY, YOU TAKE THE RIGHT FLANK, KATANA--
THAT WON'T BE NECESSARY. WELCOME TO THE CAGE.
WHO ARE YOU?
I'D EXPLAIN...
...BUT YOU WON'T REMEMBER ANY OF THIS ANYWAY.
UH... WHAT WAS I SAYING?

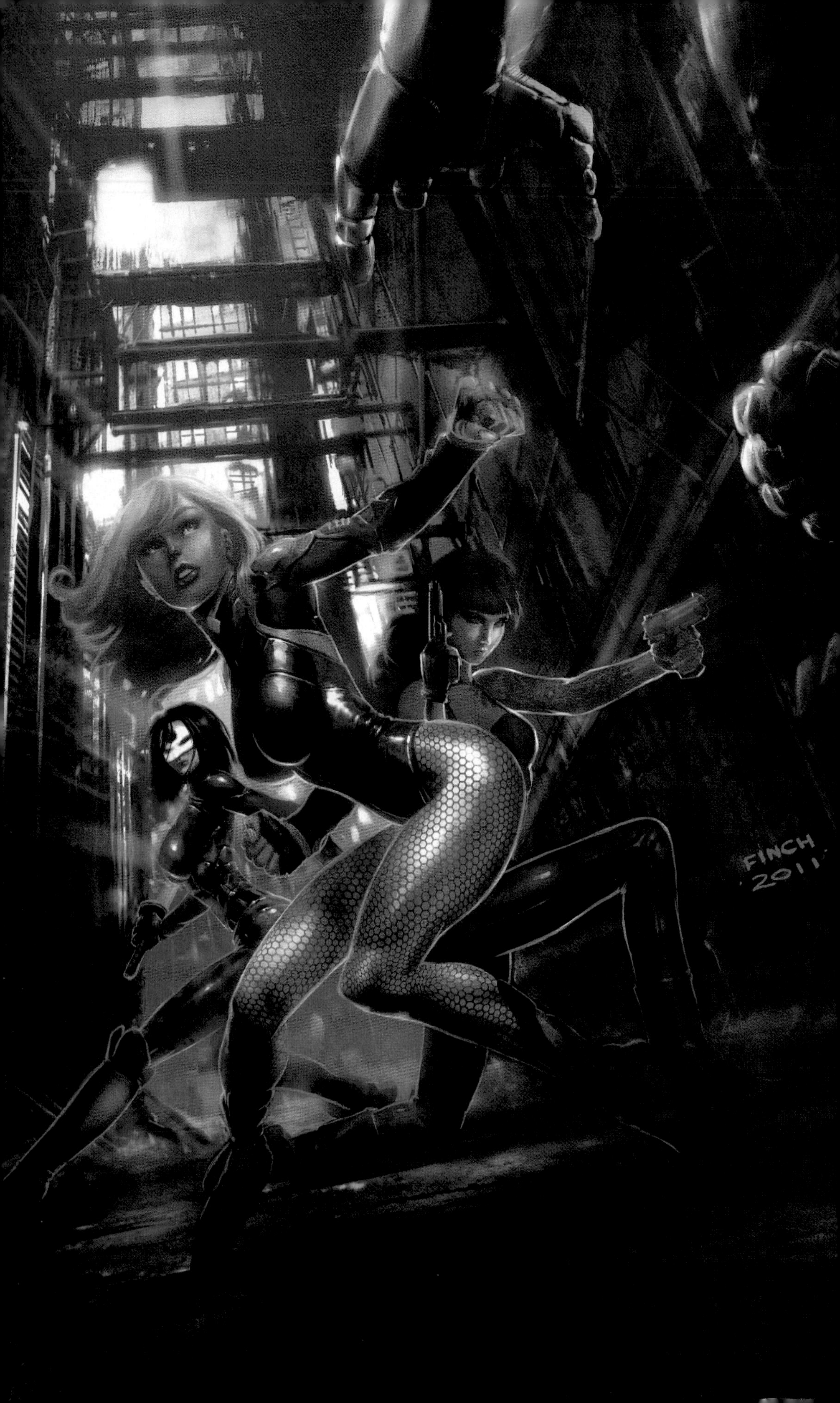
FINCH
2011

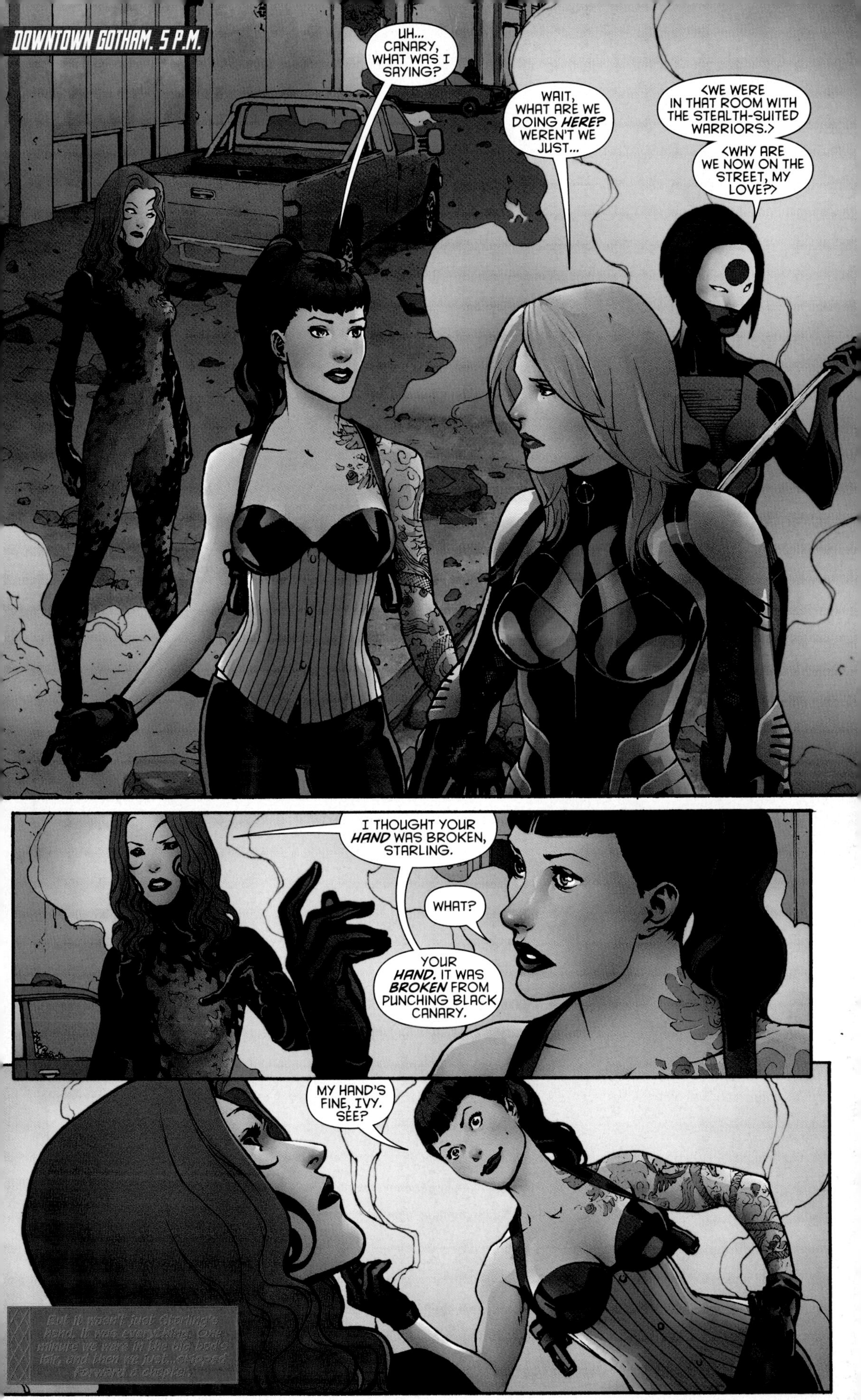

DOWNTOWN GOTHAM. 5 P.M.
UH... CANARY, WHAT WAS I SAYING?
WAIT, WHAT ARE WE DOING HERE? WEREN'T WE JUST...
<WE WERE IN THAT ROOM WITH THE STEALTH-SUITED WARRIORS.>
<WHY ARE WE NOW ON THE STREET, MY LOVE?>
I THOUGHT YOUR HAND WAS BROKEN, STARLING.
WHAT?
YOUR HAND. IT WAS BROKEN FROM PUNCHING BLACK CANARY.
MY HAND'S FINE, IVY. SEE?
But it wasn't just Starling's hand. It was everything. One minute we were in the big bad's lair, and then we just... skipped forward a chapter.

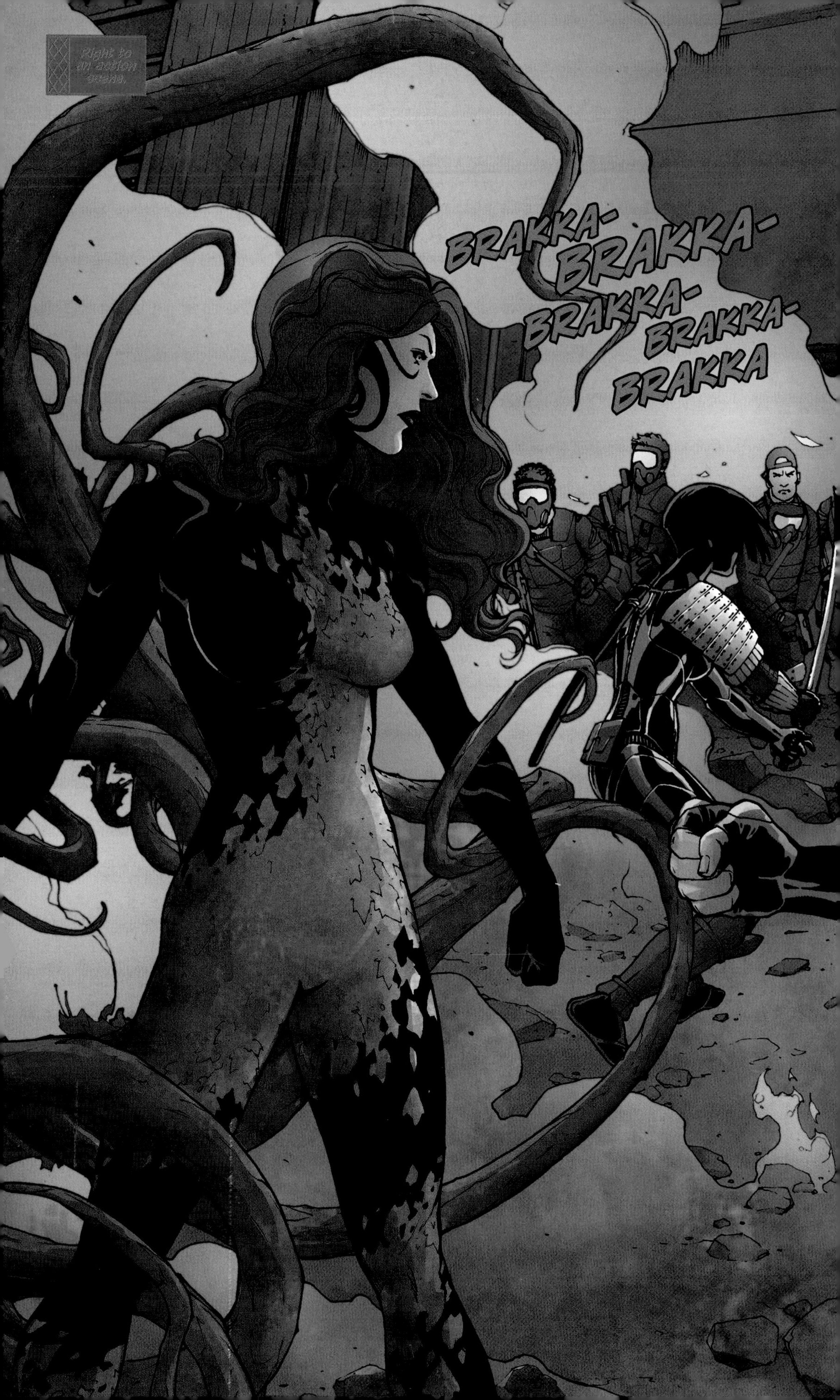
Right to an action scene.
BRAKKA-BRAKKA-BRAKKA-BRAKKA-BRAKKA

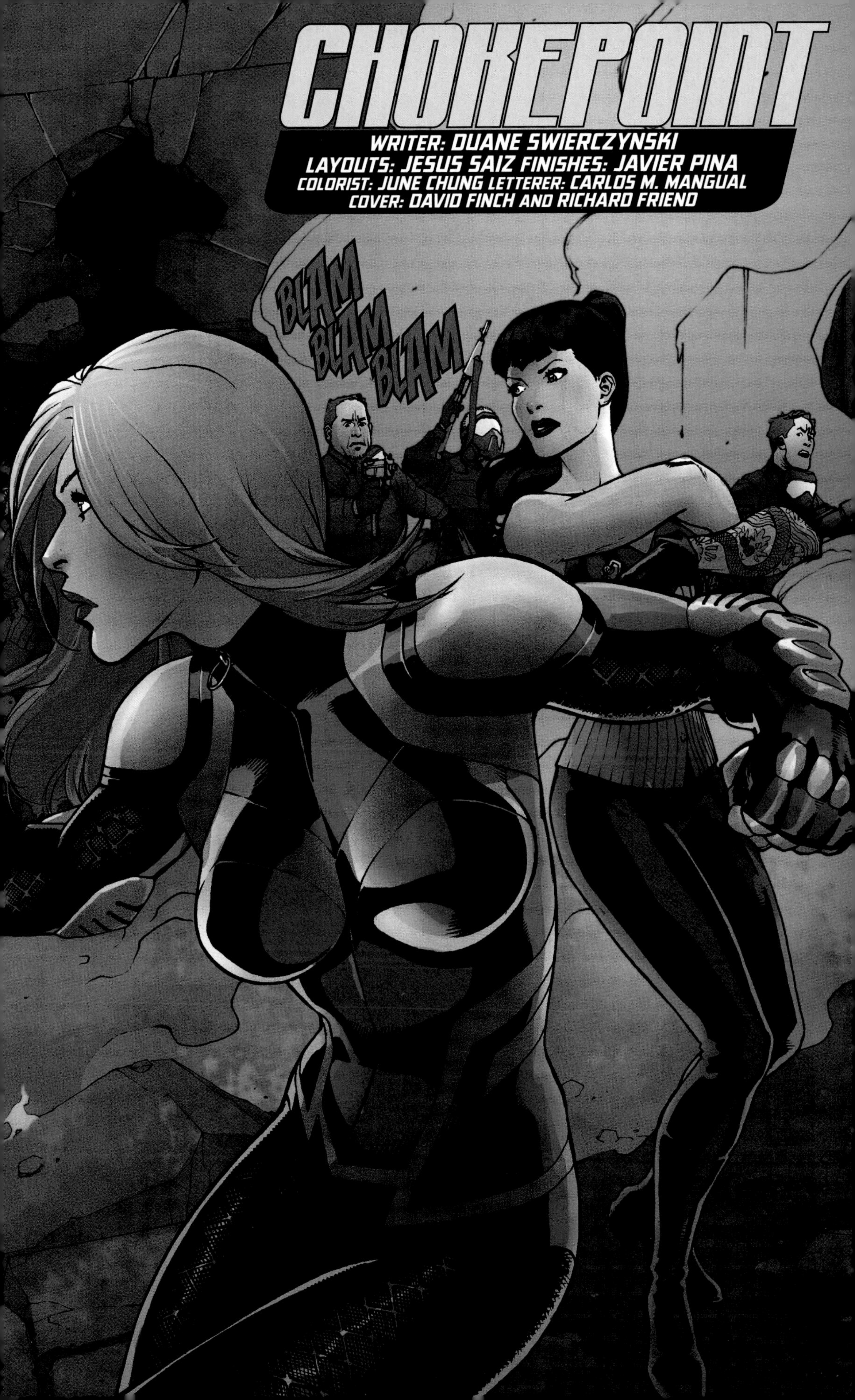
CHOKEPOINT
WRITER: DUANE SWIERCZYNSKI
LAYOUTS: JESUS SAIZ FINISHES: JAVIER PINA
COLORIST: JUNE CHUNG LETTERER: CARLOS M. MANGUAL
COVER: DAVID FINCH AND RICHARD FRIEND
BLAM BLAM BLAM

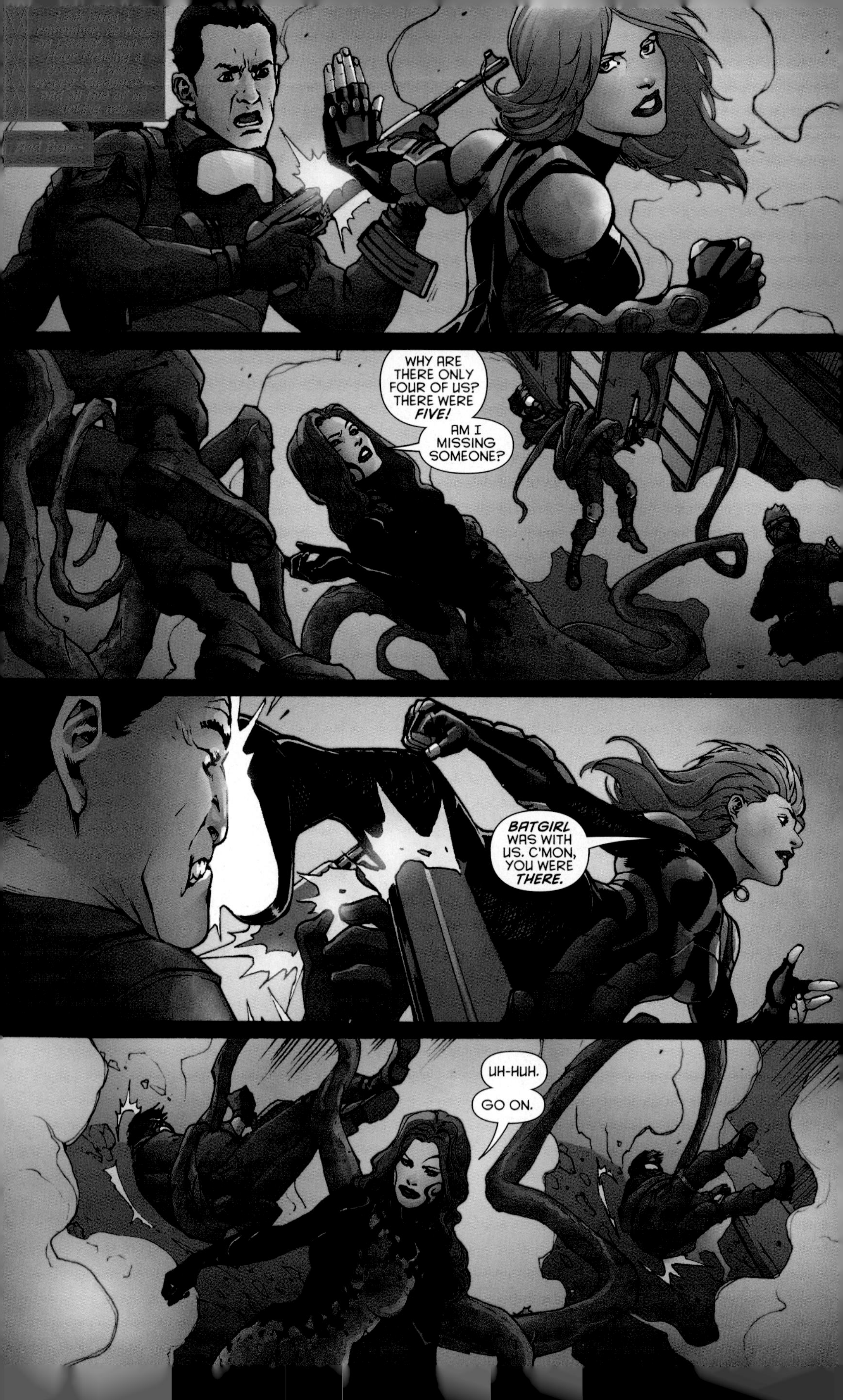
And then--
WHY ARE THERE ONLY FOUR OF US? THERE WERE FIVE!
AM I MISSING SOMEONE?
BATGIRL WAS WITH US. C'MON, YOU WERE THERE.
UH-HUH.
GO ON.

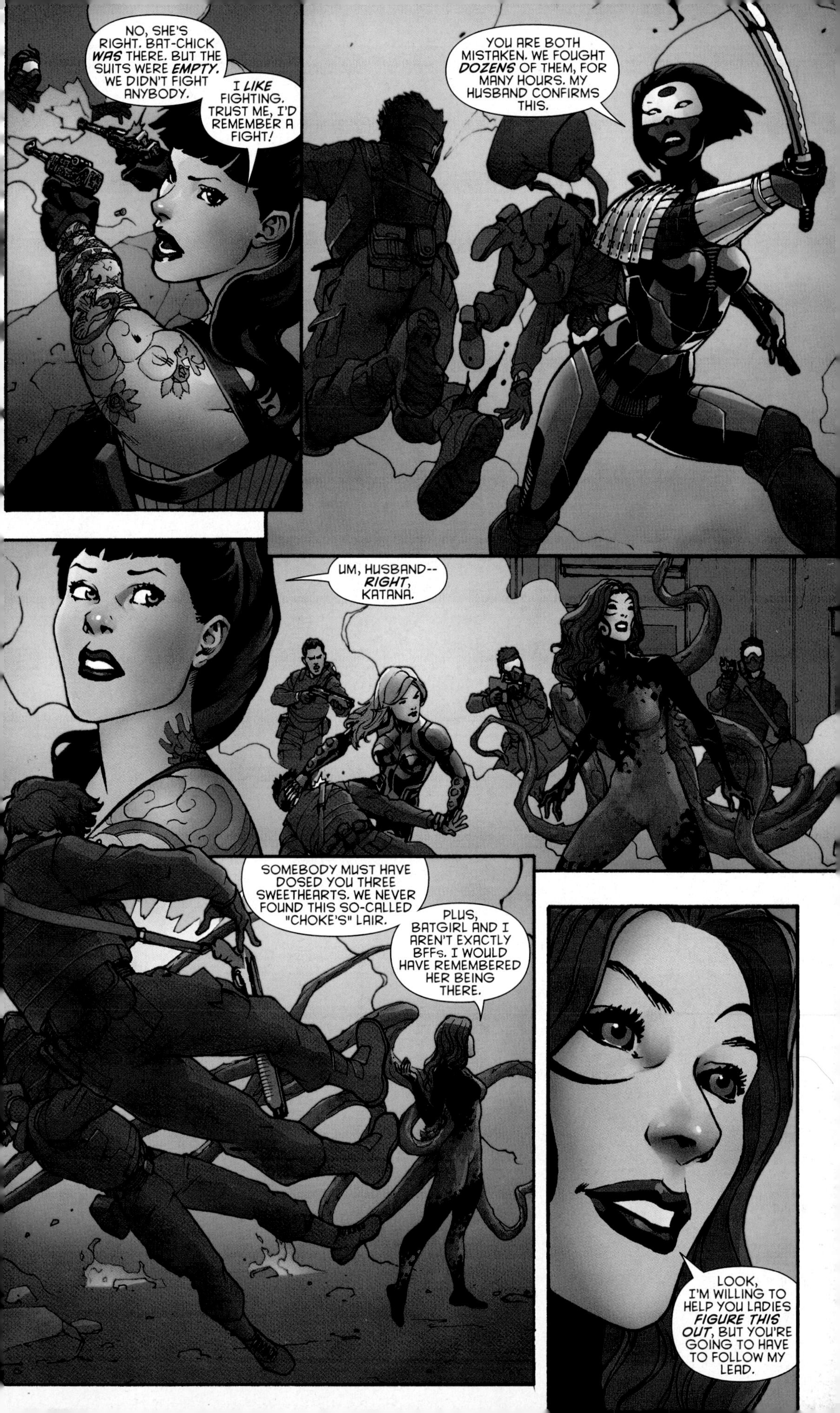

NO, SHE'S RIGHT. BAT-CHICK *WAS* THERE. BUT THE SUITS WERE *EMPTY*. WE DIDN'T FIGHT ANYBODY.
I *LIKE* FIGHTING. TRUST ME, I'D REMEMBER A FIGHT!
YOU ARE BOTH MISTAKEN. WE FOUGHT *DOZENS* OF THEM, FOR MANY HOURS. MY HUSBAND CONFIRMS THIS.
UM, HUSBAND-- *RIGHT*, KATANA.
SOMEBODY MUST HAVE DOSED YOU THREE SWEETHEARTS. WE NEVER FOUND THIS SO-CALLED "CHOKE'S" LAIR.
PLUS, BATGIRL AND I AREN'T EXACTLY BFFs. I WOULD HAVE REMEMBERED HER BEING THERE.
LOOK, I'M WILLING TO HELP YOU LADIES *FIGURE THIS OUT*, BUT YOU'RE GOING TO HAVE TO FOLLOW MY LEAD.

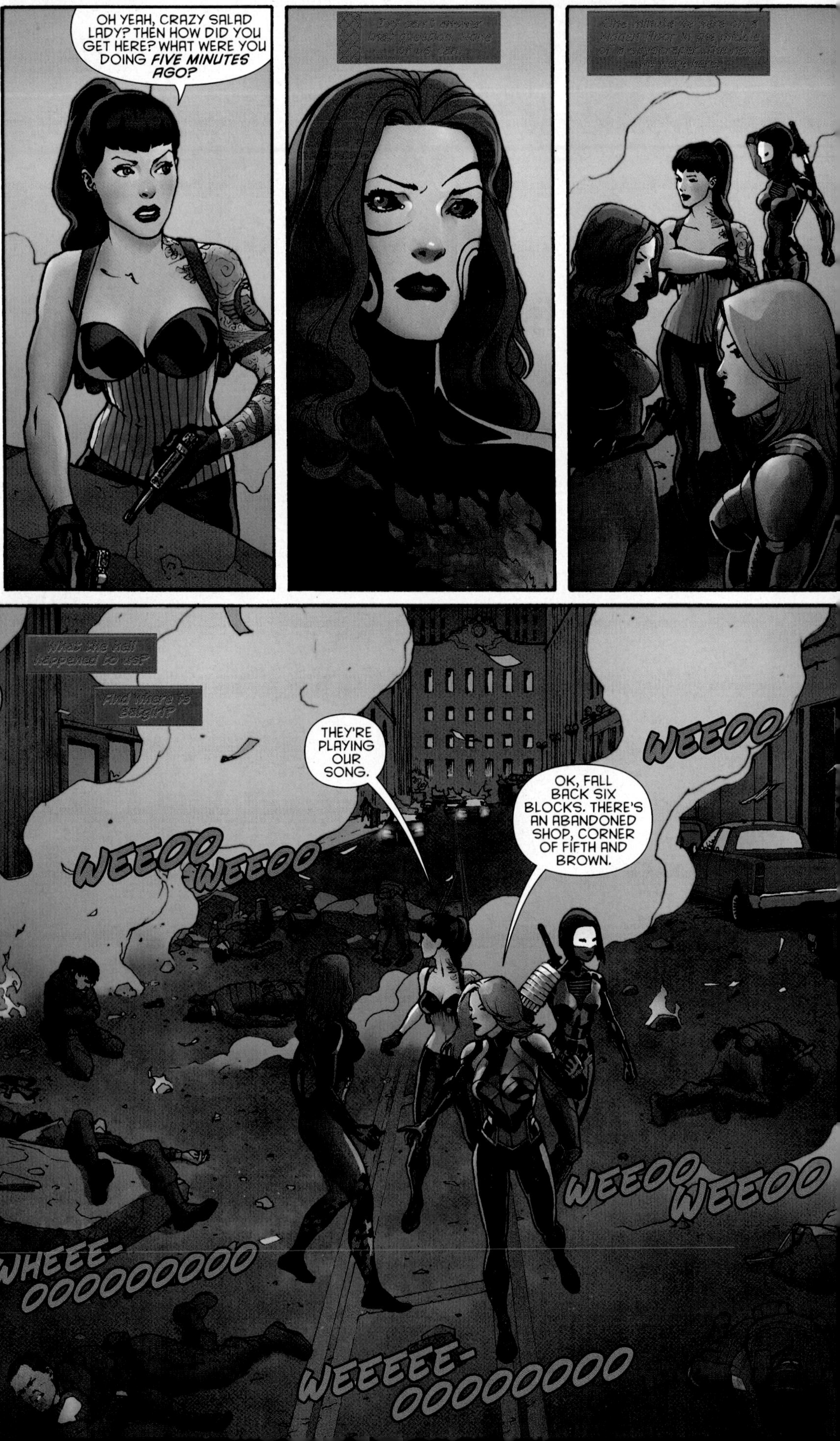
OH YEAH, CRAZY SALAD LADY? THEN HOW DID YOU GET HERE? WHAT WERE YOU DOING FIVE MINUTES AGO?
What the hell happened to us?
And where is Batgirl?
THEY'RE PLAYING OUR SONG.
WEEOO
OK, FALL BACK SIX BLOCKS. THERE'S AN ABANDONED SHOP, CORNER OF FIFTH AND BROWN.
WEEOO WEEOO
WEEOO WEEOO
WHEEE-OOOOOOOOO
WEEEEE-OOOOOOOO

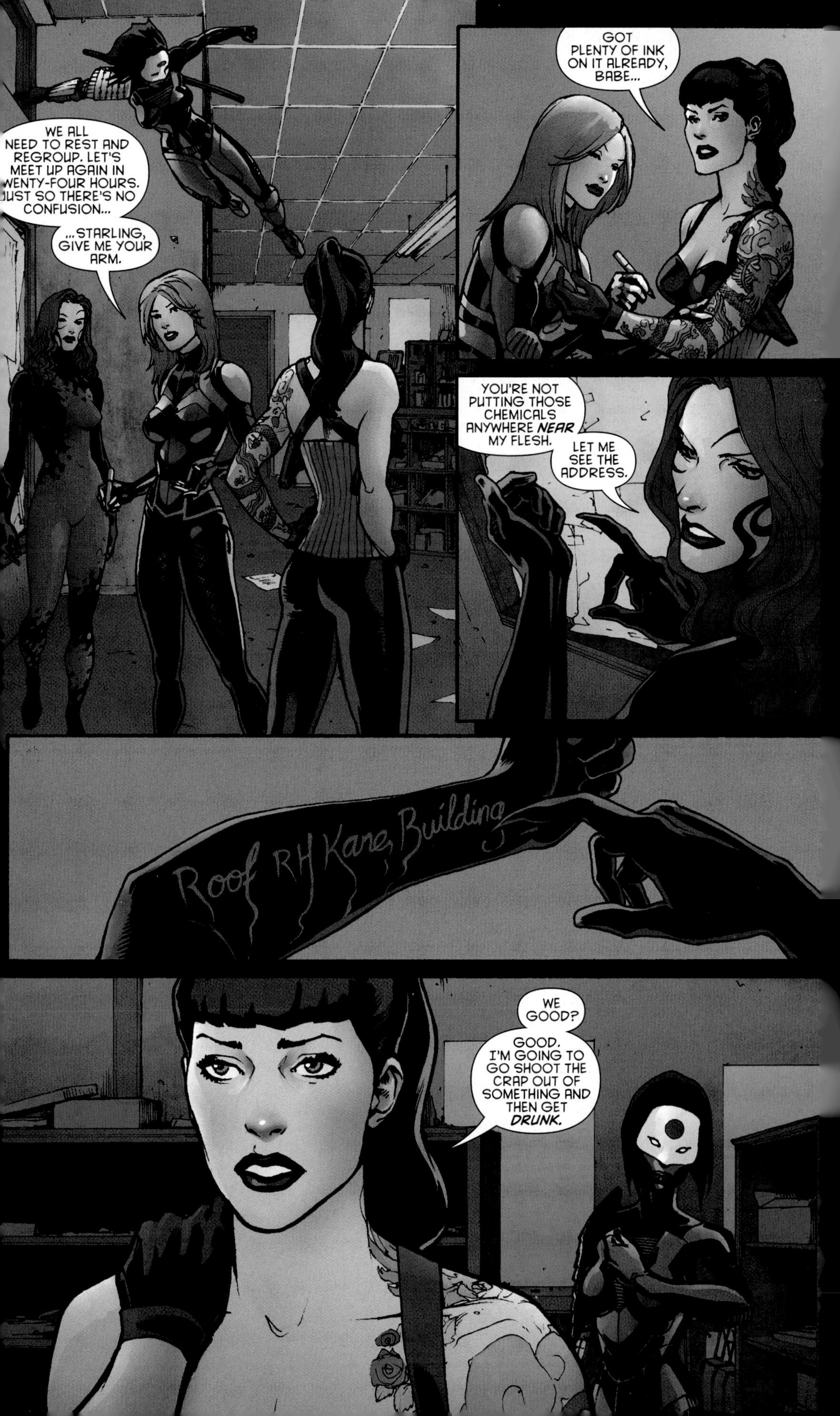
WE ALL NEED TO REST AND REGROUP. LET'S MEET UP AGAIN IN WENTY-FOUR HOURS. JUST SO THERE'S NO CONFUSION...
...STARLING, GIVE ME YOUR ARM.
GOT PLENTY OF INK ON IT ALREADY, BABE...
YOU'RE NOT PUTTING THOSE CHEMICALS ANYWHERE NEAR MY FLESH.
LET ME SEE THE ADDRESS.
Roof RH Kane Building
WE GOOD?
GOOD. I'M GOING TO GO SHOOT THE CRAP OUT OF SOMETHING AND THEN GET DRUNK.

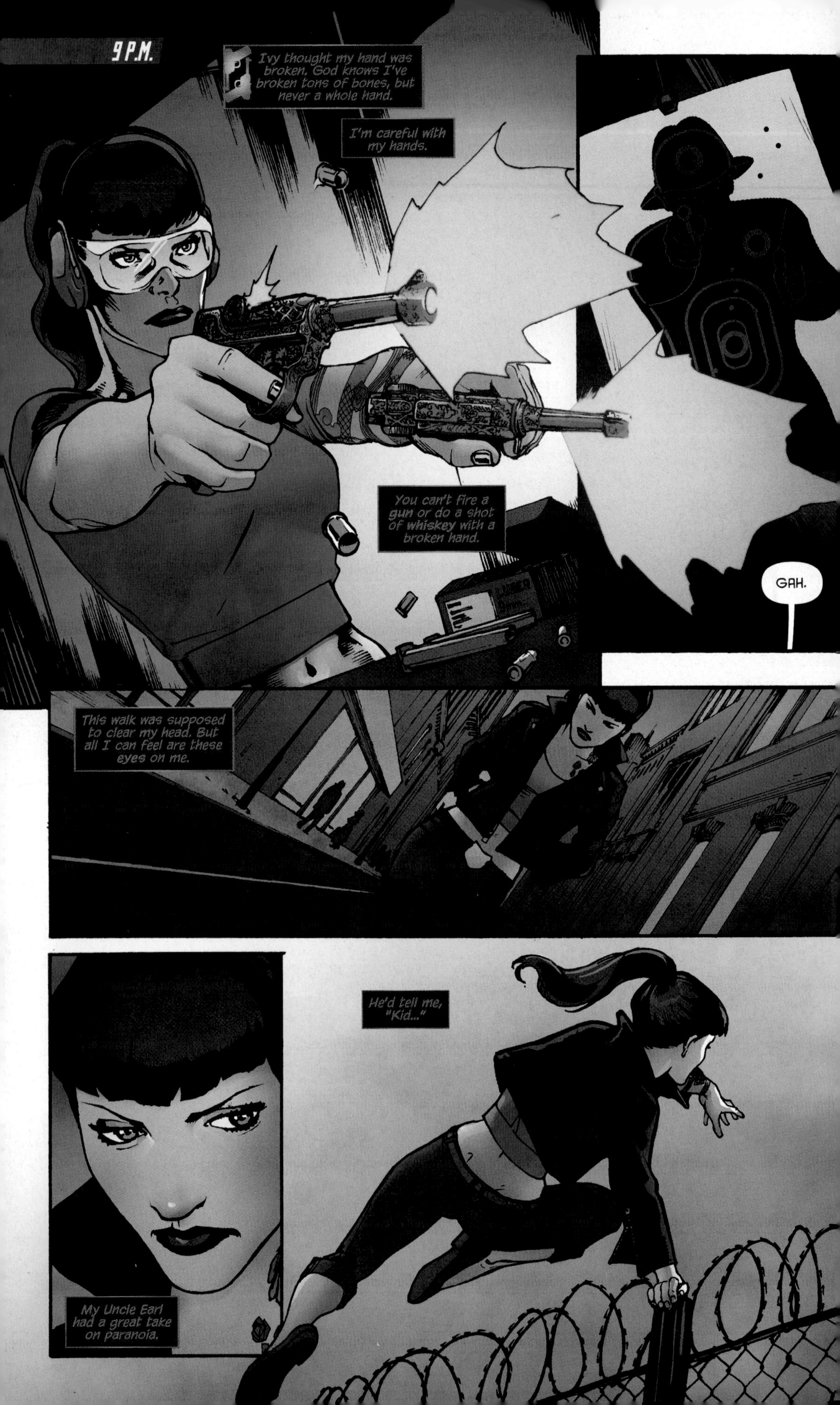
9 P.M.
Ivy thought my hand was broken. God knows I've broken tons of bones, but never a whole hand.
I'm careful with my hands.
You can't fire a gun or do a shot of whiskey with a broken hand.
GAH.
This walk was supposed to clear my head. But all I can feel are these eyes on me.
My Uncle Earl had a great take on paranoia.
He'd tell me, "Kid..."

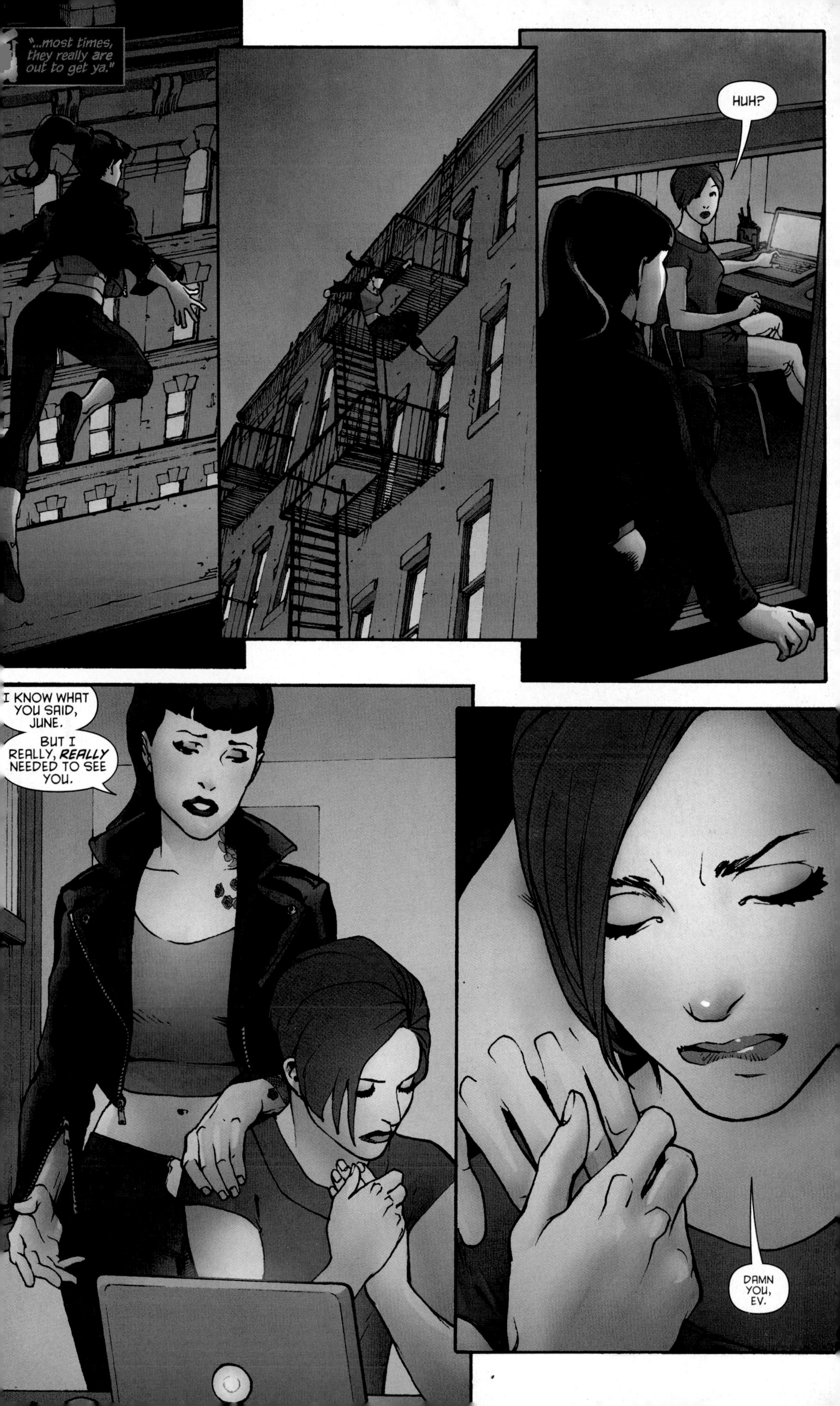
"...most times, they really are out to get ya."
HUH?
I KNOW WHAT YOU SAID, JUNE.
BUT I REALLY, *REALLY* NEEDED TO SEE YOU.
DAMN YOU, EV.

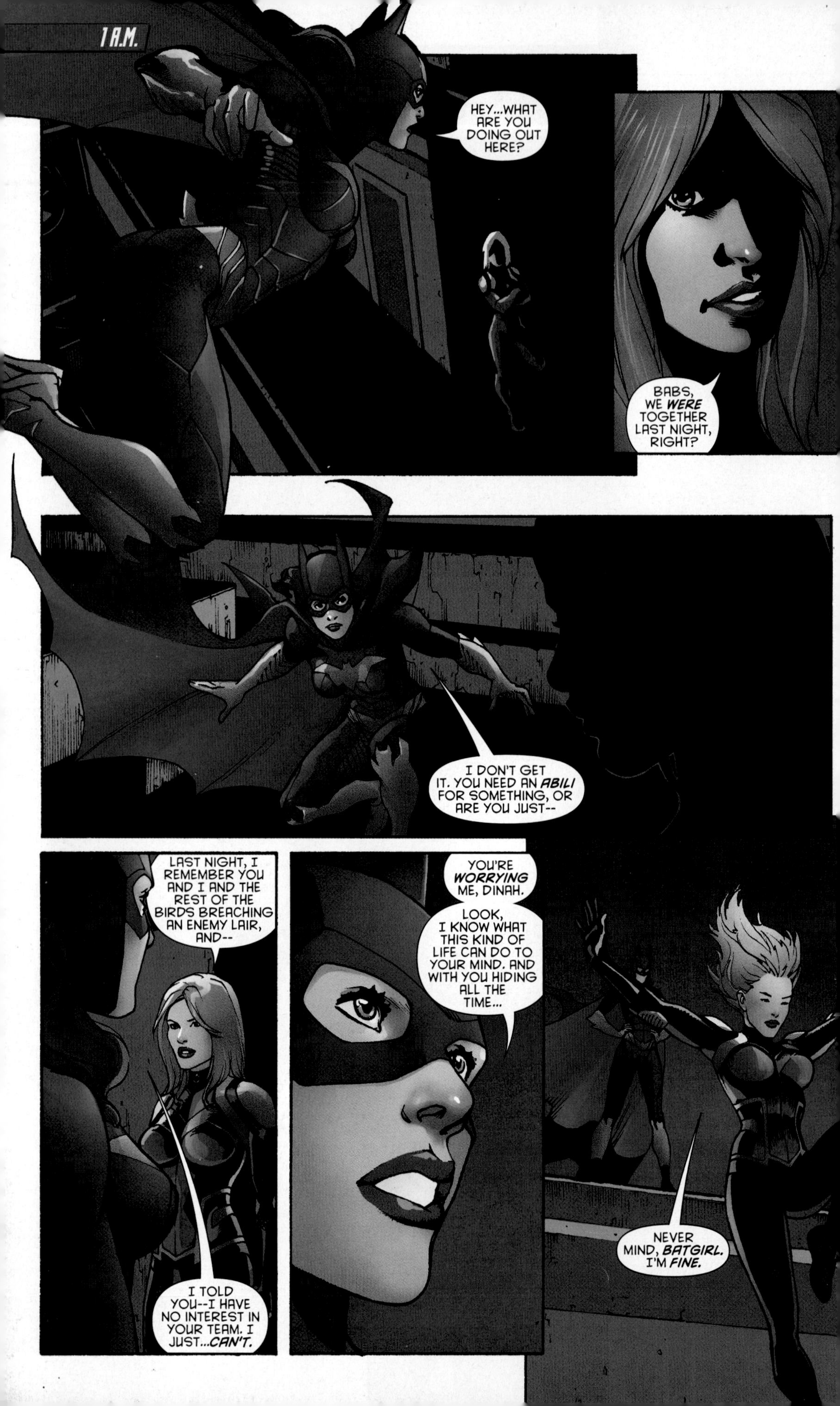
1 A.M.
HEY...WHAT ARE YOU DOING OUT HERE?
BABS, WE WERE TOGETHER LAST NIGHT, RIGHT?
I DON'T GET IT. YOU NEED AN ABILI FOR SOMETHING, OR ARE YOU JUST--
LAST NIGHT, I REMEMBER YOU AND I AND THE REST OF THE BIRDS BREACHING AN ENEMY LAIR, AND--
I TOLD YOU--I HAVE NO INTEREST IN YOUR TEAM. I JUST...CAN'T.
YOU'RE WORRYING ME, DINAH.
LOOK, I KNOW WHAT THIS KIND OF LIFE CAN DO TO YOUR MIND. AND WITH YOU HIDING ALL THE TIME...
NEVER MIND, BATGIRL. I'M FINE.

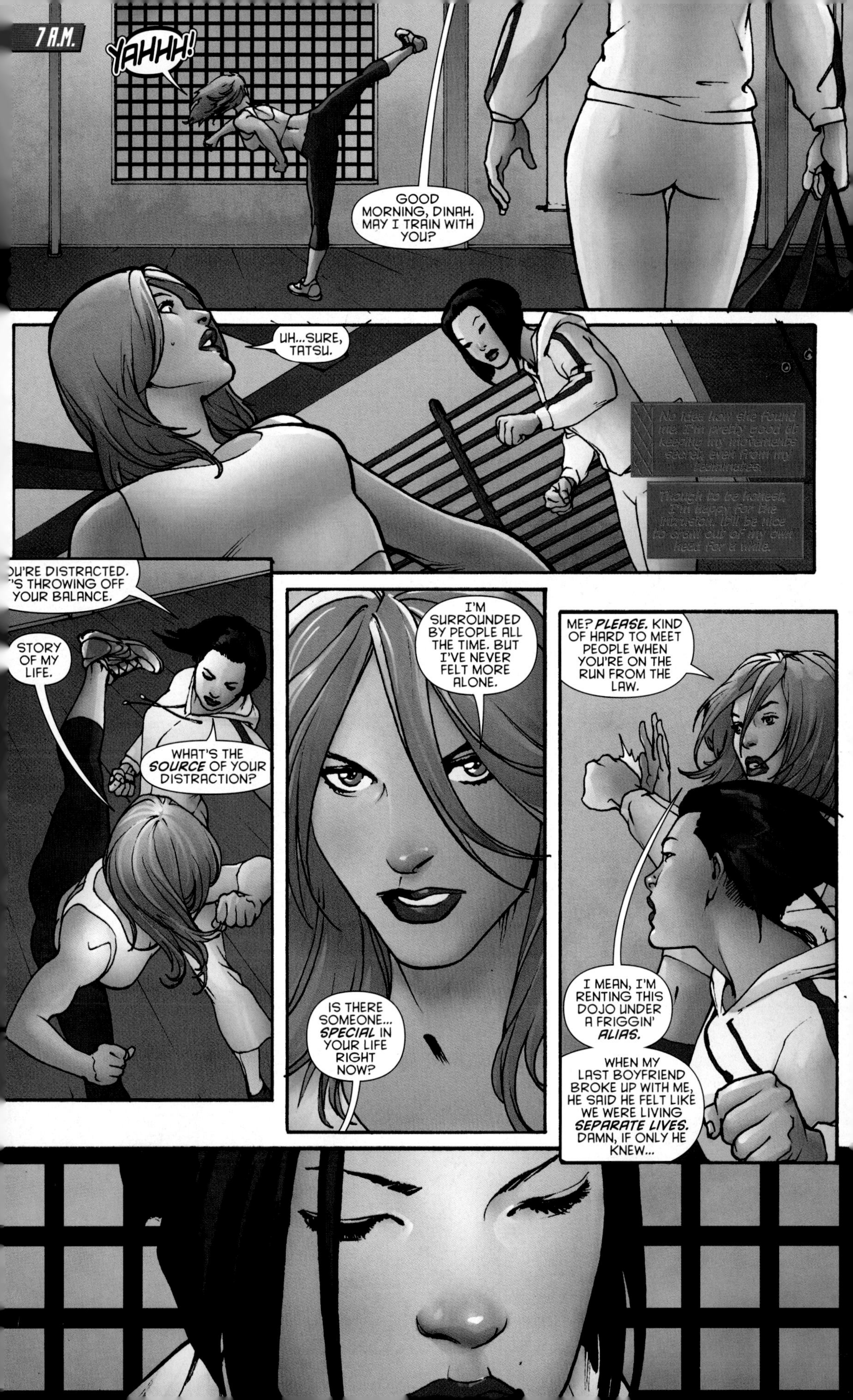
7 A.M.
YAHHH!
GOOD MORNING, DINAH. MAY I TRAIN WITH YOU?
UH...SURE, TATSU.
No idea how she found me. I'm pretty good at keeping my movements secret, even from my teammates.
Though to be honest, I'm happy for the intrusion. It'll be nice to crawl out of my own head for a while.
OU'RE DISTRACTED. 'S THROWING OFF YOUR BALANCE.
STORY OF MY LIFE.
WHAT'S THE SOURCE OF YOUR DISTRACTION?
I'M SURROUNDED BY PEOPLE ALL THE TIME. BUT I'VE NEVER FELT MORE ALONE.
IS THERE SOMEONE... SPECIAL IN YOUR LIFE RIGHT NOW?
ME? PLEASE. KIND OF HARD TO MEET PEOPLE WHEN YOU'RE ON THE RUN FROM THE LAW.
I MEAN, I'M RENTING THIS DOJO UNDER A FRIGGIN' ALIAS.
WHEN MY LAST BOYFRIEND BROKE UP WITH ME, HE SAID HE FELT LIKE WE WERE LIVING SEPARATE LIVES. DAMN, IF ONLY HE KNEW...

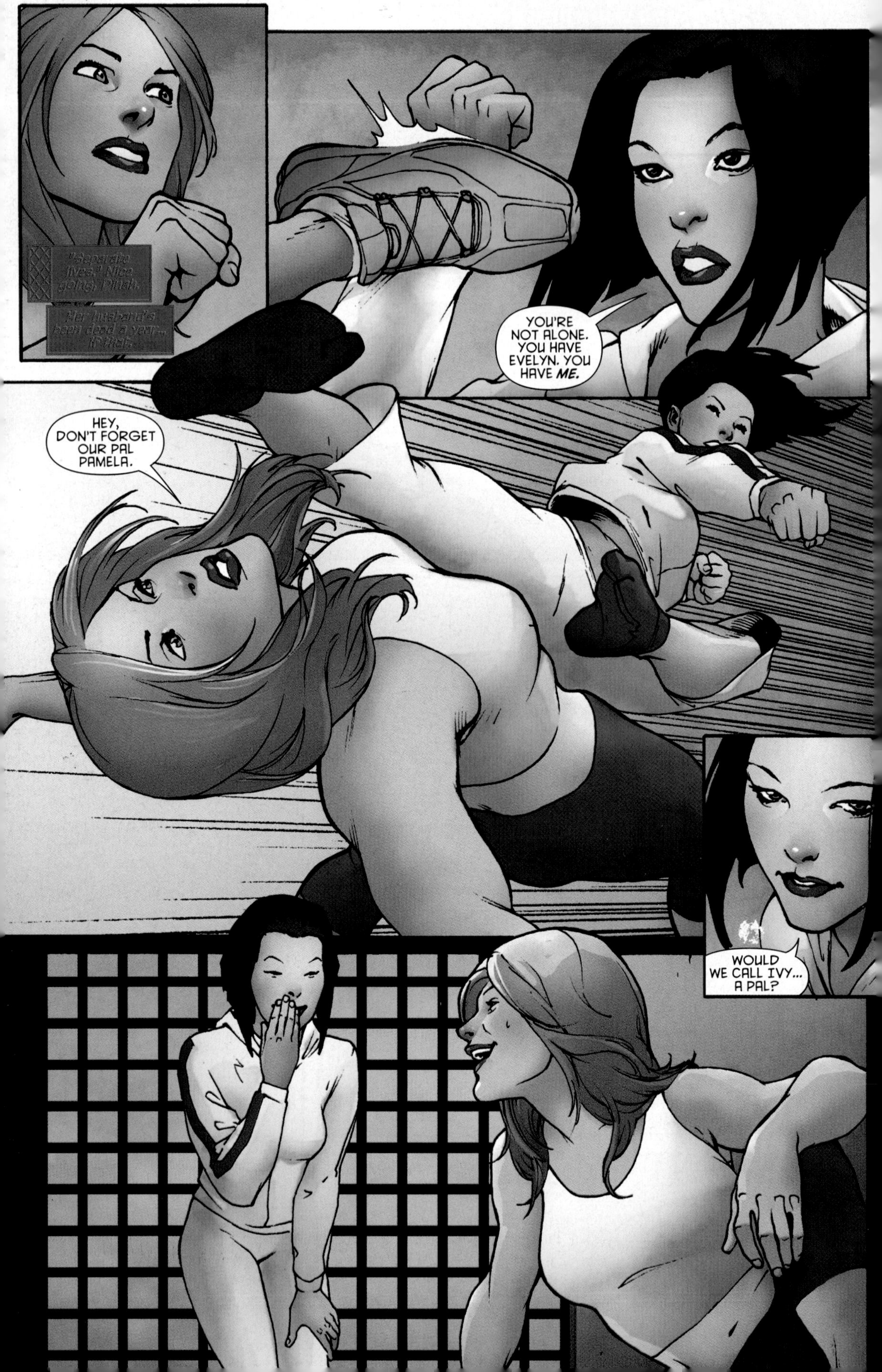
"Separate lives." Nice going, Dinah.
Her husband's been dead a year...
YOU'RE NOT ALONE. YOU HAVE EVELYN. YOU HAVE ***ME.***
HEY, DON'T FORGET OUR PAL PAMELA.
WOULD WE CALL IVY... A PAL?

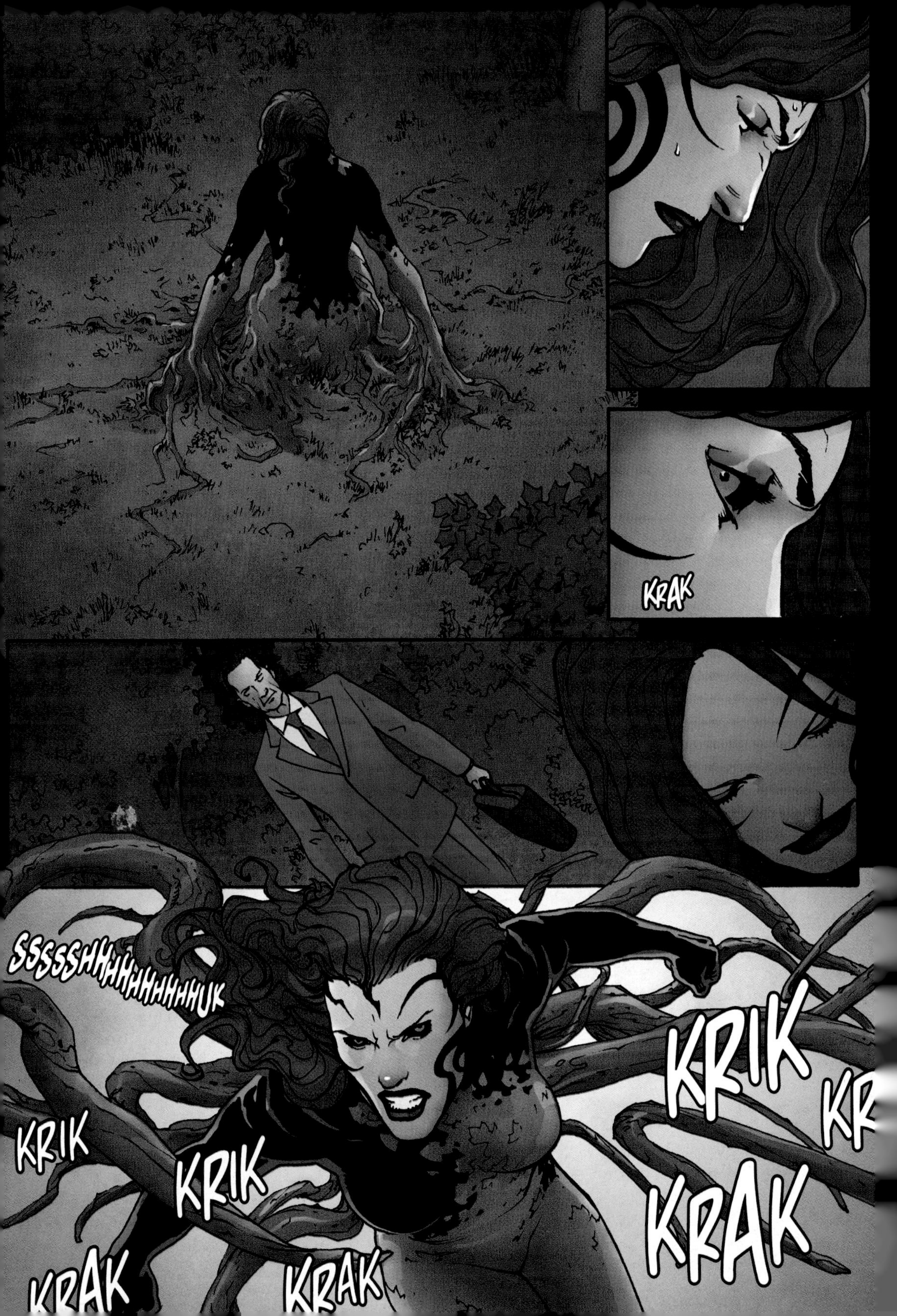
KRAK
SSSSSHHHHHHHHHHUK
KRIK
KR
KRIK
KRIK
KRAK
KRAK
KRAK

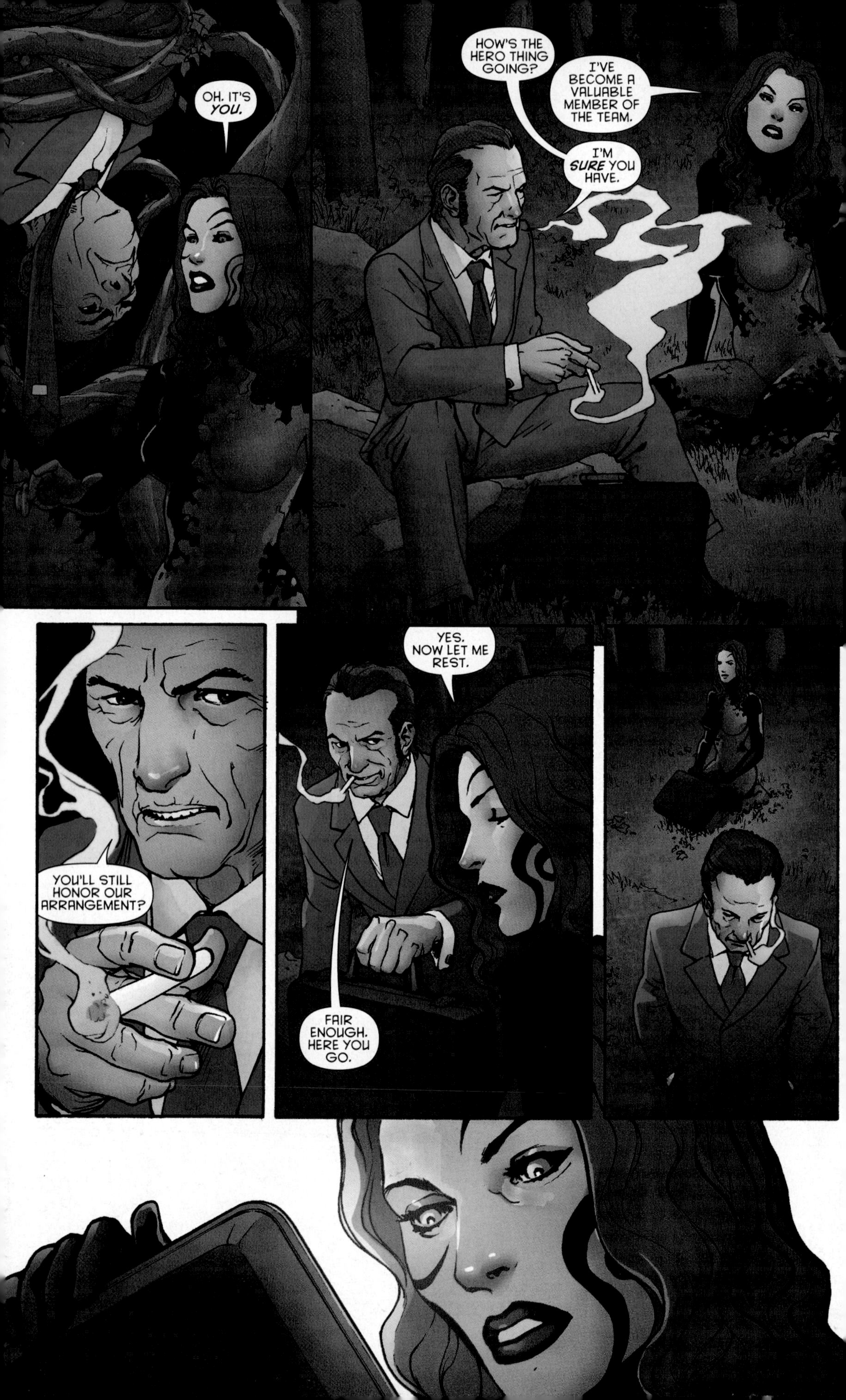
OH. IT'S *YOU.*
HOW'S THE HERO THING GOING?
I'VE BECOME A VALUABLE MEMBER OF THE TEAM.
I'M *SURE* YOU HAVE.
YOU'LL STILL HONOR OUR ARRANGEMENT?
YES. NOW LET ME REST.
FAIR ENOUGH. HERE YOU GO.

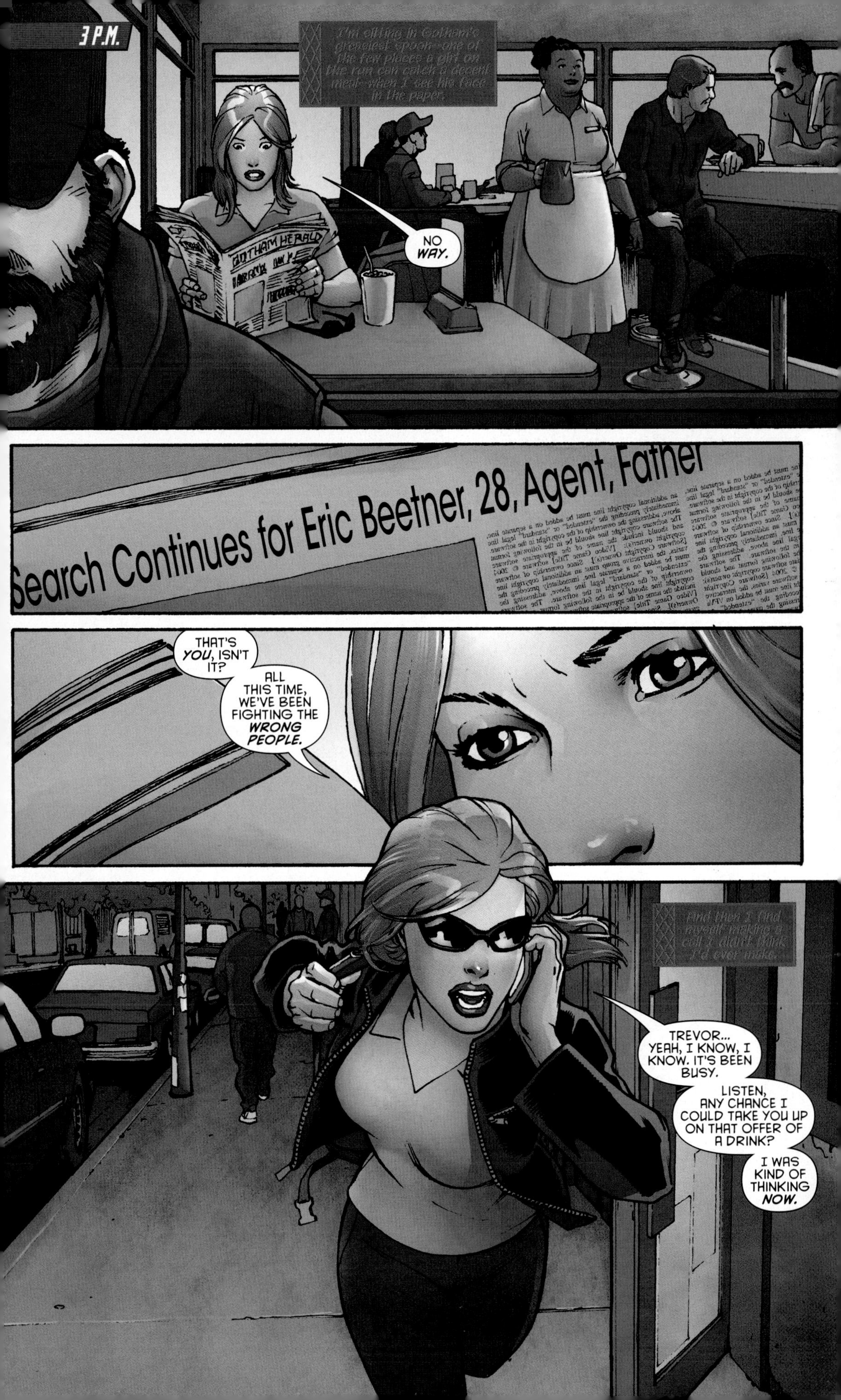

3 P.M.
I'm sitting in Gotham's greasiest spoon--one of the few places a girl on the run can catch a decent meal--when I see his face in the paper.
GOTHAM HERALD
NO WAY.
Search Continues for Eric Beetner, 28, Agent, Father
THAT'S YOU, ISN'T IT?
ALL THIS TIME, WE'VE BEEN FIGHTING THE WRONG PEOPLE.
And then I find myself making a call I didn't think I'd ever make.
TREVOR... YEAH, I KNOW, I KNOW. IT'S BEEN BUSY.
LISTEN, ANY CHANCE I COULD TAKE YOU UP ON THAT OFFER OF A DRINK?
I WAS KIND OF THINKING NOW.

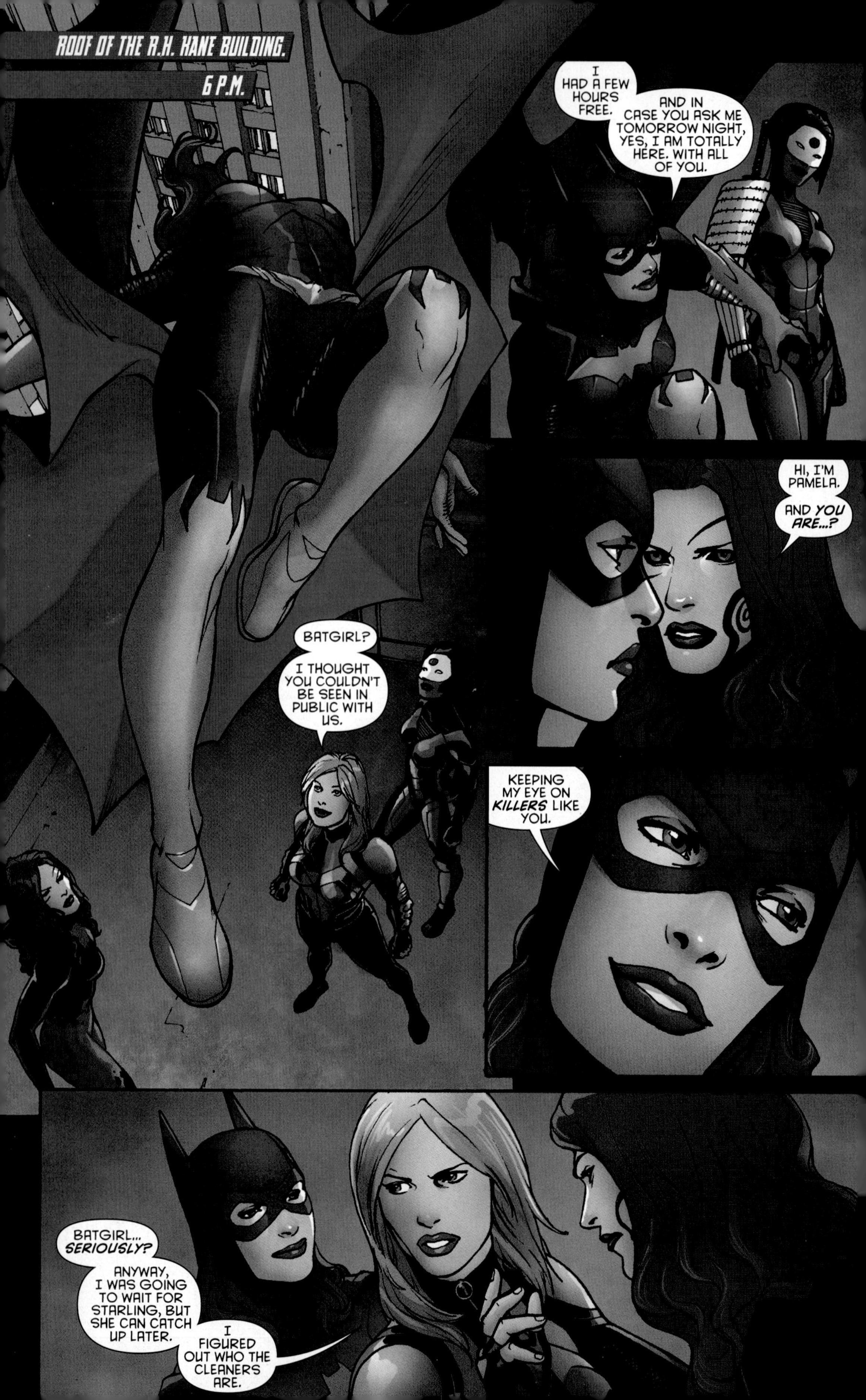
ROOF OF THE R.H. KANE BUILDING.
6 P.M.
I HAD A FEW HOURS FREE.
AND IN CASE YOU ASK ME TOMORROW NIGHT, YES, I AM TOTALLY HERE. WITH ALL OF YOU.
BATGIRL?
I THOUGHT YOU COULDN'T BE SEEN IN PUBLIC WITH US.
HI, I'M PAMELA.
AND YOU ARE...?
KEEPING MY EYE ON KILLERS LIKE YOU.
BATGIRL... SERIOUSLY?
ANYWAY, I WAS GOING TO WAIT FOR STARLING, BUT SHE CAN CATCH UP LATER.
I FIGURED OUT WHO THE CLEANERS ARE.

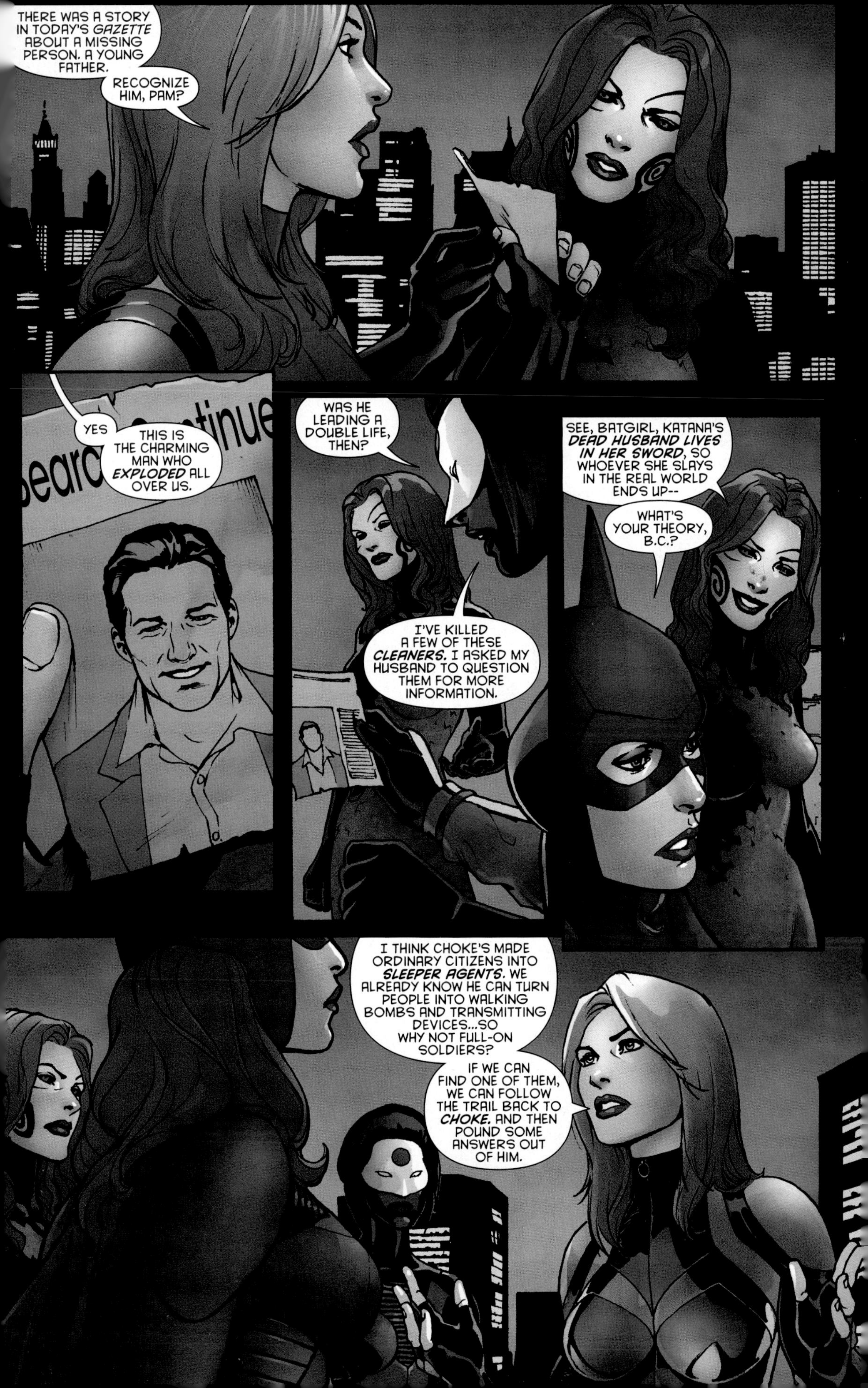

THERE WAS A STORY IN TODAY'S *GAZETTE* ABOUT A MISSING PERSON. A YOUNG FATHER.
RECOGNIZE HIM, PAM?
YES
THIS IS THE CHARMING MAN WHO *EXPLODED* ALL OVER US.
WAS HE LEADING A DOUBLE LIFE, THEN?
I'VE KILLED A FEW OF THESE *CLEANERS.* I ASKED MY HUSBAND TO QUESTION THEM FOR MORE INFORMATION.
SEE, BATGIRL, KATANA'S *DEAD HUSBAND LIVES IN HER SWORD*, SO WHOEVER SHE SLAYS IN THE REAL WORLD ENDS UP--
WHAT'S YOUR THEORY, B.C.?
I THINK CHOKE'S MADE ORDINARY CITIZENS INTO *SLEEPER AGENTS*. WE ALREADY KNOW HE CAN TURN PEOPLE INTO WALKING BOMBS AND TRANSMITTING DEVICES...SO WHY NOT FULL-ON SOLDIERS?
IF WE CAN FIND ONE OF THEM, WE CAN FOLLOW THE TRAIL BACK TO *CHOKE.* AND THEN POUND SOME ANSWERS OUT OF HIM.

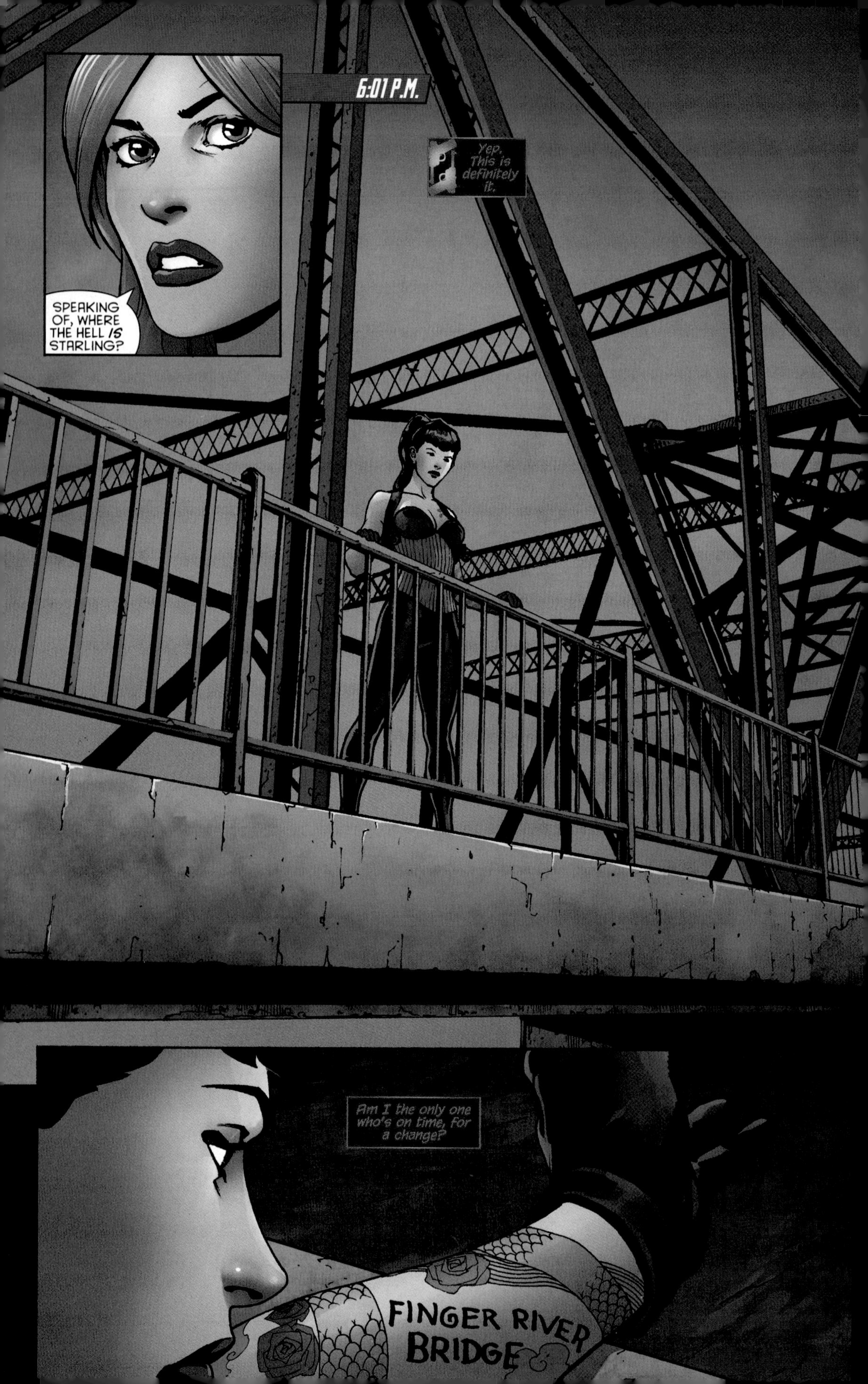
SPEAKING OF, WHERE THE HELL IS STARLING?
6:01 P.M.
Yep. This is definitely it.
Am I the only one who's on time, for a change?
FINGER RIVER BRIDGE

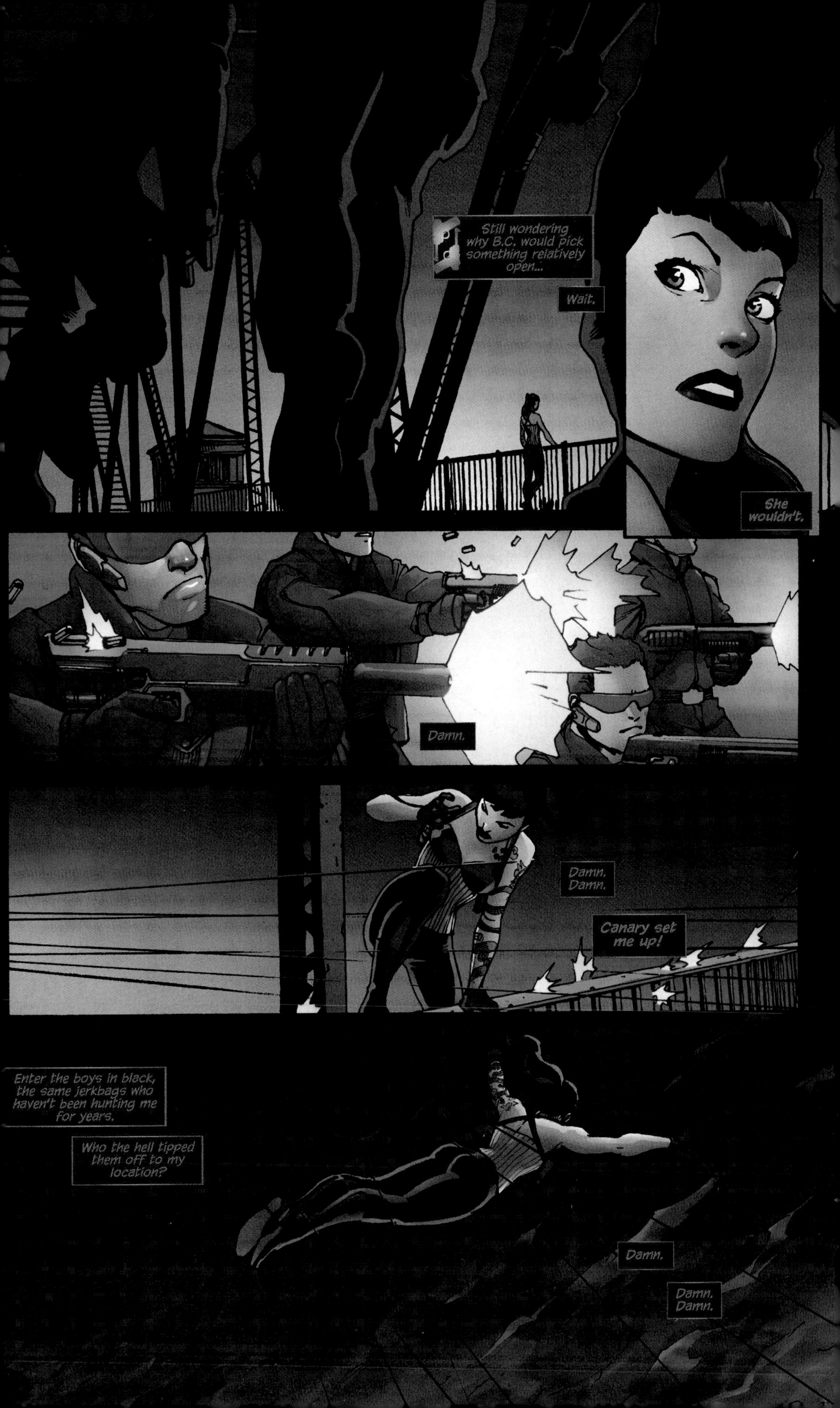
Still wondering why B.C. would pick something relatively open...
Wait.
She wouldn't.
Damn.
Damn. Damn.
Canary set me up!
Enter the boys in black, the same jerkbags who haven't been hunting me for years.
Who the hell tipped them off to my location?
Damn.
Damn. Damn.

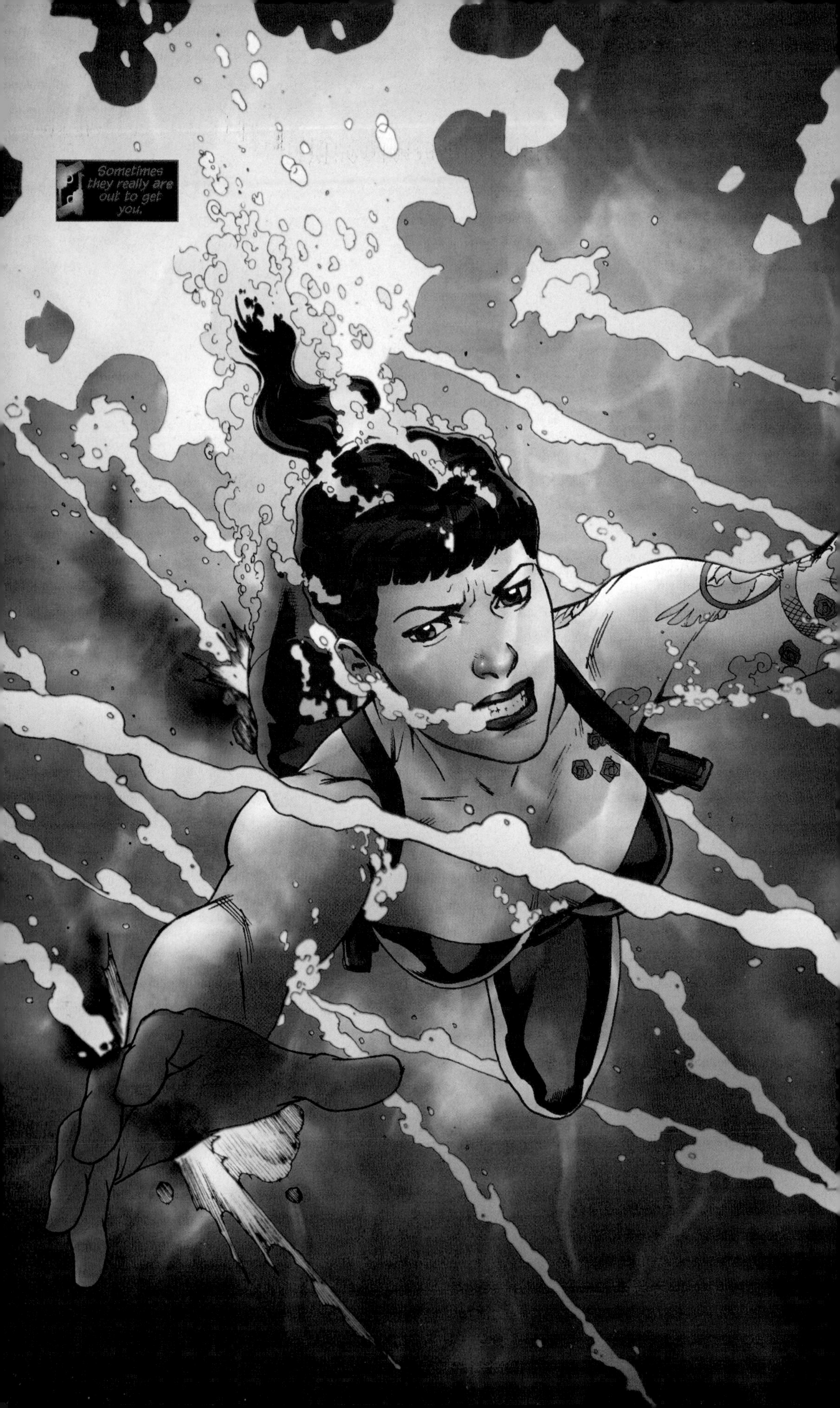
Sometimes they really are out to get you.

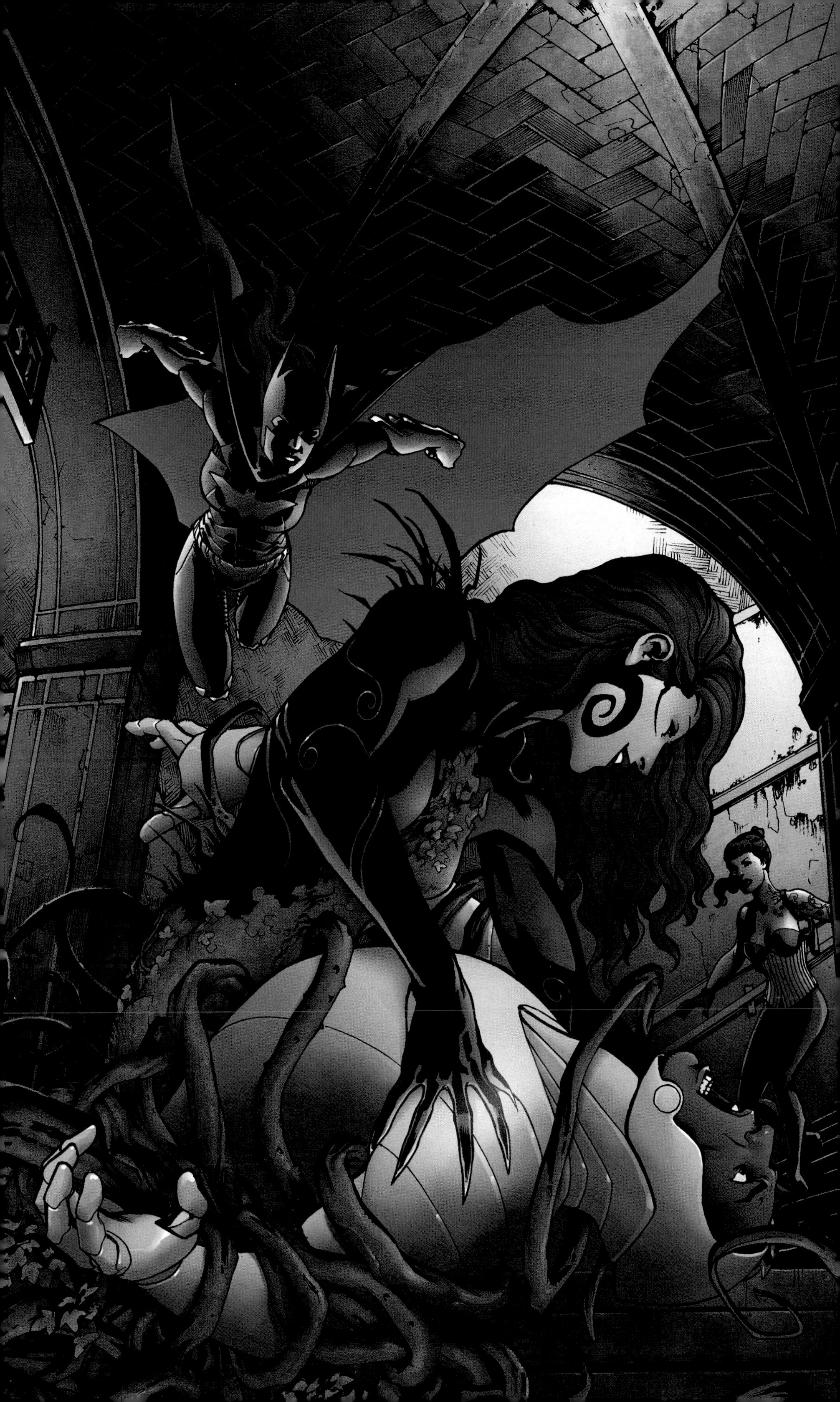

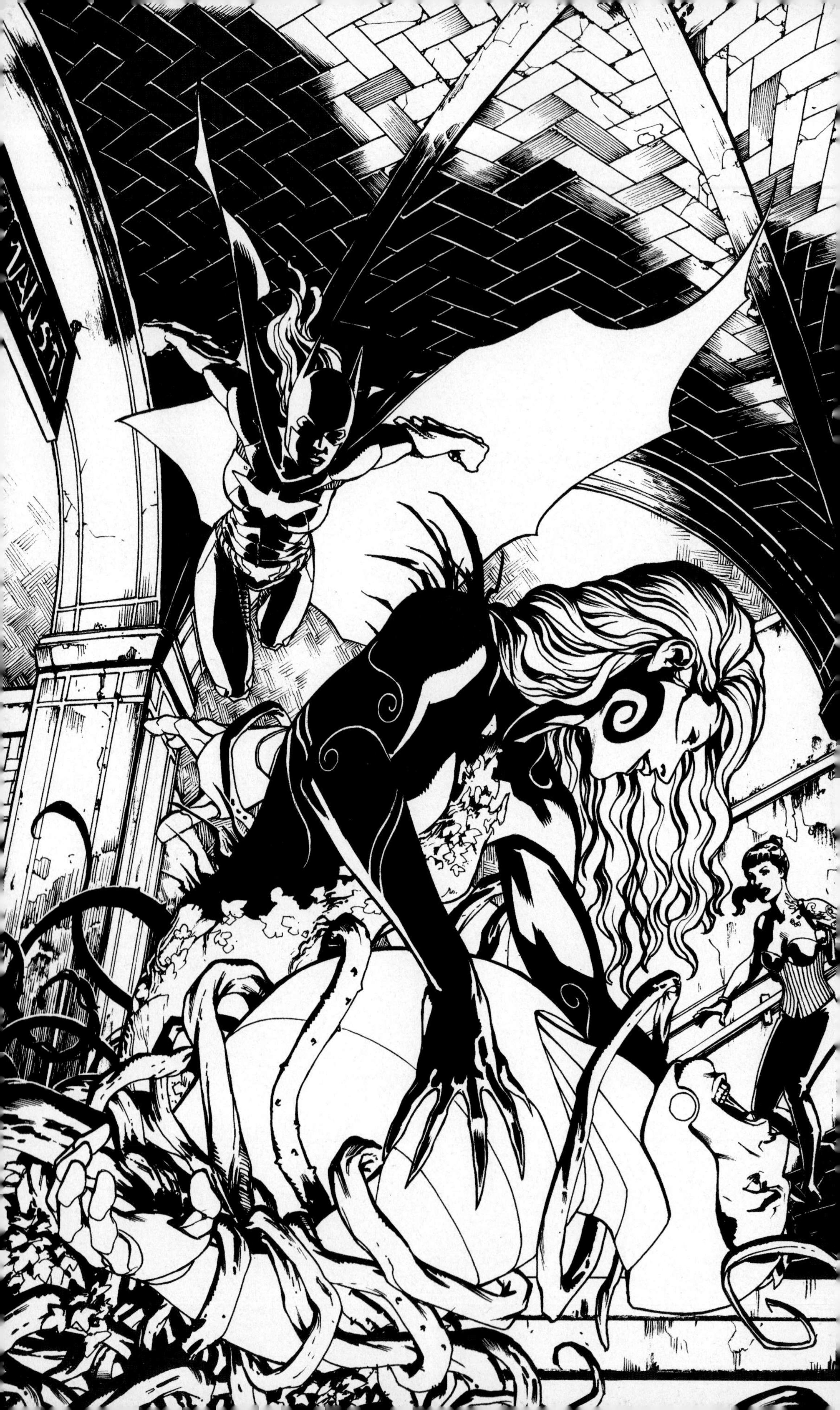

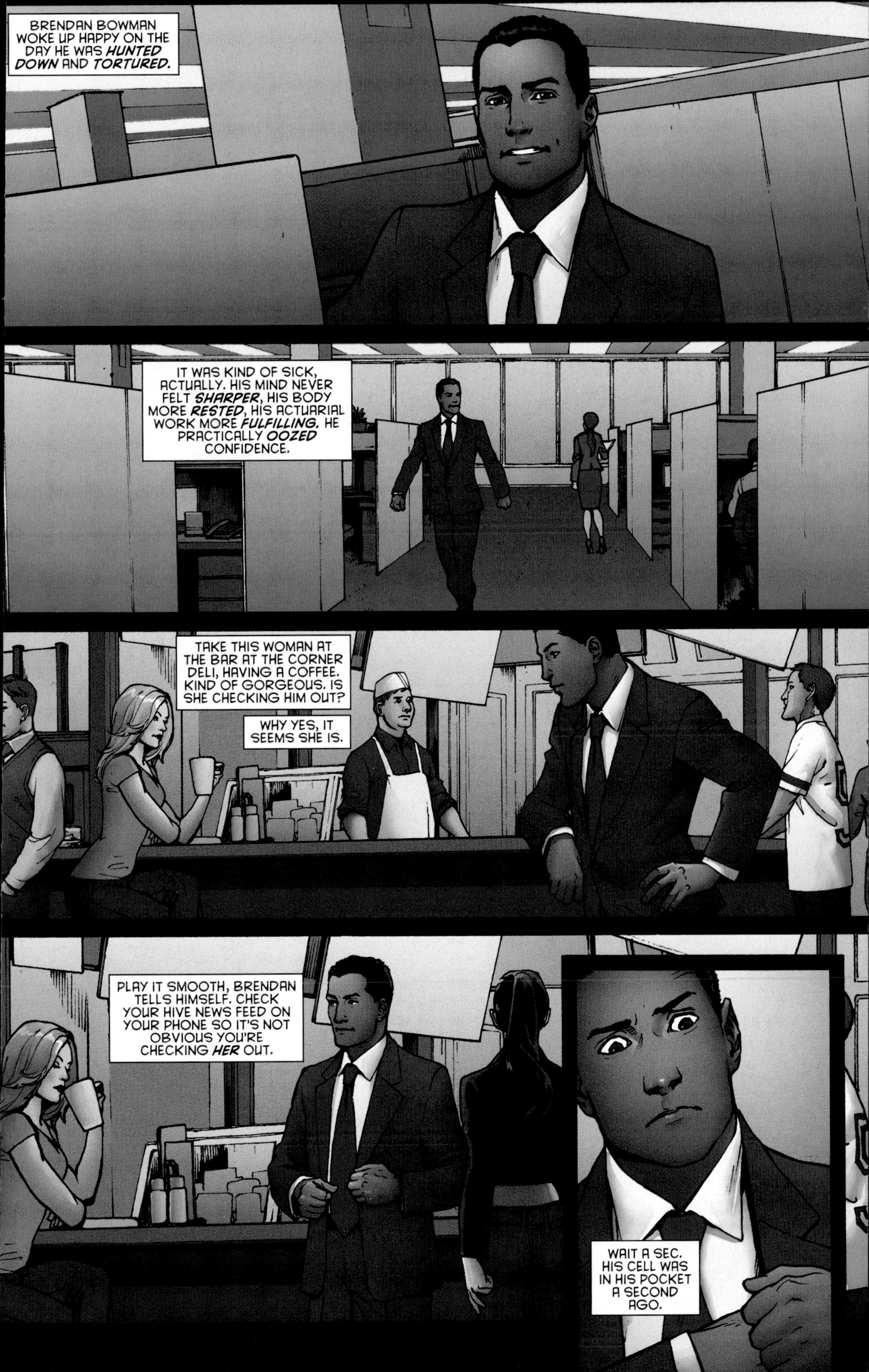
BRENDAN BOWMAN WOKE UP HAPPY ON THE DAY HE WAS ***HUNTED DOWN*** AND ***TORTURED.***
IT WAS KIND OF SICK, ACTUALLY. HIS MIND NEVER FELT ***SHARPER***, HIS BODY MORE ***RESTED***, HIS ACTUARIAL WORK MORE ***FULFILLING.*** HE PRACTICALLY ***OOZED*** CONFIDENCE.
TAKE THIS WOMAN AT THE BAR AT THE CORNER DELI, HAVING A COFFEE. KIND OF GORGEOUS. IS SHE CHECKING HIM OUT?
WHY YES, IT SEEMS SHE IS.
PLAY IT SMOOTH, BRENDAN TELLS HIMSELF. CHECK YOUR HIVE NEWS FEED ON YOUR PHONE SO IT'S NOT OBVIOUS YOU'RE CHECKING ***HER*** OUT.
WAIT A SEC. HIS CELL WAS IN HIS POCKET A SECOND AGO.

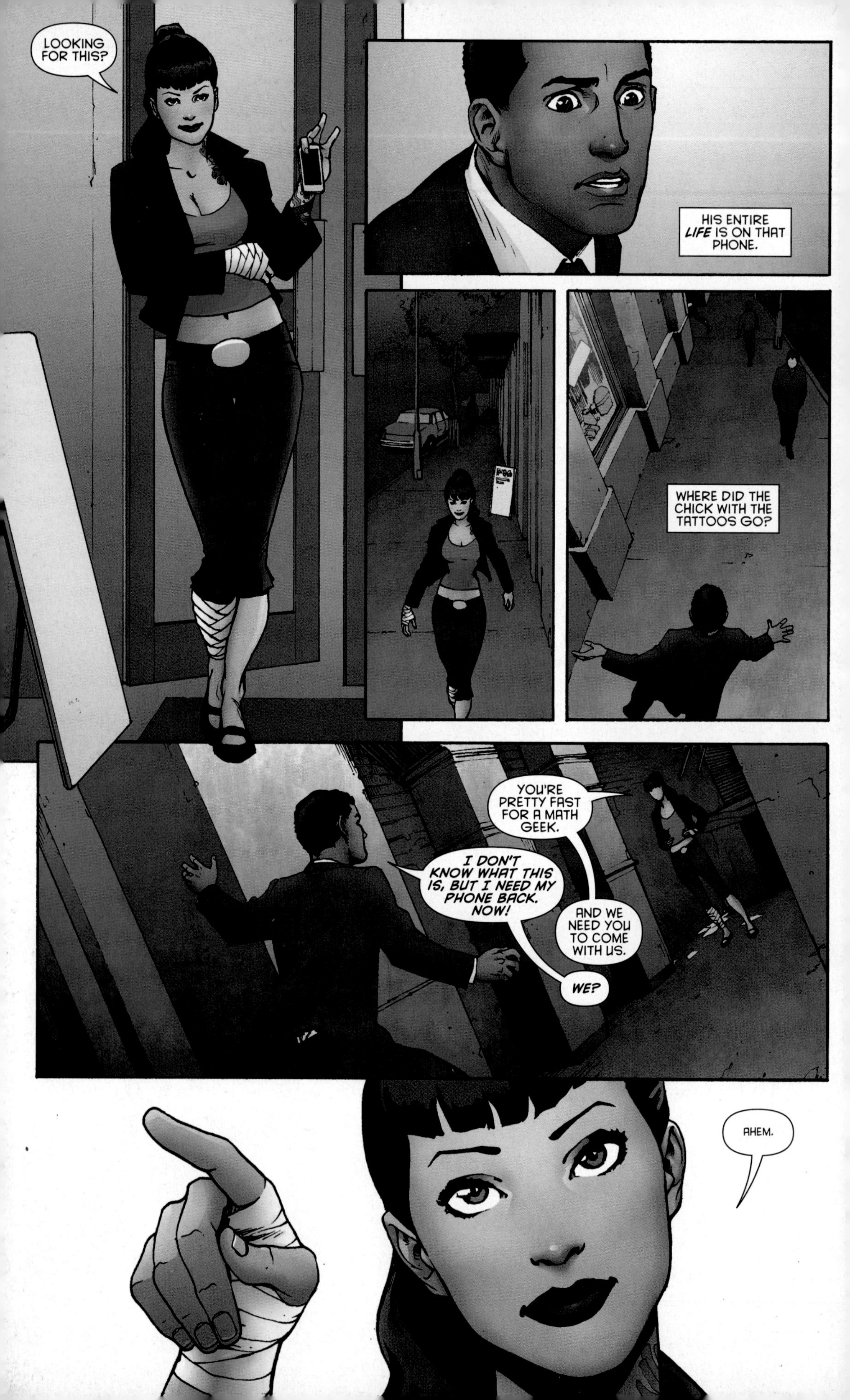
LOOKING FOR THIS?
HIS ENTIRE *LIFE* IS ON THAT PHONE.
WHERE DID THE CHICK WITH THE TATTOOS GO?
YOU'RE PRETTY FAST FOR A MATH GEEK.
I DON'T KNOW WHAT THIS IS, BUT I NEED MY PHONE BACK. NOW!
AND WE NEED YOU TO COME WITH US.
WE?
AHEM.

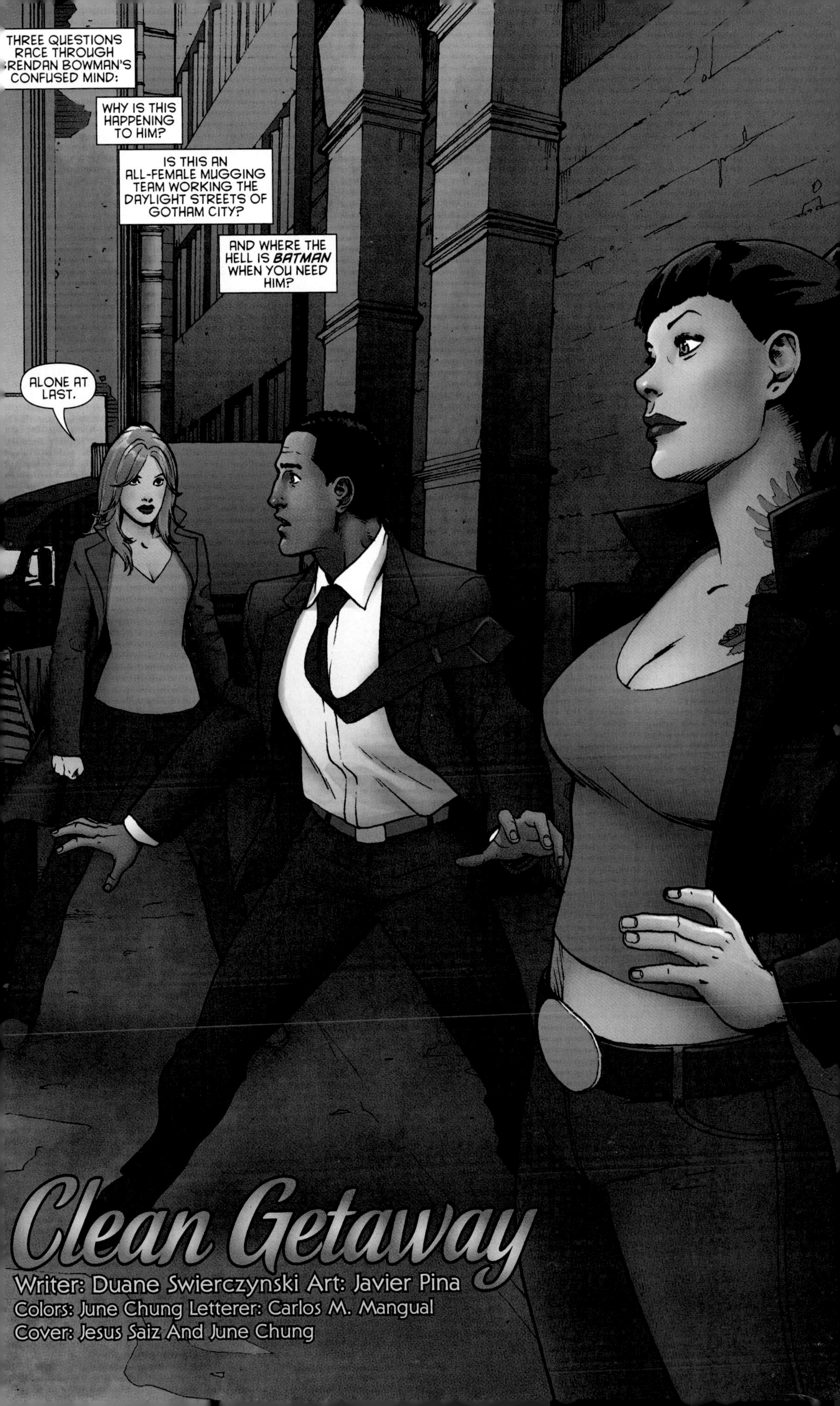
THREE QUESTIONS RACE THROUGH BRENDAN BOWMAN'S CONFUSED MIND:
WHY IS THIS HAPPENING TO HIM?
IS THIS AN ALL-FEMALE MUGGING TEAM WORKING THE DAYLIGHT STREETS OF GOTHAM CITY?
AND WHERE THE HELL IS BATMAN WHEN YOU NEED HIM?
ALONE AT LAST.
Clean Getaway
Writer: Duane Swierczynski Art: Javier Pina
Colors: June Chung Letterer: Carlos M. Mangual
Cover: Jesus Saiz And June Chung

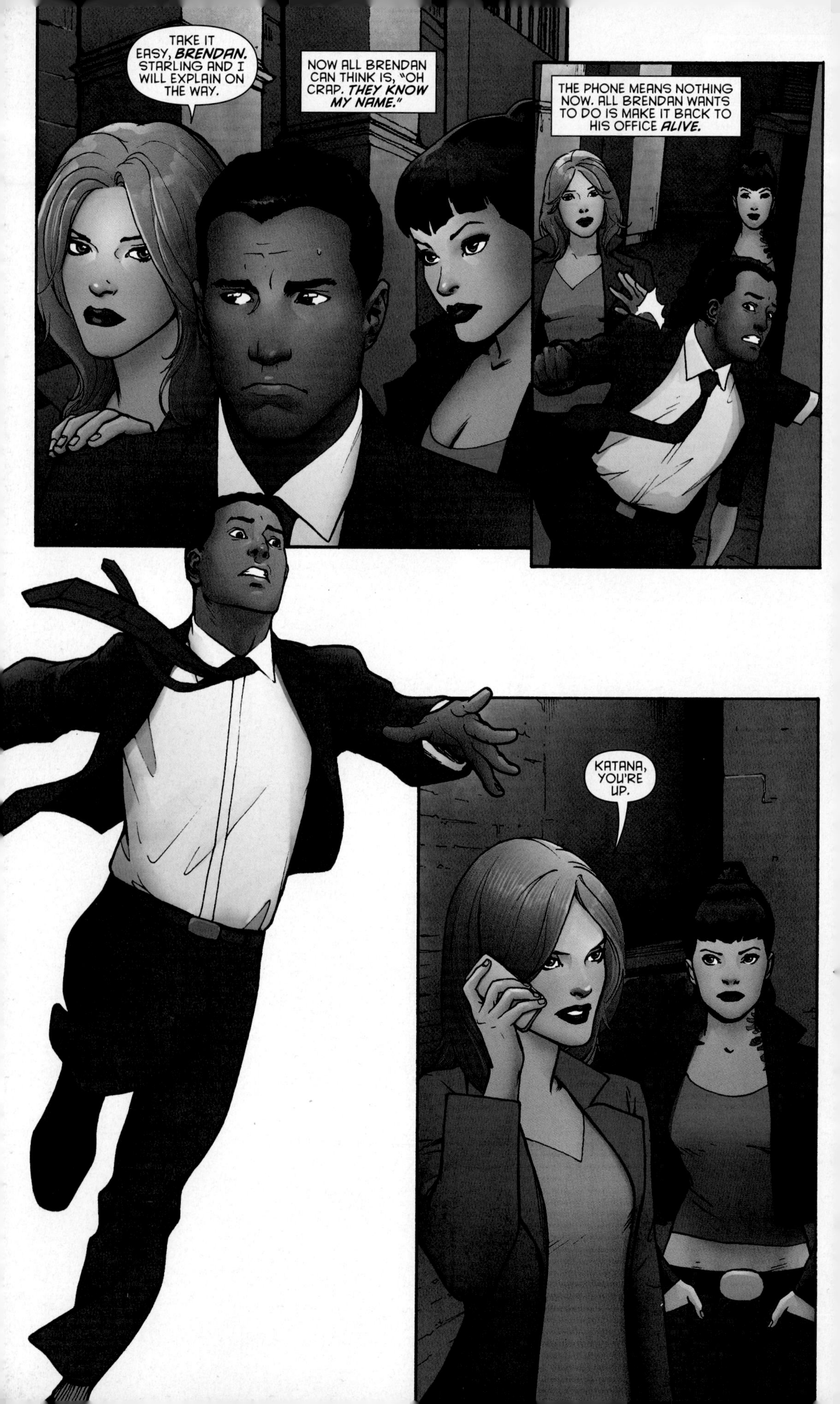

TAKE IT EASY, BRENDAN. STARLING AND I WILL EXPLAIN ON THE WAY.
NOW ALL BRENDAN CAN THINK IS, "OH CRAP. THEY KNOW MY NAME."
THE PHONE MEANS NOTHING NOW. ALL BRENDAN WANTS TO DO IS MAKE IT BACK TO HIS OFFICE ALIVE.
KATANA, YOU'RE UP.

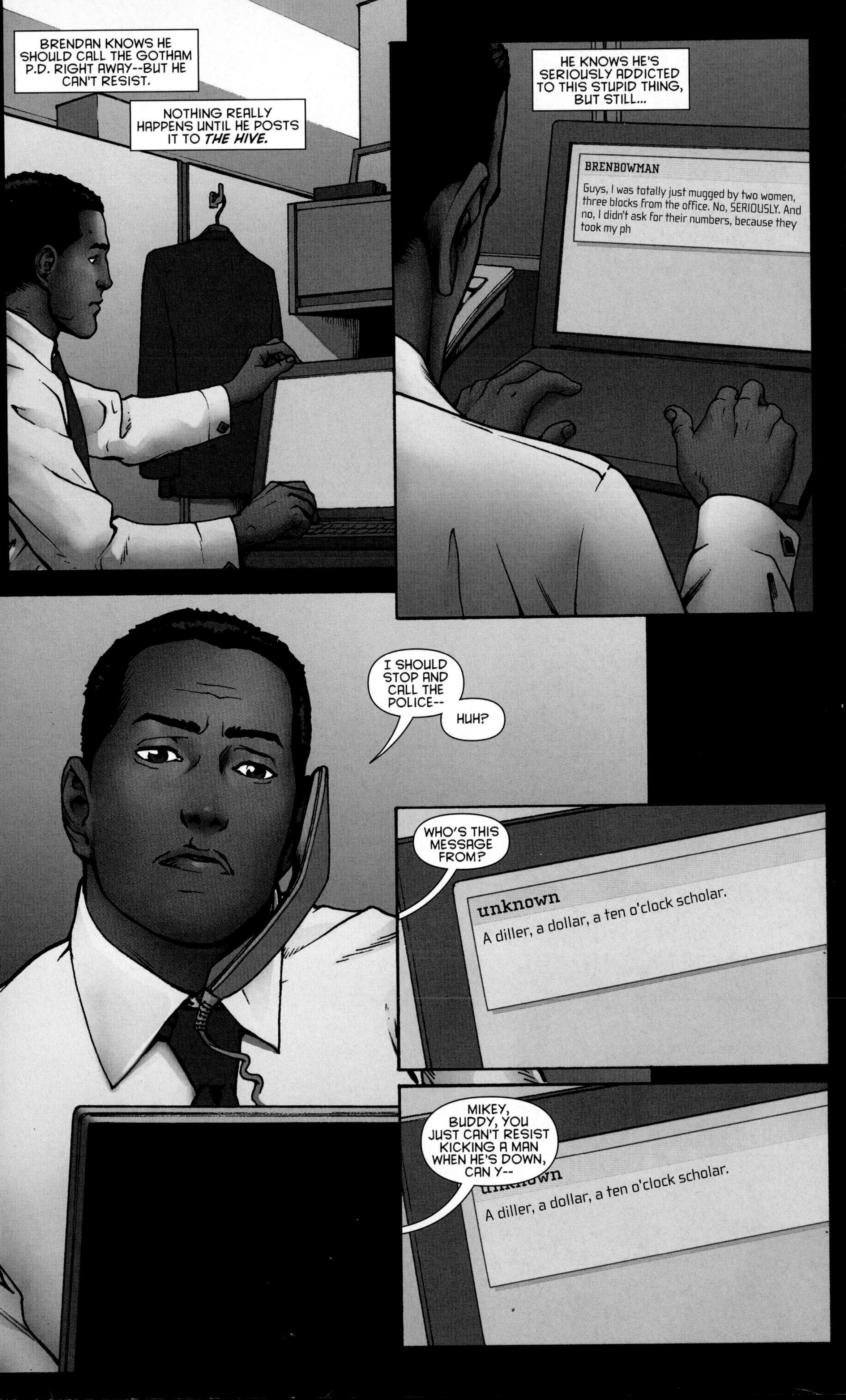
BRENDAN KNOWS HE SHOULD CALL THE GOTHAM P.D. RIGHT AWAY--BUT HE CAN'T RESIST.
NOTHING REALLY HAPPENS UNTIL HE POSTS IT TO *THE HIVE.*
HE KNOWS HE'S SERIOUSLY ADDICTED TO THIS STUPID THING, BUT STILL...
BRENBOWMAN
Guys, I was totally just mugged by two women, three blocks from the office. No, SERIOUSLY. And no, I didn't ask for their numbers, because they took my ph
I SHOULD STOP AND CALL THE POLICE--
HUH?
WHO'S THIS MESSAGE FROM?
unknown
A diller, a dollar, a ten o'clock scholar.
MIKEY, BUDDY, YOU JUST CAN'T RESIST KICKING A MAN WHEN HE'S DOWN, CAN Y--
A diller, a dollar, a ten o'clock scholar.

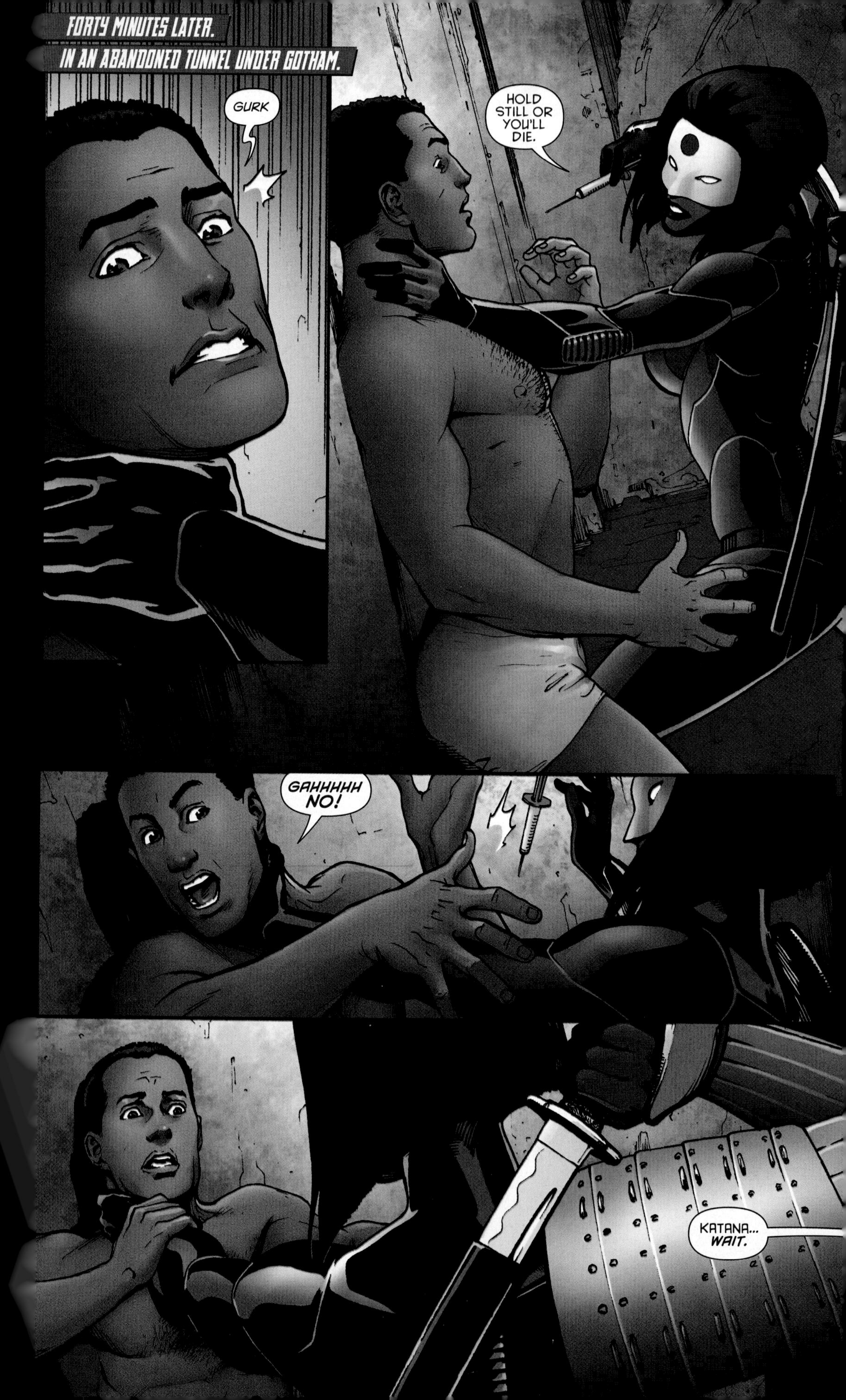
FORTY MINUTES LATER.
IN AN ABANDONED TUNNEL UNDER GOTHAM.
GURK
HOLD STILL OR YOU'LL DIE.
GAHHHHH NO!
KATANA... WAIT.

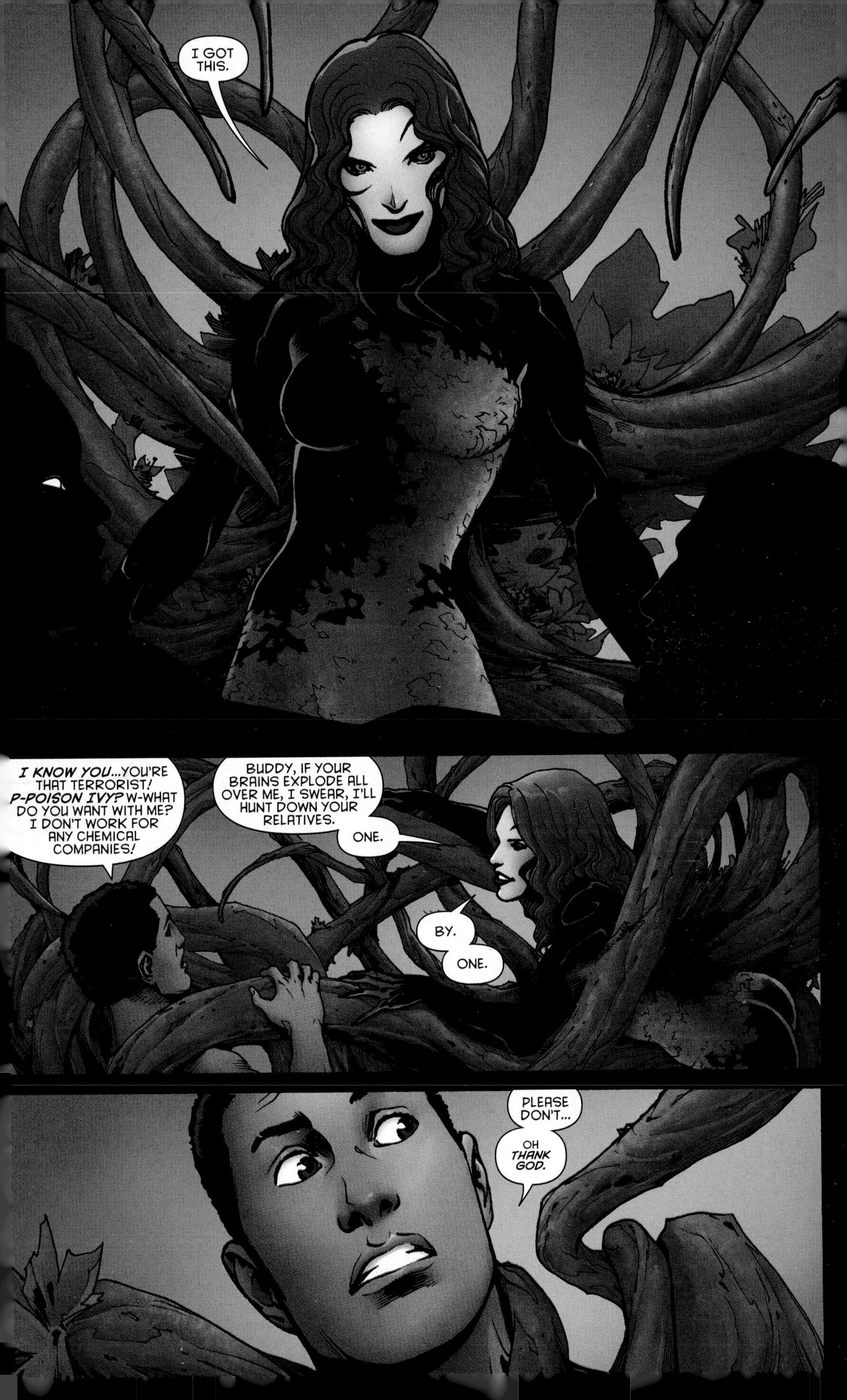
I GOT THIS.
I KNOW YOU...YOU'RE THAT TERRORIST! *P-POISON IVY?* W-WHAT DO YOU WANT WITH ME? I DON'T WORK FOR ANY CHEMICAL COMPANIES!
BUDDY, IF YOUR BRAINS EXPLODE ALL OVER ME, I SWEAR, I'LL HUNT DOWN YOUR RELATIVES.
ONE.
BY.
ONE.
PLEASE DON'T...
OH *THANK GOD.*

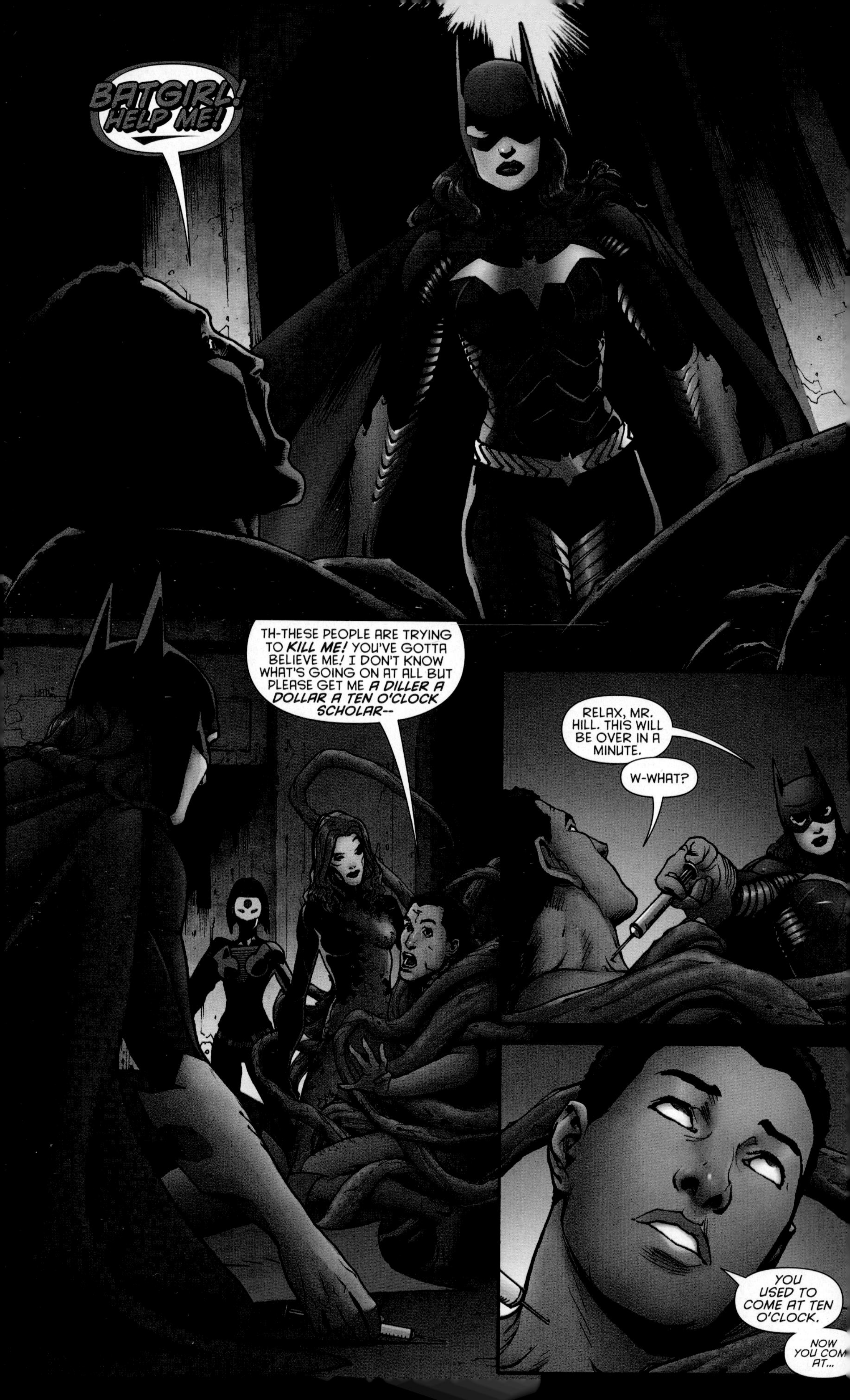
BATGIRL! HELP ME!
TH-THESE PEOPLE ARE TRYING TO KILL ME! YOU'VE GOTTA BELIEVE ME! I DON'T KNOW WHAT'S GOING ON AT ALL BUT PLEASE GET ME A DILLER A DOLLAR A TEN O'CLOCK SCHOLAR--
RELAX, MR. HILL. THIS WILL BE OVER IN A MINUTE.
W-WHAT?
YOU USED TO COME AT TEN O'CLOCK.
NOW YOU COM AT...

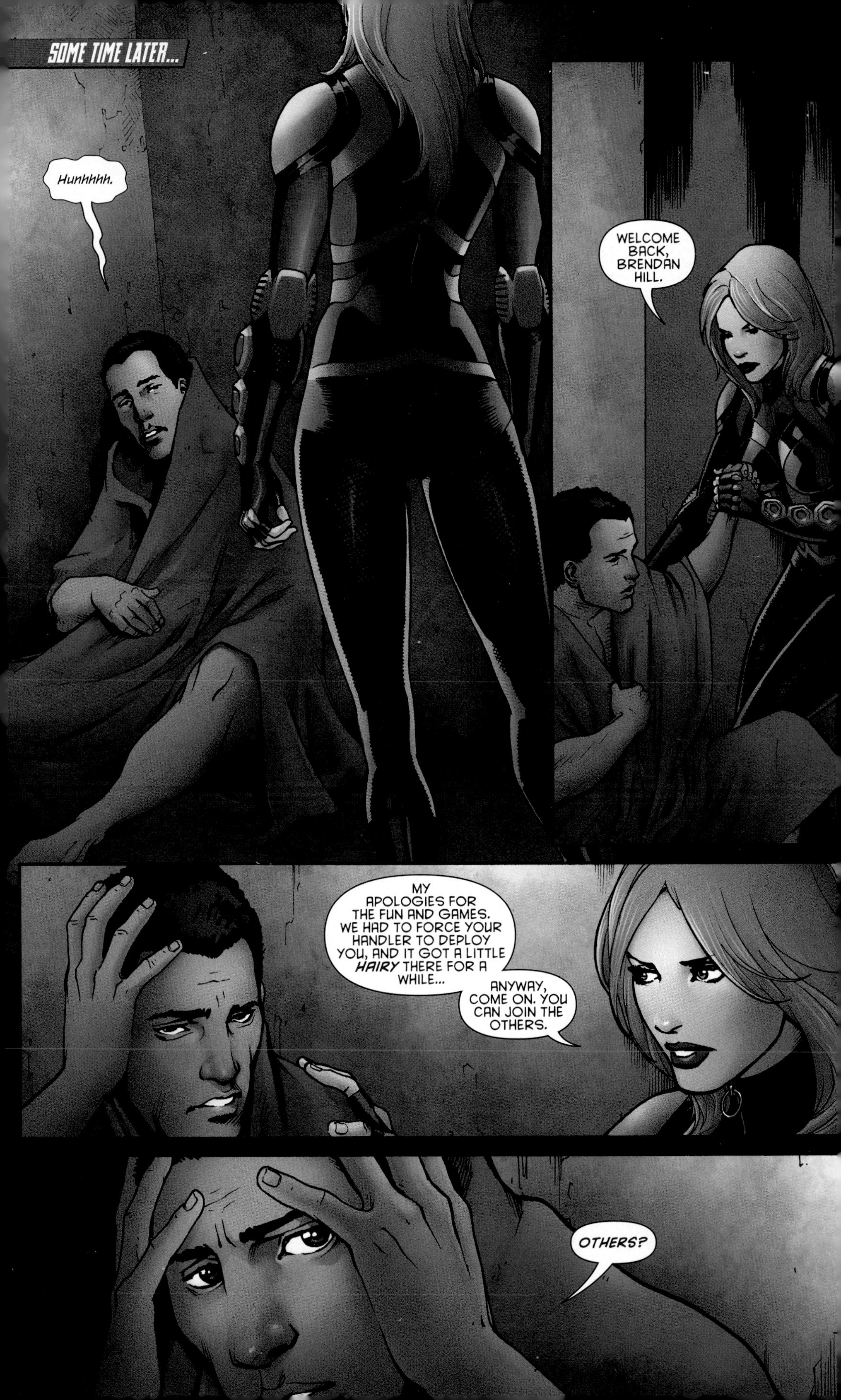
SOME TIME LATER...
Hunhhhh.
WELCOME BACK, BRENDAN HILL.
MY APOLOGIES FOR THE FUN AND GAMES. WE HAD TO FORCE YOUR HANDLER TO DEPLOY YOU, AND IT GOT A LITTLE HAIRY THERE FOR A WHILE...
ANYWAY, COME ON. YOU CAN JOIN THE OTHERS.
OTHERS?

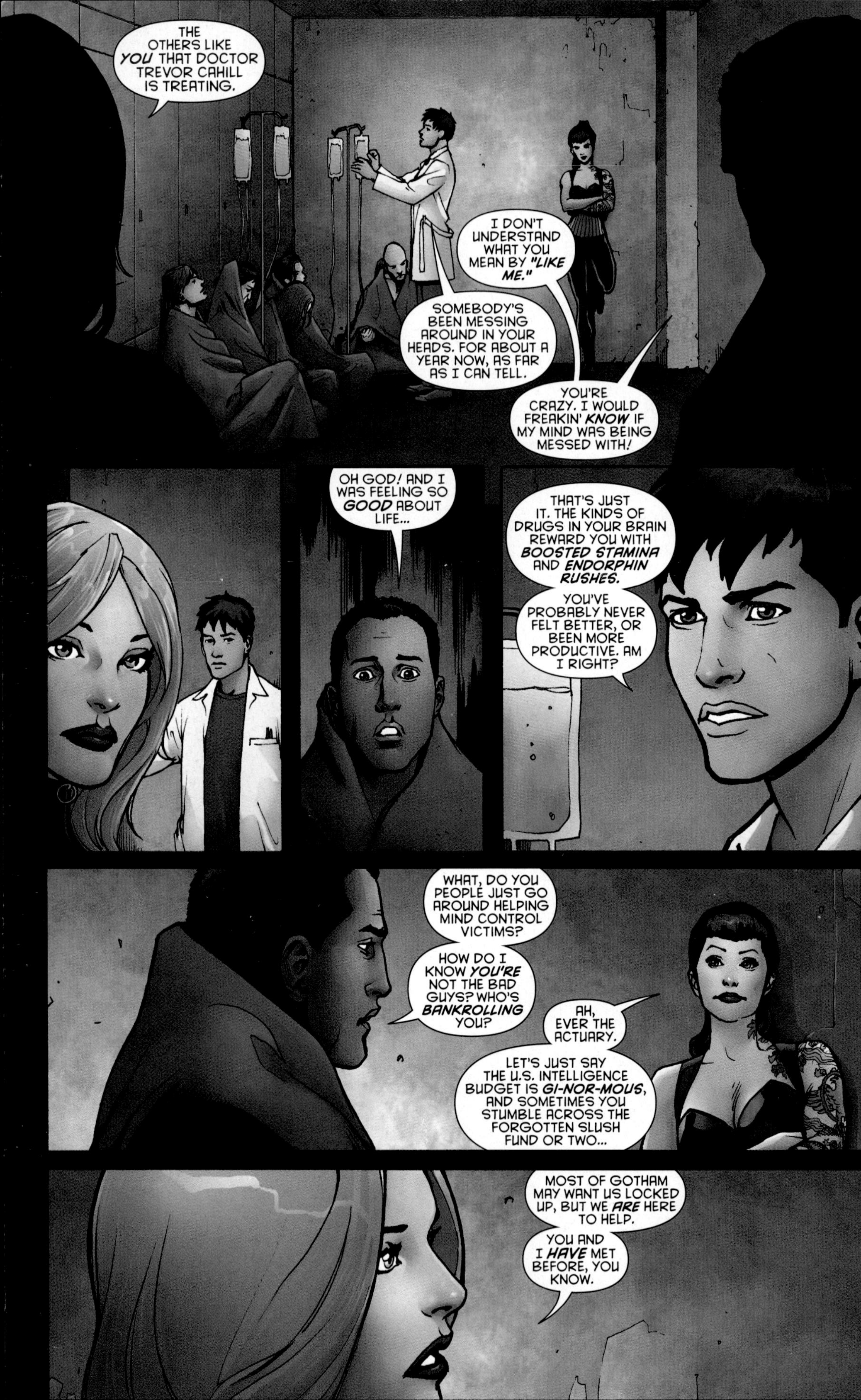
THE OTHERS LIKE *YOU* THAT DOCTOR TREVOR CAHILL IS TREATING.
I DON'T UNDERSTAND WHAT YOU MEAN BY *"LIKE ME."*
SOMEBODY'S BEEN MESSING AROUND IN YOUR HEADS. FOR ABOUT A YEAR NOW, AS FAR AS I CAN TELL.
YOU'RE CRAZY. I WOULD FREAKIN' *KNOW* IF MY MIND WAS BEING MESSED WITH!
OH GOD! AND I WAS FEELING SO *GOOD* ABOUT LIFE...
THAT'S JUST IT. THE KINDS OF DRUGS IN YOUR BRAIN REWARD YOU WITH ***BOOSTED STAMINA*** AND ***ENDORPHIN RUSHES.***
YOU'VE PROBABLY NEVER FELT BETTER, OR BEEN MORE PRODUCTIVE. AM I RIGHT?
WHAT, DO YOU PEOPLE JUST GO AROUND HELPING MIND CONTROL VICTIMS?
HOW DO I KNOW *YOU'RE* NOT THE BAD GUYS? WHO'S ***BANKROLLING*** YOU?
AH, EVER THE ACTUARY.
LET'S JUST SAY THE U.S. INTELLIGENCE BUDGET IS *GI-NOR-MOUS*, AND SOMETIMES YOU STUMBLE ACROSS THE FORGOTTEN SLUSH FUND OR TWO...
MOST OF GOTHAM MAY WANT US LOCKED UP, BUT WE *ARE* HERE TO HELP.
YOU AND I *HAVE* MET BEFORE, YOU KNOW.

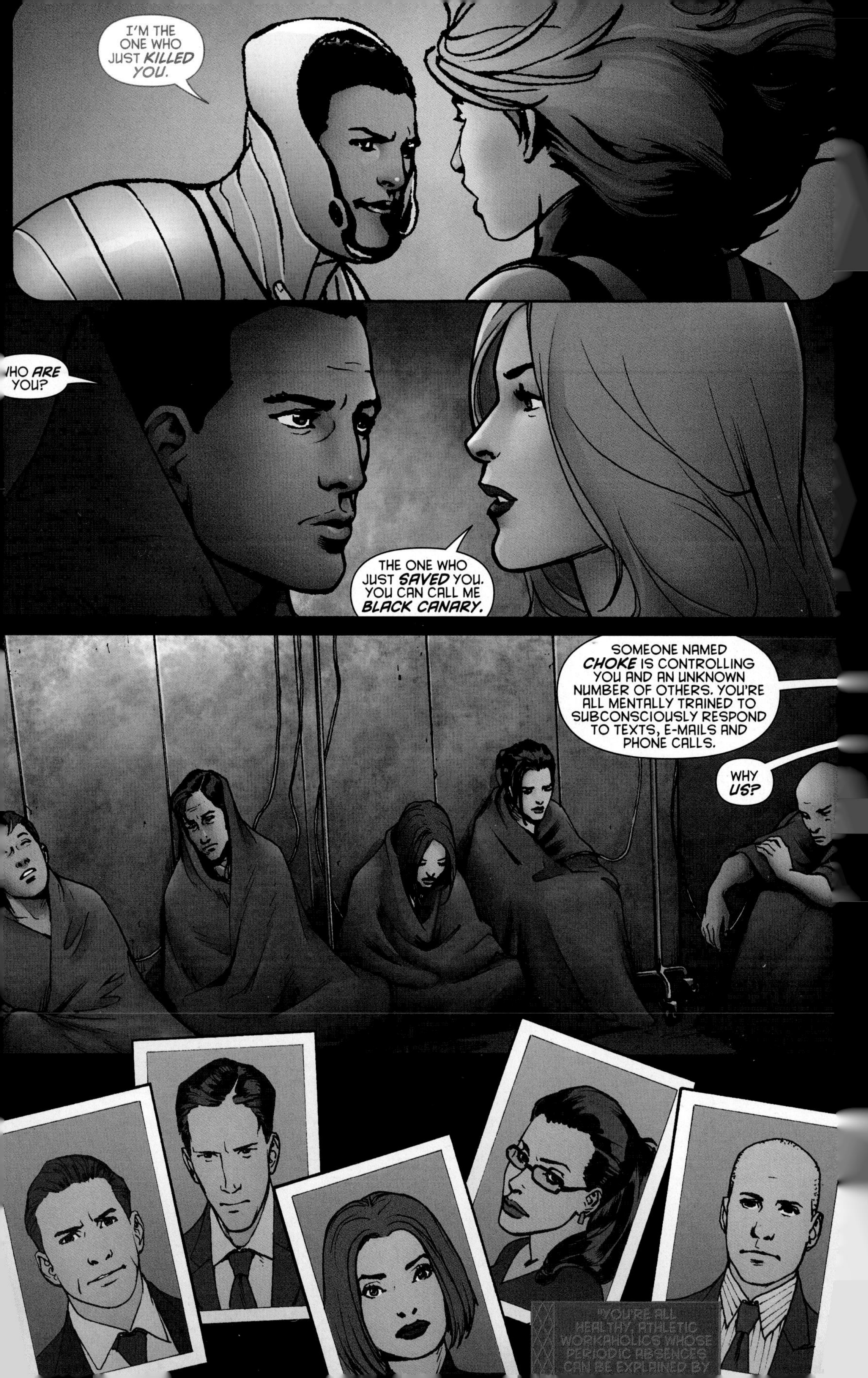
I'M THE ONE WHO JUST KILLED YOU.
WHO ARE YOU?
THE ONE WHO JUST SAVED YOU. YOU CAN CALL ME BLACK CANARY.
SOMEONE NAMED CHOKE IS CONTROLLING YOU AND AN UNKNOWN NUMBER OF OTHERS. YOU'RE ALL MENTALLY TRAINED TO SUBCONSCIOUSLY RESPOND TO TEXTS, E-MAILS AND PHONE CALLS.
WHY US?
"YOU'RE ALL HEALTHY, ATHLETIC WORKAHOLICS WHOSE PERIODIC ABSENCES CAN BE EXPLAINED BY

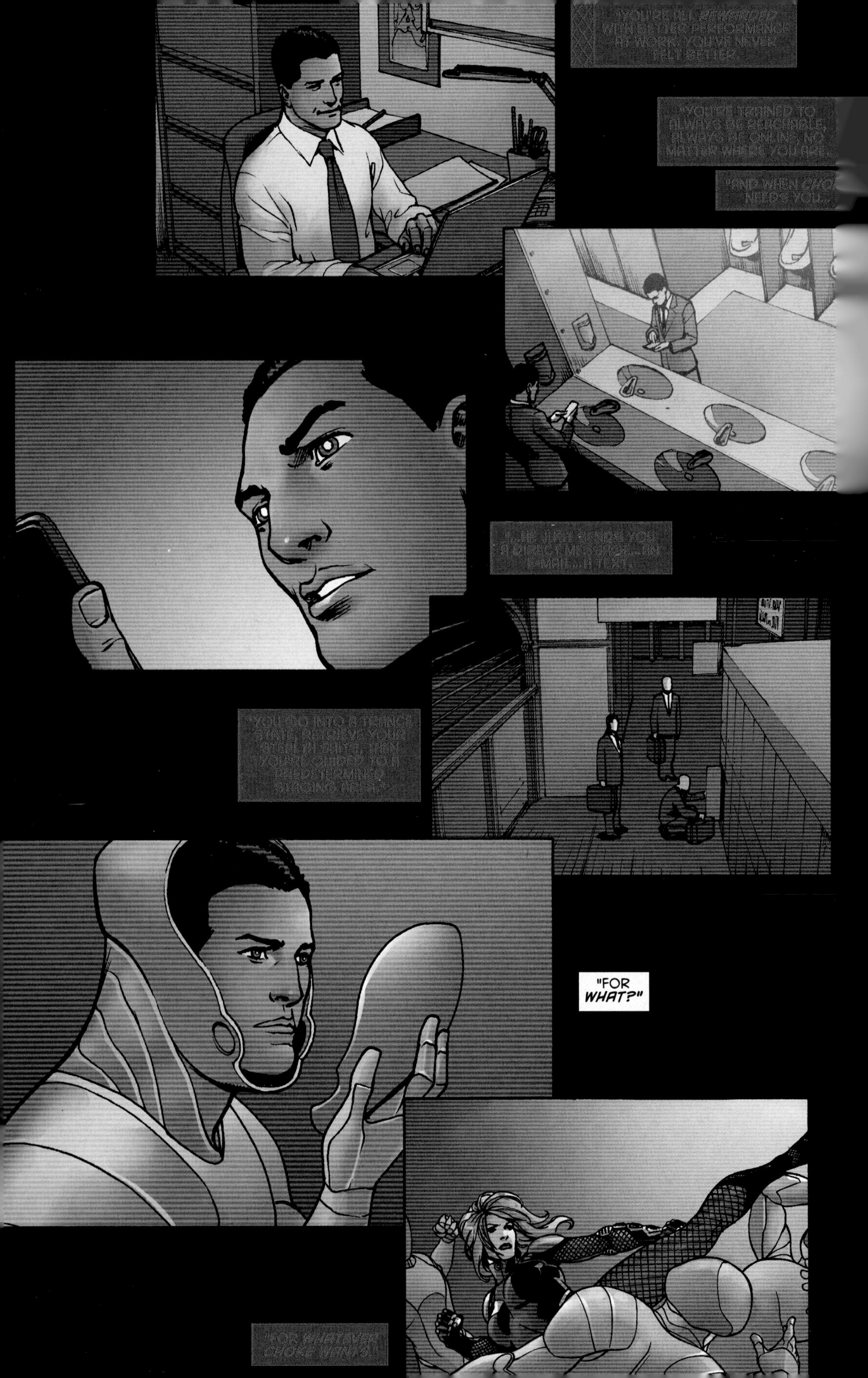
"YOU'RE ALL ENERGIZED WITH BETTER PERFORMANCE AT WORK. YOU'VE NEVER FELT BETTER.
"YOU'RE TRAINED TO ALWAYS BE REACHABLE, ALWAYS BE ONLINE, NO MATTER WHERE YOU ARE.
"AND WHEN CHO
NEEDS YOU...
"...HE JUST SENDS YOU A DIRECT MESSAGE...AN EMAIL...A TEXT.
"YOU GO INTO A TRANCE STATE, RETRIEVE YOUR SUIT...
"FOR WHAT?"
"FOR WHATEVER CHOKE WANTS!"

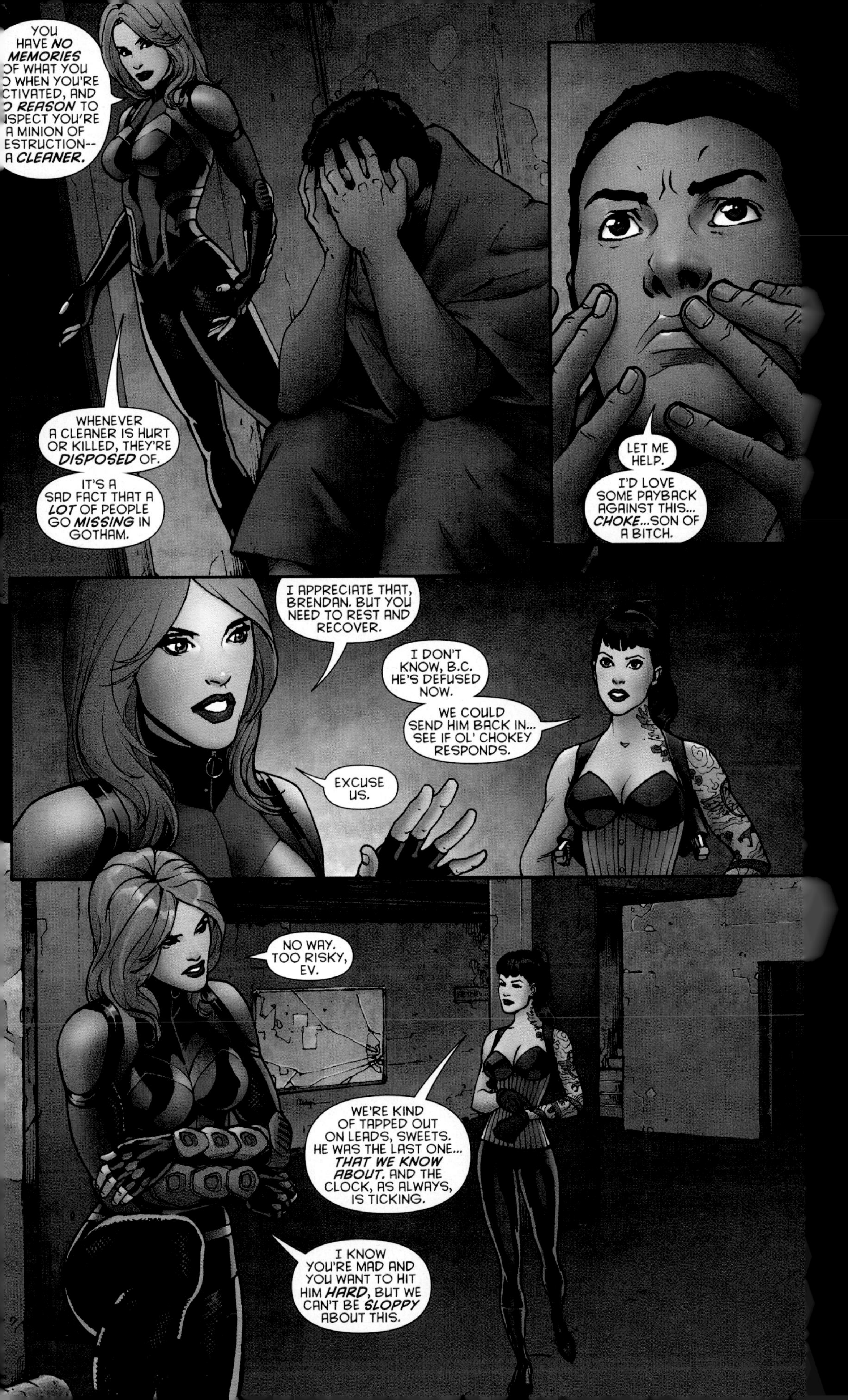
YOU HAVE NO MEMORIES OF WHAT YOU O WHEN YOU'RE CTIVATED, AND O REASON TO JSPECT YOU'RE A MINION OF ESTRUCTION-- A CLEANER.
WHENEVER A CLEANER IS HURT OR KILLED, THEY'RE DISPOSED OF.
IT'S A SAD FACT THAT A LOT OF PEOPLE GO MISSING IN GOTHAM.
LET ME HELP.
I'D LOVE SOME PAYBACK AGAINST THIS... CHOKE...SON OF A BITCH.
I APPRECIATE THAT, BRENDAN. BUT YOU NEED TO REST AND RECOVER.
I DON'T KNOW, B.C. HE'S DEFUSED NOW.
WE COULD SEND HIM BACK IN... SEE IF OL' CHOKEY RESPONDS.
EXCUSE US.
NO WAY. TOO RISKY, EV.
WE'RE KIND OF TAPPED OUT ON LEADS, SWEETS. HE WAS THE LAST ONE... THAT WE KNOW ABOUT. AND THE CLOCK, AS ALWAYS, IS TICKING.
I KNOW YOU'RE MAD AND YOU WANT TO HIT HIM HARD, BUT WE CAN'T BE SLOPPY ABOUT THIS.

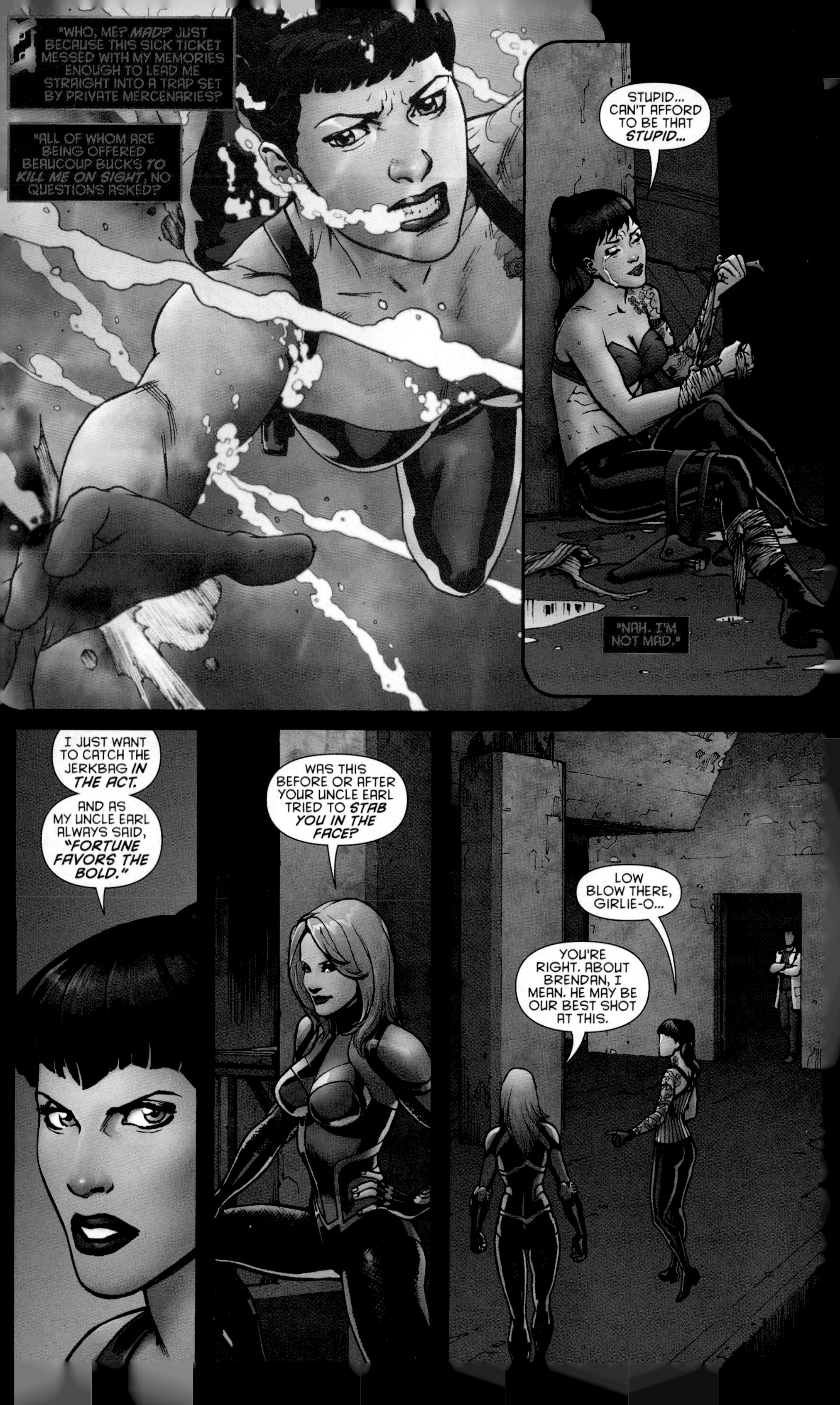
"WHO, ME? MAD? JUST BECAUSE THIS SICK TICKET MESSED WITH MY MEMORIES ENOUGH TO LEAD ME STRAIGHT INTO A TRAP SET BY PRIVATE MERCENARIES?
"ALL OF WHOM ARE BEING OFFERED BEAUCOUP BUCKS TO KILL ME ON SIGHT, NO QUESTIONS ASKED?
STUPID... CAN'T AFFORD TO BE THAT STUPID...
"NAH. I'M NOT MAD."
I JUST WANT TO CATCH THE JERKBAG IN THE ACT.
AND AS MY UNCLE EARL ALWAYS SAID, "FORTUNE FAVORS THE BOLD."
WAS THIS BEFORE OR AFTER YOUR UNCLE EARL TRIED TO STAB YOU IN THE FACE?
LOW BLOW THERE, GIRLIE-O...
YOU'RE RIGHT. ABOUT BRENDAN, I MEAN. HE MAY BE OUR BEST SHOT AT THIS.

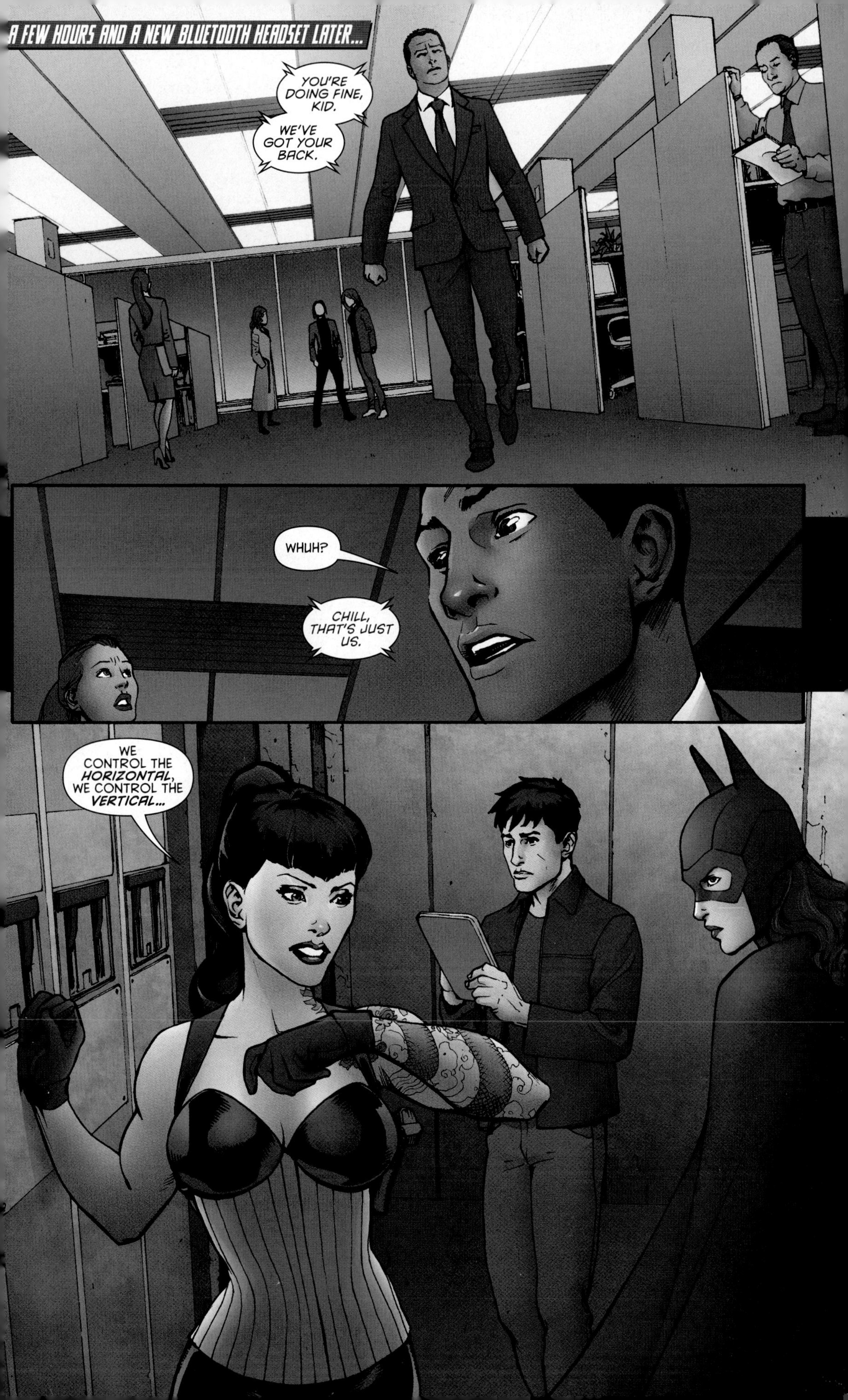
A FEW HOURS AND A NEW BLUETOOTH HEADSET LATER...
YOU'RE DOING FINE, KID.
WE'VE GOT YOUR BACK.
WHUH?
CHILL, THAT'S JUST US.
WE CONTROL THE *HORIZONTAL*, WE CONTROL THE *VERTICAL*...

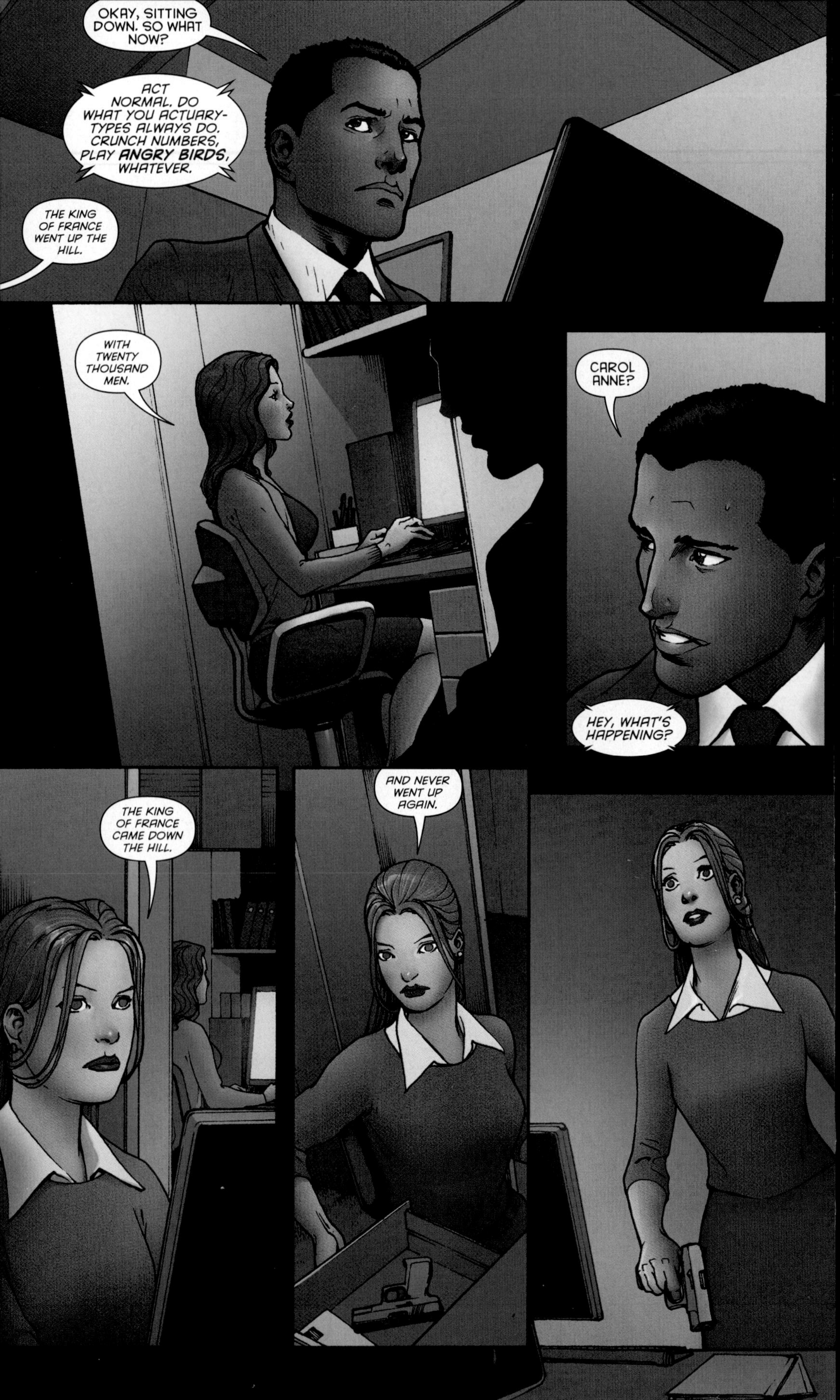
OKAY, SITTING DOWN. SO WHAT NOW?
ACT NORMAL. DO WHAT YOU ACTUARY-TYPES ALWAYS DO. CRUNCH NUMBERS, PLAY **ANGRY BIRDS**, WHATEVER.
THE KING OF FRANCE WENT UP THE HILL.
WITH TWENTY THOUSAND MEN.
CAROL ANNE?
HEY, WHAT'S HAPPENING?
THE KING OF FRANCE CAME DOWN THE HILL.
AND NEVER WENT UP AGAIN.

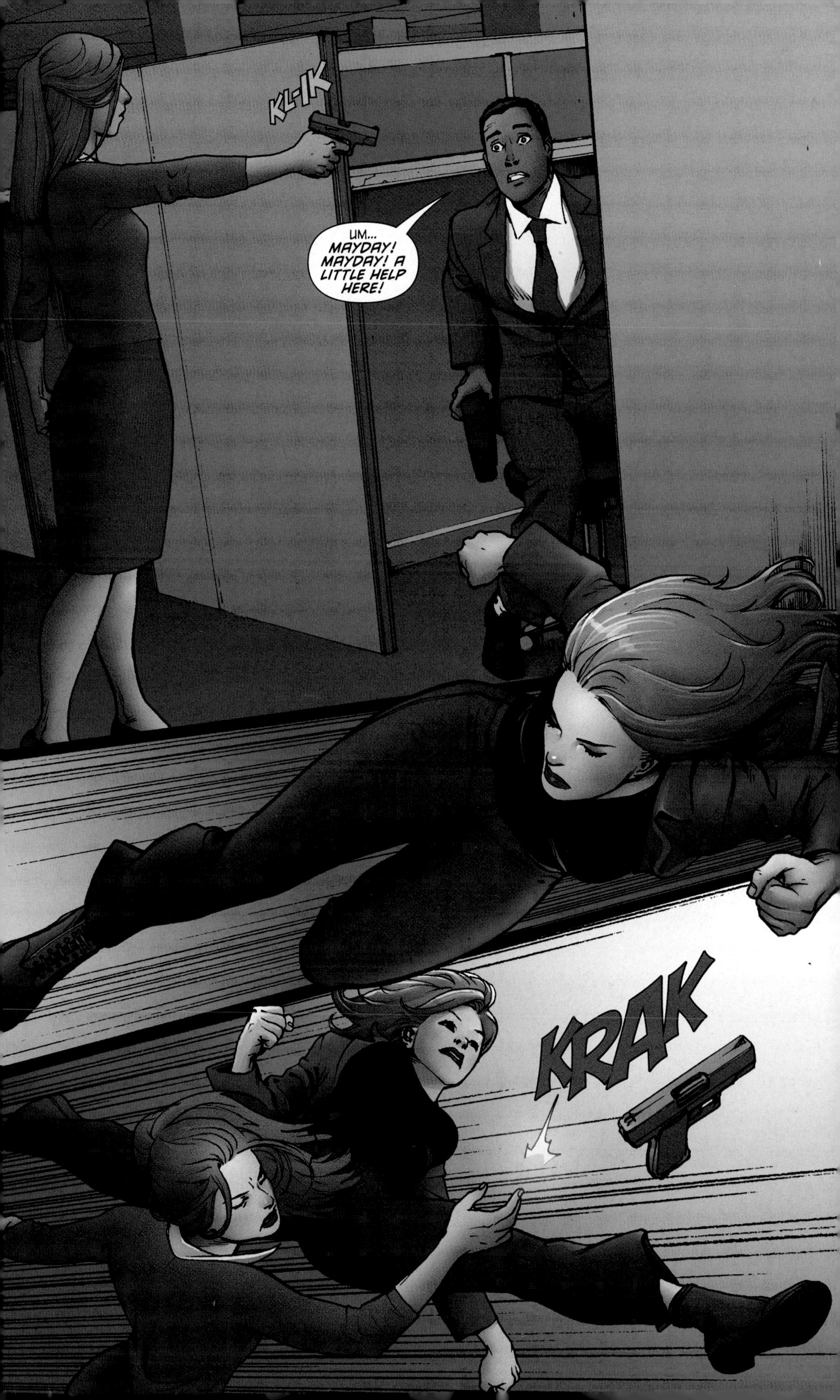
KL-IK
UM... MAYDAY! MAYDAY! A LITTLE HELP HERE!
KRAK

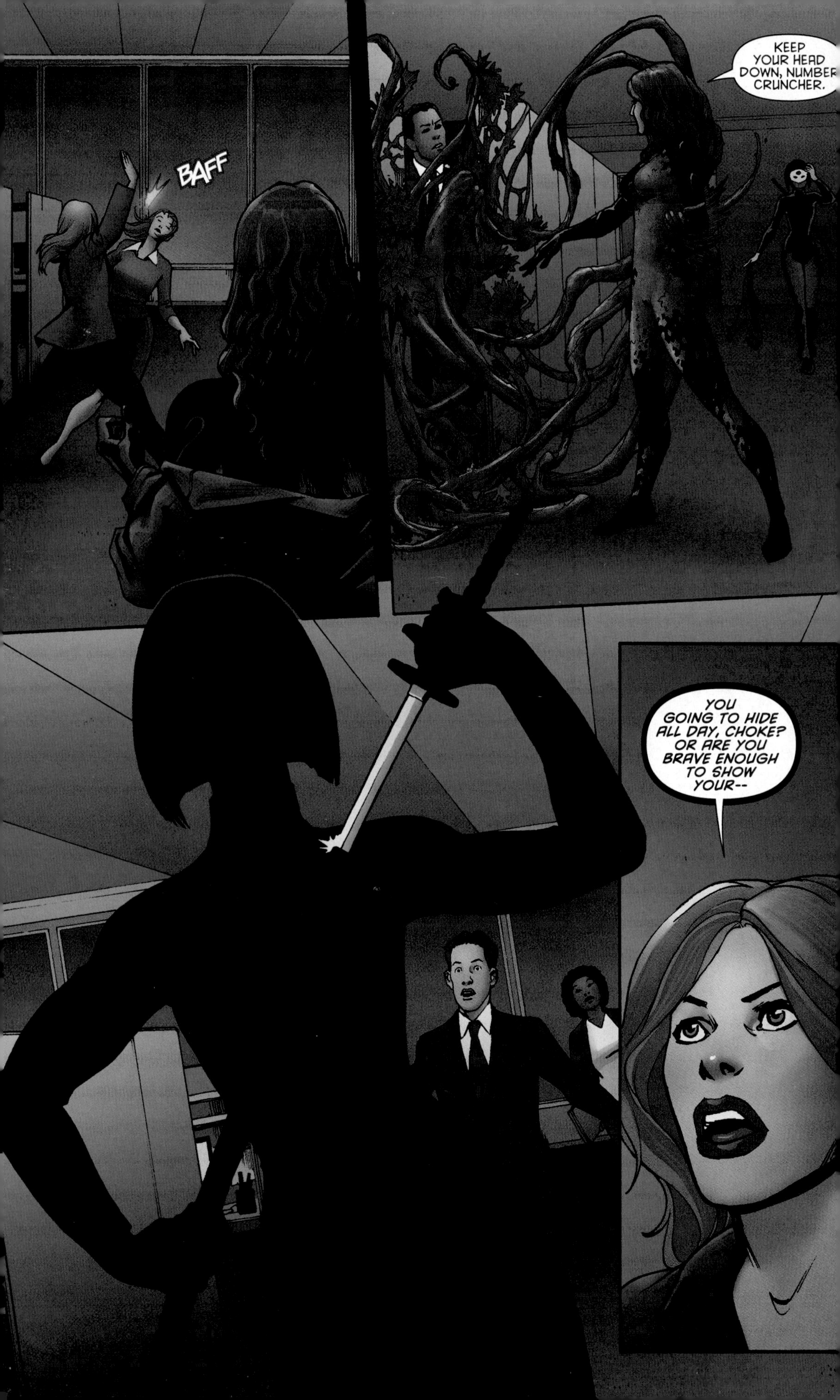
BAFF
KEEP YOUR HEAD DOWN, NUMBER CRUNCHER.
YOU GOING TO HIDE ALL DAY, CHOKE? OR ARE YOU BRAVE ENOUGH TO SHOW YOUR--

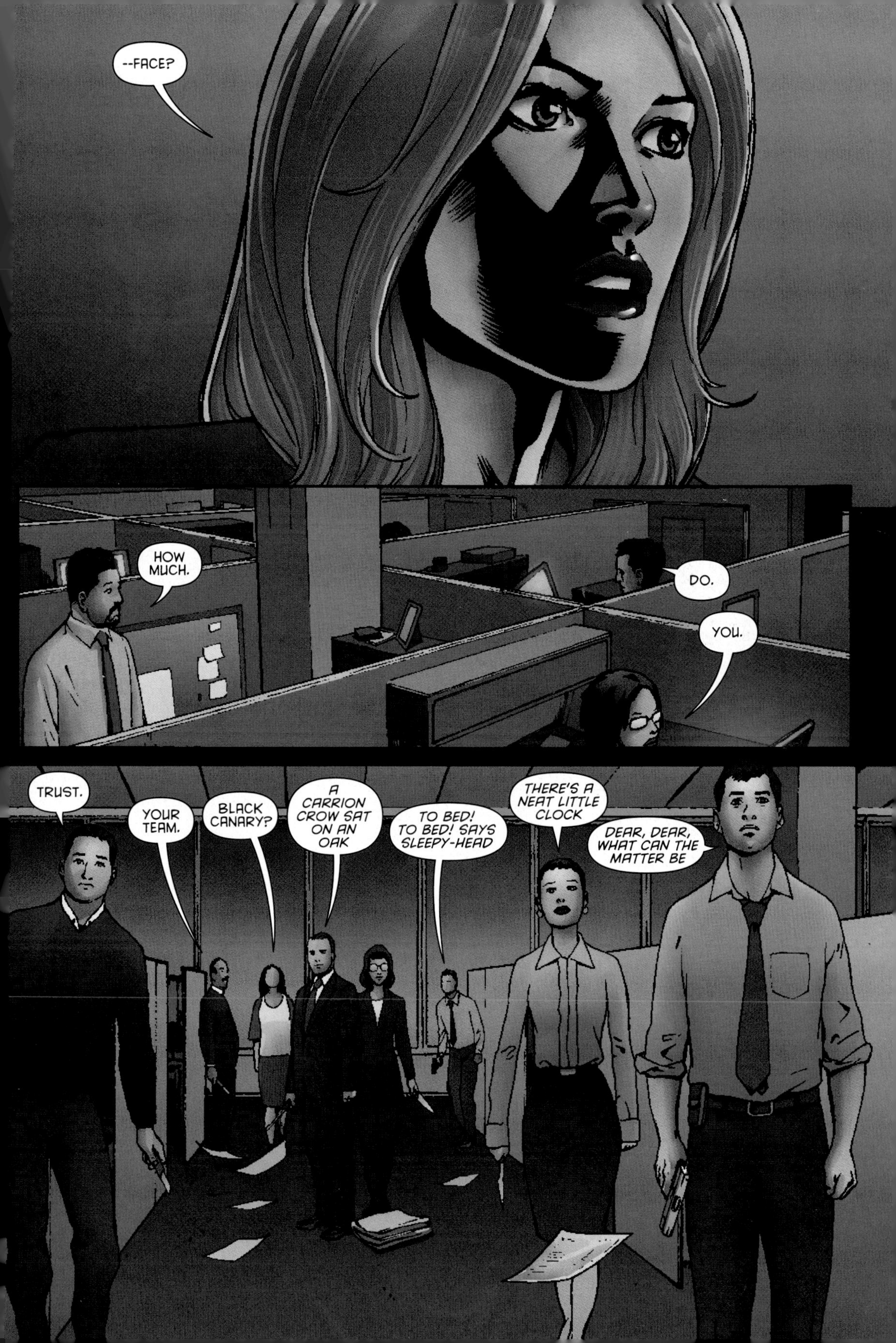
--FACE?
HOW MUCH.
DO.
YOU.
TRUST.
YOUR TEAM.
BLACK CANARY?
A CARRION CROW SAT ON AN OAK
TO BED! TO BED! SAYS SLEEPY-HEAD
THERE'S A NEAT LITTLE CLOCK
DEAR, DEAR, WHAT CAN THE MATTER BE

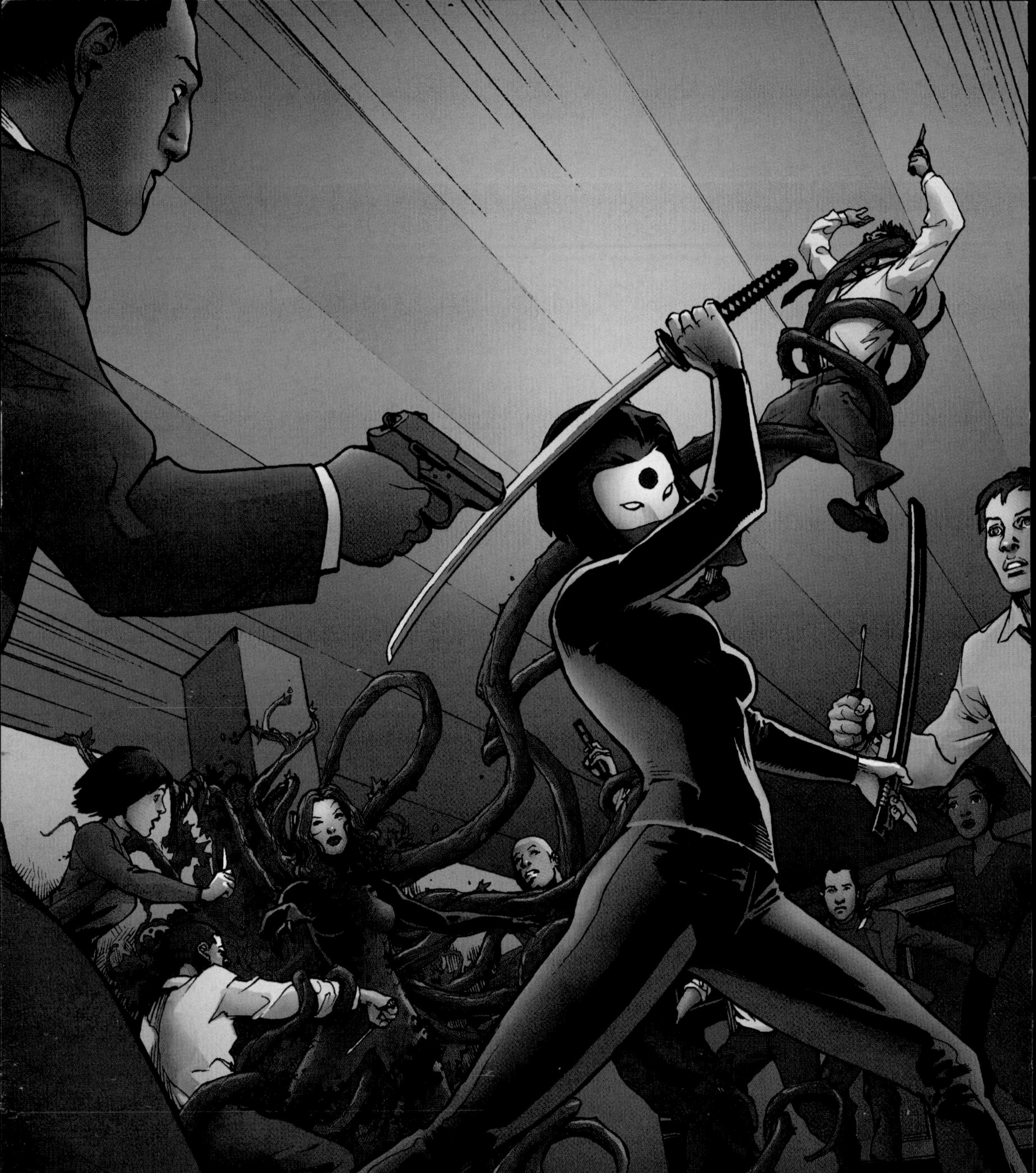

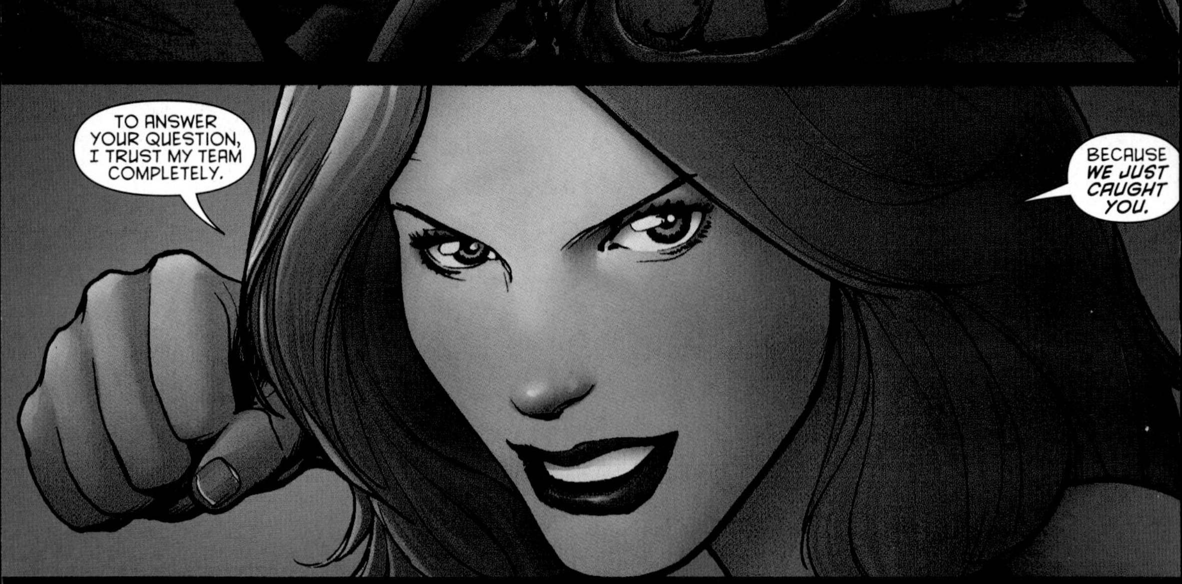
TO ANSWER YOUR QUESTION, I TRUST MY TEAM COMPLETELY.
BECAUSE WE JUST CAUGHT YOU.

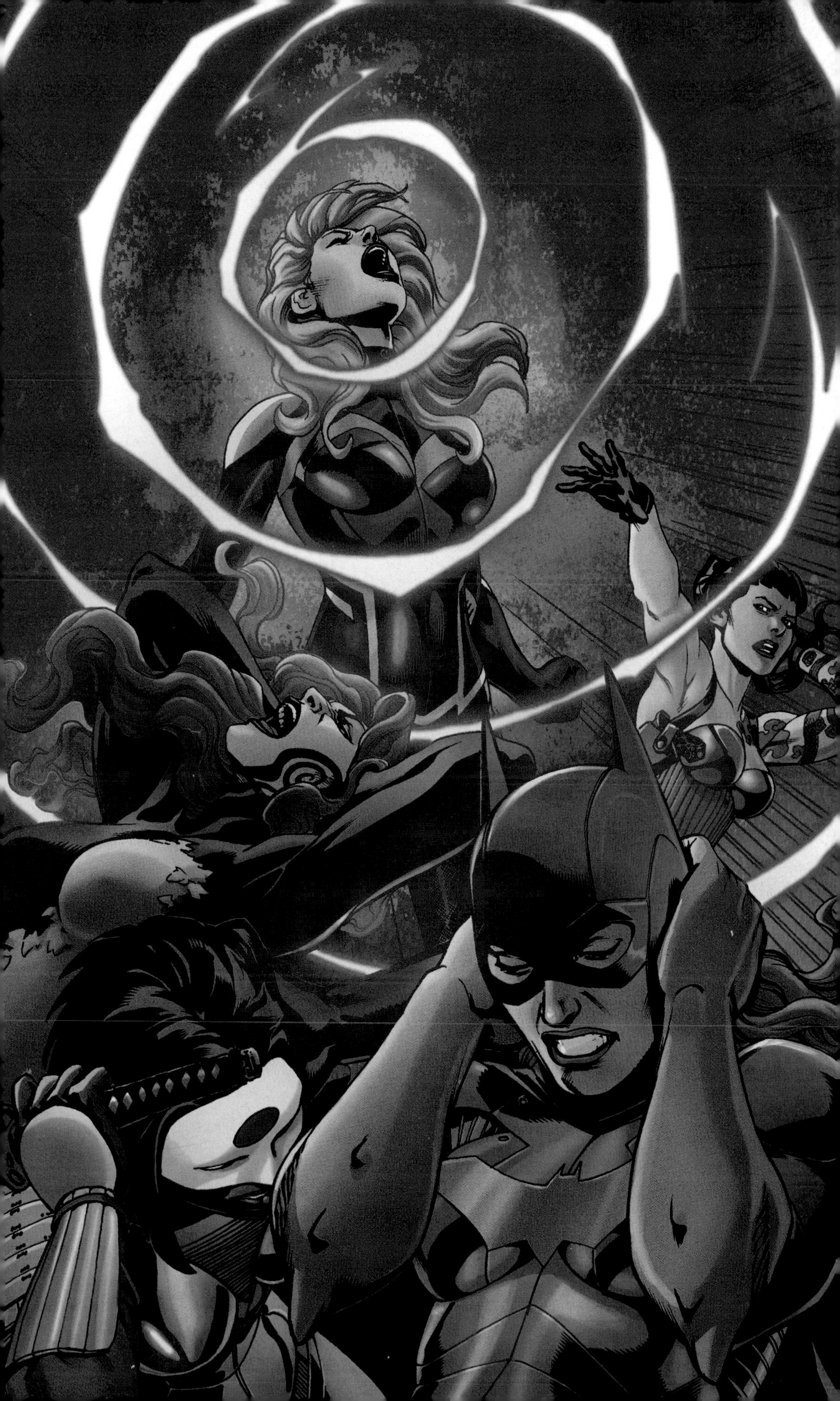

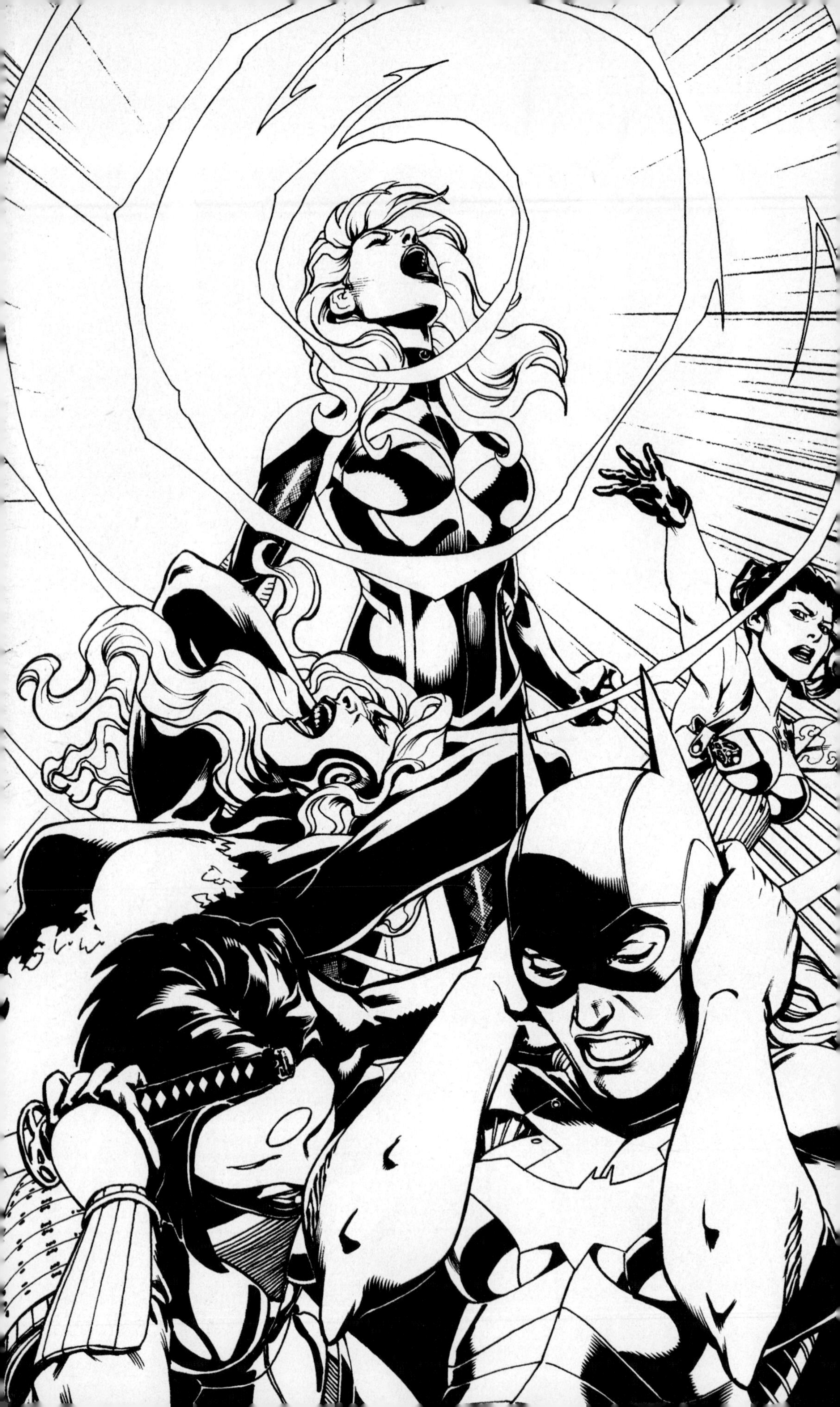

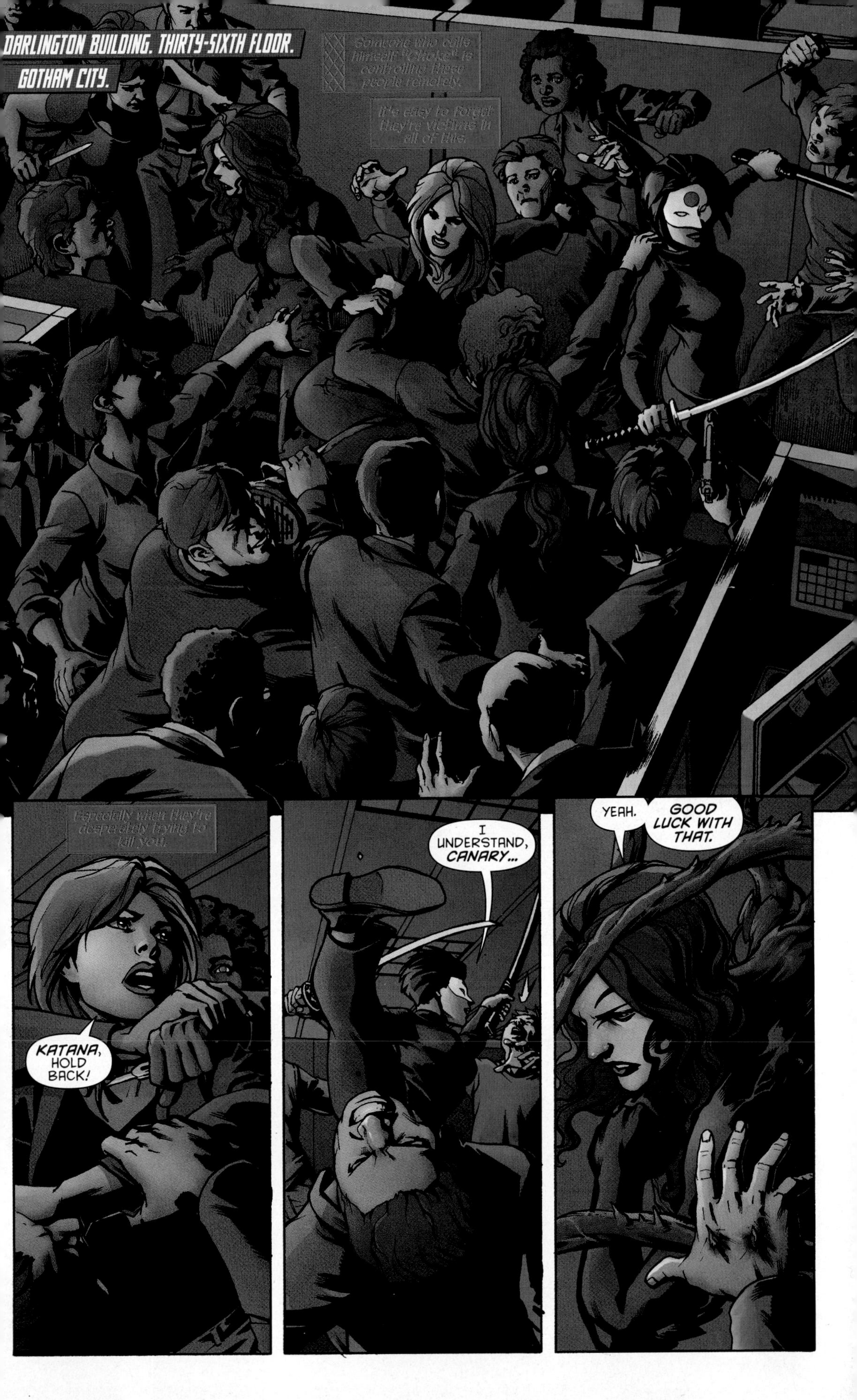
DARLINGTON BUILDING. THIRTY-SIXTH FLOOR.
GOTHAM CITY.
Someone who calls himself "Choke" is controlling these people remotely.
It's easy to forget they're victims in all of this.
Especially when they're desperately trying to kill you.
KATANA, HOLD BACK!
I UNDERSTAND, CANARY...
YEAH.
GOOD LUCK WITH THAT.

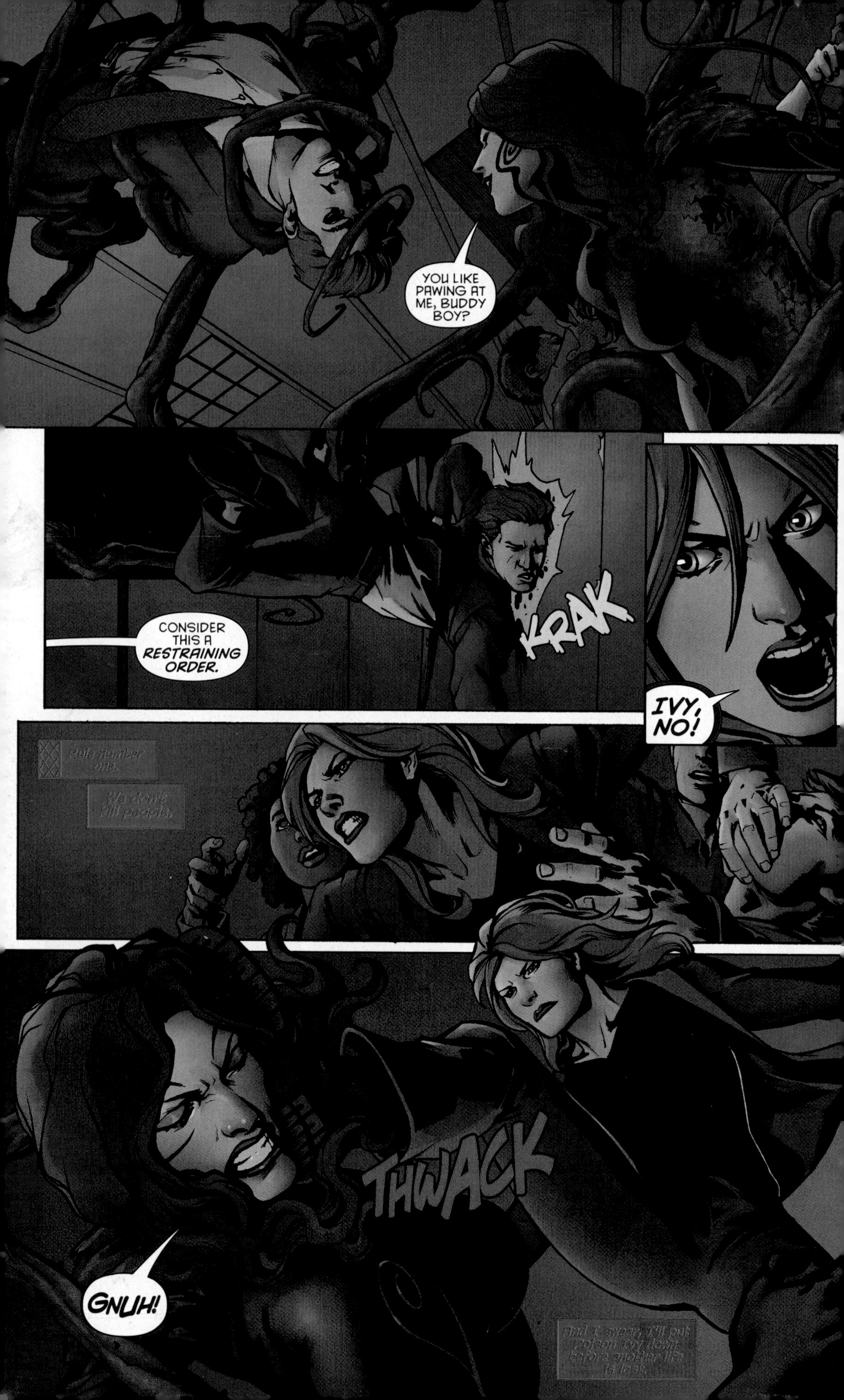
YOU LIKE PAWING AT ME, BUDDY BOY?
CONSIDER THIS A RESTRAINING ORDER.
KRAK
IVY, NO!
Rule number one.
We don't kill people.
THWACK
GNUH!
And I swear, I'll put Poison Ivy down before another life is lost.

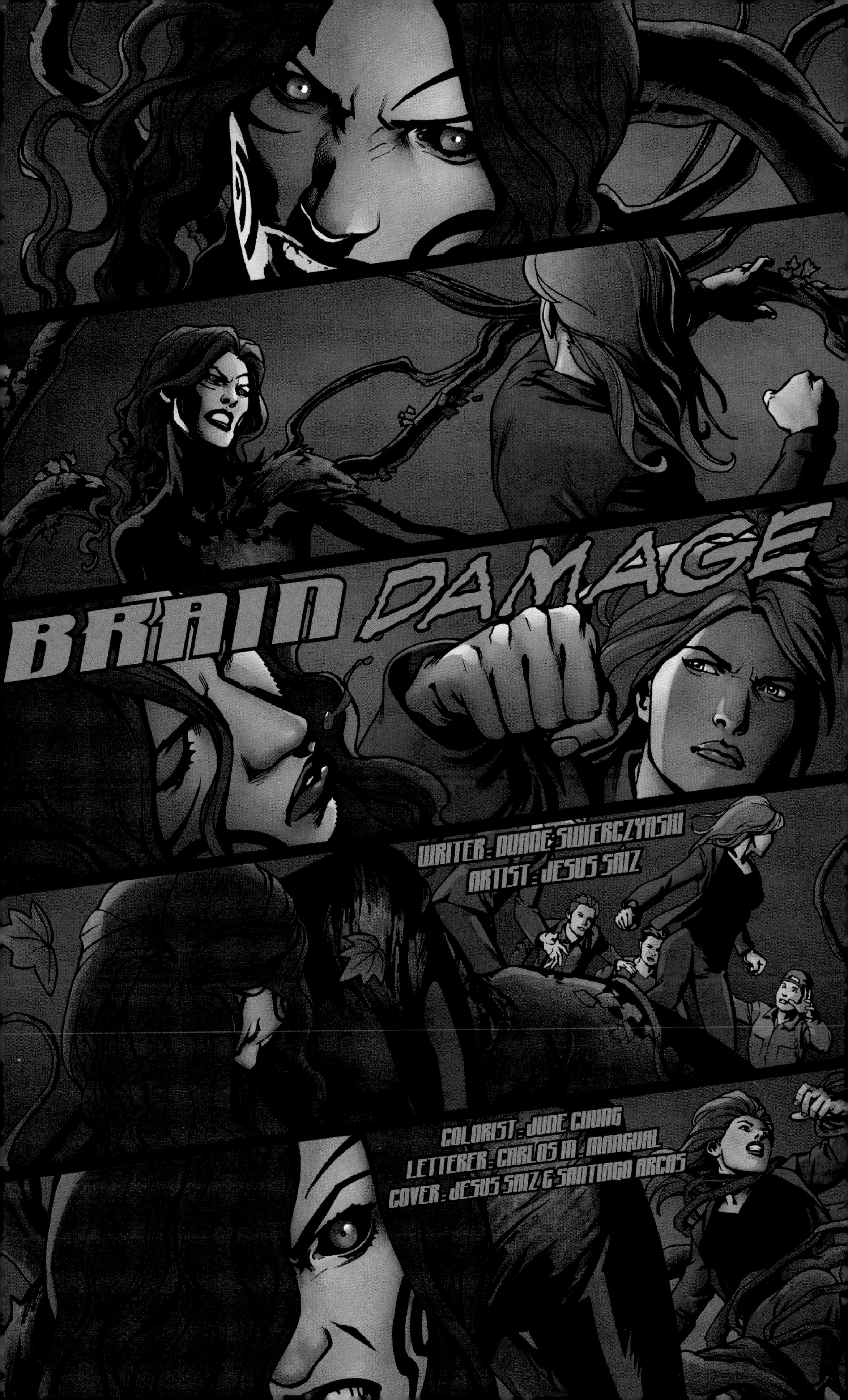
BRAIN DAMAGE
WRITER: DUANE SWIERCZYNSKI
ARTIST: JESUS SAIZ
COLORIST: JUNE CHUNG
LETTERER: CARLOS M. MANGUAL
COVER: JESUS SAIZ & SANTIAGO ARCAS

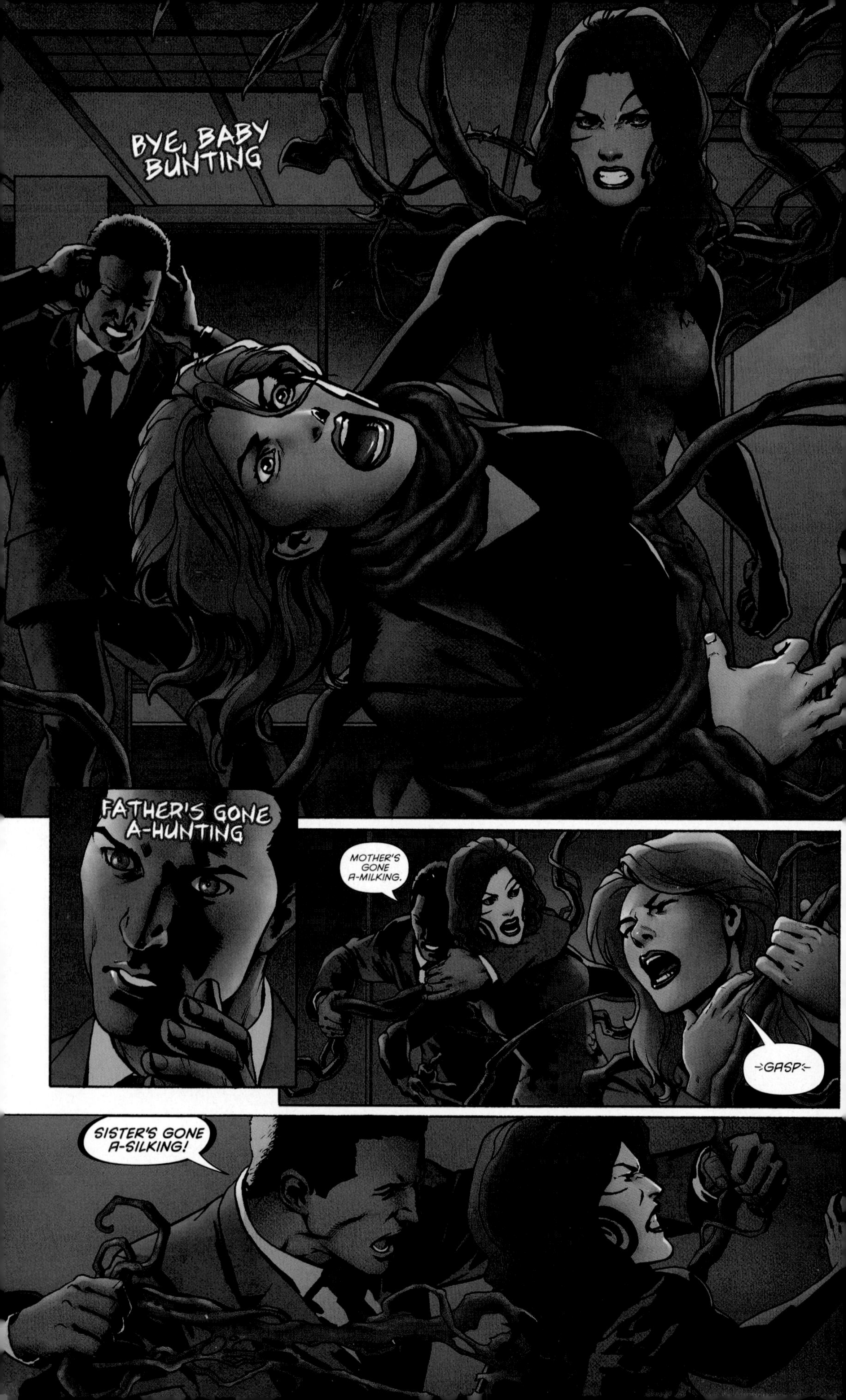
BYE, BABY BUNTING
FATHER'S GONE A-HUNTING
MOTHER'S GONE A-MILKING.
-GASP-
SISTER'S GONE A-SILKING!

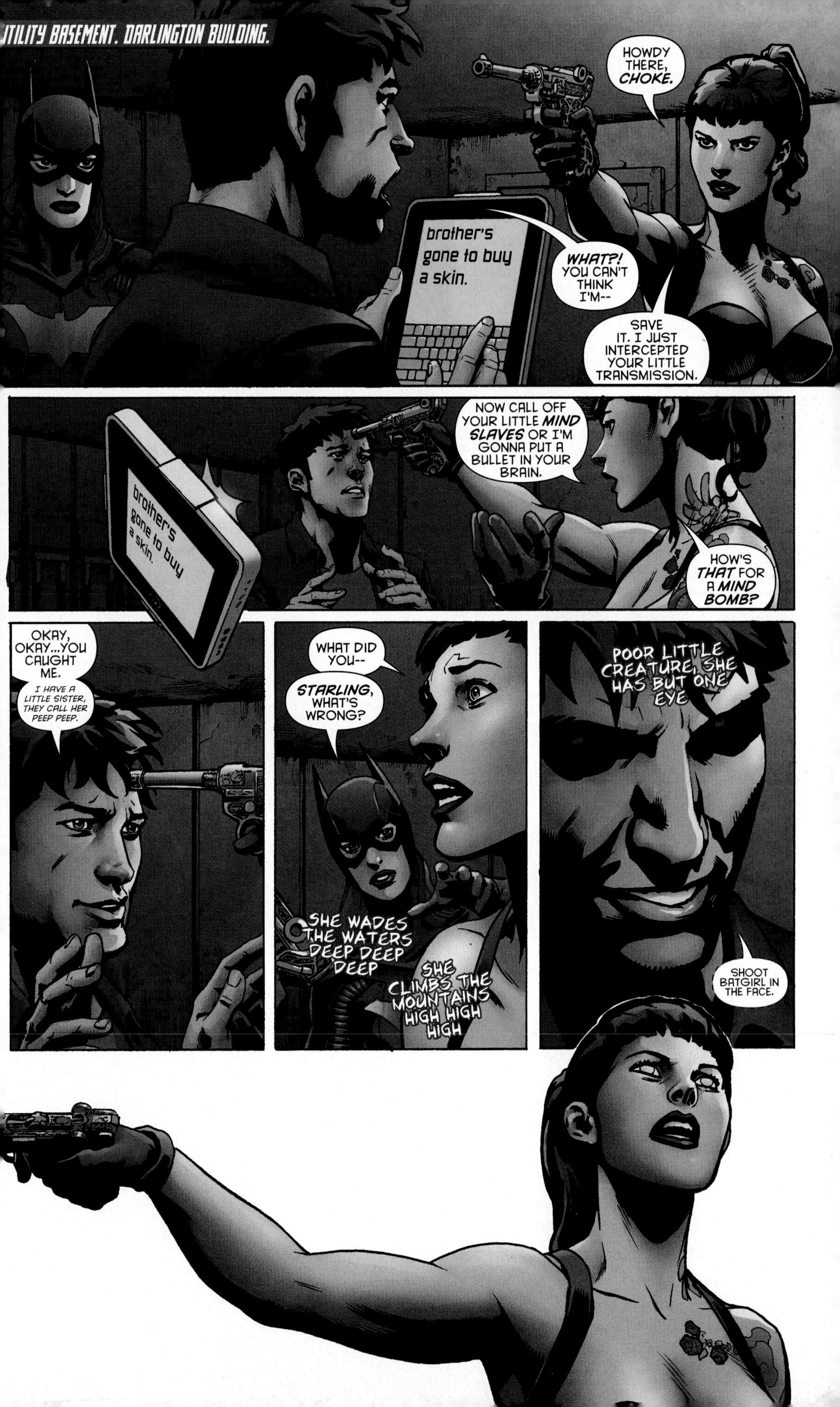

UTILITY BASEMENT. DARLINGTON BUILDING.
HOWDY THERE, CHOKE.
brother's gone to buy a skin.
WHAT?! YOU CAN'T THINK I'M--
SAVE IT. I JUST INTERCEPTED YOUR LITTLE TRANSMISSION.
brother's gone to buy a skin.
NOW CALL OFF YOUR LITTLE MIND SLAVES OR I'M GONNA PUT A BULLET IN YOUR BRAIN.
HOW'S THAT FOR A MIND BOMB?
OKAY, OKAY...YOU CAUGHT ME.
I HAVE A LITTLE SISTER, THEY CALL HER PEEP PEEP.
WHAT DID YOU--
STARLING, WHAT'S WRONG?
SHE WADES THE WATERS DEEP DEEP DEEP
SHE CLIMBS THE MOUNTAINS HIGH HIGH HIGH
POOR LITTLE CREATURE, SHE HAS BUT ONE EYE
SHOOT BATGIRL IN THE FACE.

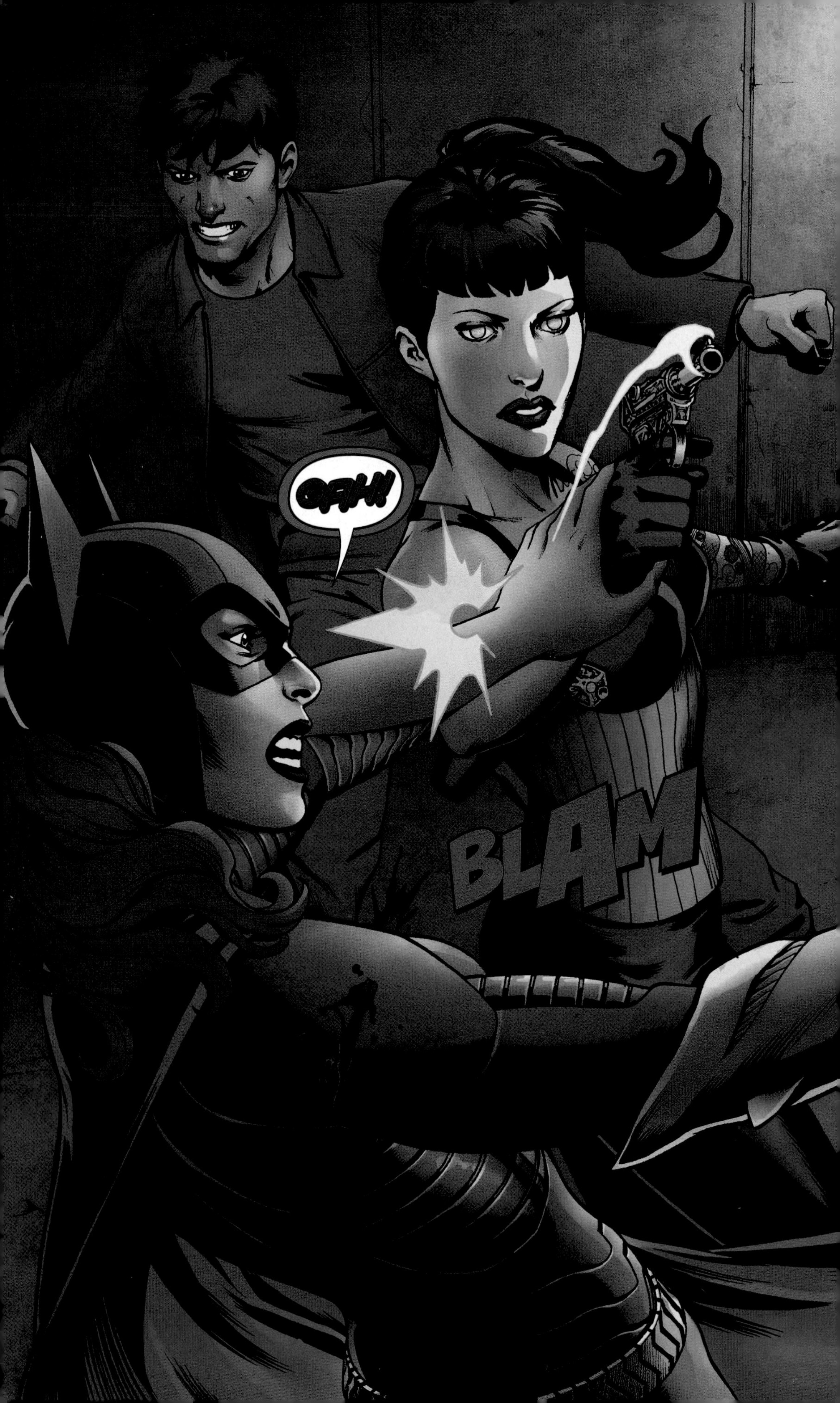
OFH!
BLAM

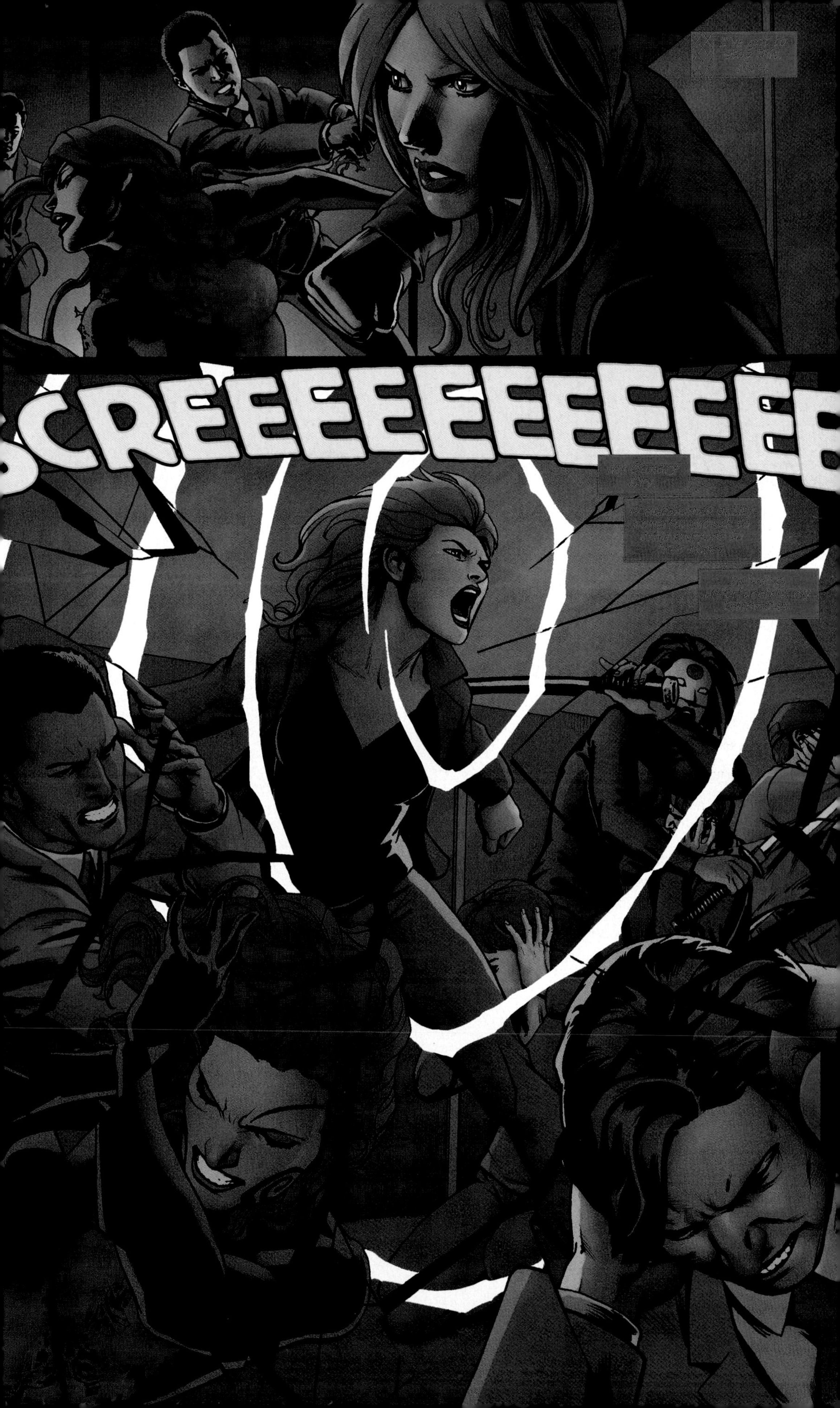
SCREEEEEEEEEEEE

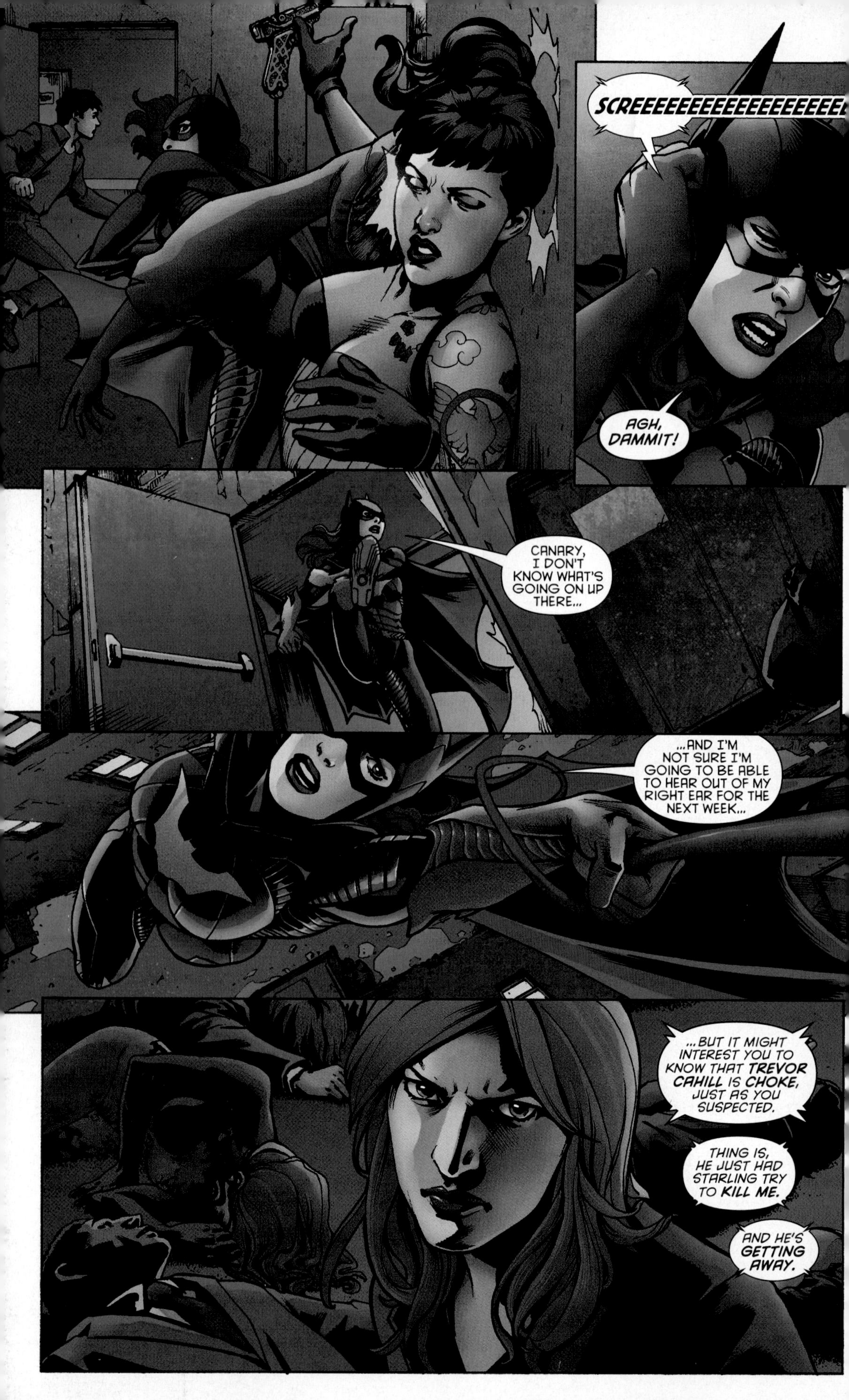

SCREEEEEEEEEEEEEEEEEE
AGH, DAMMIT!
CANARY, I DON'T KNOW WHAT'S GOING ON UP THERE...
...AND I'M NOT SURE I'M GOING TO BE ABLE TO HEAR OUT OF MY RIGHT EAR FOR THE NEXT WEEK...
...BUT IT MIGHT INTEREST YOU TO KNOW THAT TREVOR CAHILL IS CHOKE, JUST AS YOU SUSPECTED.
THING IS, HE JUST HAD STARLING TRY TO KILL ME.
AND HE'S GETTING AWAY.

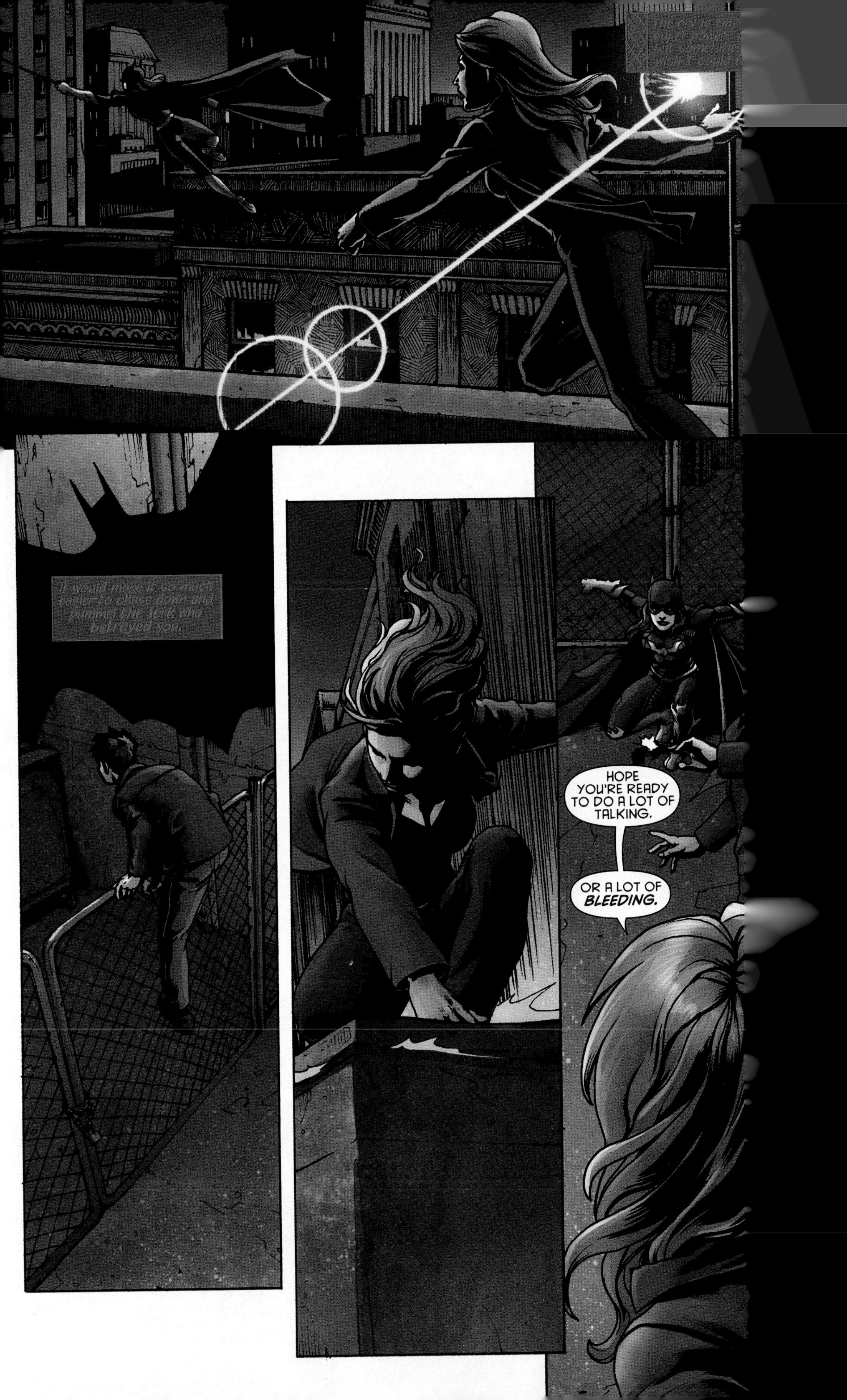
The city is
super
but
wish I could
It would make it so much easier to chase down and pummel the jerk who betrayed you.
HOPE YOU'RE READY TO DO A LOT OF TALKING.
OR A LOT OF *BLEEDING.*

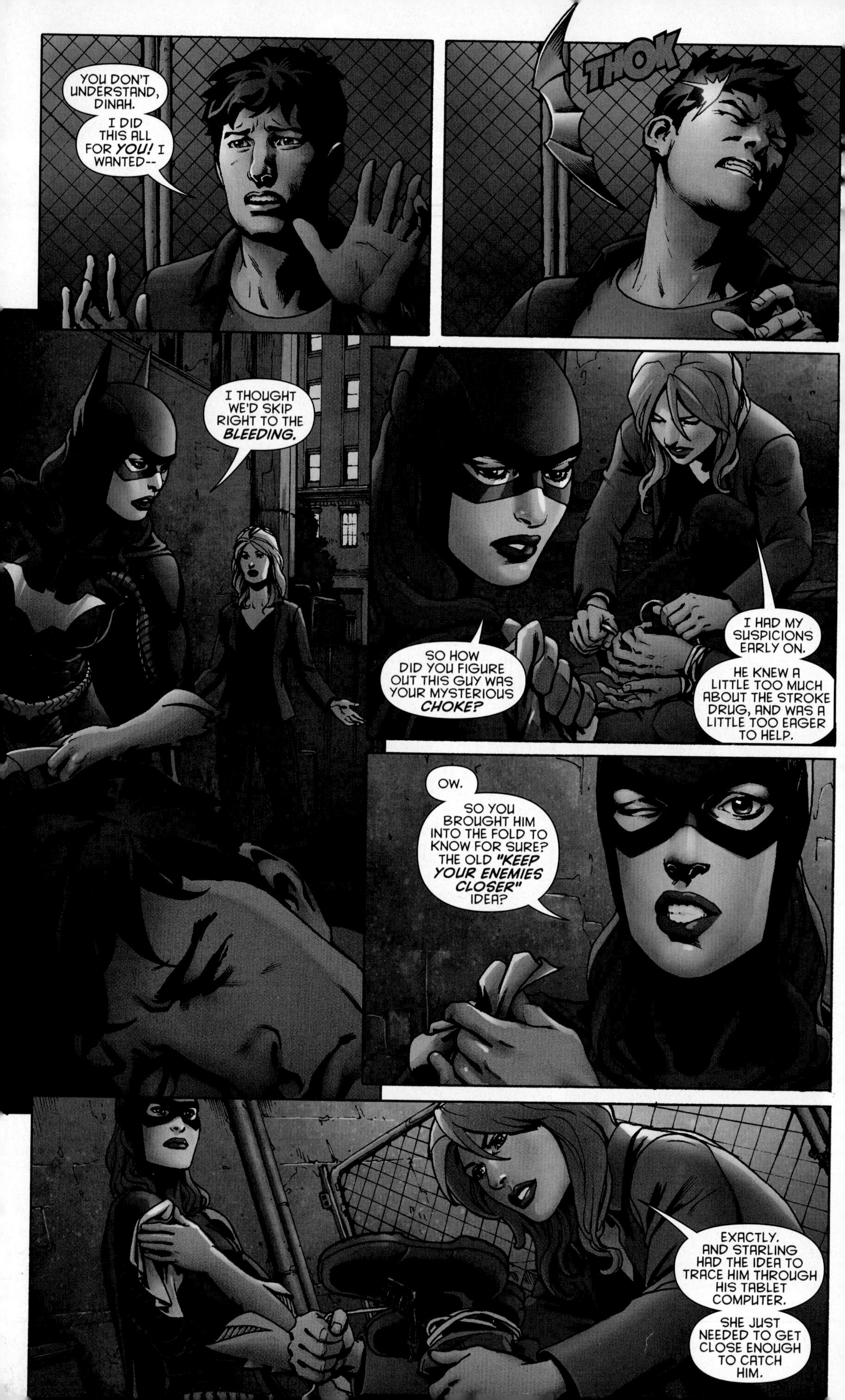
YOU DON'T UNDERSTAND, DINAH.
I DID THIS ALL FOR YOU! I WANTED--
THOK
I THOUGHT WE'D SKIP RIGHT TO THE BLEEDING.
SO HOW DID YOU FIGURE OUT THIS GUY WAS YOUR MYSTERIOUS CHOKE?
I HAD MY SUSPICIONS EARLY ON.
HE KNEW A LITTLE TOO MUCH ABOUT THE STROKE DRUG, AND WAS A LITTLE TOO EAGER TO HELP.
OW.
SO YOU BROUGHT HIM INTO THE FOLD TO KNOW FOR SURE? THE OLD "KEEP YOUR ENEMIES CLOSER" IDEA?
EXACTLY. AND STARLING HAD THE IDEA TO TRACE HIM THROUGH HIS TABLET COMPUTER.
SHE JUST NEEDED TO GET CLOSE ENOUGH TO CATCH HIM.

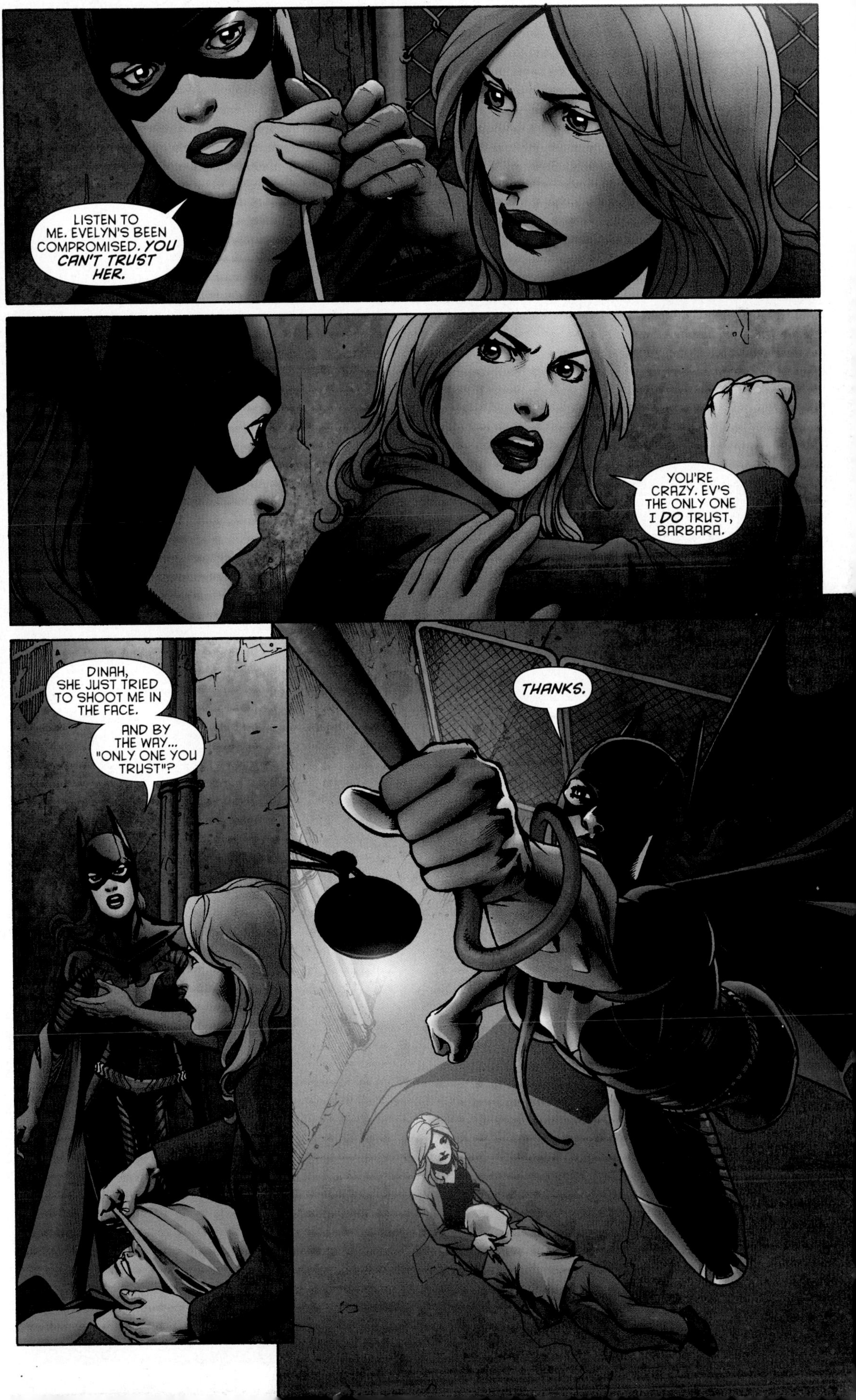

LISTEN TO ME. EVELYN'S BEEN COMPROMISED. *YOU CAN'T TRUST HER.*
YOU'RE CRAZY. EV'S THE ONLY ONE I *DO* TRUST, BARBARA.
DINAH, SHE JUST TRIED TO SHOOT ME IN THE FACE.
AND BY THE WAY... "ONLY ONE YOU TRUST"?
THANKS.

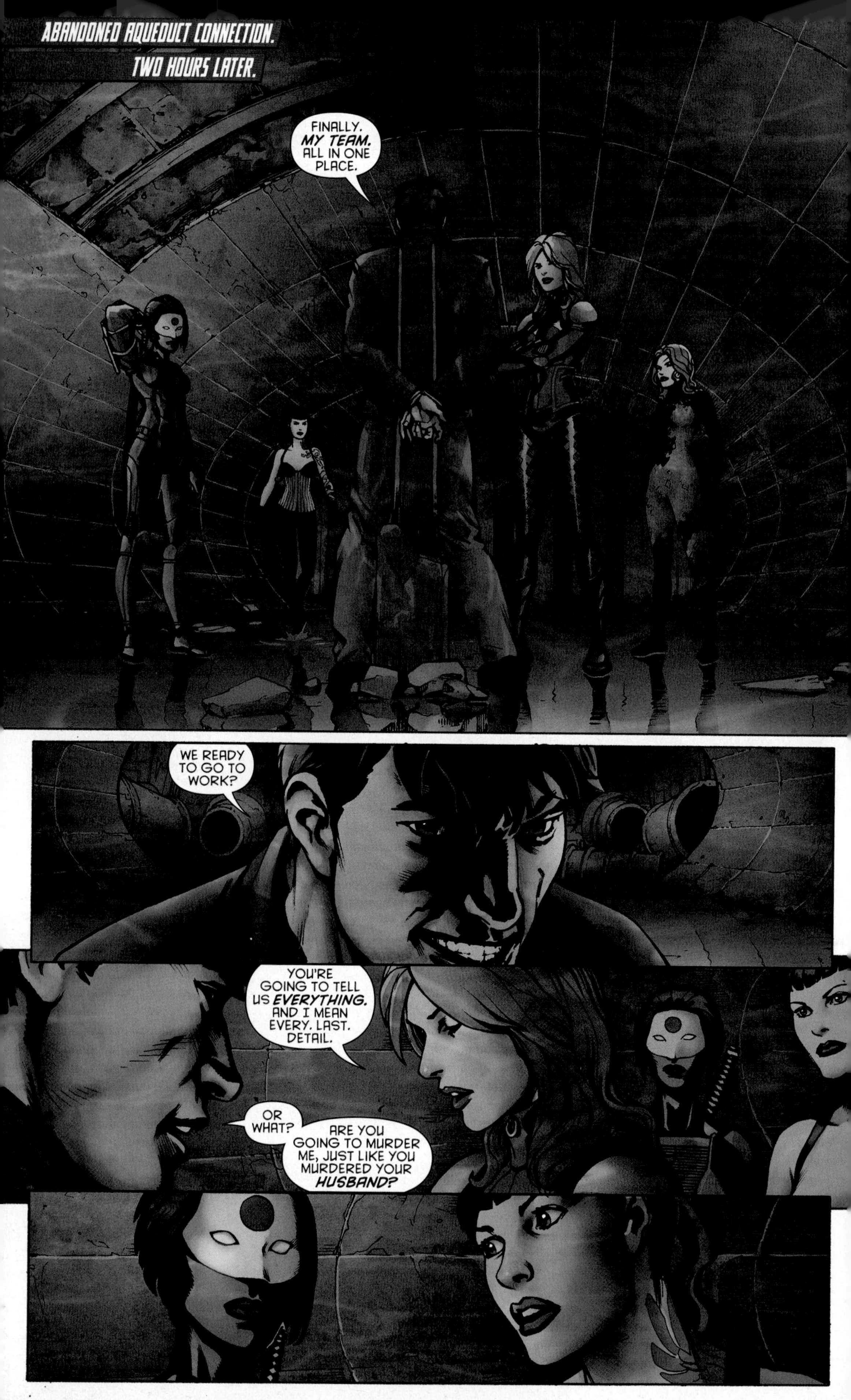
ABANDONED AQUEDUCT CONNECTION.
TWO HOURS LATER.
FINALLY. *MY TEAM.* ALL IN ONE PLACE.
WE READY TO GO TO WORK?
YOU'RE GOING TO TELL US *EVERYTHING.* AND I MEAN EVERY. LAST. DETAIL.
OR WHAT?
ARE YOU GOING TO MURDER ME, JUST LIKE YOU MURDERED YOUR *HUSBAND?*

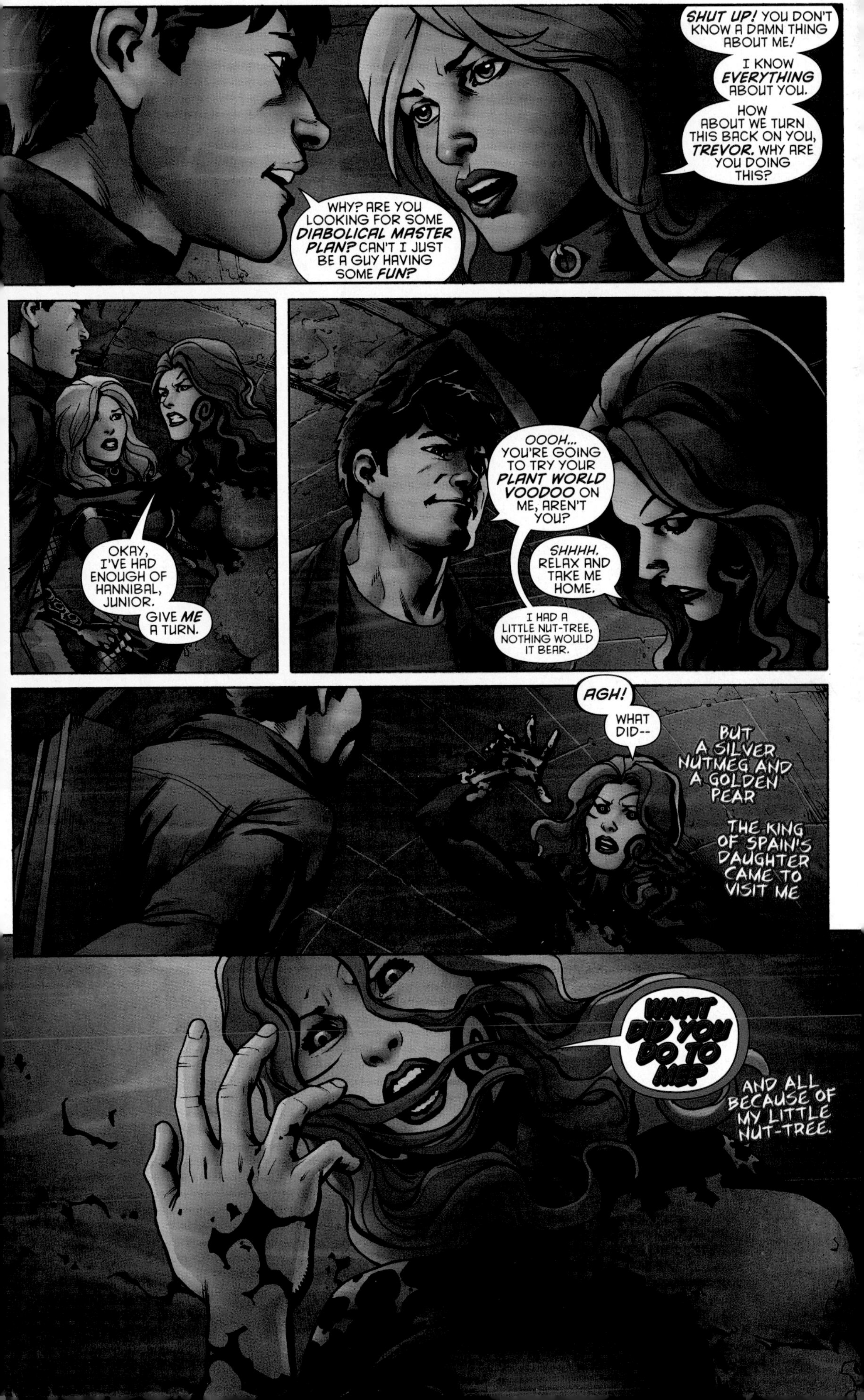

SHUT UP! YOU DON'T KNOW A DAMN THING ABOUT ME!
I KNOW EVERYTHING ABOUT YOU.
HOW ABOUT WE TURN THIS BACK ON YOU, TREVOR. WHY ARE YOU DOING THIS?
WHY? ARE YOU LOOKING FOR SOME DIABOLICAL MASTER PLAN? CAN'T I JUST BE A GUY HAVING SOME FUN?
OKAY, I'VE HAD ENOUGH OF HANNIBAL, JUNIOR.
GIVE ME A TURN.
OOOH... YOU'RE GOING TO TRY YOUR PLANT WORLD VOODOO ON ME, AREN'T YOU?
SHHHH. RELAX AND TAKE ME HOME.
I HAD A LITTLE NUT-TREE, NOTHING WOULD IT BEAR.
AGH!
WHAT DID--
BUT A SILVER NUTMEG AND A GOLDEN PEAR
THE KING OF SPAIN'S DAUGHTER CAME TO VISIT ME
WHAT DID YOU DO TO ME?
AND ALL BECAUSE OF MY LITTLE NUT-TREE.

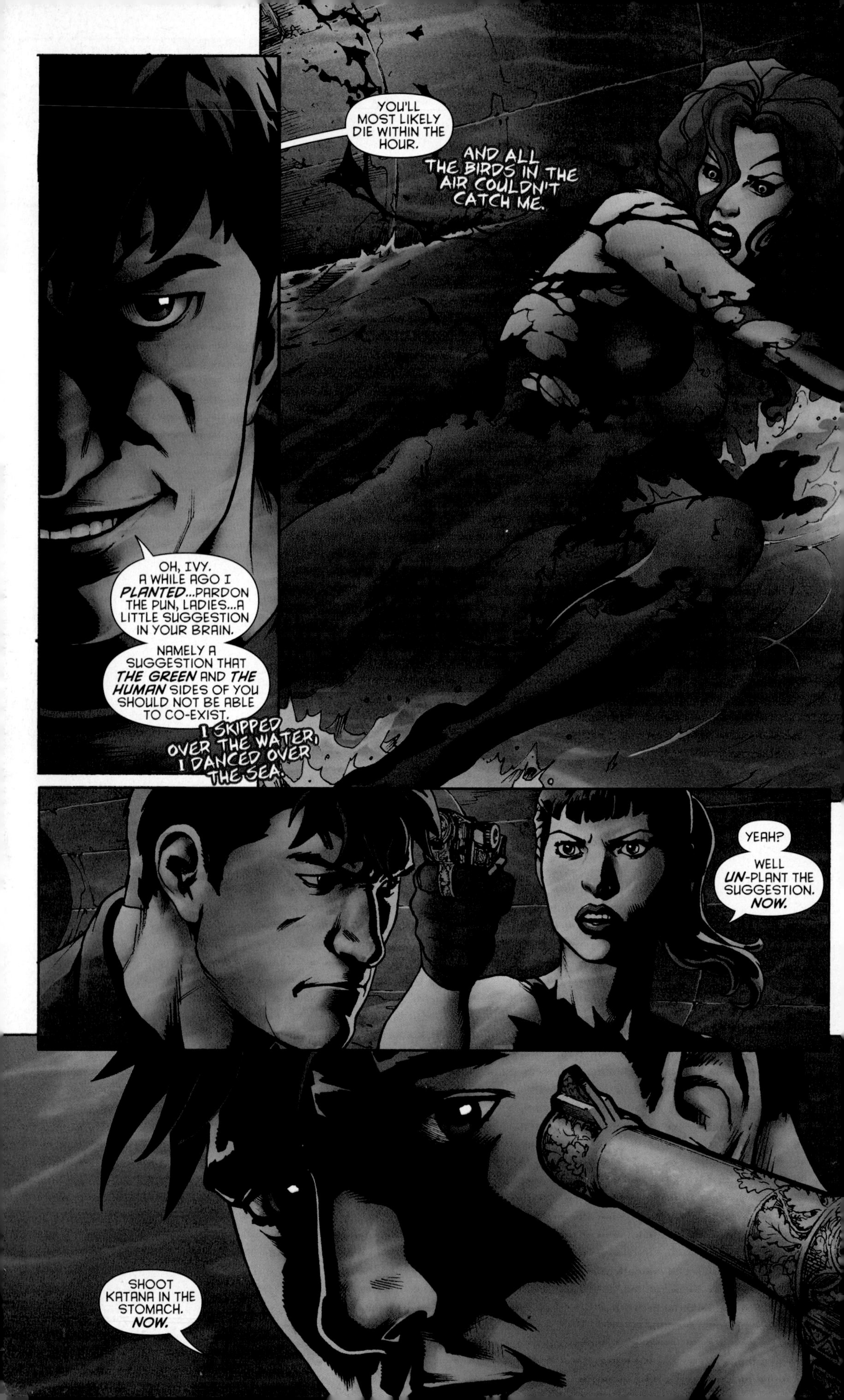

YOU'LL MOST LIKELY DIE WITHIN THE HOUR.
AND ALL THE BIRDS IN THE AIR COULDN'T CATCH ME.
OH, IVY. A WHILE AGO I *PLANTED*...PARDON THE PUN, LADIES...A LITTLE SUGGESTION IN YOUR BRAIN.
NAMELY A SUGGESTION THAT *THE GREEN* AND *THE HUMAN* SIDES OF YOU SHOULD NOT BE ABLE TO CO-EXIST.
I SKIPPED OVER THE WATER, I DANCED OVER THE SEA.
YEAH?
WELL *UN*-PLANT THE SUGGESTION. *NOW.*
SHOOT KATANA IN THE STOMACH. *NOW.*

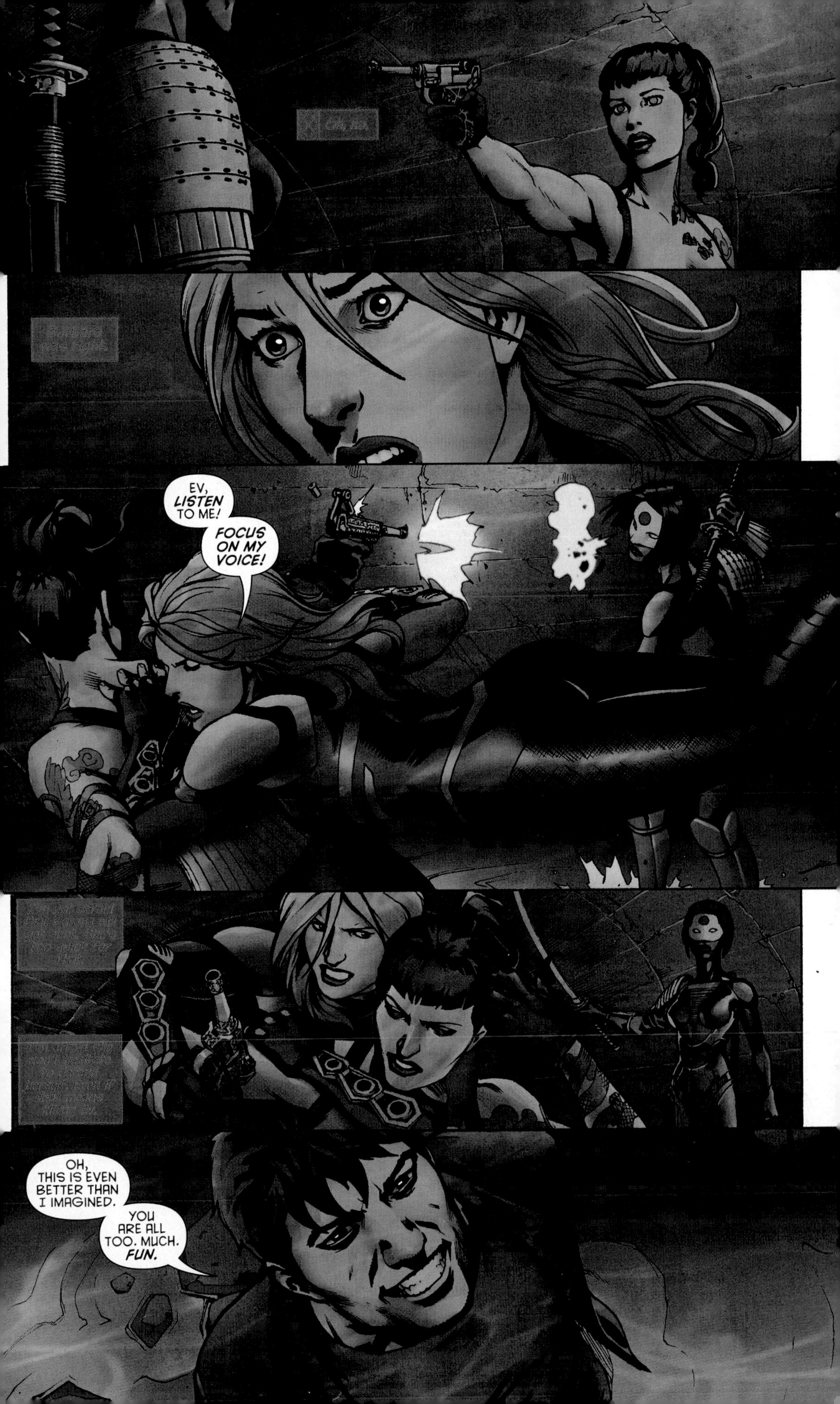
EV, *LISTEN* TO ME!
FOCUS ON MY VOICE!
OH, THIS IS EVEN BETTER THAN I IMAGINED.
YOU ARE ALL TOO. MUCH. *FUN.*

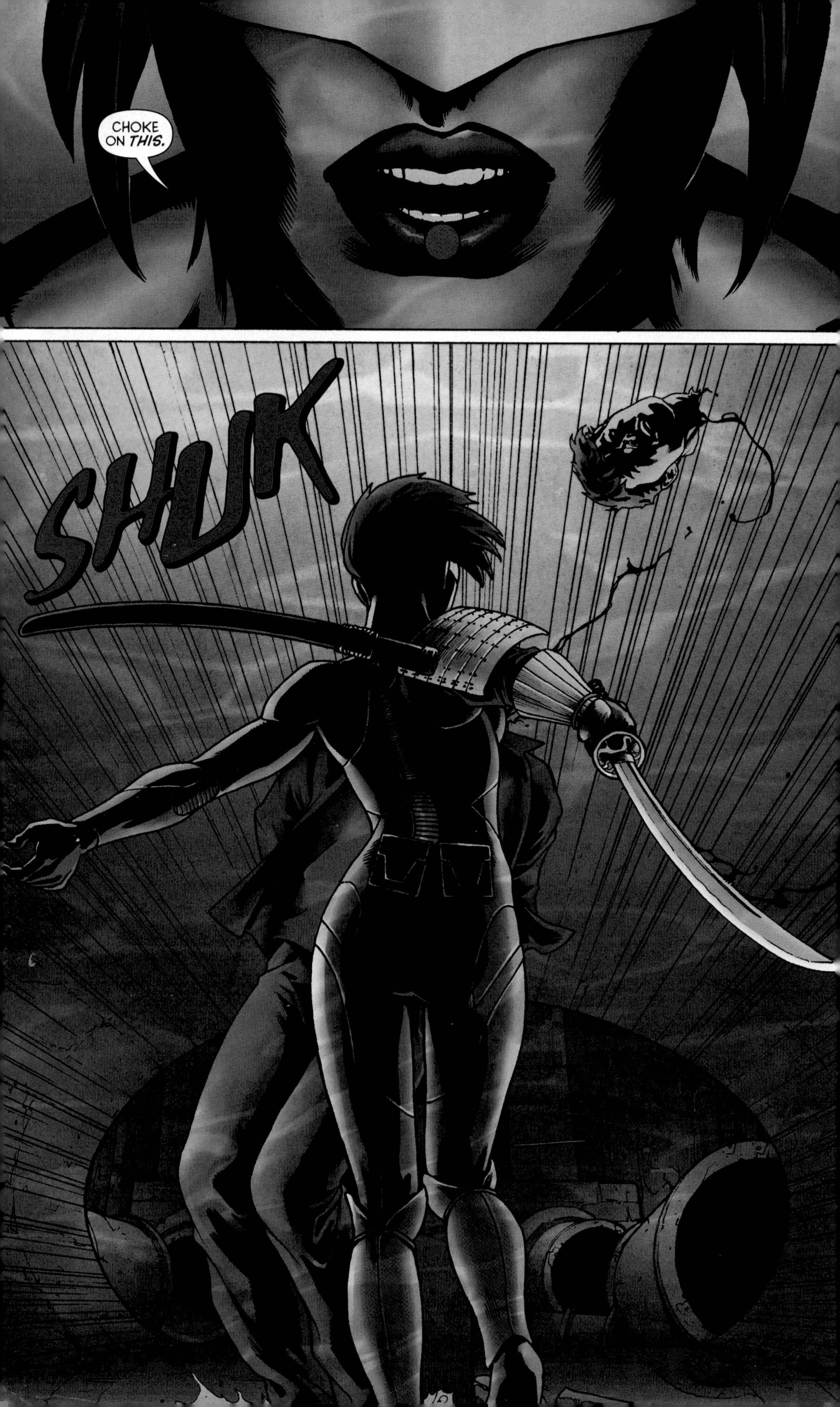
CHOKE ON THIS.
SHUK

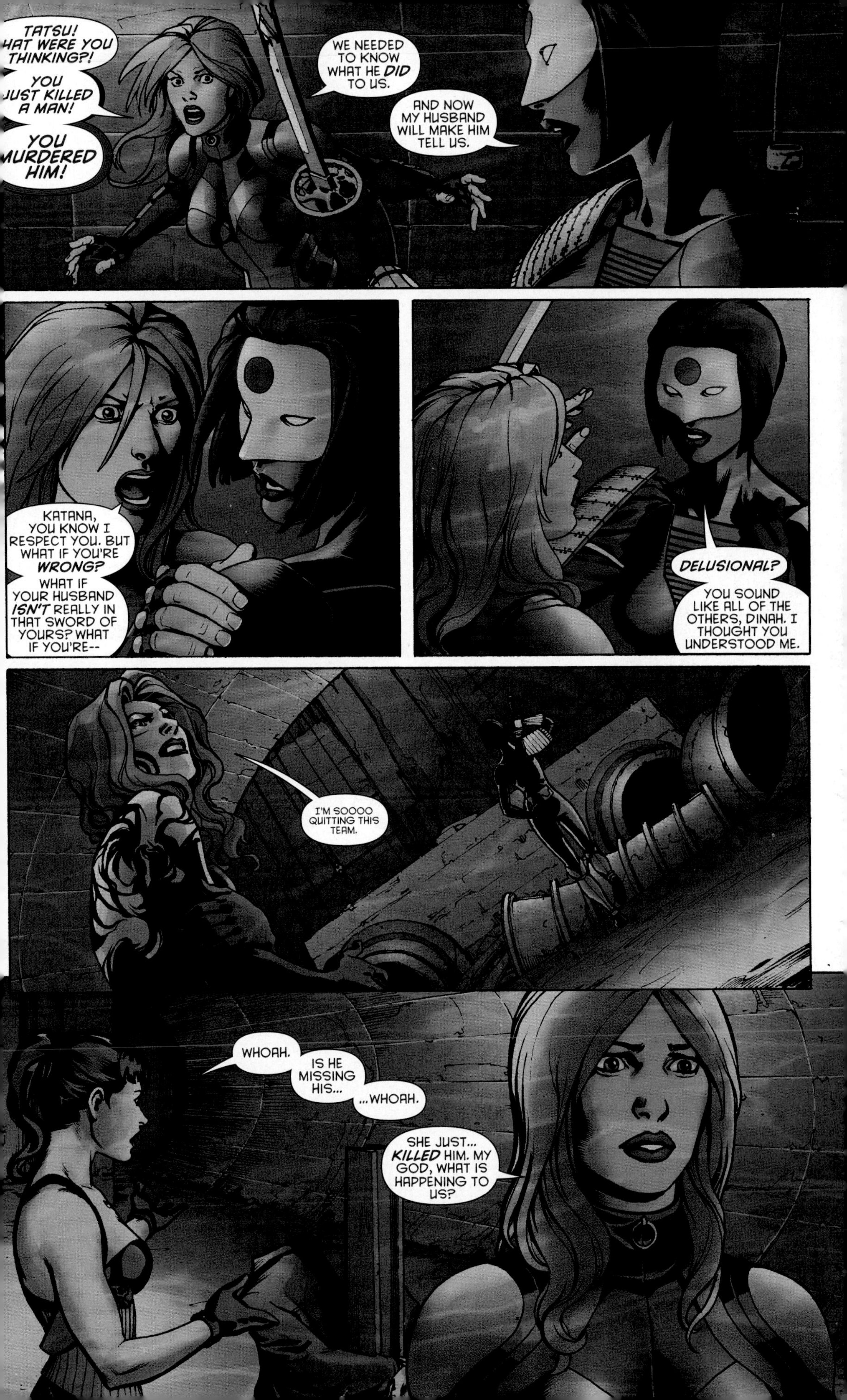
TATSU! HAT WERE YOU THINKING?!
YOU JUST KILLED A MAN!
YOU MURDERED HIM!
WE NEEDED TO KNOW WHAT HE DID TO US.
AND NOW MY HUSBAND WILL MAKE HIM TELL US.
KATANA, YOU KNOW I RESPECT YOU. BUT WHAT IF YOU'RE WRONG? WHAT IF YOUR HUSBAND ISN'T REALLY IN THAT SWORD OF YOURS? WHAT IF YOU'RE--
DELUSIONAL? YOU SOUND LIKE ALL OF THE OTHERS, DINAH. I THOUGHT YOU UNDERSTOOD ME.
I'M SOOOO QUITTING THIS TEAM.
WHOAH. IS HE MISSING HIS... ...WHOAH.
SHE JUST... KILLED HIM. MY GOD, WHAT IS HAPPENING TO US?

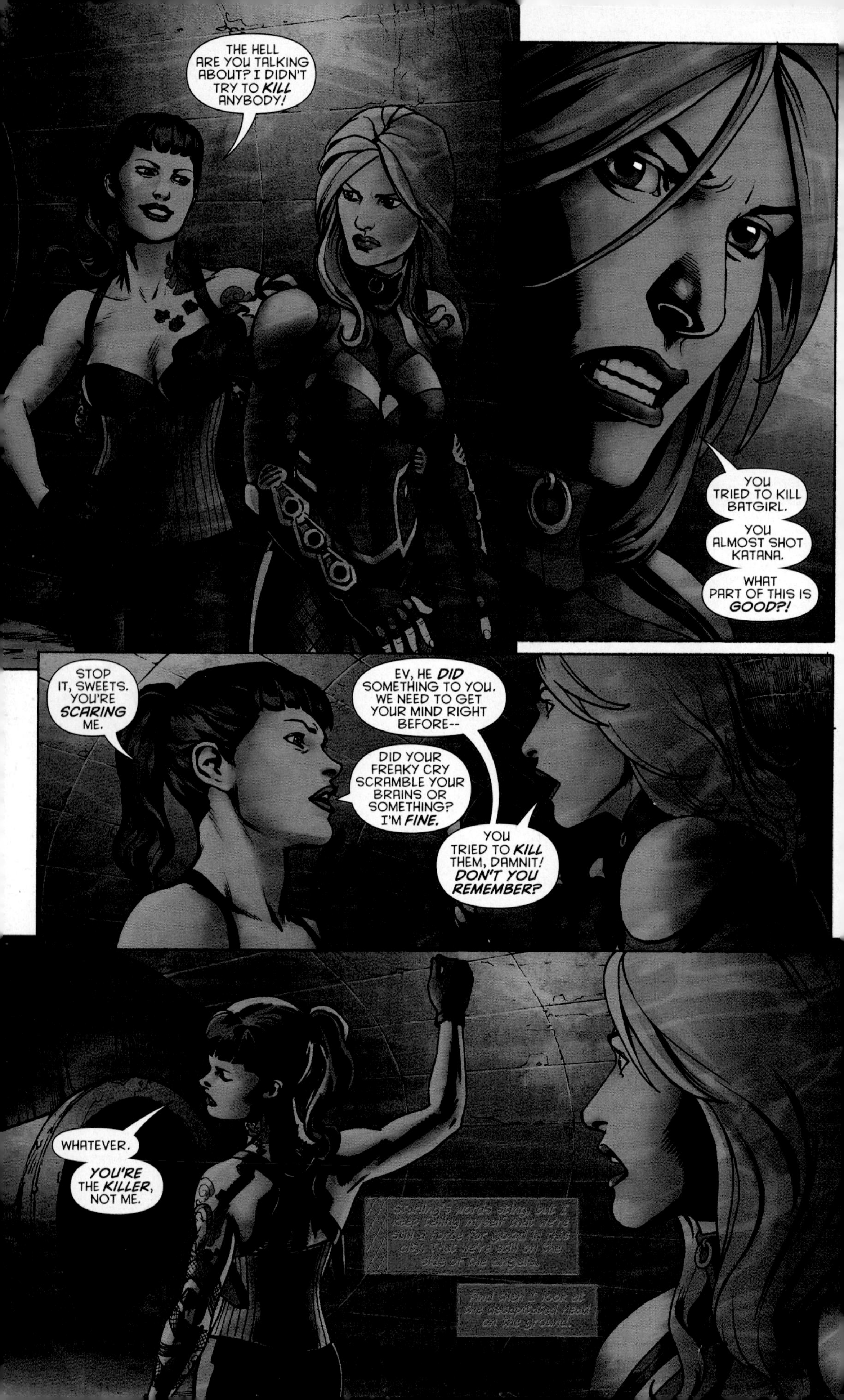
THE HELL ARE YOU TALKING ABOUT? I DIDN'T TRY TO *KILL* ANYBODY!
YOU TRIED TO KILL BATGIRL.
YOU ALMOST SHOT KATANA.
WHAT PART OF THIS IS *GOOD?!*
STOP IT, SWEETS. YOU'RE *SCARING* ME.
EV, HE *DID* SOMETHING TO YOU. WE NEED TO GET YOUR MIND RIGHT BEFORE--
DID YOUR FREAKY CRY SCRAMBLE YOUR BRAINS OR SOMETHING? I'M *FINE.*
YOU TRIED TO *KILL* THEM, DAMNIT! *DON'T YOU REMEMBER?*
WHATEVER.
YOU'RE THE *KILLER*, NOT ME.
Starling's words sting, but I keep telling myself that we're still a force for good in this city. That we're still on the side of the angels.
And then I look at the decapitated head on the ground.

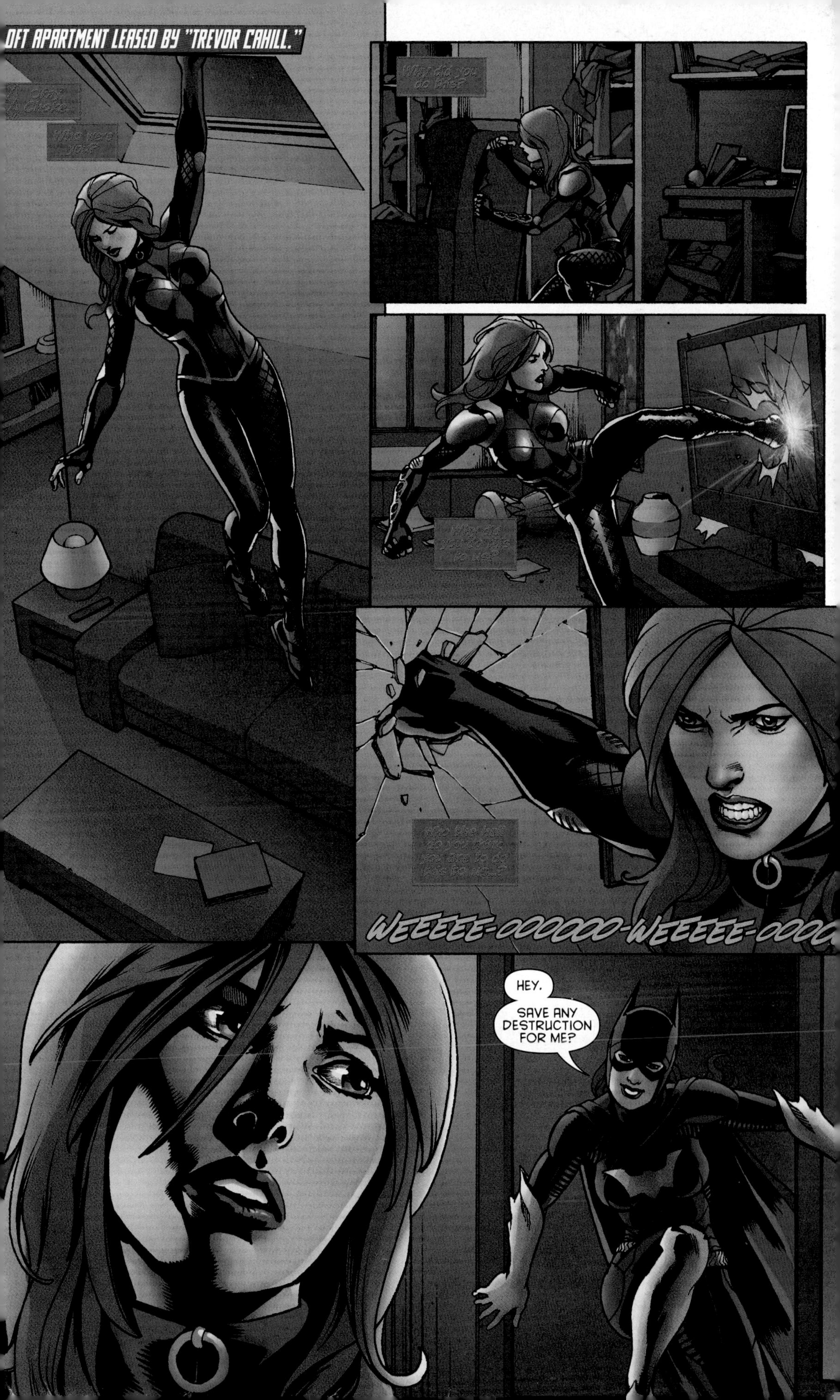
OFT APARTMENT LEASED BY "TREVOR CAHILL."
WEEEEE-OOOOOO-WEEEEE-OOOO
HEY.
SAVE ANY DESTRUCTION FOR ME?

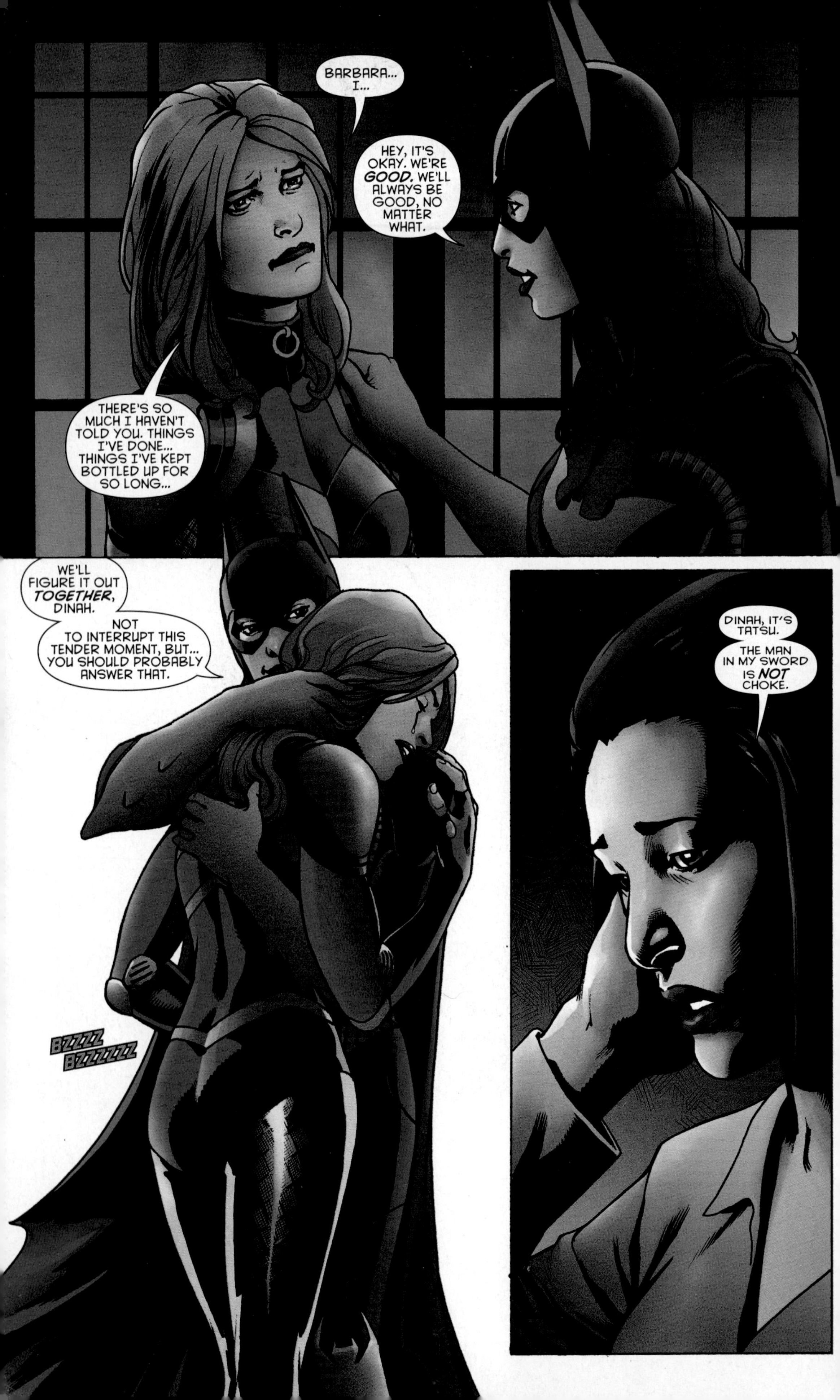
BARBARA... I...
HEY, IT'S OKAY. WE'RE GOOD. WE'LL ALWAYS BE GOOD, NO MATTER WHAT.
THERE'S SO MUCH I HAVEN'T TOLD YOU. THINGS I'VE DONE... THINGS I'VE KEPT BOTTLED UP FOR SO LONG...
WE'LL FIGURE IT OUT TOGETHER, DINAH.
NOT TO INTERRUPT THIS TENDER MOMENT, BUT... YOU SHOULD PROBABLY ANSWER THAT.
BZZZZZ BZZZZZZZ
DINAH, IT'S TATSU.
THE MAN IN MY SWORD IS NOT CHOKE.

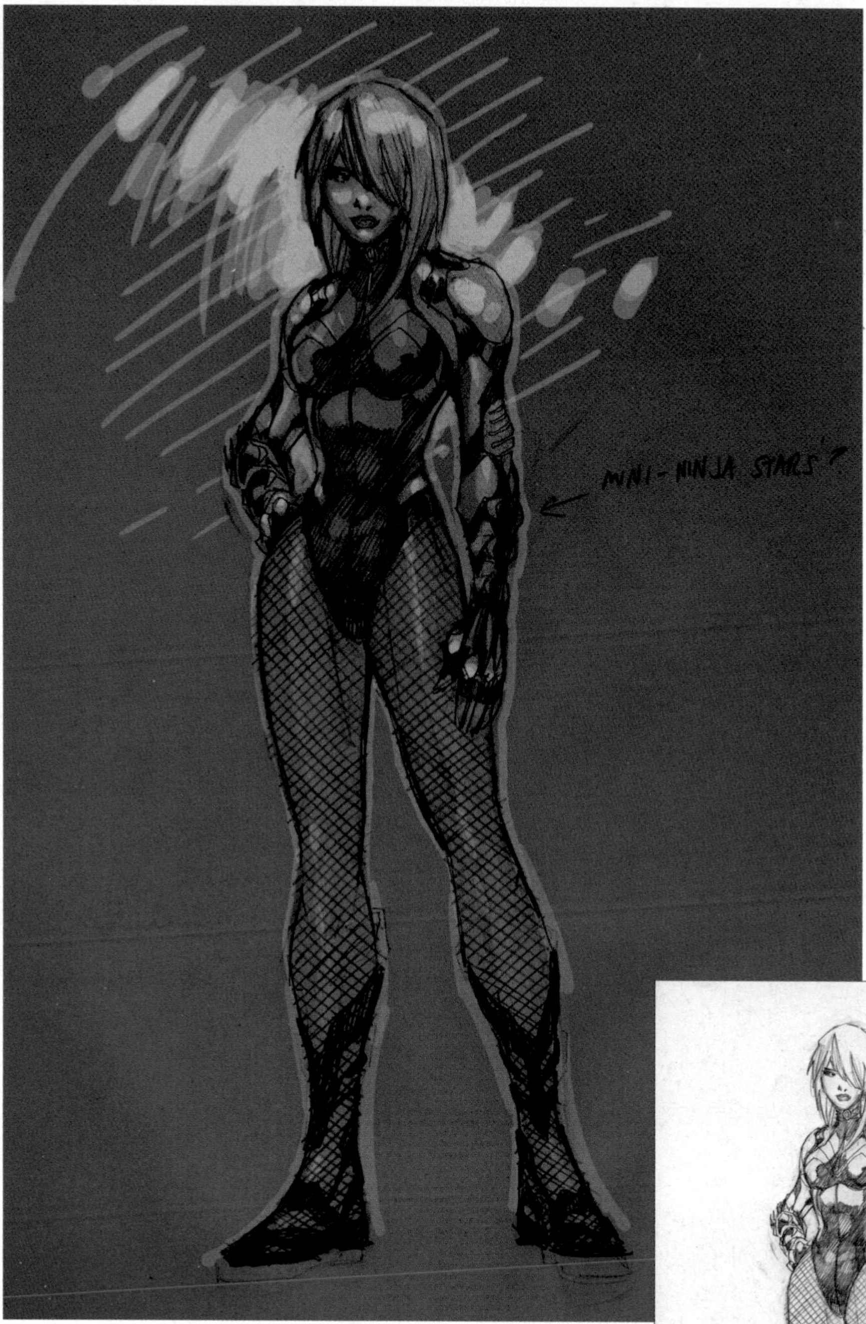
MINI-NINJA STARS?

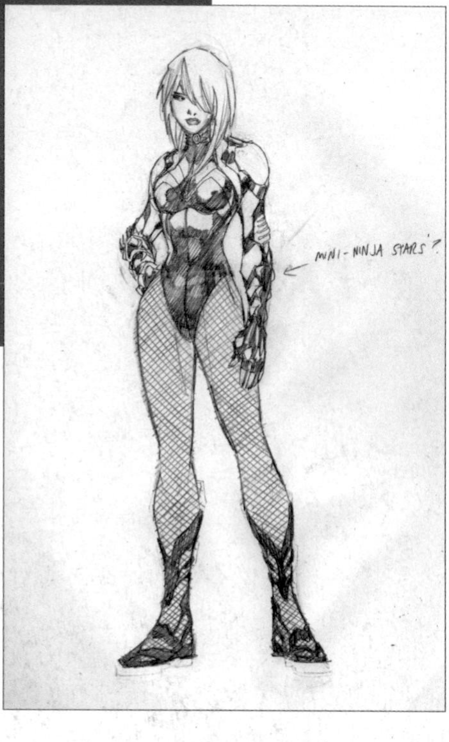
MINI-NINJA STARS?

BIRDS OF PREY

STARLING CHARACTER SKETCH BY JIM LEE

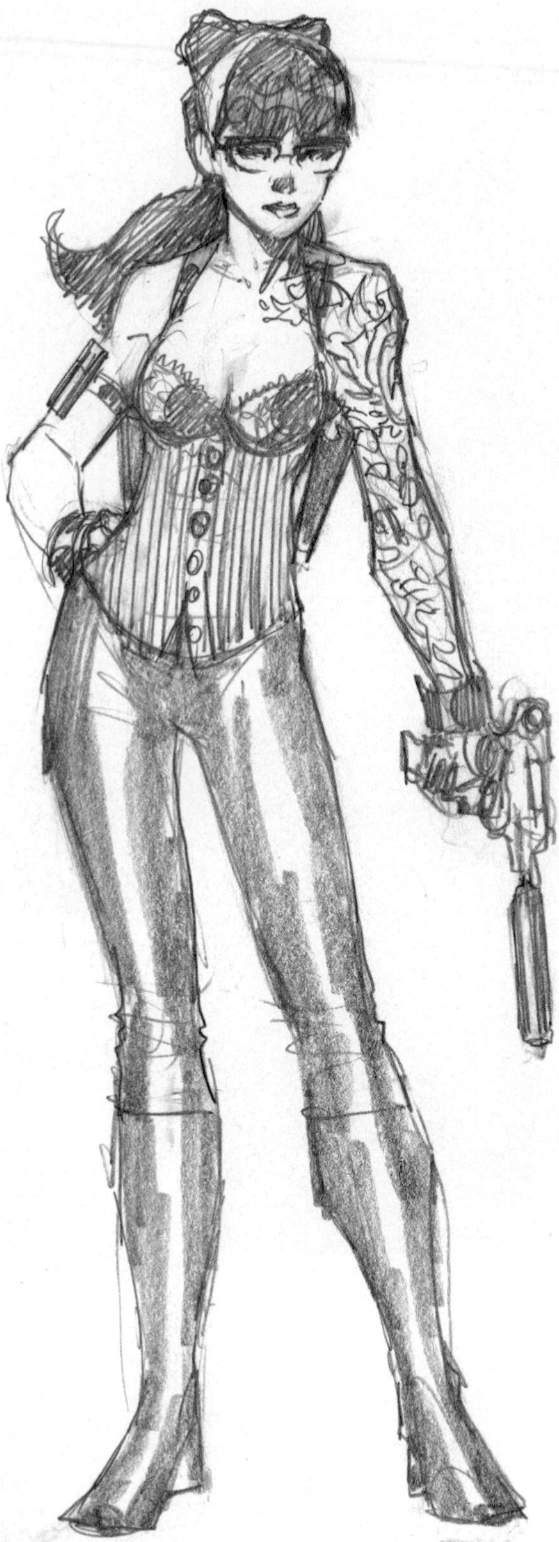

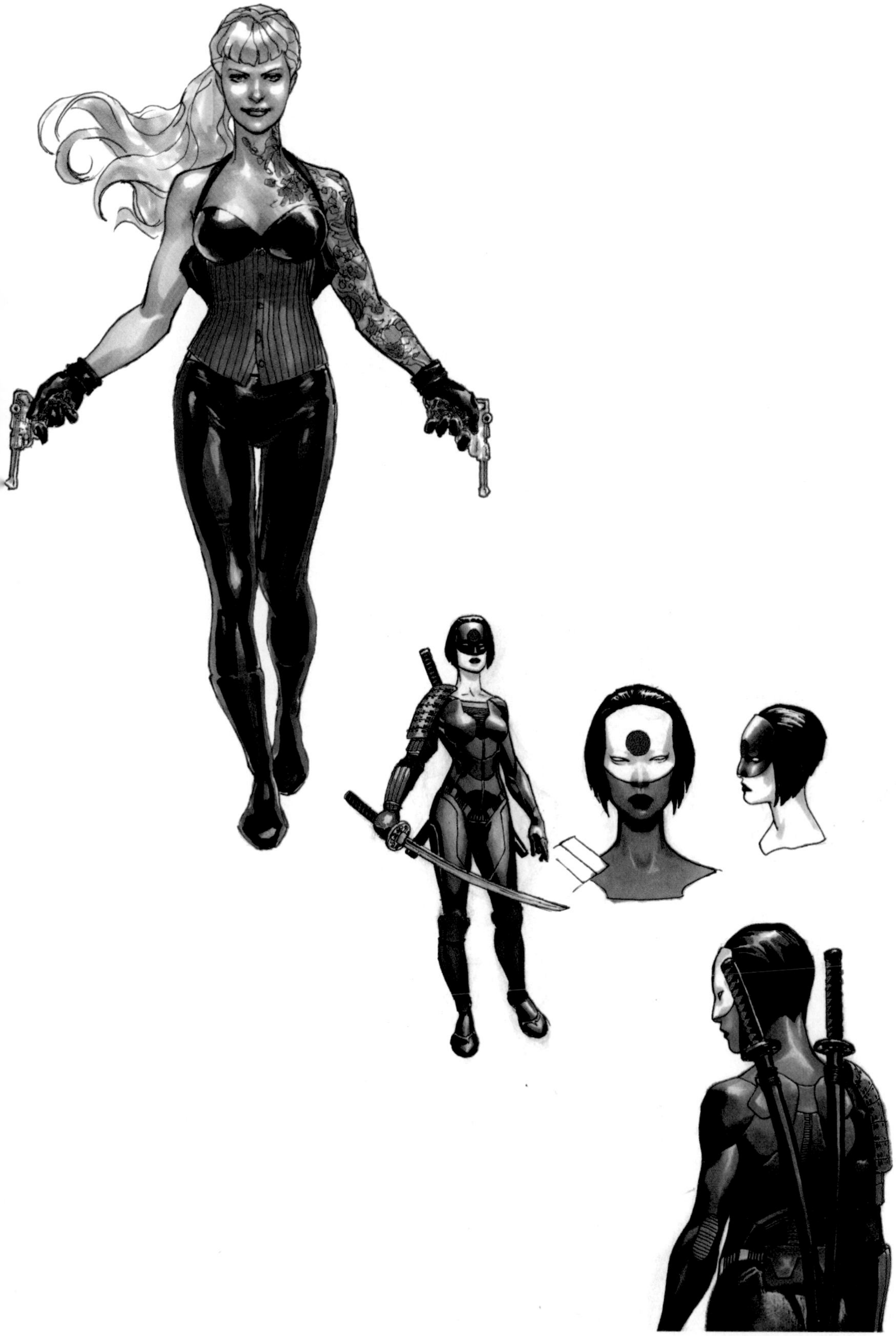

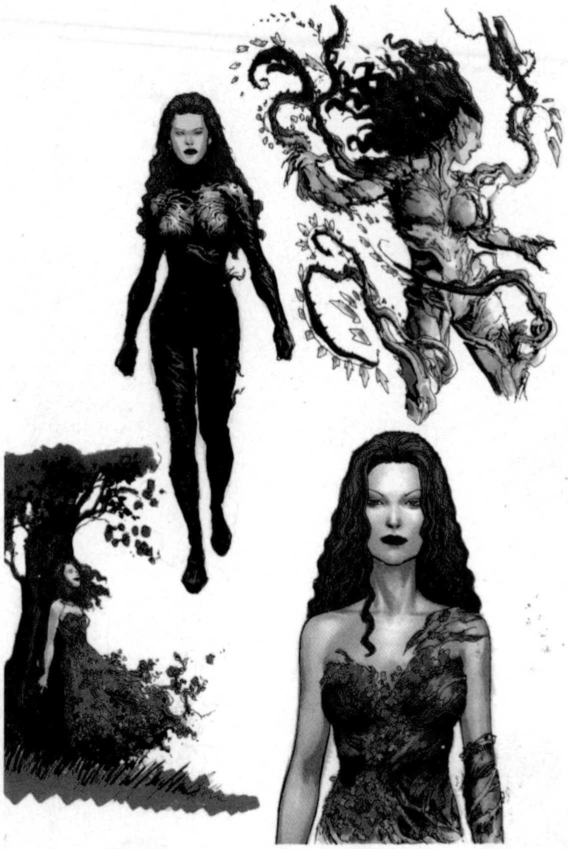

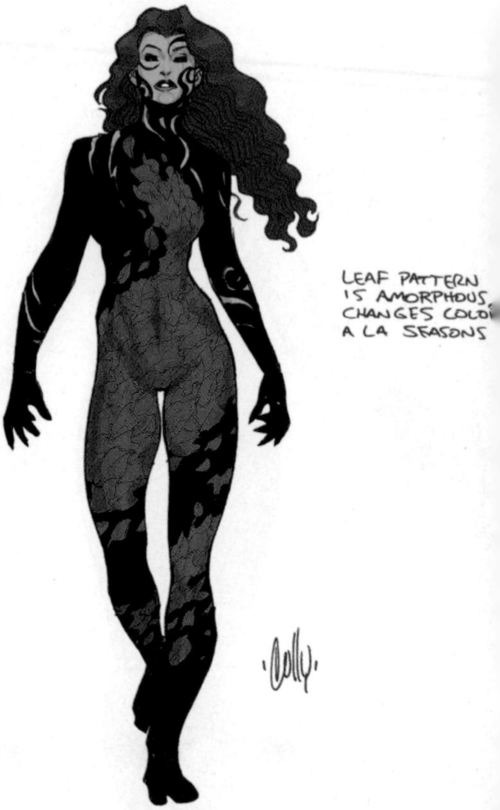
LEAF PATTERN
IS AMORPHOUS,
CHANGES COLO
A LA SEASONS

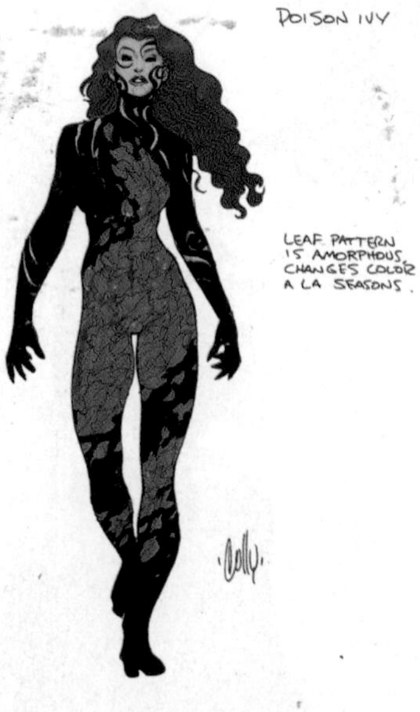
POISON IVY
LEAF PATTERN
IS AMORPHOUS,
CHANGES COLOR
A LA SEASONS.

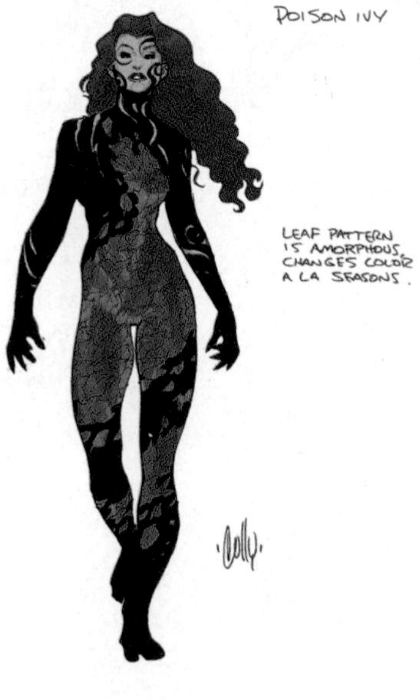
POISON IVY
LEAF PATTERN
IS AMORPHOUS,
CHANGES COLOR
A LA SEASONS.

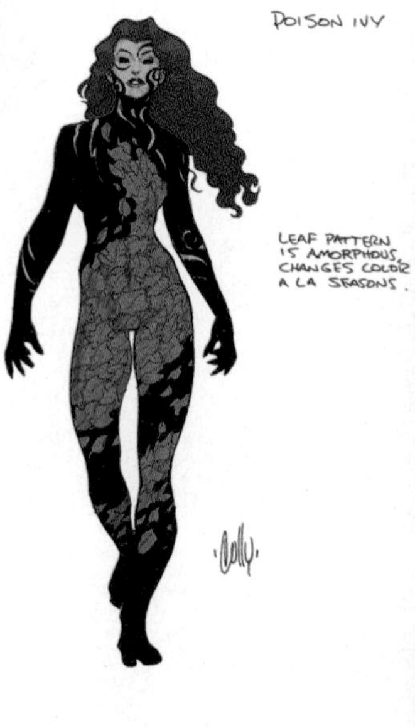
POISON IVY
LEAF PATTERN
IS AMORPHOUS,
CHANGES COLOR
A LA SEASONS.